GIANTS
OF
STEAM

Jonathan Glancey

Atlantic Books
London

First published in hardback in Great Britain in 2012 by Atlantic Books,
an imprint of Atlantic Books Ltd.

This paperback edition published in Great Britain in 2013 by Atlantic Books.

Copyright © Jonathan Glancey, 2012

The moral right of Jonathan Glancey to be identified as the author of this work
has been asserted by him in accordance with the Copyright, Designs and Patents
Act of 1988.

1 2 3 4 5 6 7 8 9

A CIP catalogue record for this book is available from the British Library.

ISBN: 978 184354 773 0

Text design and layout: carrdesignstudio.com
Printed in Italy by ꦣ Grafica Veneta

Atlantic Books
An imprint of Atlantic Books Ltd
Ormond House
26–27 Boswell Street
London
WC1N 3JZ

www.atlantic-books.co.uk

CONTENTS

Here is the most marvellous of all machines . . . of which the mechanism most closely related is that of animals. Heat is the principle of its movement. It has in its various pipework a circulatory system like that of blood in veins with valves that open and close appropriately.

Bernard Forest de Belidor, *L'architecture hydraulique*, vol. 2 (1739)

I cannot express the amazed awe, the crushed humility, with which I sometimes watch a locomotive take its breath at a railway station, and think what work there is in its bars and wheels, and what manner of men they must be who dig brown iron-stone out of the ground, and forge it into THAT! What assemblage of accurate and mighty faculties in them; more than fleshly power over melting crag and coiling fire, fettered, and finessed at last into the precision of watchmaking; titanium hammer-strokes beating, out of lava, these glittering cylinders and timely-respondent valves, and fine ribbed rods, which touch each other as a serpent writhes, in noiseless gliding, and omnipotence of grasp; infinitely complex anatomy of active steel, compared with which the skeleton of a living creature would seem, to careless observer, clumsy and vile.

John Ruskin, *The Cestus of Aglaia* (1865)

Somewhere in the course of manufacture, a hammer blow or a deft mechanic's hand imparts to a locomotive a soul of its own.

Émile Zola, *La Bête Humaine* (1890)

Steam has had a very good run for its money, and has lasted far longer than it was reasonable to expect. It has so lasted because retention of the pure Stephensonian form in its successive developments produced a machine which for simplicity and adaptability to railway conditions was very hard to replace.

E. S. Cox, *Locomotive Panorama* - vol. 2 - (1966)

THE OLD STRAIGHT TRACK

It was 10 o'clock in the morning on Tuesday, 19 December 1933. Fog lay low across Swindon, the Wiltshire town that, since 1840, had been the mechanical heart of the Great Western Railway (GWR). The late-running Paddington to Fishguard express nosed its way cautiously west through the station and along past the great engineering works where its locomotive, 4085 *Berkeley Castle*, had been built eight years earlier. The driver of this fleet and powerful, 79 ton locomotive would have been unaware as the outer edge of its front buffer beam struck the bald head of an elderly gentleman who had been stooping down to inspect the condition of the tracks.

George Jackson Churchward, deaf and partially blind, was killed instantly. Colourful and autocratic, yet kindly and adored by his staff, he was already a legend by the time of his sudden death by steam, famed throughout Britain and its empire wherever a steel rail had made its impact on the landscape and the rhythmic beat of an engine could be heard. Born in 1857, the son of a yeoman farmer, in Stoke Gabriel, a village on the river Dart in South Devon, Churchward was one of the most important of all steam railway locomotive engineers, sharing a hall of fame with George and Robert Stephenson, creators of the steam locomotive as most of us know it, and André Chapelon, the French engineer who was taking this most charismatic and loved of machines to new heights of efficiency at much the same time as the GWR engineer was struck down by *Berkeley Castle*.

A part of the tragedy – the stuff, in fact, of an ancient Greek play – is that Churchward, the retired chief mechanical engineer of the GWR, was killed by one of his successor's locomotives. It was as if the old king had been ritually slaughtered to make way for a new order. Certainly, Churchward was a very different character from Charles Benjamin Collett, the quiet, if forceful, engineer who had followed in his footsteps in 1921. Where Churchward was a radical, albeit one who looked and sounded like a tweedy English country squire, Collett was quietly conservative. Born at Grafton Manor, Worcestershire, a house built in the sixteenth century and rebuilt into the twentieth, he was educated at Merchant Taylors' School before being apprenticed to a firm of marine engineers, after which he joined the GWR. He was happy to take up his predecessor's mantle and to develop the hugely impressive machines for which the older man had been responsible, including the Saint and Star class passenger express 4-6-0s, which were among the most puissant and efficient of Edwardian steam locomotives. But where Churchward was very much a designer heading a highly talented design team, as well as an experienced workshop engineer, Collett was a production man, more interested in manufacturing – at which he was very good – than locomotive design.

The difference between the two – one an outgoing fellow with a love of modern engineering and traditional country pursuits, the other an inward-looking spiritualist, hypochondriac, and keen vegetarian – is well illustrated by a story from the mythology of Swindon works. One day, the pair were inspecting the fire-box of a locomotive together at the works. 'Pass me the illuminant,' said Collett, a touch pompously, to a fitter, who had no idea what he meant. After a frustrating pause, Churchward popped his head out of the copper fire-box and barked, 'Pass the bloody light.' Here was a man who was at once down to earth and highly imaginative. This has been a quality shared by all the truly great steam locomotive engineers; the steam railway engine has always responded best to those who are just as capable of wielding a heavy spanner as understanding the laws of thermodynamics.

Churchward was a consummate steam man. Unmarried, he dedicated his life – when not out fishing – to the development of the steam locomotive, in a career that began in 1873 with an apprenticeship at the South Devon Railway works at Newton Abbot. For him, the steam locomotive was as much a passion as a practical means of ferrying railway traffic. When teased about his bachelor status at a GWR dinner, Churchward retorted humorously: 'A lot of you are big men – important men doing big jobs, where what you say goes. But what are you when you get home? Worms! Bloody worms!' For Churchward, as for his great admirer André Chapelon, there was no time for wife or family. Their offspring, though, were some of the most impressive and best loved machines of any era or genre.

From early on, Churchward began plotting the idea of standard types, or classes, of locomotive, which would be designed with maximum interchangeability of components and would also make the most efficient use of the steam generated in the boiler. The latter was important not just for fast and free running but also to cut coal and water consumption to a minimum. Churchward was concerned, too, to get the maximum work from his engines, and standardization of components would ensure a fast turnaround during repairs and maintenance.

With his knowledge of locomotive design in the United States, where engines were robustly made and highly practical, and developments in France, where the quest was for maximum thermal efficiency, Churchward set about producing a fleet of modern steam locomotives which would be second to none, when he took charge of design at Swindon in 1902. His engines, and those of his successor, Collett, were so good that they could be relied on to provide the necessary power to run crack passenger express services, as well as the heaviest goods trains, right up until the phasing out of steam on the former GWR lines in 1965.

The basic design of Churchward's locomotives was a major advance on those running on most other British railways. The engines featured high-pressure boilers, superheating, long-travel, long-lap valves, and large axle-box bearing surfaces – elements that, taken together, made for exceptionally efficient and reliable machines. In comparison with rivals from Crewe and other contemporary locomotive works, they were more expensive to build. When asked by the board of the GWR why the London and North Western Railway (LNWR) could build three 4-6-0s for the price of two of his 4-6-0s, Churchward is alleged to have replied in exasperation, threatening to resign: 'Because one of mine could pull two of their bloody things backwards!'

This was not entirely true, although Churchward's solitary Pacific, *The Great Bear*, of 1908, certainly looked as if it might. As its stellar name suggests, this was a great beast of an engine, far bigger than anything running on Britain's railways at the time. The concept had come from Churchward's keen interest in American design practice where, since 1901, the Pacific had been emerging as the new and most effective type of passenger express locomotive. With its trailing wheels behind the main coupled driving wheels, a Pacific could carry a large and wide fire-box, sufficient to meet increased steam demands for higher power over long distances. *The Great Bear*, however, was too heavy for the majority of GWR main lines and its route availability was severely restricted. The GWR's traffic department was perfectly happy with Churchward's superb two-cylinder Saint and four-cylinder Star class 4-6-0s, as it was to be with Collett's four-cylinder Castle and King class 4-6-0s in the 1920s. The Pacific type was not introduced on GWR lines again until the arrival of the British Railways Britannias in the early 1950s.

The Great Bear was something of an anomaly, although Churchward was particularly fond of it. Essentially, it was an experimental locomotive built to evaluate a large, wide fire-box. It was later converted into a Castle, losing its trailing wheels and wide fire-box boiler in the process. This was shortly before Nigel Gresley, the dynamic young chief mechanical engineer of the Great Northern Railway (GNR), unveiled the first of a long line of magnificent three-cylinder Pacifics which was to culminate in *Mallard*'s flight down Stoke Bank between Grantham and Peterborough at 126 mph – a world record for steam – in the summer of 1938. When Churchward got wind of the new Pacific, *Great Northern*, he commented, with the characteristic wit and generosity of most steam men: 'Gresley could have had our *Bear* to play with if only we had known in time.'

Churchward was a junction box between the Victorian steam age and the subject of this book, the last of the great steam locomotive engineers, who, in spite of what eventually proved to be overwhelming opposition from the diesel and electric lobbies, drove the design of machines which, right up to the end, were recognizably the offspring of the Stephensons' *Rocket*. But where *Rocket* could generate 25 hp and canter up to 30 mph, the last great American steam locomotives were capable of producing up to 8,500 ihp and galloping up to 125 mph – with the promise of even more in the hands of André Chapelon. Chapelon aimed, ultimately, to raise these figures to at least 16,000 dbhp and 167 mph with locomotives fitted with triple-expansion drives, water-tube fire-boxes, and steam-jacketed cylinders. There was nothing unrealistic in this: Chapelon's meticulous extrapolations were based on repeated tests with his own locomotives.

The key to the development from the Stephensons' *Rocket*, through Churchward's Saints, Stars, and *The Great Bear*, to the super-power steam locomotives of the mid-twentieth century was the efficient use and optimum flow of steam, with minimum restriction, through boiler, valves, cylinders, and exhaust system. If many steam locomotives were inefficient, it was largely because they were not designed on a scientific basis. Because the vast majority of locomotives went about their business as capably as railway traffic management required, there had often been little incentive to increase absolute efficiency, or speed and power, by leaps and bounds, as the generation of steam engineers working from the 1920s to the 1950s was able, and even encouraged, to do.

Intriguingly, the first engineering discussion, in English, on the nature of free-flowing steam cycles through locomotives can be found in a book published two years before Churchward was born. This was *Railway Machinery* (1855), by Daniel Kinnear Clark, who for a brief spell was locomotive superintendent of the Great North of Scotland Railway. But if Kinnear wrote about it, it was Thomas Russell Crampton who put theory into practice, building from 1846 some three hundred free-running and efficient locomotives capable of a sustained 75 mph. These employed many of the same principles that would see British, American, and German engines of the 1930s reaching maximum speeds of around 125 mph, modestly sized French locomotives of the same period flattening hills as they generated herculean power outputs, and American steam expresses of up to 1,000 US tons (892 imperial tons), weighed down with cocktail bars, restaurant cars, sleeping compartments, cinemas, and observation cars, averaging 100 mph for mile after mile over gently falling gradients.

Understanding that the easy flow of steam through wide tubes heated by a large fire-box was all-important for speed and efficiency, Crampton, who had previously worked for the great civil engineer Marc Brunel, as well as for the GWR, built his first long, lean, big-wheeled express engine for the British-run Namur & Liège railway in Belgium. Although he created the impressive 6-2-0 *Liverpool* for the LNWR five years later – it won a gold medal at the Great Exhibition held in Joseph Paxton's Crystal Palace – which is said to have reached 79 mph, a lightning pace for the time, Crampton was unable to persuade British railway managers of the desirability of his highly original locomotives. *Liverpool* was, in any case, too heavy for existing tracks. But Crampton's locomotives proved popular on the continent, particularly in France and Germany. For many years in France '*prendre le Crampton*' meant to catch an express train, and these charismatic machines have subsequently been described rather nicely as 'Napoleon III's TGVs'.

The basic knowledge, then, needed to create the fast, powerful, and efficient steam locomotives that emerged as a new breed from the late 1920s had existed from very early on in the life of the steam railway locomotive. Yet it was not until particular economic and political pressures began to force themselves on to the railway industry after the First World War that the early researches and engineering practices of the likes of Clark and Crampton, and other progressive spirits such as Henry Alfred Ivatt of the GNR in England and Jean Gaston du Bousquet of the Nord railway in France, began to hold sway. Indeed, it was Churchward who, along with the French engineers he admired – du Bousquet and Alfred George de Glehn of the Société Alsacienne de Constructions Mécaniques – made the first truly effective attempt to reinvigorate the steam locomotive at the very time when electric traction was making a substantial impact on railways and – in Switzerland, in 1912 – the Sulzer company was about to create steam's nemesis in the form of the first diesel-electric locomotive.

Churchward's importance is that as a child of the early steam railway age he brought together the best theory and practice from France, Germany, and the United States, fusing these with British craftsmanship and finesse. Despite the way he looks in his photographs, Churchward was – although he would never have used the word – a 'modern'. He owned a motor car from the word go. He rarely stood on ceremony. He adapted engineering developments that would improve his locomotives whatever their source. Here was no narrow-minded nationalist. No sentimentalist either: in 1906 he scrapped two of the GWR's historic broad-gauge locomotives – *North Star* (built 1837) and *Lord of the Isles* (built 1851) – because they took up space in the Swindon works that could be given over to the construction of new engines.

As for design, Churchward even attempted to modernize the graceful, Victorian look that GWR engines, no matter how dynamic, were never to lose, even when pulling express trains in and out of Paddington after The Beatles had released their first LP. 'In my opinion,' he said when accused of producing 'ugly' machines like No. 100, his first 4-6-0, built in 1902, 'there is no canon of art in regard to the appearance of a locomotive or a machine, except that which an engineer has set up for himself by observing from time to time types of engines which he has been led from his nursery days upwards to admire.' Even so, Harry Holcroft, one of his assistants, was quickly drafted in to help smooth out the appearance of Churchward's early, American-influenced designs.

When Churchward retired in 1921, all he would accept as a present was a salmon and trout rod and tackle; the rest of the considerable sum raised by members of his staff was used to create a charity, now known as the Churchward Trust. It is not difficult to imagine what this great steam man would have thought of the fate that has overtaken his beloved Swindon works – now covered by the Churchward Village 'regeneration' project, centred on the Swindon Designer Outlet shopping centre and the headquarters of the National Trust, an organization that would have shuddered at the destruction of *North Star* and *Lord of the Isles*.

As it was, the influence of this distinguished engineer was to percolate through the British railway industry until the end of main-line steam construction. One of Churchward's assistants, William Stanier, went on to become the highly effective chief mechanical engineer of the London Midland & Scottish Railway (LMS). In turn, a trio of Stanier's assistants – Robert Riddles, Ernest Stewart Cox, and Roland Bond – formed the core of the team responsible for the design of British Railways' Standard class steam locomotives of the 1950s. The last of these, 92220 *Evening Star*, was one of the exceptionally free-steaming class 9F 2-10-0s, freight locomotives that could run, occasionally, at 90 mph and were loved by crews and management alike. *Evening Star* was built at Swindon in 1960 and finished like a true GWR locomotive, painted in Brunswick green, lined in black on orange, and with a copper-capped chimney. The engineering and aesthetic legacy alike, both stretching back to Churchward, were there for anyone to see.

Churchward lived and died by the steam locomotive. He also lived to see the arrival of the competitors that would very nearly kill it off: electric and diesel-electric locomotives. Churchward, though, provided much of the ammunition needed for the generation that followed him to push the steam locomotive to limits that would have seemed improbable when he took office in 1902. Quite what he thought of the new forms of motive power one can only guess; what is certain is that he believed that steam locomotives would continue to be built for many years to come, and that it was the proper concern of the engineer to ensure that they were developed to achieve maximum efficiency and reliability. By the first decade of the twentieth century, the steam locomotive was just about one hundred years old. It would continue in regular main-line service for the next hundred years, with steam only now finally disappearing from the hard-working colliery railways of China.

Although there are those who will argue that the effort invested in the development of the steam locomotive between, and especially after, the two world wars was wasteful, merely a case of holding back the clock, George Churchward himself would be fascinated to learn that it has not quite reached the end of the line. As the supply of oil becomes ever more tangled up with nasty global politics, bitter local wars, and vicious terrorism, the diesel-electric, currently so universal, may be heading towards the buffers. There is an enduring love of steam locomotives and an increasing demand around the world to ride on steam specials. Research into the more efficient steam locomotives of the twenty-first century therefore pushes ahead. Indeed, a triple-expansion machine, working at a boiler pressure of 580 psi, as envisaged by Chapelon, would give a thermal efficiency of 19 per cent for boiler and cylinders. This would compare with a figure of 38 per cent for a modern diesel. But if the cost of fuel per heat unit for steam were less than half that of diesel oil, a convincing case could still be made for steam.

Steam technology has been around for a very long time indeed. We rely on it increasingly. And we may yet get to ride behind a new generation of steam locomotives – perhaps even past the Swindon works itself.

RAISING STEAM

We live in the Steam Age. This might seem an odd, even an eccentric thing to say, and yet without the conversion of water into vapour much of our modern life would grind to a halt. When you plug the latest digital gadget into the wall to recharge the thing, it receives electric current generated in power stations which, for the most part, are steam-powered. Whether heated by nuclear rods, coal, or other fuels, mighty boilers at the heart of power stations produce steam at very high temperatures which is directed at great pressure to the blades of turbines which, spinning at speeds that make the raciest internal combustion engine seem sluggish, generate prodigious quantities of the electricity we need to make our world turn comfortably and even – it has to be said – decadently.

Our desire for ever more goods, roads, cars, supermarkets, and gadgets means that we need more and more of these supremely reliable steam engines. In the United States alone, more than 85 per cent of the nation's energy is generated by steam turbines. As a by-product of electricity generation, some one hundred thousand buildings in Manhattan are heated by steam coursing through the pipes of a centralized system. Anyone familiar with New York in winter will have delighted in, or perhaps just been puzzled by, the plumes of steam rising from beneath the city's grid of streets and avenues.

We use steam to sterilize medical instruments, to unblock our sinuses, to warm our homes – the domestic boiler powering your central-heating system is a steam producer – and to cook, wash, and clean. And from childhood stories, whether apocryphal or not, of the young James Watt holding down the lid of the kettle boiling on the range at home in Greenock, we know – almost instinctively – that just as the sun's rays will light a fire if directed through the lens of a magnifying glass, so steam when compressed has a restless, animal-like power. In fact, when water boils it increases by 1,600 times in volume. One would not have thought it required a great deal of imagination to reason that if this gaseous expansion could be harnessed in some way, it might work a machine of some sort. A pump, perhaps, or some sort of turbine, or a reciprocating engine with cylinders, valve gear, and wheels, so that if you placed it on rails, it might just pull a train.

Steam is not going to go away, no matter how hard anyone tries to persuade us that the Steam Age is a part of a sooty Victorian era, long gone. Steam is an elemental force we depend on to an ever-increasing extent. What has changed, worldwide, over the past half century is the landscape of our railways. The decision to abandon steam on many of the world's railways was taken just after the Second World War, although the production of main-line steam locomotives continued in Britain until 1960, in India until 1972, and in China until as recently as 1988. The decline and fall of the steam railway locomotive, however, was not as inevitable as is often thought. In fact, at the very same time that the decision was taken, notably in France and the United States, to put an end to steam development and production, the men who are at the core of this book – the world's last generation of great steam locomotive engineers – were producing machines that were fast, powerful, reliable, and relatively efficient. This generation of steam locomotives reached its zenith between the early 1930s and the late

1940s, and it was characterized by machines that were individually more powerful than the diesels that did so much to cause their rapid demise.

What I hope to show here is that this final great flowering of steam locomotive design, in an era when the steam locomotive was still very much part of everyday life, was not a technical dead end. The engineers whose stories and achievements are told here were pushing the boundaries of a technology that was on the verge of making the quantum leap it needed not just to stay the course against the new diesels, but to prove that 'dieselization' was neither entirely logical nor even necessary.

Remarkably, though, steam development has continued against the odds. This is partly because steam locomotives continue to be in regular use in various parts of the world and, understandably, those who operate them have wanted to lower their fuel consumption, increase their reliability, and make them as up to date as possible. As a result, men such as the visionary Argentine engineer Livio Dante Porta, who died only in 2003, and the British engineer David Wardale, who has developed designs for a new generation of high-speed steam locomotives, have been able to keep the flame alive into the twenty-first century.

If steam development had been allowed to continue, it is astonishing to think what magnificent machines might be running on our railways today. Most would resemble the steam locomotives we know from childhood, from histories, films, and museums, and from the railway preservation movement, which has kept steam vigorously alive ever since enthusiasts with a practical bent as well as a love of steam took over the running of the narrow-gauge Talyllyn Railway in North Wales in 1951. The differences, though, between a steam locomotive of *Flying Scotsman*'s generation, in the early 1920s, or even *Evening Star*'s, and its modern counterpart would be profound.

With modern servicing facilities available around the clock, as epitomized by those at Shaffers Crossing on the Norfolk and Western

Railway in the 1950s, a modern locomotive with half a century of continuous research and development behind it would be a formidable machine. It would be able to run as fast as any train in Britain today. The heat haze – rarely more – from its chimney would do little to upset environmentalists; although Chapelon suggested that even with well-controlled firing there would be some smoke emission for fifteen to thirty seconds when firing rates were increased. With its reciprocating, piston-driven machinery, the modern steam locomotive would still make the compelling, rhythmic, musical sounds many of us love to hear and, as a bonus, it would still trail plumes of white steam – clean water vapour – behind the train and across the landscape in cold weather. These machine-made clouds might, though, be a little less luxuriant than they were in the past if much of the water vapour exhausted from the hard-working cylinders was condensed inside the locomotive and returned to its tender or tanks to be used again.

Burning a variety of clean fuels and with improved control of combustion conditions, the modern steam locomotive would no longer be associated with the volcanic emission of soot and cinders. Footplate crews would work in clean conditions. The servicing and cleaning of locomotives would be mechanized. A shed of modern steam locomotives could never be a stand-in for a hospital surgery, but it would bear little resemblance to the steam depots of an era when labour was cheap and dirt, and even danger, was a part of a working man's day. And what my story will show is that steam engineers did in fact come remarkably close to realizing this vision of the modern steam locomotive. So what stopped them? The answer is not simple, but it is one that emerges as steam locomotive development rose to new heights in the 1930s and 1940s, and as competing technologies pressed their advantages and politics had their day with the railways.

The steam locomotive has always been far more than a machine. Warm-blooded by nature, it is a kind of living, breathing animal fashioned from metal. No wonder that, in Britain at least, some of the very fastest of its kind were named after racehorses or fast-flying birds. Not only does the steam locomotive tug at the heart, as well as delighting the ear and eye, it also boasts an ancestry that takes us back to the great civilizations of the past.

Hero of Alexandria, a Greek mathematician and engineer, and citizen of the Roman Empire, published notes on an early form of steam turbine which he called the *aeolipile* – the Ball of Aeolus (the Greek god of the wind). A boiler set a ball (made of bronze, perhaps) spinning, using steam directed through a pair of pipes. The steam escaped through curved nozzles set on opposite sides of the ball. Shooting out as a pair of opposed jet streams, it began to turn the ball and set it spinning – 'as in the case of dancing figures', as Hero described its action. I know it worked: I think I was seven years old when I was given a Tri-ang model of the Hero Steam Turbine. It came complete with a bust of the inventor, and it spun happily under steam. At much the same time, I was given my first reciprocating steam engine, a Mamod SE2a, made by Rovex Scale Models of Margate. Fuelled by noggins of mauve methylated spirit, it was an intoxicating device. Its flywheel rotated at great speed, although the engine was a stationary one and went nowhere. It frightened the dogs and cats, and also took the skin off my left hand after I experimented with increasing the power by restraining the safety valve.

Just as my Mamod SE2a served no practical purpose, so Hero's *aeolipile* appears to have been nothing more than a toy. This is significant because it seems possible that Hero got the idea from reading Vitruvius, the Roman architect and engineer, who refers to an *aeolipile* in his *De Architectura*, published towards the end of the reign of Augustus Caesar. In turn, although Vitruvius may well have seen an *aeolipile* revolving, the idea might just have come from the Alexandrian Greek mathematician Ctesibius, who wrote what appears to have been the first treatises on compressed air and pneumatics, and who may well also have invented the water pump, along with other useful devices such as the siphon. Significantly, when the steam engine first went to work, it was as a water pump.

Given that Ctesibius had very probably built mechanical pumps and an *aeolipile* of some kind, why did the Roman Empire treat the first steam engines as nothing more than a curiosity? The Romans were a practical people and were inventive engineers and masterly builders – just think of what they could have done with steam. (There is a funny drawing in W. Mills's whimsical *4ft 8½ and All That: A Sort of Railway History* in which a Roman senator, a centurion, and a curly-haired schoolboy watch, with some disquiet, a steam train rumbling over the top of a fine viaduct – the carriage is labelled SPQR, as in GWR or LNWR.)

The most likely explanation is that the Romans simply had no need of such machinery. With vast armies of slaves as well as well-trained soldiers, they were able to build on an epic scale without the need for steam, while well-built roads and powerful quinqueremes gave them mastery of land and sea. Indeed, in his short story 'Envoy Extraordinary', William Golding tells of a fictional Greek inventor, Phanocles, who is taken to see the Roman emperor. The emperor is amused by the inventions Phanocles shows to him: a compass, a printing press, a cannon, a pressure cooker, and a steam ship. One way or another, he finds them all enchanting but useless and even unsettling. His oarsmen take against the steam ship because it will rob them of their work and, as slaves, if they have no work, they might well be slaughtered. In any case, the ship goes out of control in the harbour and sets fire to the city around it. The pressure cooker is fun, but given that the emperor can call up a banquet in seconds with a click of his fingers, he has no need of such a device. But to reward Phanocles, while damning him with faint praise and effectively rejecting his work, he appoints him envoy extraordinary and plenipotentiary to China. No Roman, so far as we know, ever reached even the borders of the Chinese Empire.

Nonetheless, copied as they were by medieval European monks and Arab scribes, descriptions of early water pumps and steam engines haunted the imagination of later generations of inventors. Sporadic attempts to harness steam power were made from the sixteenth century onwards. In 1543, Blasco de Garay, a Spanish sea captain, is said to have demonstrated a 200 ton paddle steamer, the *Trinidad*, in the harbour at Barcelona. The story lacks authentication and it may simply have been a romantically wilful misreading of an historical document by a Spanish librarian at the time of the opening of the Stockton & Darlington Railway in 1825 – an attempt to prove that the brave and glorious Spaniards had invented the steam engine before the perfidious English.

What does seem to be true is that a century later, just before the outbreak of the English Civil War, Edward Somerset, 2nd Marquis of Worcester, built a working steam pump at Raglan Castle, his family home in South Wales. Although Somerset, impoverished by his support for the royalists, failed to capitalize on his invention, he did write about it in a treatise completed in 1655. Eight years later, this was printed in London by J. Grismond under the snappy title *A Century of the names and scantlings of such inventions as at present I can call to mind to have tried and perfected which (my former notes being lost) I have, at the instance of a powerful friend, endeavored now, in the year 1655, to set these down in such a way, as may sufficiently instruct me to put any of them to practice.*

In 1698, Thomas Savery, a Devon-born military engineer, who had read Somerset's book of inventions, patented a steam pump based on the Raglan Castle design. This was a clever ruse, because, although he built a few more or less successful engines, Savery was not the presiding genius of the emerging steam world he would have liked to have been. But his patent was such that when, probably in 1710, Thomas Newcomen, the Devon-born ironmonger and Baptist preacher, made what was perhaps the first truly successful practical steam engine, he was forced to go into partnership with the canny Savery – and throughout, and even beyond, his life, royalties were payable to the Savery estate for each Newcomen engine built.

In fact, Newcomen owed as much to the writings of Denis Papin, the

17

French Huguenot physicist who invented the steam pressure cooker between 1676 and 1679, while working with Robert Boyle at the Royal Society in London. Although he was obliged to flee to Germany when French Protestants were persecuted under the Edict of Nantes, and later died a pauper's death in unknown circumstances, it is good to know that it is to Papin that we owe the creation of the very first self-propelled steam vehicle, a paddle boat he made in 1704 while in exile in Kassel.

Papin's description, meanwhile, of the workings of a piston operating in a cylinder at atmospheric pressure (14.7 psi), in his paper *Nouvelle méthode pour obtenir à prix bas des forces considérable* (A New Method for Obtaining Large Forces at Low Cost), had been published in Leipzig in 1690, and it was to have a galvanizing effect on Newcomen. From 1710, Newcomen's steam pumps began working in the tin mines of Cornwall, although precise dates and locations are uncertain, and in the Black Country, where an engine was installed at the Conygree Coalworks, near Dudley, in 1712. By the time of his death, Newcomen had installed at least one hundred steam engines in various parts of newly industrializing Britain, as well as in France, Belgium, Spain, Hungary, Sweden, and the United States, where evidence of a Newcomen engine was uncovered at a coal mine at Midlothian, Virginia, in 2010.

Newcomen's engines worked, but they were big and slow and, by the standards of the Stephensons' much later *Rocket* locomotive, deeply inefficient. The key problem was that the cylinder was heated and cooled each time the piston was pushed up and then encouraged down, since water was poured into the top of it in order to create the vacuum necessary to prompt the downstroke. Keeping the cylinder warm is essential to the efficiency of a reciprocating steam engine, as engineers were to realize when they finally developed the steam jacket for precisely this purpose.

The problem was solved by James Watt, the Scottish inventor who by 1765 had transformed Newcomen's engine into the machine that accelerated the Industrial Revolution to full speed. By creating a cylinder the walls of which stayed warm on both upstroke and downstroke, Watt increased the performance and efficiency of Newcomen's engine several times over. Watt discovered that no less than 80 per cent of the steam generated in Newcomen's engines was wasted in heating the cylinder rather than doing useful work. Watt's patent, 'A Method for Lessening the Consumption of Steam in Steam Engines – the Separate Condenser', was first registered in January 1769.

Although a febrile inventor, Watt was no businessman. It was only when he teamed up with Matthew Boulton, owner of the Soho Foundry, near Birmingham, that he became a wealthy man. Founded in 1794, Boulton & Watt built 1,164 steam engines over the following quarter of a century. Intriguingly, many of these vast machines – some 25 feet high, with cylinders measuring a massive 50 inches in diameter (the largest to be used in a steam locomotive was an exceptional 41 inches, in the United States, in the low-pressure cylinder of John E. Muhlfeld's two-cylinder, high-pressure, cross-compound 2-8-0 of 1924) – were supported with iron pillars tricked up as Greek and Roman columns. This was not a homage to Hero of Alexandria, but it was an unwitting reference to Vitruvius, who not only described the early steam turbine but also left a body of writing that, when taken up by Italian Renaissance architects, sparked the rise of Neo-Classical design. So while Boulton and Watt were simply reflecting design values of their time, they were nonetheless reinforcing the idea that the steam engine had a classical pedigree.

What Boulton and Watt did not do was to build a steam locomotive, although they might have been the first to do so. In 1777, William Murdoch, a young Scottish inventor whose reputation had been conveyed to Watt by James Boswell, the biographer of Samuel Johnson, walked more than three hundred miles from his home in Cumnock, East Ayrshire, to Birmingham to ask Watt for a job. Murdoch made many improvements to Boulton & Watt engines, particularly when working in Cornwall, but most importantly he made

Britain's first working model of a steam locomotive. This was intended for the roads rather than rails, but the scale model of a three-wheeler carriage he made in 1784, with the engine slung beneath the two large back wheels, puffed eagerly around his living room in Redruth. This was the first time a man-made machine had travelled under its own steam in Britain.

Murdoch was aware that the French inventor Nicolas-Joseph Cugnot had got there first with his three-wheeled steam tractors for the army, the first of which moved under its own power in 1769. But, admirable though his achievement was, Cugnot's steam vehicles were extremely heavy and unstable, had a maximum speed of 4 or 5 mph, and had to stop every fifteen minutes to allow the boiler to recover its working pressure. No one, however, should underestimate the importance of these historic machines and the 1771 model on display at the Musée des Arts et Métiers in Paris is an evocative sight.

If it had been built to full scale, Murdoch's road locomotive might have been a spritely machine. Watt, though, believed there was no future in self-propelled road carriages, although Murdoch made a second working model in 1785 and demonstrated it to a wide-eyed public at the King's Head Hotel in Truro. Watt was also alarmed by Murdoch's design of a higher-pressure boiler; given the quality of existing materials available for boiler-making, Watt believed in using only atmospheric pressure. While his engines were indeed based to some extent on the principle of a boiling kettle, not wanting to take any undue risk, Watt was wary of the sort of pressures that would be found necessary in the coming years to make a success of the steam railway locomotive. A full-scale working replica of Murdoch's model was eventually built in Redruth by the Murdoch Flyer Project between 2004 and 2007.

Murdoch remained an employee of Boulton & Watt, but he kept his models. Sometime in 1797–8, he showed them to Richard Trevithick, the Cornish inventor and mining engineer who was then his neighbour and had seen Murdoch's first model working under steam in 784.

Trevithick went on to build two steam carriages of his own: *Puffing Devil* in 1801, and *London Steam Carriage* in 1803. The following year he created the world's first steam railway locomotive.

Any child who finds school difficult should take heart from Trevithick's story. One teacher from his village school in Camborne reported him as 'a disobedient, slow, obstinate, spoiled boy, frequently absent and very inattentive'. But the young Trevithick was busy, out and about from school, watching steam pumping engines at work in local mines. Observation, imagination, and a degree of genius allowed Trevithick to develop an engine with a double-acting cylinder, with steam admitted through a four-way valve and exhausted not through Watt's condenser, but through a chimney. He was getting close to the machinery necessary to make a steam railway locomotive work.

Next, Trevithick demonstrated a boiler compressed not to Newcomen and Watt's 14.7 psi but to 145 psi, at which pressure steam forced in and out of double-acting cylinders works hard and powerfully. Trevithick's bold experiments came to fruition in 1804, assuring him his place in history, while he was working at the Pen-y-Darren Ironworks in Merthyr Tydfil, in South Wales. He mounted a new stationary engine, designed to work a steam hammer, on wheels. Delighted with the ingenuity of the machine, Samuel Homfray, owner of the ironworks, made a bet with a rival ironmaster, Richard Crawshay: fifty guineas said that Trevithick's (unnamed) locomotive could pull 10 tons of iron along the 9.75 miles of the Merthyr Tydfil tramway from Pen-y-Darren to Abercynon.

It did. And more. On 21 February 1804, with George III on the throne and Napoleon Bonaparte shortly to be crowned emperor of France, the first railway locomotive hauled not just 10 tons of coal but seventy passengers too, all the way to Abercynon, in four hours and five minutes, at an average speed of 2.4 mph. The locomotive had triumphed, but because of its great weight – 4 tons – it distorted the cast-iron track made for horse-drawn trains. As a result, its wheels were removed and it returned to duty as a steam hammer at Pen-y-Darren. Once a year, a replica steams slowly along a track at the National Waterfront Museum, Swansea.

The early steam railway locomotive was restricted to use in collieries and ironworks, notably in Cornwall and Northumberland, although in 1808 Trevithick demonstrated a new locomotive, *Catch me who can*, to the public in a timber-fenced ring laid out in Euston Square. For a shilling a time, Londoners could spot their first steam railway locomotive and ride on a train for the first time. The 'Steam Circus' was not as popular as Trevithick hoped it would be. It would be another twenty-eight years before trains and steam locomotives returned to the capital. By then, Trevithick had been three years in his grave. After many failures and a number of hair-raising adventures – in Costa Rica he was very nearly eaten by an alligator – he was engaged to work on the design of an early form of steam turbine for a ship being built by J. & E. Hall Ltd at Dartford in Kent. There he contracted pneumonia and died a pauper in bed at the Bull Hotel on 22 April 1833.

Between Trevithick's 'Steam Circus' and the opening of the Liverpool & Manchester Railway in 1830, it had been unclear whether or not the steam railway locomotive would take off. Mail coaches, which could average 9 mph from London to what must have seemed like all points of the British compass, and a network of turnpike roads and canals, had revolutionized transport in Britain over the preceding half century. The few steam railway locomotives that existed were slow, lumbering things which led lives well away from the public gaze. A memoir of the early steam days in the collieries of the North-East written by Thomas Summerside, a friend of the Stephensons, tells how *Blücher*, an 0-4-0 locomotive built by George Stephenson for the Killingworth colliery in 1814, had a habit of breaking down and could be a pig to start. (*Blücher* was named, presumably the following year, after Gebhard Leberecht von Blücher, the Prussian general who came to Wellington's rescue at the battle of Waterloo in 1815.) George Stephenson would call to his buxom sister-in-law Jinnie, cutting the grass beside the track to feed her cows: 'Come away, Jinnie, and put your shoulder to her.' It was her job, too, to get up at the crack of dawn to light *Blücher*'s fire.

These first locomotives might have been crude and they were certainly no beauties, yet Trevithick had evidently set something important in motion; his Pen-y-Darren 0-4-0, however, had steamed a little too early in the day to be an economic proposition. The event that set the steam locomotive on its untrammelled metal course around the world was the Rainhill Trials of October 1829. Here was the opportunity for George Stephenson, and his son Robert, to prove that a steam locomotive could be fast, exciting, and attractive. *Rocket*, a canary-yellow and white 0-2-2, was a pretty machine, a locomotive wholly unlike its crudely presented predecessors, whether on the Stockton & Darlington Railway or working collieries and ironworks. *Rocket* was designed for passenger service. During the Rainhill Trials some fifteen thousand people saw *Rocket*, and its rivals, in action.

The Rainhill Trials determined what type of traction would haul the trains of the Liverpool & Manchester Railway, the world's first inter-city service. There was no guarantee that locomotives would win the day. The answer might have been rope haulage with a succession of stationary steam engines pulling trains between the two Lancashire cities. *Rocket*, though, was a new type of locomotive. Her boiler contained not a single large flue, with a fire at one end to heat the water and raise steam, but, at the suggestion of Henry Booth, the scientifically minded treasurer of the Liverpool & Manchester Railway, twenty-five small copper flues, or tubes, which would greatly increase the boiler's surface area and hence both the quantity and rate of steam produced. This coincided with the first application of a multi-tubular boiler in France, by Marc Seguin. A separate copper fire-box was fitted to the back of *Rocket*'s boiler. A blast-pipe exhausting steam from the cylinders created a vacuum drawing heat from the fire and through the boiler tubes.

The completed locomotive, with its boiler tested to 70 psi (its working pressure was 50 psi), was disassembled and packed off by horse and cart from Newcastle to Carlisle, and then by canal lighter to Bowness-on-Solway, where the crates were loaded on to a boat to Liverpool, the journey taking the best part of six days. *Rocket* ran very well indeed and easily won the Rainhill Trials. Eight further members of the class were built in time for the public opening of the Liverpool & Manchester Railway in September 1830. The later locomotives featured water-jacketed fire-boxes, considerably increasing steam production, smoke-boxes to collect unburned fuel and char through the boiler tubes, and cylinders mounted close to the horizontal (*Rocket*'s were angled at 45 degrees) to provide smoother movement with less stress on the track – *Rocket* had tended to waddle along. Capable of at least 36 mph, these Stephenson machines launched not just the steam locomotive in public service, but the very idea of the trunk railway rushing passengers from city to city.

Just three years later, a locomotive emerged from the works of Robert Stephenson which is largely forgotten but remains key to the story of the steam railway. This was *Patentee*, an inside-cylindered 2-2-2, designed for service on the Liverpool & Manchester Railway, the Grand Junction Railway connecting Manchester and Birmingham, and other new railways which were springing up as fast as parliament could pass acts in their favour. Its design set the style and general arrangement of thousands of British locomotives built over the next century. With a more effective blast-pipe in the smoke-box channelling exhaust steam from the cylinders and mixing it with combustion gases drawn through the boiler tubes as a result of the vacuum, *Patentee* was a major advance on *Rocket*. *Patentee*'s cylinders were inside the frames and under the smoke-box to keep them warm, minimizing condensation losses and increasing efficiency, and allowing the engine to run more smoothly than *Rocket*'s due to better balancing of the driving forces.

If *Patentee* had a fault – as did so many of these early locomotives – it lay in the fact that her construction was disharmonious. These were truly early days: not only was the steam locomotive new, but the materials used in its construction were still largely untested, especially in the rough and tumble of regular everyday passenger and goods services over long distances, uphill and down. Many locomotives of this generation would virtually shake themselves to pieces, suffering severe vibratory stresses and fractured components which entailed frequent repairs. Their lives were short, if colourful. Yet half a century on, British 2-2-2 and 4-2-2 locomotives – descendants of Stephenson's *Patentee* – were running at speeds of up to 90 mph and clocking up mileages of over a million miles before being withdrawn from service. All the great steam locomotive engineers of the future would possess a very sound understanding of materials – just as they all served long apprenticeships, beginning with the making of bolts and screws, before they were let anywhere near the drawing board.

Even so, something was missing in the 1830s to make the Stephensonian locomotive a world-beater. This was the reversing link motion, invented in 1842 by William Howe, a pattern-maker with the Robert Stephenson works in Newcastle-upon-Tyne. Howe's invention, known as Stephenson's Link Motion, allowed the driver progressively to cut off steam admission into the cylinders. While a locomotive often needs the full force of steam rushing into the cylinders to get a train moving, or to climb a severe gradient, it needs far less steam once it is up to speed. Howe's lever-controlled motion linkage meant that the driver could choose the percentage of piston stroke during which steam would be admitted to produce the required power. When starting, he might admit steam for 75 or even 80 per cent of the piston stroke; as the train accelerated he could 'link up' or 'notch up' so that the volume of steam admitted to the cylinders per stroke was progressively reduced. The most efficient steam locomotives might streak along with an express passenger train on level track at full regulator and yet with a 'cut-off' of as little as 15 or even 10 per cent, with much of the power being developed from the steam that had been admitted expanding in the cylinders. Howe's invention gave the steam locomotive the equivalent of the gears used in a car. A cut-off of

75 per cent is rather like being in first gear, 50 per cent second, 35 per cent third, and so on. Rewarded by Robert Stephenson with a bonus of twenty guineas, Howe saved railway companies huge amounts of money as fuel bills fell when their drivers were trained to run well 'linked up'.

Now, four of the five fundamental engineering characteristics of the classic Stephensonian locomotive had been established. The five components were like five commandments, forged in iron and handed down from Robert Stephenson and Company in Newcastle-upon-Tyne to drawing offices and engineering workshops in Britain and around the world. These commanding characteristics were as much a part of *Evening Star*, the last main-line locomotive to be built for regular service in Britain, as they were of Stephenson engines of a century and a half earlier. They were: (i) two cylinders with cranks at right angles, unless power requirements called for three or four cylinders; (ii) the blast-pipe exhaust, giving induced draught to force the fire to produce the heat necessary for the required steam production; (iii) the multi–tubed boiler with separate fire-box; (iv) expansion valve motion; and (v), the one major characteristic that nineteenth-century locomotives lacked, the smoke-tube superheater, a device that would eliminate cylinder condensation when a locomotive was on the move and would greatly increase the volume and effectiveness of steam at any given pressure, increasing power by 20 to 25 per cent.

Over the following sixty years, between Howe's link motion for Robert Stephenson and George Churchward's appointment as locomotive superintendent at the GWR, many thousands of steam locomotives were built in Britain, and then in Europe, the United States, and, more slowly, in other parts of the world, which rarely differed from the pattern of design set in those pioneering days. National and regional characteristics emerged, with such distinctive designs as the all-purpose American 4-4-0, with its prominent cowcatcher, bulbous chimney stack designed to catch (or 'arrest') sparks, outside cylinder drive, powerful headlamp, sonorous bell, and mournful whistle; French locomotives, covered in ancillary equipment of all sorts intended to increase their efficiency; and the classic Victorian British locomotive, shaped – oh so elegantly – as if it had no moving parts whatsoever, galloping through the landscape like a thoroughbred hunter.

Despite outward appearances, design changes came slowly and steadily in the second half of the nineteenth century, rather than in a rush. This is understandable, given that few railways demanded great speeds until the twentieth century, and that most passenger trains were very light before the advent of corridor-connected, double-bogie carriages, restaurant cars, kitchens, lavatories, air conditioning, and other conveniences and luxuries. It is also true that, for the most part, labour – even skilled labour – was cheap and, until trade unions developed muscle, management was able to rule the railway roost on its own terms.

Cheap and plentiful labour also meant that nineteenth-century steam locomotives tended to be beautifully turned out, immaculate in their astonishing variety of liveries, from cream, through Stroudley's improved engine yellow, Brunswick green, Prussian blue, and crimson lake, to the glossiest blackberry black. This must surely have been one reason why the steam locomotive, and the steam railway as a whole, won admiration so very quickly from the wider public. From the ungainly, smoke-belching monsters of the colliery days before the Liverpool & Manchester Railway, the steam locomotive had turned into the most elegant and prized machine.

Generations of nineteenth-century schoolboys wanted to become engine drivers or, as they grew up, locomotive engineers. A new generation of professional men – and a very few women, too – was quick to realize that railways were good for business. Ideas as well as people could hurry between towns and cities at speeds that no one could have imagined before George Stephenson first opened out the regulator of *Rocket* at Rainhill in 1829. Finally, it was possible to travel faster than by horse.

*

'I am such a locomotive being always flying about,' wrote the prolific architect Augustus Welby Pugin, as he sped around the country whenever, it seemed, a new railway opened, in his mission to build Gothic Revival churches the length and breadth of Britain. Architectural styles had begun to travel too, and one wonders whether the railways were to blame for the sheer eclecticism of High Victorian design as architects raced about the country, rather than working locally, and with local materials, as in the days before steam.

Railways, though, and the steam locomotive in particular, had a character and an aesthetic of their own. The ways they looked, moved, and sounded were new and special. From early on, artists attempted to capture the spirit of the steam locomotive in oil on canvas. J. M. W. Turner's *Rain, Steam, and Speed*, showing one of Daniel Gooch's broad-gauge 2-2-2s blazing across Maidenhead viaduct between Paddington and Reading at the head of a GWR express, was painted in 1842. It is a brilliant, awe-inspiring evocation of a steam train in full flight, part fairy-tale dragon, part factory furnace, a fiery and fleet herald of the industrial world that had shaped it, at once frightening and compelling.

If artists and, later, photographers became enchanted with the steam locomotive, so did musicians. Steam locomotives sing a universally popular song, a song with an insistent regular beat which has been the direct inspiration for many forms of music: orchestral, jazz, blues, boogie-woogie, folk, country and western, pop, and rock. In an interview in 1923, Arthur Honegger, the Swiss-born French composer, said: 'I have always had a passionate liking for locomotives; for me, they are living things and I love them as others love women or horses.' Honegger's *Pacific 231* (1923) is a piece of music that captures, in its own modern way, the excitement and musical intensity of a train journey spun through the landscape by a relentless French État railway Pacific locomotive. And even before Honegger's overt orchestral paean to the steam locomotive, Jean Sibelius had worked the sounds of a steam train into his *Night Ride with Sunrise*, as had Anton Bruckner in his Fourth Symphony, Dvořák in the scherzo of his D minor Symphony, and Igor Stravinsky in *The Rite of Spring*.

Black plantation workers from Texas, Mississippi, and Louisiana rode a mix of passenger and freight trains north to Chicago to find work and a new life after the American Civil War. This internal emigration continued for many decades. The sound of all those steam engines, the clickety-clack of the rail joints, lonesome whistles, and a sense of hope, yearning, and nostalgia, all railroaded into one new sensibility, helped give rise to the blues. To jazz and boogie-woogie, too, through the rocking pianos of Jimmy Yancey, Albert Ammons, and Meade 'Lux' Lewis. Just listen to 'Lux' Lewis's 'Honky Tonk Train Blues' (1926).

From an earlier time, here is a wonderful poem, 'From a Railway Carriage', by Robert Louis Stevenson, published in *A Child's Garden of Verses* (1885):

Faster than fairies, faster than witches,
Bridges and houses, hedges and ditches;
And charging along like troops in a battle
All through the meadows the horses and cattle:
All of the sights of the hill and the plain
Fly as thick as driving rain;
And ever again, in the wink of an eye,
Painted stations whistle by.

Here is a child who clambers and scrambles,
All by himself and gathering brambles;
Here is a tramp who stands and gazes;
And there is the green for stringing the daisies!
Here is a cart run away in the road
Lumping along with man and load;
And here is a mill, and there is a river:
Each a glimpse and gone for ever!

How cleverly, and in so few lines, Stevenson, born seven years before G. J. Churchward and just twenty years after the opening of the Liverpool & Manchester Railway, catches the sound of the locomotive and of the carriages tearing after it – and how, too, his soundscape gives us the train now racing along the level, now climbing a hill, and, finally, streaking off into the unheeding distance.

W. H. Auden managed much the same with his memorable script for the GPO Film Unit's *Night Mail* (1936). As we watch 6108 *Seaforth Highlander*, a three-cylinder Royal Scot class 4-6-0, climb the long gradient to the summit at Beattock, Auden recites:

> This is the Night Mail crossing the border,
> Bringing the cheque and the postal order,
> Letters for the rich, letters for the poor,
> The shop at the corner and the girl next door.
> Pulling up Beattock, a steady climb:
> The gradient's against her, but she's on time.

Stately. Dignified. But with the punch and pull of pistons pounding in hard-pressed cylinders. And, then, as the LMS locomotive streaks down the fells towards Glasgow, the poet accelerates too:

> Letters of thanks, letters from banks,
> Letters of joy from the girl and the boy,
> Receipted bills and invitations
> To inspect new stock or visit relations,
> And applications for situations
> And timid lovers' declarations
> And gossip, gossip from all the nations,
> News circumstantial, news financial,
> Letters with holiday snaps to enlarge in,
> Letters with faces scrawled in the margin,

Letters from uncles, cousins, and aunts,
Letters to Scotland from the South of France,
Letters of condolence to Highlands and Lowlands
Notes from overseas to Hebrides
Written on paper of every hue,
The pink, the violet, the white and the blue,
The chatty, the catty, the boring, adoring,
The cold and official and the heart's outpouring,
Clever, stupid, short and long,
The typed and the printed and the spelt all wrong.

Here you can hear the rhythm of the rail joints as well as the insistent chatter of valves, letting steam in, letting steam out.

As for films, perhaps it is significant that the very first moving picture shown to the public was of a train. This was the Lumière brothers' fifty-second short, *L'arrivée d'un train en gare à La Ciotat*, filmed on a family holiday in July 1895. The sequence shows a tall-chimneyed Paris–Lyon–Mediterranean 2-4-2 pulling into a seaside station between Marseilles and Toulon and passengers getting on and off. The sight of the locomotive heading towards the screen when the film was projected in the basement of the Grand Café on the Boulevard des Capucines in Paris on 28 December 1895 caused several members of the audience to duck their heads behind the seats in front.

The steam locomotive created a rich world of art, culture, and enthusiasm around itself. For the men whose work is celebrated here, it was a world in the round. Brought up in an era in which the steam locomotive was all around them, it was no wonder that the future mechanical engineers who shaped the last generation of great main-line steam locomotives were so smitten with them. For some, as we will see, it was steam to its limits, even though most were well aware of the competing demands of new forms of traction. There was, though, always going to be a difference between a machine that seemed to be alive, abounding in character and imbued with a soul, and smooth anonymous boxes on wheels which moved trains along tracks with little apparent effort. This attitude was summed up well by British Railways design engineer E. S. Cox when he wrote in 1965:

> Professionally, the diesel and the mechanical parts of electric locomotives have given me just as absorbing an interest and challenge as ever did their steam predecessors, and I shall watch their future progress with the closest interest when I have no longer any contribution to make. Privately, steam has been a lifelong love, from the lineside, in the erecting shop, on the footplate and above all in the countless aspects of design and development with which it has been my good fortune to be concerned. When the time comes, not far distant now, when the steam locomotive in this country is only to be seen in museums or on small enthusiast-sponsored light railways, the magnificent sound of crashing exhausts, and the distant wail of the chime whistle will remain in memory's ear as unforgettable recollections of an age which has gone.

Quite simply, steam had a magic quality, a spirit that was difficult for those brought up with steam railways in their Victorian and Edwardian heyday, when all was spick and span and colourful, even to want to consider giving up. There came, though, a later generation of politicians and professional men and women who believed in modernization at all costs, whether promoting high-rise council estates, motorways, and supermarkets, with the concomitant destruction of so many historic buildings and town centres, or conducting an attack on the steam locomotive which, even at the time, seemed the stuff of a zealous and blinkered iconoclasm.

As it was, I was born at the very end of steam in regular main-line service. And yet, like so many generations of boys – and a number of girls – before me, I was captivated the moment I first saw and listened to a steam engine. There were Britannia class Pacifics named after British heroes and all-purpose Stanier class 5 4-6-0s at Marylebone, the delightfully quiet and quintessentially Edwardian terminus hidden behind the roaring traffic of the Marylebone Road, where steam-hauled semi-fasts raced the electric trains of London Transport's Metropolitan Line through Kilburn and Neasden, then up the steep Chiltern banks to Amersham and on across the Vale of Aylesbury, along the magnificently aligned route that Sir Edward Watkin had built to more generous continental dimensions in the late 1890s, dreaming of a direct service from Manchester through Sheffield, Nottingham, Leicester, Aylesbury, and Neasden, and on through central London to Paris, via the South Eastern & Chatham Railway and a Channel Tunnel.

There were the ex-GWR red 0-6-0 pannier tanks, based at Neasden depot, which could be heard chuffing around the Circle Line at night with their maintenance trains. There was an unforgettable day at the Dagenham works of the Ford Motor Company where I got to drive a steam locomotive for the first time. I had to stand on a wooden box to see out of the circular cab window of Ford's No. 8, a Peckett 0-6-0 saddle tank which was used, together with a small fleet of identical engines, to pull goods inwards from Dagenham Docks on the Thames and goods outwards, in the form of cars, to the boats that would take them to the continent. I can still remember the sheer thrill of opening a regulator for the first time. That slight delay between moving the lever and the steam pushing the two pistons in and out. The clouds of steam shooting out from the cylinder cocks as the fireman exhausted condensation from the cylinders after the locomotive had been standing idle. The sudden chuff from the chimney as the industrial engine rumbled down from behind the massive factory towards the docks.

I remember the driver, from the nearby Becontree Estate, built by the London County Council in the 1920s, covering my hand and guiding it through the various positions of the brake valve. There were instructions on how to use the 'blower', a valve that opens to shoot steam up through the blast-pipe whenever the regulator is shut, to ensure a draught through the fire-box and boiler tubes; without this, a sudden downdraught or the compression of air when passing through a tunnel could blow back down the chimney and force flames and hot gas out on to the footplate, threatening the crew with the very real danger of severe, or even fatal, burns. No. 8 was painted green, with the distinctive Ford signature logo on the bulbous saddle tank. She was no beauty, yet locomotives like this were very much a behind-the-scenes part of the working life of industrial Britain. I wonder what became of her? Perhaps she went the way of 99 per cent of Ford Cortinas. Hopefully, though, she is delighting a new generation of children on a preserved railway somewhere, a generation for whom steam, despite the allure of digital Twittery, retains its elemental sorcery. In her vastly popular Harry Potter books, the first of which was published in 1997, J. K. Rowling instinctively knew that her fictional Hogwarts Express had to be a steam train. In the equally successful Harry Potter films, the locomotive used to pull the Hogwarts Express is an ex-GWR, Hall class two-cylinder 4-6-0, *Olton Hall* (renamed *Hogwarts Castle*) designed under the direction of Charles Collett and built at Swindon in 1937. Both author and directors gauged the mood of children at the turn of the twentieth century exactly. It is still possible to be intrigued by steam, and even to love the steam locomotive, while living in an age of global digital communications and computer design and technology.

I rode the footplate of another Peckett 0-6-0 saddle tank some years later, at the Betteshanger colliery in Kent. Today, in the era of Facebook and air-conditioned edge-of-town shopping malls, the idea of a coal mine in the plush Home Counties, complete with cage lifts and the skeletal wheeled towers that lowered miners into Hadean depths, must seem highly improbable. But the Kent mines were real enough, and very old-fashioned indeed by the time I got to see them in action. Somewhere, my old school friend Paul Kutarski, a former army medic and today a consultant surgeon, has an 8 mm film of the occasion. He says he cannot find it. I wish he could. It would be the stuff of museum archives now. Betteshanger was the last colliery in Kent. It closed in 1989.

I remember a thrilling ride on the 08.30 express from Waterloo, for the first time, to greet the RMS *Queen Elizabeth*, the Cunard liner, at Southampton Docks. Our locomotive was a filthy West Country Pacific – 34001, shorn of its nameplate, *Exeter* – originally built to the radical designs of Oliver Bulleid for the Southern Railway in 1945 and modified by Ron Jarvis for the Southern Region of British Railways in 1957. We sat in the first coach, an elegantly curved, malachite-green Bulleid Open Brake Second, ventilators wide open, as I listened with the intensity of a young child to the compulsive three-cylinder jazz beat of *Exeter* as she raced south-west, her performance belying her appearance. At the end of steam, British Railways management seemed determined, unlike railway managements in France, Germany, or South Africa, to prove to the public that steam was inherently unclean – although perhaps a shortage of workers willing to toil in sooty engine sheds in the 1960s was equally responsible.

By refusing to clean engines, stripping them of names and number plates, and maintaining them to minimal standards, and simultaneously declining to retain a suitably skilled workforce, British Railways' intention appears to have been to turn passengers against these beautiful machines in preparation for the impending launch of gleaming, if characterless, electric multiple units. Yet even in their very last days, these charismatic and modern steam locomotives – some, like 34098 *Templecombe*, had been rebuilt just six years before withdrawal – would run happily at 100 mph and more when given their head between Basingstoke and Woking, a blur of whirling, grimy motion, a triumph of design and engineering over a management blinkered by the notion of modernization at any cost.

Was the public fooled? Perhaps. One thing I was to learn, though, many years later when firing and driving regular steam trains in

Poland was that many – most? – passengers simply want to get from A to B, to commute from home to work and back, as quickly and reliably as possible. The question of whether their train is powered by steam, diesel, or electricity is largely irrelevant. On my first solo spell driving the 04.16 fast commuter train from Wolsztyn to Poznań on a savagely cold day in 2003, when the landscape was shrouded in snow and even Captain Oates might have allowed himself a grumble of complaint, I drew to a halt under the electric wires at a graffiti-sprayed Poznań station, aligning the doors of the first of the olive-green, double-deck coaches behind me with the stairs leading to the exit, exactly on time. Andrzej Macur, the moustachioed regular PKP (Polish State Railways) driver who had allowed me to drive as I saw fit for the two hours from Wolzstyn, clapped me gently on the shoulders, exclaiming: 'Bravo! Pivo! Wodka!' – which meant he would be buying the drinks back in the engineman's bar in Wolsztyn that night. I leaned out of the cab of the well-groomed, if hard-pressed, fifty-year-old, black and green PKP two-cylinder 2-6-2, 0149-69, and watched passengers stream from the train, some behind newspapers, others blowing their noses, several staring crossly at their watches. Not one, not a single one, looked up at me or spared the most cursory glance for the brutally handsome machine that had brought them safely and on time through the snow, stopping at and starting from fifteen stations along the way. Perhaps some had been hoping the train would be cancelled so they could stay at home in front of the fire – and who could blame them in such extreme weather?

I can remember, too, those Nottingham semi-fasts from Marylebone. 'Brackley? That's the steamer, son.' This was the stuff of Stephensonian wizardry to me, yet just a train, or so it seemed, to the bored-looking grown-ups in the compartment with me. I used to stand in the corridor, lower the window, and look out as the 14.38 Marylebone to Nottingham Victoria barked through the tunnels under Lord's Cricket Ground and St John's Wood on a Wednesday afternoon, red and orange sparks rising from the chimney of a Britannia Pacific or, more usually, a Stanier class 5 4-6-0, the glow from the cab flickering against blackened brick walls. As a teenager, I remember the shock of recognition when I first saw Joseph Wright of Derby's painting *An Iron Forge* (1772) in the Tate Gallery, and again, at much the same time, when I looked properly at Wright's *An Experiment on a Bird in the Air Pump* (1768) in the National Gallery. Wright had painted, in spirit if not in fact, what I had seen when looking out of the window of a maroon ex-LMS coach in the tunnels leading north-west from Marylebone.

Gradually, this made sense. Joseph Wright of Derby was one of the first artists to capture and represent the spirit, at once thrilling and demonic, of the Industrial Revolution. I suppose I had a very romantic view of the steam locomotive from very early on. I can remember stepping back into my compartment on the 14.38 and a man in a grey worsted suit with braces and Reginald Maudling glasses sliding the ventilator above the window shut with some force. 'Soot!' he said, sitting down behind his newspaper.

I never wrote down the numbers of steam locomotives or underlined them in the pages of Ian Allan ABC Locospotters books because I simply liked to look and listen to those few still busy at work when I was very young. I knew full well that they were on their way out and I was, somehow, trying to take them in, to absorb them in every last detail and sensation. Pulsating exhausts. The clank of connecting rods when there was undue play between big ends and crankpins. The chatter of piston valves. The singing of injectors that bring water at very high temperatures to thirsty boilers from tanks and tenders. (If you have a traditional Italian espresso machine, you might well use a steam injector every morning to froth the milk for the breakfast cappuccino.) The hum of blower valves. The urgent roar of steam escaping from safety valves. The shriek, wail, hoot, or chime of whistles. The backbeat of air-brake compressors. The sizzle and smell of hot oil. The glow from the fire-box. A hum from the boiler. The astonishing thing, though, is just how quiet even the biggest well-maintained steam locomotive is as it stands idling at a station. It is only when the green light gives the right of way and the guard's whistle blows that it erupts into full-blooded life. Whereas diesel and even electric locomotives standing in stations, and especially under roofs, can be very noisy indeed.

I liked to talk to drivers and firemen, and, bit by bit, I came to be fascinated by the idea of the men who, at some time in the past, had designed these enthralling machines. For many years I had a colour photograph – I think I still have it somewhere in a box of papers – of the Princess Coronation class Pacific 46254 *City of Stoke-on-Trent*. This was the thirty-fifth out of thirty-eight four-cylinder 4-6-2s designed under the direction of William Stanier, chief mechanical engineer of the LMS, to work the heaviest and fastest expresses to and from Scotland and London, over Shap and Beattock. The Coronations, or Duchesses, as these superb engines were usually called, were the most powerful steam locomotives to run in Britain. They were also fast, reliable, and much loved by crews, shed staff, management, and enthusiasts. The first was built in 1937. *City of Stoke-on-Trent* emerged from the Crewe works in 1946, painted black, as the era of austerity demanded. In 1951, at the time and, perhaps, in the spirit of the Festival of Britain, she was repainted in blue. Four years later, she became a green engine. In 1958 she changed to red and finally, in May 1960, she was shopped out from Crewe in a fresh coat of red lined in yellow – and for the first time in her brief life she looked exactly as she should have done all along. This was the occasion when an official British Railways photographer caught her on colour film, standing on the track at Crewe works with a backdrop of trees. This was the photograph that I took with me on my very first day at school and proudly showed it to the three children I was to share a desk with that year: Susan Connolly, Susan Peacock, and Philip Marshall. They all liked the red, and Philip, who was already trying to read his older brothers' Thomas the Tank Engine books – at a time when these were still being written, innocently, by the Rev. W. Awdry and had not yet become computer-generated animations on children's television – appeared greatly impressed.

I learned the principal dimensions of 46254 *City of Stoke-on-Trent* along with my times tables and catechism. I could tell my dog and the cats that the Coronations were 'introduced in 1937', that they had four cylinders with a bore of 16.5 in and a stroke of 28 in, a boiler pressure of 250 psi, 6 ft 9 in driving wheels, and weighed 105 tons. Tractive effort was 40,000 lb, power classification 8P. Of course, a number as improbable as 40,000 was meaningless to me, but that wasn't a problem. There were, after all, many aspects of the catechism that I couldn't grasp either. The real puzzle, though, was who was William Stanier?

As I came to read books, principally by Cecil J. Allen, the railway engineer, journalist, and writer, and O. S. Nock, the signal engineer, journalist, and writer, borrowed from public libraries, I began to be able to associate the names of engineers with the locomotives they built and became as interested in the nature, purpose, history, and design of these machines as I was in how fast they could go. What I was unaware of for years to come was what kind of men they really were. I was ignorant, too, of exactly how they worked, imagining that William Stanier and Nigel Gresley simply sat down, dreamed up particular classes of locomotives, and drew them, as if straight out of their heads.

Today, I know that *City of Stoke-on-Trent* and her thirty-seven siblings were the result of team work. The general principles of the design of the Coronation class had been laid down by William Stanier as a development of his Princess Royal class, but he was in India on official railway business throughout the time that the detailed design of the new locomotives came together in the drawing office of his chief draughtsman, Tom Coleman. If the Coronation class had to be assigned as the work of a single engineer, then that engineer would have to be Coleman, rather than Stanier. Even then, these superb engines owed much to Churchward, and something to Chapelon in France, while the last two members of the class, *Sir William A. Stanier*

FRS and *City of Salford*, were modified with labour-saving components devised in the United States.

This question of who actually designed what is important, and it is one with which, say, any writer on architecture will be familiar, since architectural practices tend to take their names from the founding partner. This does not, however, mean that the person whose name is on the firm's letterhead actually designed this school or that museum, even if every building emerging from the practice will have been approved by its leading light. And so it was with steam locomotives. For example, Sir Henry Fowler, one of Stanier's predecessors at the LMS, was a great organizer, a man with a scientific outlook, and an expert in metallurgy; yet although such famous locomotives as the three-cylinder Royal Scot 4-6-0s are credited to him in the ABC Locospotters books, and many other publications, he did little in the way of detailed design work, leaving that to experienced assistants or, in the case of the Royal Scots, as much to the engineers of the North British Locomotive Company in Glasgow as to his own staff at Derby and Crewe. Indeed, one day in 1929, when one of his assistants, Henry George Ivatt, who went on to become the last chief mechanical engineer of the LMS, was pointing out details of improvements being made to the Walschaerts valve gear of the excellent two-cylinder 2-6-4 tank engines ascribed to Fowler, Sir Henry turned to him and said: 'Quite honestly, I don't understand the thing.' He might, of course, have been pulling Ivatt's leg. To his credit, though, Fowler had taken members of his design team on a trip to France in 1926 in preparation for outlining an LMS four-cylinder compound Pacific – a design that was, as it turned out, rejected by the company's motive power running superintendent, J. E. Anderson, who refused to spend his department's budget on the new and longer turntables the Pacifics would have needed.

Others, like Oliver Bulleid, were very much hands-on designers. The extraordinary Merchant Navy, West Country, and Battle of Britain Pacifics built by the Southern Railway at Eastleigh, along with the ultra-austere Q1 class 0-6-0 and revolutionary Leader class 0-6-6-0 prototype – a steam locomotive that might easily have been mistaken for a diesel – could have been the work of no one else. Equally, while the very able twentieth- century German locomotive engineer Richard Paul Wagner aimed for a uniformity of mechanically excellent designs free from individualistic quirks and flourishes, no other engineer than André Chapelon could have produced the truly brilliant 240P, 242A1, and 141P classes of compound locomotives, which were the most efficient of all steam locomotives in regular service and continue to inspire steam engineers today.

Thanks to the National Railway Museum and the *Independent* newspaper, in 1990 I got to ride on the footplate of the Stanier–Coleman Pacific 6229 *Duchess of Hamilton* on the demanding Settle and Carlisle main line – an experience akin to being in very heaven for someone who, as a five-year-old boy, had carried a colour photograph of one of these engines to school with him. Some years later, I drove *Duchess of Hamilton* – at nothing more than 50 mph, sadly – on the revived stretch of the Great Central Railway between Loughborough and Leicester. It was another cold, snowy day and the experience of opening up the surprisingly sensitive regulator was a happily challenging one. Was it possible to move the train out of Loughborough station without the *Duchess*'s 6 ft 9 in driving wheels slipping? With expert guidance, yes. Linking up and feeling this great locomotive respond to an increased demand for power with such a smooth surge was very nearly enough to make me want to throw in the day job and become an engine driver. In 1994, however, there were not enough steam locomotives about to make that a practical career option, although I have been lucky enough to have oiled, fired, ridden, and driven steam locomotives around the world since then. I took up flying instead.

Sir Nigel Gresley's sister Beatrice, a talented painter, said that he had wanted to be an engine driver from the age of four. Gresley, like many talented young men of his generation, could have chosen to go on from school to university to study maths or science, but instead opted to serve an apprenticeship with the LNWR at Crewe under Francis Webb and, later, with the Lancashire and Yorkshire Railway under George Hughes at Horwich. Gresley got to drive as many locomotives as he cared to; he also designed them.

Today, such options are open to increasingly few young people, not just in Britain – a country with little apparent appetite for modern railway engineering – but in all countries where the idea of a service and consumer economy has taken root, or even taken over, and the making of things is all too often seen as a lowly and grubby activity. And now that digitalia is fast becoming virtually a medical condition of our times, and ever more people spend their working day, and even their leisure time, glued to computer screens and electronic gadgets, the thought of shaping a steam locomotive from raw materials, and turning those raw materials into a thing of stirring beauty which can also move you through real landscapes, is increasingly anathema.

The day of the great steam locomotive engineers in the mould of Churchward, Gresley, Chapelon, Stanier, and Wagner is gone. It is gone because the technology has changed and has become ever more complex: a modern locomotive could no more be designed by one individual heading a reasonably small team of engineers than could a jet fighter. Furthermore, it has been damned by the rise of the banal culture of modern management, which is more concerned with managing than with creating or innovating and which has little apparent care for manufacturing and engineering, and by the grimly persistent ideology of modernization – modernization, that is, for its own sake. The wiles of the oil lobby, meanwhile, have not simply driven steam railway locomotive development into a siding, but have also left very many countries dependent on expensive imported fuels and at the mercy of war and terrorism as well as ever-rising prices. (One key reason why, for example, the Norfolk and Western Railway stayed loyal to steam until late in the diesel day was that its routes passed through some of the richest coal seams in the United States. The fuel needed to power its trains was relatively cheap and located under and around its tracks. It did not have to be imported from thousands of miles away.) And if I repeat these arguments throughout this book, it is simply, and sadly, because they bear repetition.

As it was, the locomotive superintendents and chief mechanical engineers of Britain's railways were powerful individuals, many of whom would report directly to their company's board of directors. In many cases, this gave them creative leeway and they were able to conduct experiments, to innovate, and quite often to set the tone and, in later years, much of the press and public relations agenda of their companies. Gresley and Stanier were well known in their day, their locomotives making newspaper headlines and starring in newsreels and even in feature films. Gresley's streamlined A4 Pacific 2509 *Silver Link* was prominent in the opening sequence of the hugely popular Will Hay comedy *Oh! Mr Porter* (1937), while in the same year few cinema audiences could have failed to be moved by a newsreel showing the streamlined Stanier Pacific 6220 *Coronation* racing up to 114 mph on the final descent from Stafford to Crewe on the press run of the Coronation Scot express.

When the railways were nationalized, this kind of individualism and even flamboyance was often frowned upon. In some cases, there was no longer a chief mechanical engineer as such, but heads of various technical committees instead. The key word now was standardization, which was undoubtedly a useful means of reducing component stocks and costs. This had already taken place in countries where railways were under state control, as in Germany, or where private enterprise ruled the commercial roost, as in the United States, where the designs of the majority of locomotive types converged over the course of the twentieth century.

The killer, though, was modernization. Modernization is often a naive concept; it is also a weasel word, much used by politicians and management, from Harold Macmillan to Tony Blair, to make themselves seem like forward-looking, tough, no-nonsense, out-with-the-old-and-in-with-the-new, trains-run-on-time kinda guys. And the trouble with modernization plans is that they often presage a form of commercial Year Zero. When, in December 1954, British Railways announced and published its 1955 Modernization Plan, one of the key recommendations was for the progressive replacement of all steam locomotives through large-scale dieselization and electrification. This put a summary end to steam development at a time when the development of diesel locomotives in Britain was still at a relatively early stage.

British Railways initially ordered 171 examples of fourteen different types of main-line diesels, most with electric and, later, hydraulic transmission, which were often less reliable than the steam locomotives they replaced. The idea had been to test these engines over a period of three years to sort out the sheep from the goats. Unfortunately, the hand of Roland Bond, chief mechanical officer of British Railways, was forced by politicians and civil servants at the Ministry of Transport. Oil companies and other commercial interests convinced the ministry that a major coal strike, or series of strikes, could paralyse the largely steam-hauled railways. This had happened on the east coast of the United States in 1946–7 and it could happen in Britain too. Under political pressure, British Railways ordered a further five hundred diesels before the various prototypes could be properly evaluated.

For the most part, these main-line diesels looked strangely old-fashioned and cumbersome. They guzzled expensive imported oil, belched out poisonous fumes, and did little to raise the average speed of either express passenger or fast goods trains at the very time – in the early 1960s – when a national network of motorways was under construction and inter-city jets were about to make their debut on prime business routes from London to cities such as Glasgow, Edinburgh, Newcastle, Manchester, and Leeds. Management had argued that the latest 2,000 hp, 90 mph English Electric diesel-electrics, placed in service from 1958, should be able to do the work of the 3,000 ihp, 100 mph-plus Stanier Pacifics on the west coast route from London to Glasgow over Shap and Beattock. Given the state of the track, signalling, line occupation, and timetabling at the time, in theory this was possible. The Coronation class Pacifics were rarely asked to produce much more than 2,000 ihp in daily service in the late 1950s, while the maximum speed allowed on the line was 90 mph. There was good reason for this. British Railways management regarded 4,000 lb of coal an hour as the maximum rate for sustained hand-firing. At that rate, a Coronation would generate 25–28,000 lb of steam per hour, sufficient for 2,000 ihp or 1,400–1,450 dbhp. A 2,000 hp diesel-electric could sustain 1,450 dbhp. And, although the Pacifics had a much greater turn of speed, diesels were much quicker off the mark up to about 30 mph and therefore well suited to a busy main line like the west coast route south of Preston, where delays could be frequent and the need for rapid acceleration was imperative.

British Railways engineering management, moreover, was reluctant to introduce mechanical stokers, fearing increased locomotive maintenance costs at higher power outputs, quite apart from the cost of the stokers themselves and the higher fuel consumption. When a Southern Region Merchant Navy Pacific, 35005 *Canadian Pacific*, was fitted with a mechanical stoker, fuel consumption increased by 25 per cent. (In France, by contrast, mechanically fired locomotives were equipped with much longer fire-box brick arches, as well as superior draughting, which ensured that the coal was burned efficiently.)

A point, however, that the diesel-oriented management appears to have overlooked is that the Coronations could rise well above the occasion when necessary – to win back lost time, for example. Or when a special train for VIPs was called on to run faster than was normally allowed. One day in 1953, at a time when British express passenger trains were only very slowly getting back up to speed after the ravages caused by the Second World War, a group of 180 guests had to be taken by train from London to Glasgow and back for the opening of a new Rolls-Royce aero-engine factory at East Kilbride. Among the complement were top brass from the Royal Navy and RAF, and Duncan Sandys, minister of supply.

The party went up overnight on a heavy, fourteen-car, sleeping-car express, worked as far as Carlisle by a London crew from Camden shed in charge of the Coronation Pacific 46241 *City of Edinburgh*. Driver George Pile, one of three brothers who were all drivers at Camden, was teamed with fireman 'Nellie' Wallace and, on account of the importance of the occasion, locomotive inspector W. G. Fryer. The following day, Fryer was told that because the VIPs had to be back in London that night, they would have to make a very fast run from Carlisle back to Euston, with stops at Crewe and Watford Junction. When the train arrived at Carlisle, just before 18.00, it was formed of just seven coaches, weighing 260 tons. *City of Edinburgh* went like a rocket. Between Lancaster and Preston, Fryer allowed Pile to pile on the speed, despite a 90 mph restriction.

'At Bay Horse [in Lancashire],' wrote Fryer, some years later, 'we were on the limit and going well. Nellie gave me the thumbs-up sign. George held his pipe in his left hand still unlit. So far he had not been able to spare the concentration to light up. I looked over the side to see the connecting and side rods; at speed they were just a blur. In the moonlight I could just see the mileposts. With my stopwatch I made it 8 sec for the ¼ mile [112.5 mph] . . . The locomotive was running like a sewing machine, the click of the rail joints barely audible; the steam from the exhaust clung to the boiler and drifted over the tender. It was as if some gigantic hare was running with its ears laid back.'

The net running time, taking into account delays caused by signals and permanent-way restrictions (temporary speed limits), was about four hours and ten minutes, an average of 72 mph. This was not just very fast indeed for 1953, but a run that would have been wholly out of the question for one of the expensive 2,000 hp diesel-electrics which arrived five years later to start replacing *City of Edinburgh* and her siblings. Nor was this run wholly out of the ordinary. When pressed, the Coronation Pacifics could put up short-term performances that could only be equalled by the 3,300 hp Deltic diesel-electrics ordered for the east coast main line for delivery in 1961. These had been commissioned in the knowledge that 2,000 hp and 90 mph simply would not do in the motorway age. Gerald Fiennes, the inspired railway manager who insisted on the Deltics, said that he loved steam but diesels were, apart from anything else in their favour, more predictable in terms of performance.

If fitted with mechanical stokers, the Coronation Pacifics should have been able to match even the timings demanded by the management when the west coast line was electrified and cleared for 100 mph running over lengthy sections in 1965. Not only did a Coronation run the 158 miles from Crewe to Euston in two hours, as the new 1960s electrics were asked to do, but they would, as many locomotive inspectors and engineers, and timing experts like Cecil J. Allen and O. S. Nock, were happy to confirm, have been able to do the run in 110 minutes with the help of modern track, freshly aligned curves, new signalling, and a 100 mph line limit. Even then, these were the Coronations as designed in 1936–7 by Tom Coleman and his team. If the Second World War had not intervened, further examples would have been built with a higher boiler pressure (275 psi, rather than 250 psi) and improved steam flow, among other improvements, which would have significantly raised their performance. A much bigger and more powerful mechanically fired Stanier 4-6-4 also intended for the route would have been able to sustain a power output at least equal to that of a Deltic diesel-electric. And this had all been planned in the 1930s. Imagine what might have been achieved if steam development had accelerated from 1939.

British Railways' 1955 Modernization Plan certainly appeared to lack technical coherence. The new 2,000 hp and other diesel-electrics, for example, were equipped with steam boilers to provide heating for the carriages trailing behind them. This anachronism caused no end of problems and for several years it was necessary to keep spare locomotives on 'pilot' duty at principal stations in case of minor breakdowns. Again, the competence of the design of the Stanier Pacifics – locomotives designed to have plenty of reserve power in hand – was recognized even while they were being withdrawn from service and consigned to breakers' yards, despite the fact that they had many years front-line service left in them.

O. S. Nock was riding in the cab of a 2,000 hp English Electric diesel-electric at the head of the down Midday Scot express from Euston to Glasgow when the water tank feeding the steam-heating boiler sprang a leak just before Crewe. The replacement engine was not, as Nock expected, another diesel, but 46228 *Duchess of Rutland*, one of the red Coronation Pacifics. Unfazed by the sudden switch from the antiseptic cab of a diesel to the footplate of one of Britain's most powerful steam locomotives, driver Purcell and fireman Keen from Camden not only regained much time but gave Nock, a hugely experienced train-timer, his fastest run to date over the 141 miles from Crewe, including the formidable ascent of Shap Fell, to Carlisle. The journey on to Glasgow was marred by the need to stop for water for the best part of five minutes at Carstairs. Because the modernizers had been at work, the troughs from which *Duchess of Rutland* should have been able to scoop up water to fill her tender while still at speed had been taken out of service.

It was this lack of what, today, we call 'joined-up thinking' that characterized aspects of the modernization of Britain's railways. In Germany, steam locomotives were generally kept in tip-top condition, even during their last weeks in regular use. Passengers and crews were not made to suffer simply because steam was officially outmoded. But perhaps the most curious aspect of British Railways' dieselization policy was the replacement of steam locomotives on a like-for-like basis, in terms of power, speed, and overall performance. Instead of taking the opportunity to invest in diesels with much greater power and speed than the existing Pacifics and other express steam locomotives, diesel engines were bought that offered precious little, if any, advance on what steam engineers had achieved to date. This was partly because there were few high-powered diesels on the market at the time, but it was also a consequence of the easy schedules of most British express passenger trains in the 1950s. These were such that a Coronation Pacific running a 500 ton train from Crewe to Euston even on a mile-a-minute schedule could get by with an average of little more than 1,100 dbhp. A diesel locomotive with a rating of just 1,600 hp could match this performance quite comfortably, as George Carpenter, the British locomotive engineer and historian, found out for himself one day in 1951 when he rode the footplate of the ex-LMS 1,600 hp diesel-electric 10001, built in 1947. The diesel ran the 158 miles from Crewe to Euston with a fourteen-coach, 510 ton train at a start-to-stop average of 62 mph, a performance that matched up to Pacific standards, even though steam men on the LMS thought of the diesel as having the same power and performance as a class 4 two-cylinder 2-6-4 tank engine.

There was, of course, agreement among many European steam engineers of the last decades of regular main-line steam that high-speed passenger trains on principal routes in the future would be electric, as electric traction provided the most convenient means of obtaining the very high power outputs (10,000 hp and more) required to accelerate trains of more than 800 tons, like the French TGVs, to speeds of up to 186 mph (300 kph). Furthermore, as was made clear by Sir John Weir's 1931 report on railway electrification, the great advantage of electrification is the removal of the power source from the train itself to central power stations, with substantially reduced motive power maintenance costs.

Even so, few were prepared for the extent of the triumph of the diesel and oil lobby over steam, certainly in the United States, from the late 1930s onwards. There were many reasons for this triumph, as we shall see, but the effect was to change and distort the railway locomotive market worldwide. Many American diesels were undoubtedly excellent designs, but such was the pervasive influence of US business practice and American culture that railways around the world began to dieselize regardless.

The arrival of the diesel locomotive in the United States, and the lobby that promoted it, replete with sales managers and marketing executives, revealed an entirely new culture which must have been baffling to steam men. The great steam engineers were themselves the product of a tradition that had begun with the Stephensons, and even before. Not only did they build on precedent but, despite commercial rivalries, they often enjoyed a camaraderie which joined hands across borders. Otto Jabelmann, the Union Pacific Railroad's vice president in charge of the Department of Research and Mechanical Standards, and the driving force behind the awe-inspiring Big Boy 4-8-8-4 fast freight locomotives of 1941, certainly knew of the work of André Chapelon, as did Paul Kiefer, head of design for the New York Central Railroad, whose Niagara class 4-8-4s of 1945 were among the very finest of all passenger locomotives. In 1947 Kiefer crossed the Atlantic to give a very important paper in London on the relative costs of running steam, diesel, and electric locomotives. Jabelmann came to Britain to give advice on how to speed up the servicing and maintenance of locomotives for wartime service. In fact, he died in London in 1943.

A. I. Lipetz, chief consulting engineer with Alco – the American Locomotive Company, of Schenectady, New York – the firm that developed and built the Big Boys with Jabelmann, was a Pole who came to the United States at the time of the First World War. He had previously worked with G. V. Lomonosoff, the most famous pre-revolutionary Russian locomotive engineer. In 1935, Lipetz was in France where, on 3 October, he rode on the footplate of the Chapelon Pacific 231.726, with Chapelon himself, together with driver Gourault and fireman Miot, heading the Sud Express from Paris to Bordeaux, steam-hauled over the 217 miles from Tours. Despite a train composed of thirteen heavy Pullman cars, weighing 622 tons, on its way to meet an ocean liner berthed at Bordeaux, and a line limit of 125 kph (77.5 mph), the Chapelon Pacific ran the 122.6 kilometres (70 miles) from Poitiers to Bordeaux in 59 minutes, at an average speed of 114 kph (70.8 mph). Lipetz was astonished by the performance of this relatively small locomotive, which equalled that of a New York Central class J-1 Hudson weighing half as much again. On his return to the

USA, he told Alco vice president Joe Ennis of his observations, and this resulted in an enlarged steam-flow circuit and improved draughting for the New York Central's new class J-3 Hudsons, then under design, which raised their maximum indicated power by 20 per cent over the J-1s. Lipetz also put Chapelon's ideas into practice in the design of the Union Pacific's Challenger 4-6-6-4s as well as its FEF 4-8-4s and the New York Central's Niagara 4-8-4s of 1946.

Richard Wagner, meanwhile, gave a talk in 1935 on high-speed locomotives to the Institute of Locomotive Engineers in London and was always keen to show British engineers his latest designs for the Deutsche Reichsbahn. In 1936, Stanier rode on the footplate of one of the Deutsche Reichsbahn's streamlined 4-6-4s at a rock-steady 118 mph. These supremely fast-running machines were designed by Adolf Wolff at the Borsig works in Berlin in 1935. Previously, Wolff too had come to London, to talk to Gresley when considering conjugated valve gear – a distinctive and, to some, controversial feature of Gresley's locomotives for the London and North Eastern Railway (LNER) – for his three-cylinder locomotives. (In the end, the larger and much heavier valves of Wolff's 05 class over Gresley's A4s ruled these out.)

Raoul Notesse, the young Belgian railways locomotive design engineer, visited Stanier to study the design for the LMS four-cylinder Princess Royal Pacifics. The visit led to Notesse's own massive four-cylinder type 1 Pacific for the Belgian railways. Tragically, Notesse, who had left Belgium for England in 1940, was killed by a V-2 ballistic missile at Harrow-on-the-Hill, where the 14.38 Marylebone to Nottingham semi-fast I rode as a young boy made its first stop. As for Chapelon himself, he was a friend of Gresley and Bulleid, both of whom spoke fluent French and had enormous respect for the brilliant French engineer.

Gresley and Stanier were close friends, too. When *Mallard* captured the world speed record for steam on 3 July 1938, Stanier wrote to Gresley the following day:

My dear Gresley

What a magnificent effort. Sincerest congratulations on
the fine performance of 'The Mallard' yesterday.
I shall be very interested in seeing details of the run and
particulars of the engine working at some future time.

Yrs very sincerely,
W. A. Stanier

When Stanier was too unwell, following a trip to the United States
in 1939, to attend the annual dinner of the Institute of Mechanical
Engineers – he was president that year – Gresley took the chair, telling
members: 'I am here in the position of a stop-gap. I am very sorry that
there has been an engine failure and Stanier has run hot.' Stanier was
also close to Bulleid, despite their very different approaches to design,
and in retirement would often spend time with the Bulleids at their
home in Sidmouth on the south Devon coast.

Steam engineers of this calibre were evidently an international
fraternity. They may have been employed by commercial companies
or by state-owned railways, and yet their mission was to improve
and increase the efficiency of the steam locomotive, a machine they
loved in their bones. The word 'mission' is not used loosely here: the
great steam locomotive engineers were, and continue to be, a secular
priesthood of sorts. These were not men who worked from nine to
five, five days a week, but engineers with a big picture of their art
and profession in their generous minds' eyes. They shared knowledge
and transcended the corporate limits of the companies that employed
them. And, although some of them persuaded themselves that the
steam locomotive was coming to the end of its life, nearly all of them
would be enthralled to know not only that steam locomotives still give
pleasure to countless people today, but also that steam development
is not yet dead.

These steam men were – no matter how radical some of them might have been – part of an engineering lineage that did, indeed, take them back to the Stephensons. The career of a pure GWR man, Frederick William Hawksworth, is a perfect example. Hawksworth, the son of a GWR draughtsman, was born and died in Swindon. He began at the works as an engineering apprentice in 1898, and in 1905 was working on the design of Churchward's Pacific *The Great Bear*. Twenty years later, he was chief draughtsman and designed the mighty King class 4-6-0s for C. B. Collett. In another twenty years, he had succeeded Collett as chief mechanical engineer of the GWR and, although for some ineffable reason he refused to talk about it up until his death, he began design work on a new Pacific which would push the design of the classic GWR express passenger locomotive onwards while still linking back to *The Great Bear*.

Meanwhile, Churchward takes us back through his chief, William Dean, to Sir Daniel Gooch, whose parents could trace their lineage back to Alfred the Great – they thought of the Normans as parvenus – and frequently entertained the Stephensons, when Daniel was a young man, at their home in Bedlington, Northumberland. Those visits were one of the things – along with an innate love of engineering, as well as an appreciation of the sheer thrill of the challenge of building the new railways – that led Daniel on to become the first full-time locomotive engineer of the GWR. He was appointed chairman of the board in 1866. From Stephenson through to Hawksworth, then, this line of steam locomotive engineers was unbroken.

There are those of us who would very much like to see a new generation of highly efficient steam locomotives pushing on from the classic Stephensonian model and running alongside the sensationally fast electrics that have revolutionized inter-city and international passenger services ever since *Shinkansen*, or 'Bullet', trains began running in Japan in 1964 and the French TGVs were launched in 1981. It would be a fine thing, too, to witness a new generation of steam locomotives hard at work in parts of the world where importing oil is a complete – as opposed to a partial – nonsense. The steam engine has been with us for a very long time. It deserves a fresh look and demands the loyalties of the hearts and minds of a future generation of Staniers and Gresleys, Kiefers and Jabelmanns, Churchwards and Chapelons.

CHAPTER 1

GREAT BRITAIN
Steady Progress and
Racing Certainties

One afternoon in the spring of 1922 . . . I was making my way to the 'Local' station at King's Cross by way of the principal departure platform at the terminus – then No. 1 – when my progress was suddenly arrested. On this never-to-be-forgotten day a new articulated sleeping car was standing alongside the loading dock, and beyond that – shining, stately and strikingly impressive – the most massive locomotive that I had ever set eyes on in Great Britain until then. It was No. 1470 *Great Northern*, Gresley's first Pacific, brought to London to be exhibited to the directors of his company, the Great Northern Railway.

This was Cecil J. Allen, the Great Eastern Railway materials inspection engineer, train-timer, and technical journalist, coming face to face with what appeared to be the first truly modern British steam locomotive. The sight of *Great Northern* must have been something of a shock to eyes – and engineers – used to the small, if elegant and often energetic and purposeful, steam locomotives that haunted most British main-line stations. Churchward had built a solitary Pacific, *The Great Bear*, in 1908, but even this big machine had a Victorian look about it. In fact, all GWR engines did, even when they were as dynamic and as efficient as Churchward's four-cylinder Star class 4-6-0s of 1907.

When Cuthbert Hamilton Ellis, writer on railways, painter, and wartime MI6 agent, asked Stanier, a former GWR man, 'whether there was some nameless cabala at Swindon which ruled the styling of a Great Western locomotive, seeing that a Hawksworth locomotive [of the 1940s] looked like a Collett locomotive, and a Collett locomotive looked like a Churchward locomotive, and a Churchward locomotive ... had the rich Victorian styling of a Dean locomotive [of the 1870s],' the LMS engineer exclaimed: 'Dean? Gooch! It was traditional.' Daniel Gooch had designed the very first locomotive, *Great Western*, to emerge from Swindon works. That was in 1846. But *Great Northern* was different. Although the locomotive had some of the styling details of the Ivatt Atlantics that preceded her, her length and sheer sleekness were something new. Her size was too, of course. In fact, there was something about *Great Northern* that made her feel as much American – at least in terms of scale – as British.

In 1916, a year after he had designed a lacklustre four-cylinder Pacific which stayed on the drawing board – it was little more than a stretched Ivatt Atlantic – Gresley read a series of articles, complete with detailed drawings, in *Engineering* magazine about the Pennsylvania Railroad's hugely impressive class K4 Pacific, built by Alco from 1914. By 1928, 425 of these competent locomotives were at work. Developed over many more years, they became ever more powerful – 4,325 ihp with poppet valves, or 35 per cent more than the first of the class – and fast.

The class A1 Pacific *Great Northern* owed something to the K4s, something to Churchward, and something, of course, to Henry Alfred Ivatt, Gresley's predecessor as locomotive engineer of the GNR. But it was also very much his own machine, the locomotive that saw him ascend the ladder to his seat in the pantheon of the world's great steam locomotive engineers. With the design of the A1s, Gresley had had the full support of his management. As the GNR was about to be merged into one of the Big Four privately owned railway companies in 1923 – an intermediate stage on the iron road towards the nationalization of Britain's railways in 1948 – the company was keen to bow out in style. In the event it was, through Gresley, to stamp its mark on the locomotives of the new LNER right up to the great man's untimely death in 1941 and beyond, since Gresley's locomotives continued to run the crack express passenger trains of British Railways' Eastern, North-Eastern, and Scottish regions as late as 1966.

When the LNER was formed, the new board of directors offered the job of chief mechanical engineer to the most senior locomotive engineer from among the constituent railways brought into its capacious fold. This was John George Robinson, chief mechanical engineer from 1900 to 1922 of the Great Central Railway, for which he had designed three excellent classes of locomotives: the class 11B 'Jersey Lily' Atlantics of 1903 (their curvaceous good looks were likened to those of Lillie Langtry, the beautiful actress who caught the roving eye of Edward, Prince of Wales), the class 11E and 11F Director 4-4-0s of 1913 and 1920, and the class 8K 2-8-0s of 1911, a freight locomotive of which an extra 521 were built for the Railway Operating Division of the Royal Engineers for service in France, Belgium, the Middle East, and Persia during the First World War, and which continued in front-line freight service with British Railways until 1966.

Feeling himself too old, at sixty-seven, for a role that he felt should rightly belong to a dynamic and much younger engineer, Robinson politely refused the job, suggesting Gresley in his place. Inevitably, this rather upset Vincent Raven, who had been chief mechanical engineer of the North Eastern Railway – the upper English half of the east coast main line from London to Scotland – from 1910. Raven had unveiled a Pacific at almost exactly the same time as Gresley. The two, both with three-cylinder drive, were pitted against one another in tests and, perhaps inevitably, the Gresley A1 was chosen as the standard-bearer for GNR locomotive design. This made sense, for even while the Raven locomotives were decent machines, they looked Edwardian, or even Victorian, whereas Gresley's mechanical racehorse looked like a modern express passenger locomotive should: long, lithe, taut, and very much all of a piece. From the words 'Right away, driver', the A1 was one of those designs that could only be spoilt if anything was added to it – spoilt, too, if anything was taken away from it.

Not only did the A1 look just right, but the idea of naming these beautiful, modern, apple-green engines after racehorses was also truly inspired. The third of the class, 4472, was dubbed *Flying Scotsman* to match the 10.00 King's Cross to Edinburgh express service. First run in 1862, this had been known as the Special Scotch Express, but was renamed the Flying Scotsman by the LNER in 1924. That was the year of the British Empire Exhibition, held at Wembley, alongside the tracks of the Metropolitan Railway and the former Great Central Railway. There, the LNER displayed *Flying Scotsman* along with new coaches from the Flying Scotsman train. Gresley's imperious new Pacific stood beside the GWR's new, and considerably smaller, Collett four-cylinder 4-6-0, 4073 *Caerphilly Castle*.

Flying Scotsman weighed over 92 tons, while *Caerphilly Castle* was 13 tons lighter. *Flying Scotsman* was 70 feet long, *Caerphilly Castle* 65 feet. With a grate area of 41.25 sq ft, *Flying Scotsman*'s fire-box was much bigger than *Caerphilly Castle*'s, at 29.36 sq ft. The evaporative heating surface inside *Flying Scotsman*'s boiler and fire-box added up to 2,930 sq ft; that of *Caerphilly Castle* totalled just 1,963 sq ft. Despite these statistics, stacked overwhelmingly, or so it seemed, in the A1's favour, a notice in front of *Caerphilly Castle* stated, quite categorically, that the GWR engine was Britain's most powerful express passenger locomotive. The basis for this claim was the fact that *Caerphilly Castle* boasted a tractive effort of 31,625 lb, compared with *Flying Scotsman*'s 29,835 lb. Tractive effort is calculated as the square of the diameter of the piston, multiplied by the piston stroke, multiplied by 85 per cent of the maximum boiler pressure, divided by the diameter of the driving wheels. The final figure, based on the dimensions of a two-cylinder locomotive, should be increased by 50 per cent for a three-cylinder engine and 100 per cent for a four-cylinder engine. (The vast majority of steam locomotives have been built with two cylinders.)

What the figures for tractive effort show is the maximum (or theoretical) pulling force a given locomotive can exert on starting. It might be compared to the figures given for torque for internal combustion engines. While horsepower is the combination of force and speed, torque is the pulling power needed to get a car moving from rest, or from low speeds in high gears. Until the 1930s, locomotive engineers tended to rate the power of locomotives in terms of tractive effort alone, as this enabled the operating department to calculate the train weight a locomotive could start and could haul on varying gradients. However, this did not necessarily relate to how fast and powerful a locomotive was when running. While a high maximum tractive effort is essential for a goods locomotive, which is asked to start very heavy loads from rest, it is not required for a passenger locomotive called on to run light trains at high speeds. A better measure of performance capacity at speed is horsepower output. As speed and haulage capacity began to matter more and more, for both passenger and freight trains, so, from the 1930s, locomotive engineers increasingly evaluated horsepower outputs. For steam locomotives, the two most important measures are indicated horsepower (ihp), the power generated in the locomotive's cylinders, and drawbar horsepower (dbhp), the power a locomotive can exert to pull a train after the power needed to move itself against friction and air resistance has been extracted.

Generations of enthusiasts – in Britain and abroad – believed that the most powerful locomotives were those with the highest tractive effort. But this was not always true, and so visitors to the British Empire Exhibition would perhaps have been right to question the GWR's claim for *Caerphilly Castle*. In any case, the matter was put to the test the following year when the GWR and LNER agreed to a trial of strength. In late April 1925, 4474 *Victor Wild* was packed off with an LNER crew to run the GWR's principal express, the Cornish Riviera Limited, a demanding non-stop run from Paddington to Plymouth, leaving London with a full load weighing about 530 tons. Crew and locomotive did well. *Victor Wild* proved able to maintain the very tight schedule. However, the GWR team, with 4074 *Caldicott Castle* in the spotlight, was able to knock fifteen minutes off the schedule on a single run with a 380 ton train. More than this, *Caldicott Castle* was burning considerably less coal, with an average saving of 6 lb per mile. Over the 225.5 miles from Paddington to Plymouth, this would add up to more than half a ton. Given that *Caldicott Castle* carried just 6 tons of coal in its small, six-wheeled tender, this was both a considerable saving in what was becoming, even at that time, an increasingly expensive fuel, and an appreciable saving over the fuel consumption of *Victor Wild*. To be fair, the LNER crew had been instructed to adhere to the timetable and not to try to run ahead of it, while the long wheelbase of *Victor Wild* had to be run at lower speeds downhill due to the restrictive alignment of GWR curves. As a result, *Victor Wild* had to work harder uphill, burning more coal in the process. Following the trials, the GWR improved its curves and Gresley improved his Pacifics.

To the astonishment of the LNER management – and of enthusiasts – much the same thing happened when 4073 *Caerphilly Castle* ran test trains of up to 480 tons from King's Cross to Doncaster and back. Refusing to slip its driving wheels – which, at 6 ft 8½ in, were a half-inch larger in diameter than those of the rival A1, 2545 *Diamond Jubilee* – as it lifted its heavy trains up the greasy rails through Gas Works Tunnel immediately beyond the platform ends at King's Cross, the GWR engine was easily master of the east coast main line, while burning 6 per cent less coal.

Gresley might have designed locomotives that appeared to be more modern and powerful than the GWR Castle class, but what he had yet fully to appreciate was that, years earlier, Churchward had understood much about the need for a free-steaming boiler – which both the A1s and Castles possessed – matched to a valve design that allowed the maximum expansive use of steam and its rapid ingress and exit from cylinders, to give a free flow of steam through the locomotive's operating cycle. Despite their old-fashioned looks, the Castles were, in this respect, the more advanced of the two designs.

A part, though, of what made Gresley a great engineer was that he learned the lessons from Churchward quickly. The new class A3 Super Pacifics which emerged from Doncaster from 1928 onwards had boilers pressed to 220 psi, rather than the 180 psi of the A1s. Like many engineers, Gresley was persuaded that boiler scaling increased at pressures above 180 psi. However, his new chief chemist, the forceful T. Henry Turner, pointed out that chemical water treatment would overcome this, and its introduction by the LNER in 1928 enabled Gresley to use higher pressures.

The A3s were fitted with improved valve settings. With long-lap, long-travel valves – standard on Churchward designs – steam could now flow freely through the valves into and out of the cylinders and do more work by expansion at short cut-off. Before the advent of long-lap, long-travel valves, many British locomotives were unnecessarily choked, unable to channel steam freely enough through the cylinders to allow them to run rapidly and economically. There had been notable exceptions, especially in the designs of Patrick Stirling and Henry Ivatt for the GNR and William Adams for the London & South-Western Railway. The ideal, as Churchward and Chapelon demonstrated and explained, for a steam locomotive at speed was for the driver to open the regulator fully whenever possible and to cut off steam to the cylinders as early as possible. In 1925, *Victor Wild* and *Diamond Jubilee* were being worked at speed uphill with cut-offs of up to 50 per cent with the regulator partially opened. This was a bit like driving a fast car in third gear with the foot down on the throttle, rather than changing up to fourth or fifth and going easy on the gas.

Bert Spencer, Gresley's chief technical assistant, was very much instrumental in persuading the chief mechanical engineer of the advantages of Swindon- and French-style valve settings. The result paid off in the Pacifics: the A3s built between 1928 and 1935 were magnificent machines, while the A1s were modified with improved valve settings and, where necessary, new A3 boilers. It was not that the A1s were poor performers, but they were heavier on coal and water and not as efficient as they might have been.

Significantly, Gresley's use of the term 'Super Pacific', borrowed from the French Nord railway, coincided with the development in the United States of what was known as 'super power' at the Lima works in Ohio. The A-1 class 2-8-4 built by William E. Woodard in 1925 was, along with the work of Chapelon in France, one of the key turning points in the development of the steam locomotive, leading to a new generation of machines that were to give diesels and electrics a very good run for their money before the management tide turned against steam in Britain and the USA after the Second World War. Woodard described super power as 'horsepower at speed', the goal of most American locomotive engineers from 1925 until the end of steam construction in the USA in 1955.

The LNER's A1s, however, had been built to haul heavy expresses at moderate speed. Gresley intended them to pull 600 ton trains – 30 per cent heavier than before – at average speeds of 50 mph. Even by the standards of 1922 this was slow. There was, though, a reason. From 1895, after a summer of hair-raising railway races to the North, when the east and west coast railways from London to Scotland attempted to go ever faster on rival runs from King's Cross and Euston to Aberdeen, the companies had agreed to a truce, with a leisurely timing of 8 hours 15 minutes – an average speed of 48 mph – from Edinburgh to King's Cross. So there was no imperative to design for speed. Instead, express trains became ever more comfortable and, in consequence, very heavy indeed.

In May 1928, the LNER made the headlines with the introduction of the non-stop Flying Scotsman service. The first train was headed by 4472 *Flying Scotsman*. There was no need to hurry, the express ambling down to Edinburgh (in Britain, trains go 'up' to London and 'down' to all other destinations) in 8 hours 15 minutes. It was no mean feat, though, to maintain what was, at 393 miles, the world's longest non-stop run, on a daily basis. It was possible, in summer, partly because the engines could pick up water at speed from six troughs along the route, and partly because Gresley's new design for a corridor tender allowed crews to change halfway through the journey as the locomotive thundered on. Significantly, from the point of view of speed, the winter timetable included five intermediate stops within the same time schedule.

The relief crew of the non-stop train would 'ride on the cushions' in a reserved compartment in the leading coach, chatting, reading, staring out of the window, or snoozing until they were needed. Then driver and fireman would make their way through a corridor connection and into an 18 inch wide, 5 foot high passage inside the tender, leading to the glare of the rolling footplate. This was such a sensible invention that it seems odd that no other railway adopted it. The experience, meanwhile, of huddling through one of these Gresley corridors and out into the cab of an A1, A3, or A4 Pacific is one that few fairgrounds can rival in terms of sheer thrill and drama. I was lucky to experience it once, when riding behind the streamlined A4 Pacific 60009 *Union of South Africa* at 75 mph. The comparison my excited mind made at the time – this is what I scrawled in my notebook – was with the experience of first negotiating the claustrophobic corridors and anterooms of the Doge's Palace in Venice, before experiencing the inexplicably shocking scale and splendour of the vast and opulent Sala Maggiore at the heart of the building. The footplate of a big and powerful steam locomotive at speed is never less than an operatic spectacle.

A revolution in speed, though, was about to begin which would indeed lift the steam locomotive into a new reality of super power, and Gresley was at its forefront. The spark was ignited by the launch of high-speed inter-city diesel and steam services in Germany and long-distance streamlined diesels in the United States. These events made railway management in Britain at long last think seriously about the rise of new forms of competition, both internal and external. Traditional heavy steam express trains were being challenged by lightweight, high-speed diesel and steam trains, at the very same time as the first inter-city air services were taking off and the wealthy were able to buy fast cars which could purr elegantly and comfortably across long distances.

A step change in speed in railway travel was deemed essential – by the LNER at least – and it was this, and the need to accelerate existing heavy main-line trains, that drove the design of the steam locomotive to unprecedented heights. In Britain, Gresley was very much the steam locomotive engineer of the moment. In 1934, when the first high-speed tests were made on the LNER between London and Leeds, Gresley was fifty-eight years old. Within the next four years, he gave the British steam locomotive a new lease of life, proving that it was easily possible for a steam locomotive from Doncaster to take on Germany's revolutionary new express diesels – and to win very convincingly indeed, especially in terms of passenger comfort. He was to be dead within seven years.

Gresley was a big man in every sense. Large-framed, 6 ft 2 in tall, commanding and direct – friendly and good-humoured, too – he was born the fifth son of the Rev. Nigel Gresley, rector of Netherseal (or Nethereseale), in Derbyshire, and Joanne Beatrice, née Wilson, in June 1876. The family was aristocratic, although both its major homes, Drakelowe Hall and Netherseal Hall, were demolished in the 1930s. The future designer of *Flying Scotsman*, *Mallard*, and *Green Arrow* could trace his ancestry back to soldiers who fought with William the Conqueror at the Battle of Hastings and, through Hugh de Calvacamp, archbishop of Rouen in the tenth century, to the Viking warriors who settled in Normandy in the late ninth century.

St Peter's, Netherseal, in the churchyard of which Gresley is buried (his tomb was restored in 2009 by the Gresley Society, with the help of readers of *Steam Railway* magazine), is a modest thirteenth-century building with a fifteenth-century tower. It was largely rebuilt in 1877, while Nigel was learning to walk, by Arthur Blomfield, the church architect who employed the young Thomas Hardy (an architect before he found fame as a novelist and poet) and who, daringly, built a house for himself in concrete in East Sheen in south-west London. There is a simple Gothic bench in the church made by the young Gresley.

The Gresleys lived comfortably, with a staff that included a Swiss nursemaid who taught Nigel to say his prayers in French before he could say them in English. From Marlborough School, Gresley was taken on as a premium apprentice at the LNWR's Crewe works in 1893 under the aegis of the autocratic and eccentric, if extremely able, Francis Webb. At a dinner held in Crewe in 1919 by former apprentices and pupils, Gresley, according to Geoffrey Hughes, one of his biographers, sang a duet with Sir John Aspinall, the retired chief mechanical engineer and general manager of the Lancashire and Yorkshire Railway, who, years before, had worked for Webb at Crewe, and who had employed Gresley in his drawing office at Horwich in 1898. To the tune of 'The Holy City', a popular hymn written by Frederick E. Weatherby and scored by Stephen Adams (the pen name of the musician Michael Maybrick) in 1892, the engineers crooned the 'Crewe Steam Shed Song':

Last night I lay a-sleeping
There came a dream to me –
I stood within a Steam Shed,
A marvellous Shed to see.
The walls were clean and spotless,
And smoke troughs white as snow,
And not a spot of grease was seen
Upon the pits below.

O Loco Men! O Loco Men!
Shout loud for well you may –
'Twas the Blessed Steam Shed of Paradise
We all shall see some day.

Here, the son of the rectory (like so many steam locomotive engineers) invoked the near-religious calling of steam itself.

Before moving on to the GNR at Doncaster in 1905, Gresley had married Ethel Frances Fullager, a talented young musician and the daughter of a Bolton solicitor. They had four children and lived happily and comfortably. Devastated by Ethel's death from cancer in 1929, at the early age of fifty-four, Gresley eventually moved to Salisbury Hall, a moated Elizabethan house near St Albans, where, with the help of his daughter, Vi, he entertained in grand style between holidays in Scotland, where he shot, fished, and played golf. They spent every other weekend with the Staniers. He was particularly fond of the mallards that bred and played in the moat at Salisbury Hall, hence the name of the locomotive that was to make him world-famous in 1938.

Gresley replaced H. A. Ivatt as locomotive superintendent of the GNR in 1911, appointing Oliver Bulleid as his personal technical assistant. The two men were to work closely together until Bulleid left the LNER to become chief mechanical engineer of the Southern Railway at Eastleigh in 1937. Bulleid, a natural innovator, must have encouraged Gresley to push forward with a number of radical new locomotive designs. Between the emergence of the A1 and A3 Pacifics, Doncaster came up with a very fine class numbering just two locomotives. These were the massive, three-cylinder P1 class 2-8-2 goods engines of 1925. Designed to pull hundred-wagon coal trains and other goods trains of 1,600 tons and more along the main line, these powerful and decidedly modern engines were never fully utilized. After the economic crisis of 1929, the demand for hundred-wagon trains disappeared and Gresley's three-cylinder 02 class 2-8-

0s were able to handle the heaviest trains with aplomb. In any case, hundred-wagon trains were too long for the LNER's existing main line freight loops and this problem was only partly solved when stretches of the east coast main line were upgraded to four tracks in the 1930s.

The P1s were originally to have been even larger – 2-10-2s – but this really was a case of Gresley and Bulleid getting too far ahead of themselves. As it was, the P1s were fitted with A1 boilers, with extra power provided by an auxiliary booster engine on the trailing axles. Made by the Superheat Co. of New York, they offered a hefty increase in tractive effort when called upon to start very heavy trains up gradients or when they needed to accelerate quickly. With the booster kicked in, the starting tractive effort of the P1s was a considerable 47,000 lb. To make life more comfortable for the driver, the locomotives were fitted with steam-powered reversing gear – a feature of Bulleid's Southern Railway Pacifics of the 1940s – while steam brakes fitted to the wheels of their tenders as well as to the engines themselves gave the crews an extra degree of reassurance when stopping hundred-wagon loads, which had no continuous brakes, especially downhill and on rails slippery with rain. With their 5 ft 2 in driving wheels – larger than most British goods locomotives – the P1s had a good turn of speed, with 65 mph attained on a test with a passenger train.

Edward Thompson, Gresley's successor, had the P1s scrapped in 1945, on the grounds that they did not fit into the LNER's fleet of standard locomotives. The P1s had shown the potential for what a fast and heavy railway freight service could be as early as the mid-1920s – and just such a service became a daily feature of American railroads from 1925, soon after Woodard's A-1 2-8-4 emerged from Lima's Ohio works. Britain, however, would have to wait until the arrival of the British Railways Standard class 9F 2-10-0s in 1954 – engines that, if required, could run a twelve-car passenger train at up to 90 mph – before it had a truly fast heavy freight locomotive. Even so, what most held back the speed of goods trains in Britain was the fact the vast majority of them had no continuous braking system and were limited to just 25 mph so that they could be stopped safely within signal distances.

A year before his masterpiece, the streamlined A4 Pacific, emerged from Doncaster in 1935, Gresley and Bulleid came up with another hugely impressive 2-8-2 design. This was the P2 class, an express passenger locomotive with 6 ft 2 in driving wheels, smaller than normally used on such engines, designed for hauling 550 ton sleeping-car expresses over heavy gradients from Edinburgh across the Forth Bridge and through to Dundee and Aberdeen. Six of these formidable three-cylinder locomotives were built, and the first two, 2001 *Cock o' the North* and 2002 *Earl Marischal*, were among the most beguiling of all British steam locomotives.

Cock o' the North was a stunning-looking machine. She was very long, her lines clean as could be. Her smoke deflectors – necessary to lift the exhaust of a large-boilered locomotive with a short chimney clear of the cab and the crew's view ahead – were a forward-projecting continuation of the boiler casing, rather than being bolted on. Her eight close-coupled driving wheels were wholly exposed, giving the engine a distinctly modern appearance. Until then, and even afterwards, it was the tradition of British engineers to cover a part of the wheels of express engines with splashers on the running boards, as if there was something a little indecent about them being exposed to full view. A V-shaped cab derived from the Paris–Lyon–Mediterranean railway in France, an American chime whistle (the first to be fitted to an LNER engine, it had been a present to Gresley from Captain Jack Howey when Gresley had visited the miniature Romney, Hythe & Dymchurch Railway in Kent when it was taking delivery of its latest, US-style Pacifics, *Dr Syn* and *Black Prince*), double Kylchap exhausts, an ACFI feedwater heater in place of injectors, a massive 50 sq ft grate, a high degree of superheating, and Lentz rotary-cam poppet valves instead of the Walschaerts valve gear that Gresley normally employed – all added up to a powerful and efficient locomotive, and one that clearly embodied ideas Gresley had seen in designs by Chapelon and was keen to evaluate.

Gresley and Bulleid had first met Chapelon in 1928 at Davey Paxman & Co., the Colchester-based engineering firm that built Captain Howey's 15 in gauge Pacifics for the Romney, Hythe & Dymchurch Railway. Designed by Henry Greenly, these were based closely on the LNER A1s. Davey, Paxman & Co. was then the West European agent for the Lentz oscillating- and rotary-cam poppet valve gear which the LNER engineers were about to fit to Gresley's D49/2 class three-cylinder 4-4-0s, a variant of the D49 intermediate express passenger locomotive built between 1927 and 1935. Chapelon was at Colchester with the Paris–Orléans railway's chief design engineer, Paul Billet, to discuss the Lentz oscillating-cam poppet valve gear for what was to be the epoch-making rebuilt Pacific No. 3566. As Gresley and Bulleid both spoke French (between 1908 and his rejoining the GNR in 1912, Bulleid had been employed as assistant manager at the Westinghouse works at Freinville, near Paris) and were keen to improve the performance of their locomotives, they struck up a great friendship with the man who would become the world's greatest steam locomotive engineer, even though he was virtually unknown at the time.

For his part, Chapelon was impressed with Gresley's willingness to experiment. The results, though, could be idiosyncratic and even downright disappointing. When, in November 1934, at the suggestion of Chapelon, Bulleid took *Cock o' the North* to the French locomotive testing plant at Vitry-sur-Seine, the P2's performance was much inferior to that of Chapelon's compound Pacifics of much the same weight, let alone that of his herculean 4-8-0s. Out on the 90 mile line between Orléans and Tours, with a train composed of four P-0 class 4-6-0 brake locomotives, *Cock o' the North* exerted a maximum sustained power output of 1,910 dbhp at 68 mph.

Chapelon himself was the most persuasive and convincing exponent of the compound steam locomotive, in which steam is expanded not once, as in the conventional or 'simple' Stephensonian engine, but twice (or even three times, as in marine engines) and therefore performs greater work for the same amount of steam raised and fuel expended. He believed that only compounding would yield the super power results sought by his English friends. In *Cock o' the North*, though, the excessively large clearance volume (or dead space) in the valve and cylinder steam passages more than offset the improved freedom of steam flow, and resulted in a specific steam consumption of 30 per cent more than in the Chapelon Pacifics. This, as much a lack of compounding, ensured that the 2-8-2 had a proportionately lower output than the French Pacifics.

Even so, with their tractive effort of 43,462 lb – the highest yet for a British passenger locomotive – and eight-wheel drive, the P2s performed very well indeed on the Edinburgh to Aberdeen day and overnight expresses. *Cock o' the North*'s debut in June 1934 was a test run from King's Cross at the head of a twenty-coach, 650 ton train. With this, she ran freely at 85 mph and topped the ascent of the long Stoke Bank, between Peterborough and Grantham, at 57.5 mph, generating 2,100 dbhp. Despite their power and sure-footedness, the P2s did give problems in their earliest days, but they got into their stride and did splendid work on the difficult Edinburgh to Aberdeen line. They were much loved by drivers, if not by firemen, who had to shovel coal into their huge grates at a much greater rate than was necessary with the A1 and A3 Pacifics. In due course, they were rebuilt as rather ineffectual Pacifics by Edward Thompson, in 1943–4, and became the first LNER 4-6-2s to be withdrawn from service by British Railways.

As it was, the breakthrough Gresley and Bulleid were looking for came in 1935, and triumphantly so. Gresley had gone to Germany in 1933 to ride on the Deutsche Reichsbahn's sensational new *Fliegender Hamburger* (*Flying Hamburger*), a two-car, streamlined, diesel-electric train which ran the 178 lightly inclined miles from Berlin to Hamburg in 138 minutes at an average of 77.4 mph. The performance was undoubtedly impressive, demanding long stretches to be run at 100 mph, yet Gresley had a hunch that he could do just as well with steam in Britain. He was certainly interested to learn that the back-up train used when the diesel flyer failed had made the run, using a standard light 03 Pacific limited to 87 mph, with three standard coaches, in a scheduled 148 minutes, although this timing was capable of improvement if the maximum speed limit were raised.

Gresley was, though, very unimpressed with the spartan accommodation offered by the *Fliegender Hamburger*. There were just ninety-eight seats when the train first ran in May 1933, four months after Adolf Hitler was sworn in as Chancellor of Germany, and complaints that the seats were too cramped led to a reduction to seventy-seven. There was, of course, no dining car, although German businessmen were perfectly used to eating cold sausages, cheese, and rolls, washed down with wine or beer, when travelling. Not so their British counterparts, who were accustomed to much finer and more ample fare. When the LNER's first streamlined express, the Silver Jubilee, began service in September 1935, it offered passengers in first and third class (there was no second at the time), a choice of forty-six cocktails, including a Silver Jubilee at two shillings. The à la carte menu proffered choices of soup followed by a fish course (oysters were on offer, too), a Jubilee mixed grill, a pudding (peach melba, anyone?), and cheese and biscuits.

To provide such a service and adequate comfortable seating, Gresley needed a seven-coach train and a new class of locomotive that could race it the 268 miles from King's Cross to Newcastle in four hours flat, with a stop at Darlington. Before the dramatic unveiling and breathtaking press run of the Silver Jubilee, research into high-speed running on the east coast main line was conducted with great haste. In 1934, Gresley asked the German manufacturers of the two-car *Fliegender Hamburger* – Waggon- und Maschinenbau AG (WUMAG) – how long a 140 seat, three-car train would take to run the 185.7 miles from King's Cross to Leeds, a route that attracted heavy business traffic on a daily basis. The meticulously calculated answer was 165 minutes, including a contingency allowance for checks. The more ambitious run over the 268 miles to Newcastle would take 255 minutes.

On 30 November 1934, 4472 *Flying Scotsman* steamed out from King's Cross at the head of a four-coach test train, complete with dining car, weighing 147 tons. It was a dull and misty morning. On the footplate were driver Sparshatt and fireman Webster. Cecil J. Allen was sitting by a window in one of the coaches timing the special using the lineside mileposts and a pair of stopwatches. Nothing like this had been experienced in Britain before. *Flying Scotsman* was through Peterborough, 76.35 miles from London, in 39 seconds over the hour. She topped the final 1-in-178 gradient of the long climb to Stoke summit at 81 mph (a new record) and was into Leeds Central in 151 minutes and 16 seconds, fourteen minutes ahead of the schedule calculated for the streamlined German diesel. With two extra carriages attached, and with the train now weighing 207 tons, *Flying Scotsman* ran back to London in just over 157 minutes, racing down Stoke Bank to Peterborough at a maximum speed of exactly 100 mph. This was the first time a British steam locomotive had, for certain, run at a three-figure speed. Cecil J. Allen rushed to Broadcasting House to report the record run on the BBC's 9 o'clock news.

The German schedule had been easily beaten by a conventional train, with 140 seats, hot meals, and an eleven-year-old steam locomotive at the front without the benefits of a higher-pressure A3 boiler, a high degree of superheating, or streamlining. On 5 March 1935, a second high-speed test trip was made, this time from King's Cross to Newcastle and back, formed of six coaches weighing 217 tons, pulled by the A3 Pacific 2750 *Papyrus*. The train was taken down to Newcastle by driver Gutteridge and fireman Wightman, and up to London by Sparshatt and Webster. With Cecil J. Allen on the stopwatches again, the special took just 237 minutes and 7 seconds for the 268.35 mile journey, arriving three minutes ahead of time and undercutting the proposed German diesel timing by eighteen minutes. Without a signal stop and other delays, the run would have been made in 230 minutes.

On the return journey, Sparshatt flew down Stoke Bank, averaging 100.2 mph for 12.25 miles on end and reaching a maximum of 108 mph. *Papyrus* arrived at King's Cross in 231 minutes and 48 seconds. As Allen reported, a total of three hundred miles had been run at an average speed of 80 mph, and coal consumption, at 43 lb per mile, showed that, although running like the wind, *Papyrus* – named after the winner of the 1923 Derby – had been expertly handled and economically fired.

Anything diesel could do, steam could do better. Or so it seemed on the LNER at the time. The drive to high speed certainly galvanized Gresley's drawing office and the Doncaster works. Within a week of *Papyrus*'s record run, an 'outline diagram of suggested train' had been submitted to the LNER board. As soon as they were approved, drawings of the locomotive, to be designated class A4, and train – the Silver Jubilee coaches designed by Norman Newsome, chief technical assistant, carriage and wagon – were ordered. The frames of 2509 *Silver Link* were laid down at Doncaster on 26 June and the engine steamed for the first time on 7 September. The silver-grey streamlined train was ready on 17 September. The press run was scheduled for Friday, 27 September, and the daily service was due to start the following Monday.

Not only was every target met, and in such an extraordinarily short time, but *Silver Link* was truly raring to go. The press run made international news. Before it left King's Cross, Ralph Wedgwood, general manager of the LNER insisted: 'This is not a stunt train' – even though it must have felt like one at the time. Cecil J. Allen was on board to time the train, sitting at one point alongside an ebullient Gresley, a deeply concerned Charles Brown, the line's civil engineer, and the *Daily Mail*'s reporter, Randolph Churchill. Up front, seated on leather-upholstered bucket seats on the footplate of the wedge-shaped locomotive, its motion enclosed, were driver Taylor and fireman Luty – not that Luty would be sitting for long.

At 14.25, *Silver Link* stormed out of the station. Just beyond Stevenage she was up to 100 mph, 112.5 mph six miles north of

Hitchin and again at Sandy, averaging 100 mph for 43 miles on end. She was then through Peterborough, travelling 76.4 miles in 55 minutes and 2 seconds. Earlier, from Hatfield to Huntingdon, a distance of 41.15 miles, the train had averaged 100.5 mph. Between mileposts 30 and 55, where speed, as Allen recorded, had never fallen below 100 mph until reduced to 85 mph for a restricted curve, the average speed had been 107.5 mph. Both the Silver Jubilee and *Silver Link* were media darlings and wonders of the new age of streamlining. These eye-opening speeds had been achieved without the benefit of modern colour-light signalling, fully canted curves (where one rail is elevated above the other to ease trains smoothly around the curve at high speeds), or special training for the crew. Indeed, as 2509 was riding so smoothly, it seems possible that driver Taylor was unaware of quite how fast he was going until Gresley came through the corridor tender to tell him: 'Ease your arm, young man; there are some rather nervous elderly gentlemen in the train.' French Flaman recording speedometers were subsequently fitted to the A4s. How crews worked a train like the Silver Jubilee so successfully through bitter English winters, at high speed through dense fogs, driving snow, and pelting rain, remains not so much a mystery as something of a miracle. Small wonder these drivers were popular working-class heroes.

The train itself needed fine tuning – the suspension of the coaches was slightly modified after the boisterous test run, while the civil engineer increased the rail cant on the curves – but the A4 proved to be a brilliant design from the word go. Until a second member of the class was ready, *Silver Link* ran the up and down Silver Jubilee service by herself every day, Monday to Friday, for the first three weeks, covering eight thousand miles. This was proof that the first of a new generation of steam locomotives had arrived – a machine that was fast, powerful, and reliable, and which could be turned around quickly with precious little servicing.

The A4 was, in one sense, nothing more than a super A3, a development of what had gone before. The differences between the two classes, beneath the A4's distinctive streamlined casing, may have seemed marginal: an inch here and there in the diameter of piston valves and cylinders, a 250 psi rather than a 220 psi boiler. However, the way that Gresley, his chief technical assistant, Bert Spencer, and his chief locomotive draughtsman, Edgar Windle, ensured that steam flowed with minimum pressure-drop losses inside the A4 was most important. The LNER engineers had learned from Chapelon and now applied the Frenchman's theory very positively to British practice. When the regulator was open fully, steam flowed into the cylinders of the thirty-five A4s at virtually the same pressure at which it was raised in the boiler – these were efficient and economical engines. They were also well built and powerful. Originally designed to rush the 230 ton Silver Jubilee from London to Newcastle, later batches were used to head the most prestigious heavyweight expresses, like the 550 ton Flying Scotsman, on mile-a-minute schedules.

The Silver Jubilee proved to be very popular – as the train was nearly always full, an extra coach was added – and highly profitable too, earning the LNER a net thirteen shillings per mile, about double the income of a conventional express train. In September 1937, a second streamlined service, the Coronation – 'We want to go one better than a Pullman,' said Gresley – was brought into service between London and Edinburgh. The schedule for the 393 miles was six hours, with two stops going north and one heading south, and with the really fast running being made over the 188 miles from King's Cross to York (157 minutes, at an average of 71.9 mph, the fastest scheduled service in Britain). This was made all the more impressive by the fact that the new nine-coach train, complete with a streamlined observation car at its tail end, weighed 325 tons, 40 per cent more than the Silver Jubilee. Again, the reliability of the A4s was on public show: forty-eight of the first fifty-one runs were made behind the uncomplaining 4491 *Commonwealth of Australia*.

What these streamliners proved is not simply that steam could be run very fast, but that such inspired and demanding running could be expected as a matter of course, day in, day out. The A4s laid down a challenge for protagonists of rival forms of railway traction and they allayed the railways' own fears concerning the contemporary threat from the air. Airlines were still in their infancy in Britain and every flight was still a rather uncomfortable and even hair-raising adventure. The first regular Anglo-Scottish service, operated by the Railway Air Service, began on 20 August 1934, when a pair of brand new de Havilland DH 86 Express four-engine, ten-seat biplanes took off from Renfrew, near Glasgow, on what should have been a flight of four and a quarter hours to Croydon Airport, via Belfast, Manchester, and Birmingham. Gale-force winds meant that both flights had to be abandoned at Manchester, although one plane did finally get through to Croydon. These were early days, but it does seem a shame that, despite having such a lead over the airlines in the mid-1930s, the railways – or those charged with looking after them – let this go. If steam development alone had been kept up to the pace Gresley set in the 1930s, who knows how fast and glamorous train travel in Britain would have been in 1962, let alone 2012?

Just how fast a Gresley locomotive could run was demonstrated on 3 July 1938, when, during high-speed brake tests, 4468 *Mallard*, a brand-new locomotive fitted with double Kylchap exhaust and chimney, was sent from a starting point four miles north of Grantham over Stoke summit with a seven-coach train, including the LNER's veteran dynamometer car (used for recording locomotive performance), weighing 240 tons, with driver Duddington at the controls and fireman Bray on the shovel. The crew were from Doncaster. Accelerating rapidly to pass the summit at 74.5 mph, Duddington took *Mallard* up to 125 mph, before slowing down for the curve at Essendine. The dynamometer recorded a momentary 126 mph, enough – just enough – for the LNER to claim a world record for steam traction. The previous year, one of Adolf Wolff's streamlined Deutsche Reichsbahn 05 class 4-6-4s had reached 200.4 kph (124.5 mph). Although Wolff was on very friendly terms with his essentially apolitical British counterparts, there was inevitably much crowing as well as cheering in the British press. We had beaten the Germans.

Worked hard up Stoke – a longer run up would have made things easier for the locomotive and her crew – *Mallard* came to a stand at Peterborough, with an overheated connecting-rod big end detected when steam was shut off thirteen miles away for the Essendine slack. This was because of the very high stress reversal forces caused when steam was shut off completely. (Adolf Wolff was later to disclose that the 05s had suffered from the same problem until drivers were told never to close the regulator fully when braking from above 90 mph.) As it was, *Mallard* was quickly repaired and back in regular service almost immediately after her record run. The test train, meanwhile, continued to King's Cross behind a veteran Ivatt Atlantic – and staff on board the dynamometer car were quick to hand out photographs of *Mallard* in case the press published images of the Atlantic instead of the Pacific.

Given an unrestricted run up to Stoke, *Mallard* may have well reached 130 mph or more. This performance, though, had demanded, at one stage, an output of 3,100 ihp, meaning that the Kylchap-fitted A4s were one of a very select band of 3,000 hp British steam locomotives. The others were the Stanier Coronations, and – just – Bulleid's Merchant Navy Pacifics and Arthur Peppercorn's post-war A1s. The Kylchap exhaust gave the A4s a 300 ihp boost. Indeed, on one occasion in 1963, the last year the A4s ran from King's Cross, *Mallard* was at the head of the eleven-coach, 405 ton, 14.00 Newcastle express. A signal stop before Stevenage and other signal and permanent-way restrictions delayed the train. Late through Peterborough, *Mallard*, with driver Coe of King's Cross, arrived in Grantham just ahead of time. Climbing Stoke at between 80 and 82 mph, with a slight drop on the final 1-in-178 rise to the summit, *Mallard* was producing a sustained 2,450 bhp, with a maximum of about 3,200 ihp.

During the Second World War, the A4s performed heroically, displaying herculean muscle. The Rev. G. C. Stead timed 4901 *Capercaillie* at the head of a twenty-one-coach Flying Scotsman, weighing 730 tons, covering a 25 mile stretch of more or less level track between Darlington and York in just under twenty minutes, at an average speed of 76 mph. This required a continuous output of 1,700 dbhp, or 2,400 ihp. From the outbreak of the war, speed was nominally limited to 60 mph, but the Flaman recording speedometers had been removed and stored.

As for *Silver Link*, on 5 April 1940, this high-speed record-breaker was charged with lifting a twenty-five-coach, 850 ton express out of King's Cross on a 1-in-105 gradient. It took no fewer than sixteen minutes to climb the 2.5 miles to Finsbury Park, but once on the move from Potters Bar, the A4 was running well and was just eleven minutes late on stopping at Grantham, having averaged 50 mph from Finsbury Park. This huge train was then worked on to Newcastle – a further 163 miles – losing just four minutes on its schedule.

The A4s continued to impress in British Railways days. A non-stop, eleven-coach, 390 ton express, the Elizabethan, averaged a mile a minute from London to Edinburgh, demanding the very best from crews, signalmen, shed staff, and operating management at a time when the railways were still struggling to get up to speed after the war and the long period of austerity. A twenty-minute black-and-white film of the train, *Elizabethan Express*, directed by Tony Thompson and produced by Edgar Anstey, was made by British Transport Films in 1954. The cheeky verse commentary by Paul Le Saux is irritating, but the shots of *Silver Fox* galloping effortlessly up the east coast main line, and life aboard an express train in the era before mobile phones, booming personal stereos, and non-stop announcements, are nothing less than delightful. To many, steam expresses were always more than a way of getting from A to B in the shortest possible time.

Gresley produced a number of other fine engines for the LNER, including the fast and powerful three-cylinder V2 class 2-6-2s of 1936, with slightly shortened A3 boilers and 6 ft 2 in driving wheels, the first named *Green Arrow* after a new high-speed main-line goods service running at up to 60 mph. A further 183 were built. Like all Gresley's big locomotives, they proved invaluable during the war, when trains could be very heavy indeed, and the 2-6-2s could stand in for Pacifics. For service over the tortuous but beautiful Scottish line from Glasgow to Mallaig via Fort William, Gresley devised the three-cylinder K4 class 2-6-0s with 5 ft 2 in driving wheels. These six compact engines, built between 1936 and 1939, had a tractive effort of 36,599 lb, and were very useful on a line with many starts and stops, tight curves, steep gradients, and multiple speed restrictions. They also meant that train weights for a single locomotive could be raised from 220 to 300 tons.

Gresley's final shot at an all-purpose locomotive primarily for secondary lines was the three-cylinder V4 class 2-6-2, an exquisitely engineered class of just two prototype locomotives, the first named *Bantam Cock*, the second nicknamed *Bantam Hen*. The idea was that these bantamweights would be able to work very nearly 80 per cent of the LNER's route mileage, bringing modern traction to lines often reliant on Victorian locomotives.

Bantam Cock made her debut just weeks before Gresley died. There is no doubt that the great engineer had become exhausted as the war progressed. Believing it to be his duty to put in as much effort as anyone else, he took to working seven days a week, despite a known heart problem. There was still so much to do. A mechanically fired three-cylinder 4-8-2, with a P2 boiler, for heavy passenger services, was on the drawing board, as well as an A4 with its boiler pressed to 275 psi to give a 10 per cent higher tractive effort. Meanwhile, the first main-line electric locomotive designed under Gresley's supervision ran for the first time on the Manchester to Sheffield line in February 1941. In March, Bulleid invited Gresley to the unveiling of his first Pacific, *Channel Packet*, but his old boss and friend was unable to attend. He died on 5 April 1941 and was buried alongside his wife in the churchyard at Netherseal.

Gresley was that glorious English thing, a radical in the unaffected guise of a country gentleman with an office and a club, or two, in town. A lieutenant colonel in the Engineer and Railway Staff Corps in the First World War, captain of his local golf club when he lived with his family in Hadley Wood, a member of the Junior Carlton Club and Brooke's, an honorary DSc and a knight of the realm, he reinvigorated the British steam locomotive to remarkable effect. Like Churchward, he introduced the best, or most appropriate, developments from France and the United States. He experimented continually and had high hopes of setting up, with William Stanier of the LMS, a national locomotive testing plant to ensure that the engines of the future would be scientifically evaluated. Work on such a plant began at Rugby in 1938, but was halted after the declaration of war in September 1939. When the facility was completed in 1948, the first locomotive to be tested was the A4 Pacific *Sir Nigel Gresley*.

Gresley brought dash and panache to steam engineering and design, and while aware that electric traction was on the way – he actively promoted it – he was determined to raise the standard of steam design to new heights. His three-cylinder locomotives were to be much maligned by Edward Thompson, his immediate successor at the LNER, on account of their patent conjugated valve gear, which, when properly set up and maintained, was an effective way of eliminating the inaccessible third set of valve gear between the frames of the locomotive and replacing it with a simple horizontal lever system, normally placed in front of the cylinders. And yet those who cared for Gresley's locomotives at most depots had them working superbly throughout the 1950s and well into the 1960s. As late as May 1959, an attempt on the British steam speed record was made when driver Hoole and fireman Hancox of King's Cross streaked down Stoke Bank at the controls of 60007 *Sir Nigel Gresley*, at the head of an eight-coach, 295 ton Stephenson Locomotive Society special. Hoole had already allegedly achieved 117 mph in November 1955 with *Sir Nigel Gresley* at the head of the Tees–Tyne Pullman. In the event, he was still accelerating at 112 mph when he was ordered by Fred Dixon, the locomotive inspector on the footplate, to ease off. Might *Mallard*'s record have been broken? We will never know; but it is hard not to think of the spirit of Sir Nigel Gresley himself, an engineer and railway enthusiast to the core, willing on the locomotive that bore his name – and which still runs on main-line specials today – to unprecedented heights.

*

Another locomotive that might have broken *Mallard*'s record was 6220 *Coronation*, the magisterial LMS four-cylinder Pacific which seems to have reached 114 mph approaching Crewe station one summer day in 1937, when it was brand-new. The streamlined locomotive, as free steaming as an A4 and with even greater power, was accelerating well and given the kind of long downhill run the LNER enjoyed between Grantham and Peterborough, it might well have crested 120 mph and possibly run faster than that. One of a class of thirty-eight express passenger locomotives built at Crewe between 1937 and 1948, the Coronation class 4-6-2s were, along with Gresley's A4s, among the greatest of all British steam engines. Designed under the direction of Sir William Stanier and named after British cities, British royalty, and, of course, the coronation of King George VI in 1937, these 105 ton, 3,000 hp, 100 mph machines were true monarchs of the rails.

The Coronations were certainly special and were much loved by everyone who came into contact with them, and yet they were no more and no less than the crowning glory of a fleet of highly standardized modern locomotives put into service by the LMS between 1933 and the company's absorption into British Railways in 1948. Even then, as we will see, these Stanier locomotives – which ranged from powerful, compact 2-6-4 tank engines through mixed-traffic 4-6-0s and 2-8-0s designed for heavy freight duties and wartime service in Egypt, Turkey, Iran, and Iraq, to express passenger three-cylinder 4-6-0s and heavy-duty Pacifics – were to be the direct inspiration for the British Railways Standard class locomotives built up until 1960.

Looking back, the design and general arrangement of these fine and purposeful machines owed an incalculable debt to Churchward and the

GWR. This was hardly surprising, for William Stanier was a GWR man through and through, from his birth at Swindon in March 1876 – three months before Gresley was born in Derbyshire – until, at the age of fifty-five, he was tempted away to take up the post of chief mechanical engineer of the LMS.

The move must have been a wrench for Stanier. He liked to say that he had the letters G W R embroidered in the seat of his trousers. The son of W. H. Stanier, a GWR man who had held many posts on the railway, including that of chief clerk, Stanier joined the company in 1892, the year that Brunel's 7 ft 0¼ in broad gauge finally gave way to the national standard gauge of 4 ft 8½ in. Apprenticed at the age of sixteen, he rose to be works manager at Swindon and rebuilt the famous engineering works so that by 1923, when the vast majority of Britain's railways were grouped into four regional companies, the Big Four, it was the most advanced in the country.

Stanier became assistant to Charles Collett in 1921. He was soon in the thick of locomotive design. Collett was hard hit by the death of his wife in 1923 and this very private man retreated ever further into himself. It was left to Stanier to see the new Castle class 4-6-0 through its final design and production. By this time, Stanier, who had loved working with tools since he was a toddler, was one of the best railway engineering production managers in the country. More than that, he was also a major figure in Swindon society, a largely self-contained world which revolved almost entirely around the GWR. A happily married father of two children, he was a founder member and president of the Swindon Rotary Club, a governor of Swindon secondary school, a director of both the Swindon Gas Company and the Swindon Permanent Building Society, and chairman of the local Toc H committee (the Christian fellowship and charity founded by Neville Talbot and Philip 'Tubby' Clayton, two First World War army chaplains). He took a keen interest, as his father had done, in the education of the working men of the GWR, and gave many technical addresses. A keen swimmer, tennis player, and ice-skater, Stanier was also president of the Swindon rugby and athletics clubs. He was to remain robust, decisive, and a famously fast walker, until his early eighties. And, despite a superficially brusque manner when he was in a hurry, as he often was, Stanier was, without the shadow of a doubt, a kind, warm, and good-natured man.

How, then, could he consider leaving Swindon as he did in 1932, so late in his career? The answer was twofold. First, Stanier was just five years younger than his chief, Collett, who had no interest in retiring before he was seventy, in 1941. Stanier would have stepped into Collett's shoes, but he would have enjoyed just a very few years to make his mark before his own retirement. Second, the offer put to him by the LMS was impossible to refuse.

Stanier had been groomed for the LMS job by Sir Harold Hartley, a vice president of the LMS and the railway's director of scientific research, who was also a fellow of the Royal Society, a fellow of Balliol College, Oxford, and, as Brigadier General Hartley, had been controller of the chemical warfare department during the First World War. Hartley had been assigned the task of finding a new chief mechanical engineer for the LMS by the extraordinary Sir Josiah Stamp, who was the son of a railway-station bookstall manager from Wigan and in 1926 had moved to the LMS as its first president from Nobel Industries Ltd (which later became Imperial Chemical Industries, or ICI – later, in 1961, a director of ICI, Richard Beeching, would become the much-criticized chairman of the board of British Railways).

The LMS was by far the biggest of the Big Four, but, unlike the GWR, it was an empire bristling with rivalries and possessed a fleet of disparate locomotives designed by engineers from Derby, Crewe, Horwich, and other works, who seemed incapable of seeing eye to eye. The public referred to the LMS as an ''ell of a mess'. By 1932 it was way past time to sort out a situation that had not significantly improved since the company had been formed in 1923. Although there were a number of very able locomotive engineers from its constituent companies at work in the LMS, the various design departments had still to gel. They needed to be forced to do so, but the man who could achieve this had yet to be found.

The railway's first chief mechanical engineer had been George Hughes. An affable and much-liked Fenland farmer's son, he had held the same position from 1907 with the Lancashire and Yorkshire Railway at Horwich, and from 1922 with the LNWR. Hughes did his best to break the stranglehold of the dominant, Derby-based, ex-Midland Railway faction within the LMS, which believed in locomotives of moderate size to run relatively light express trains. Such engines were certainly economical, but Midland Railway locomotive development appeared to have frozen by the time of the First World War. Nevertheless, J. E. Anderson, the Midland Railway's chief locomotive draughtsman, had been appointed motive power running superintendent at Derby in 1923, and he believed that a locomotive should have the least number of wheels possible to do the work it was asked to do. He strongly advocated the small-engine school of thinking that dogged the early days of the LMS, even on the former LNWR main lines from London to Liverpool, Manchester, and Glasgow, where trains had long been much heavier than those running on the Midland Railway.

This policy resulted in the need for double-heading – two locomotives coupled together – to work the heaviest express passenger and goods trains. This was clearly a waste of resources. To meet demand, Hughes had proposed a four-cylinder Pacific in 1924, with a 2-8-2 heavy goods version of the same machine. These projects had come to nothing because Anderson put a spoke in Hughes's wheel when he refused to spend the money necessary for new and longer turntables for the putative Pacifics. As it was, one of the young men working on the design of the Hughes Pacific and 2-8-2 was Ernest Stewart Cox, who went on to become one of Stanier's key men and, after the nationalization of the railways in 1948, was appointed head of design for British Railways steam locomotives.

When Hughes retired in 1925, his successor, Henry Fowler, the son of a cabinet-maker from Evesham, was another nice fellow who proved unable to break Anderson's obstruction of larger LMS locomotive designs. One promising design, however, was for an enlarged Midland compound. These highly successful 4-4-0s had been Derby's crowning achievement, and Fowler now suggested a more modern and powerful 4-6-0 version. With a tractive effort of 32,270 lb, it would have been comparable to the later Royal Scots and might well have been a very useful machine. Again, though, Anderson's influence ensured that it was rejected.

In October 1925, Fowler organized and led a trip to France with other LMS engineers, along with the LNER's Bulleid, who acted as translator, to study the latest in French compound locomotive design. Enthused by the 12–15 per cent fuel savings that French engineers claimed – accurately – for their compounds, Fowler, a compound enthusiast, came back eager to resurrect the Hughes Pacific in compound form. The result was the design of an impressive-looking, four-cylinder compound Pacific with 6 ft 9 in driving wheels, twinned with a 2-8-2 goods engine with 5 ft 3 in driving wheels, and boasting a tractive effort of 44,400 lb. Fowler himself was no expert in detailed design, but his team did a terrific job and it looked as if the LMS finally had the super power it needed.

It seems that casting work on the cylinders had already begun when Anderson, determined that a four-cylinder Pacific was too big for the LMS, played a surprising trump card. In September 1926, he invited the GWR to send a Castle class 4-6-0 for trials between Euston and Carlisle. Anderson knew that greater power would soon be needed for the fifteen-car Royal Scot train which would run non-stop over the 299 mile route the following year, but he was not prepared to sanction Pacifics.

The Collett-designed Castle was set against a four-cylinder LNWR Claughton class 4-6-0, an older and less dynamic machine, and no one was really surprised when 5000 *Launceston Castle* demonstrated her clear superiority over her rival, a design by Charles Bowen Cooke dating from 1913. What *Launceston Castle* proved to Anderson and the operating department was that nothing bigger than a 4-6-0 was needed for even the most demanding west coast work. They convinced the LMS board, and Swindon was asked if it could supply fifty new Castles. The answer was a very firm no. The upshot of this was the Royal Scot class three-cylinder 4-6-0s of 1927, largely designed and wholly built by the North British Locomotive Company of Glasgow. The Pacific was abandoned and Fowler's name, a touch ironically, was from then on attached to the very locomotives that had scuppered his finest moment. Anderson's tactics had worked. The Royal Scots were far from perfect in their original form, but they were nevertheless fast and powerful engines which did away, for the most part, with double-heading on the principal west coast expresses. But while the Royal Scots solved one problem, much of the LMS locomotive fleet remained as diverse and old-fashioned as it had been at the time the railway was formed in 1923.

When, by 1930, even the Royal Scots were performing at near their limits and more power was deemed necessary, Anderson – independently and over the head of the chief mechanical engineer – approached Beyer Peacock in Manchester, manufacturers of the superb, if unconventional, articulated Garratt locomotives, and suggested an express passenger compound Garratt with 6 ft 9 in wheels. Beyer Peacock's design team were quick to understand that what Anderson really wanted was a kind of twin Midland compound 4-4-0. They dutifully drew up an arrangement for a 4-4-2 + 2-4-4 compound, but – in a lovely touch – added drawings of what they thought should be built instead. This was a 4-6-2 + 2-6-4 compound with 6 ft 9 in driving wheels, long-lap, long-travel valves, a massive 220 psi boiler, and a tractive effort of close to 50,000 lb – and there was every indication that it would have been a truly special machine which would have romped up Shap and Beattock with small towns in tow. Anderson was presumably not amused, but the idea of the express passenger Garratt lingered until the arrival of Stanier and his decidedly big Pacifics.

Fowler was promoted sideways into a top-level research role in 1930 and Ernest Lemon took the reins while a chief mechanical engineer who could deliver Sir Josiah Stamp's vision of a fully integrated railway could be found. GWR practice, meanwhile, had certainly impressed LMS management. Sir Harold Hartley used the GWR as a matter of course on his way up and down from London to Oxford; a rational man, he was impressed by the high level of standardization and efficiency found on Stanier's railway. As for Stamp himself, he wanted rationalization at any cost. After the Treaty of Versailles, he had been on the Dawes committee in Germany which helped to establish the Deutsche Reichsbahn in 1922, a newly integrated state railway set up on commercial lines and one step removed from full state control. His continuing, eager interest in the ways of the German economy were to lead him, along with many other British businessmen sympathetic to Nazi Germany, into serious errors of political judgement. In 1936, he wrote to *The Times* calling for British academics to attend the 550th anniversary of Heidelberg University even though, under Nazi control, it had unceremoniously sacked forty Jewish lecturers. He wrote for Hermann Göring's lavishly produced *Die Vierjahresplan* (*Four-Year Plan*) magazine and, as a guest of Hitler, attended the Nuremberg Rally in 1938. That same year he was raised to the peerage, but on the night of 16 April 1941, Stamp, his wife, and his eldest son, Wilfred, were killed in a Luftwaffe bombing raid. His house, Shortlands, in Kent, had received a direct hit.

At the time of his death, Stamp was serving as the government's adviser on economic coordination. He was one of the 'Guilty Men' accused in the book of that title published by Victor Gollancz in 1942. Written by 'Cato', the pen name of a trio of writers representing the three major British political parties – Michael Foot, Frank Owen, and Peter Howard – *Guilty Men* pointed an angry finger at the architects of appeasement. Stamp, however, was accused not for his fondness for Nazi Germany's apparent administrative efficiency (a not uncommon trait among the British ruling and senior administrative class at that time), but for spending too much money on the LMS. 'The soldiers of Britain had insufficient tanks and airplanes to protect them,' Cato railed, 'for the simple reason that insufficient money had been spent to buy them. It was not really Lord Stamp's fault. He was only half guilty. The nation's railways must be carried on.'

Stamp's pro-German views did not, however, prevent the LMS from commissioning a brilliant poster by the Viennese artist Lili Réthi, titled *Crewe Works: Building 'Coronation' Class Engines*, which was issued in 1937 in the run-up to the launch of the Coronation Scot express from Euston to Glasgow. When 'invited' to produce art glorifying the Third Reich, Réthi chose to emigrate to London, and eventually to New York.

Stanier, meanwhile, a big man with a Wiltshire accent which never left him, was as apolitical as most steam locomotive engineers. Coming from a Churchward background, however, he did believe in standardization, simplicity, and ease of maintenance. His biggest single problem on joining the LMS on 1 January 1932 lay with the infighting going on around him. Once in his stride, he shaped an impressive team of designers and production engineers, allowing him to produce, starting with the two-cylinder class 5 mixed-traffic 4-6-0s, a family of locomotives that would be among the very last steam locomotives in regular service with British Railways. Stanier's class 5 4-6-0 of 1934, and its heavy goods sibling, the class 8F 2-8-0 of the following year, were manufactured by LMS and other works in vast numbers. A total of 842 'Black 5s' was built between 1934 and 1951, along with 852 of the 2-8-0s between 1935 and 1946.

The Black 5s were, without doubt, one of the best all-round steam locomotives to run in Britain. A development of the GWR Hall class two-cylinder 4-6-0s built between 1927 and 1950, the Stanier class 5 could run on most routes of the LMS and, from 1948, many lines of all British Railways regions. They were simple, free-steaming machines which were timed at up to 96 mph. They could exert peak outputs of up to 1,800 ihp and were equally at ease at the head of goods, parcels,

William Stanier, pictured here in 1936, became the highly effective Chief Mechanical Engineer of the LMS in 1932.

The quietly brilliant Tom Coleman, posing here at his desk for the railway's official photographer in 1936.

Stanier and Coleman's masterwork was the Coronation class Pacific. In this mid-1950's scene at Carlisle Citadel, 46231 *Duchess of Atholl* [left] prepares to take over from 46244 *King George VI* for the northward run of the *Royal Scot* express from London to Glasgow.

The *Night Ferry* prepares to leave London Victoria on 15 December 1947, behind the 'air-smoothed' Bulleid West Country Pacific 21C56 *Croydon*. Built at the beginning of that year, it was rebuilt in 1960 and withdrawn from service in May 1967.

The compelling sight – and sound – of express steam in full flight is captured in this stirring shot of Merchant Navy Pacific, 35018 *British India Line* racing through Raynes Park on a London Waterloo to Bournemouth train on 16 December 1962.

For a brief spell, the Great Western Railway's *Cheltenham Flyer* was the world's fastest train. Here it is in April 1937, behind one of Charles Collett's Castle class 4-6-0s, 5004 *Llanstephen Castle*. Built in 1927, the *Cheltenham Flyer* remained in front line service until April 1962.

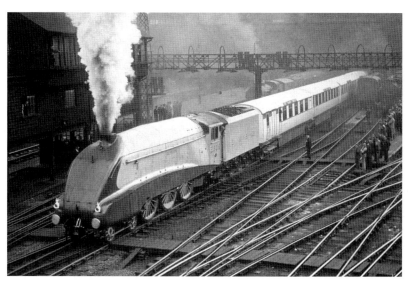

Thermodynamic principles learned from the Great Western's Castles were embodied in Nigel Gresley's magnificent streamlined A4 Pacifics for the LNER. Here, brand new 2509 *Silver Link* roars out of London Kings Cross with the press run of the *Silver Jubilee* on 7 September 1935.

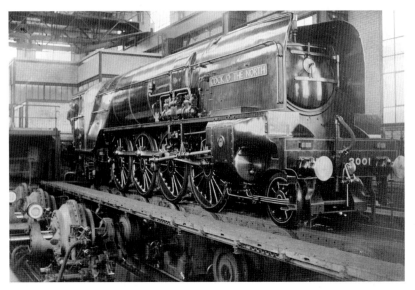

Co-operation between Nigel Gresley and Andre Chapelon led to the scientific testing of the striking new LNER P2 2-8-2, 2001 *Cock o' the North*, at Vitry, near Paris, in 1934.

After the Second World War, extensive tests were made between rival forms of traction. In this British Railways poster of 1949, a brand new Stanier Class 5 4-6-0 competes with a pair of equally new 1,600 hp LMS diesel-electrics, both overtaking a suburban electric multiple unit of 1927 vintage.

Stanier's experimental LMS Turbomotive at Euston station on 27 June 1935. This was the first turbine locomotive built in Britain. Stanier wanted to build fifty improved Turbomotives, but the financial and operating strictures imposed by the Second World War intervened. The handsome 2,600 hp 6202 was rebuilt as a conventional Pacific in 1952, but destroyed in a horrific crash that year.

The experimental water-tube boilered four-cylinder compound, 10,000, has arrived at Kings Cross, on time, at the head of the non-stop *Flying Scotsman*. From left to right: Nigel Gresley, the locomotive's designer-in-chief; drivers J. Gascoigne and R. Eltringham; and firemen H. A. Brayston and J. W. Ritchie; 31 July 1930.

Adolf Wolff's magnificent Deutsche Reichsbahn 05 001 4-6-4 parades for newsreel cameras at Borsig works, Berlin, 1 March 1935. Sister locomotive, 05 002, reached 200.4 kph [124.5mph] the following year. These supremely fast and reliable red engines lost their streamlined casings in 1944 and were rebuilt in 1951. Sadly, 05 002 was scrapped in 1960; 05 001 has been preserved.

One of 6,719 Class 52 Kriegsloks built across the Nazi Reich from 1942, 52 301 is at the head of a post-war Austrian State Railways freight train. They ran in Austria until 1976, and in East Germany until 1988.

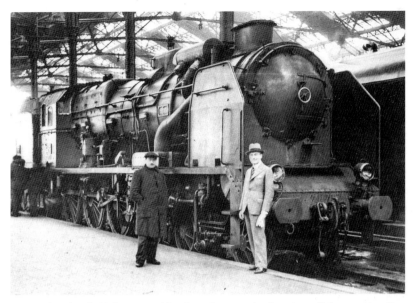

Andre Chapelon (left), has just ridden from Lyon on the footplate of his sensationally efficient 240-705, here on test at Paris Gare du Lyon in 1938. Erwin Mulotte (right), President of the Association Francaise des Amis des Chemins de Fer, looks suitably impressed.

The 240P compound 4-8-0 was a development of the 240-700 series. This is 240P 10 at Laroche in 1947. Built in 1940–1, these twenty-five locomotives were Chapelon's favourites. They were retired in the early 1950s.

Dressed in Givenchy, Audrey Hepburn poses in front of 232-U1, an equally stylish SNCF de Caso 4-6-4. The scene, at Gare du Nord, is from *Funny Face* filmed in 1956.

Chapelon's solitary 242A1, a three-cylinder compound 4-8-4, was a rebuild of an ineffective Etat Railway 4-8-2 and could sustain power outputs unknown outside the USA. Built in 1946, 242A1 was scrapped – scandalously – in 1960.

stopping passenger, and express trains. True maids-of-all-work, they were known as 'engineman's friends' and, especially when clean (a rare condition in late British Railways service), they were particularly handsome machines. They also set the tone for the look of all standard Stanier locomotives.

Where did this enduring aesthetic come from? From the drawing board of Tom Coleman at Horwich works, who, in 1935, became Stanier's chief draughtsman. All Stanier's greatest engines were effectively designs by Coleman: the class 5 4-6-0s, the class 8F 2-8-0s, the rebuilt three-cylinder Royal Scot and Patriot 4-6-0s, and, most famously, the Princess Coronation Pacifics. Coleman himself was the most self-effacing of men. Born in Endon, Staffordshire, in 1885, he served an apprenticeship with locomotive builders Kerr, Stuart & Co. at Stoke-on-Trent at much the same time as Reginald Mitchell, who went on to become chief designer for Supermarine and gave us the Spitfire. Coleman himself moved on to the North Staffordshire Railway, also based in Stoke-on-Trent, in 1905, rising to the rank of chief draughtsman. The chief mechanical engineer there was George Hookham, whose daughter was Margot Fonteyn, the famous ballet dancer. Coleman was transferred to Horwich in 1926.

Once he had discovered this quiet, unassuming giant of a man – Coleman had played centre forward for Port Vale FC in the 1908–9 season, scoring fifteen goals in twenty-two games – Stanier was dependent on him. Coleman, the very best of backroom boys, had no interest in self-promotion. He wrote few technical papers and left no memoirs. But no matter how bluff and crag-like he must have seemed, Coleman did have a sense of humour. When Stanier had his arm twisted by management at Euston into producing a series of streamlined Pacifics, he said: 'Let them have their bloody streamliners if they want them, but we will build five proper ones as well.' The nameplate on the non-streamlined Pacific that Coleman drew up for Stanier bears (or bares) the legend *Lady Godiva*. In retirement, Stanier told Coleman's son-in-law, G. A. Lemon, that without Coleman he would not have succeeded on the LMS and might well have left. Coleman was an artist of sorts: he knew instinctively how to draw handsome and fully resolved locomotives which, visually, were just so and all of a piece. It is a real gift to be able to make a highly functional machine into a thing of true elegance and even beauty, and in Coleman's case the gift was innate. Indeed, industrial stylists have never been able to better the design work of the finest locomotive engineers.

Coleman's genius, like that of Stanier, Gresley, and Churchward, was to gather a team of like-minded engineering disciples around him, not just from within his own department but from wherever he could find the talent he needed. Among his first-division players were two men brought in from outside the LMS – L. Barraclough from the North British Railway and G. R. Nicholson from the Yorkshire Engine Co. – along with D. Willcocks from Horwich, his own home base, and J. Francis from Crewe. E. S. Cox and E. A. Langridge were already at Derby when Coleman took over there in 1936 and they too became part of Coleman's impressive design team for Stanier.

In his first two or three years with the LMS, Stanier's star was at mid-point. His three-cylinder Jubilee class express passenger 4-6-0s were unreliable steamers. His class 3P two-cylinder 2-6-2 tank engines were ineffectual. His first two Pacifics, 6200 *Princess Royal* and 6201 *Princess Elizabeth*, were neither as powerful nor as economical as their size and specification suggested. And even the first Black 5s were not as effective as they should have been. The problem was simple enough. Coming from Swindon, where only that amount of superheating that would dry steam was considered necessary, Stanier had continued with a superheating practice which he thought was readily transferable, until he realized that servicing conditions on the LMS were very different from those on the GWR. With a higher degree of superheating, and other modifications, the Jubilees and Princess Royals were transformed. Tests on low- and high-superheat Black 5s showed that the upgraded engines used 12 per cent less coal and 14 per cent less water for the same work.

But while Stanier's main concern was with building up a consistently modern fleet of locomotives – and carriages, too – the age of streamlining and high-speed railways soon caught up with him. A good friend of Gresley's, he was well aware of developments on the LNER. He was never a convert to the streamlining of locomotives, believing that the savings in horsepower requirements that could be achieved as a result of the reduced air resistance, as demonstrated in wind tunnels, were relatively insignificant at speeds up to 100 mph, and, more importantly, that streamlining meant that machinery was hard or even impossible to access, which was something he normally opposed. The siren voices of speed and streamlining were, however, impossible to ignore.

On Monday, 16 November 1936, when Stanier was in India as a member of Sir Allan Mount's committee of inquiry into serious derailments of Pacific locomotives on the Indian railways, a high-speed run was made from London to Glasgow and back. The journey was planned in typically meticulous detail by one of Stanier's up and coming team, R. A. 'Robin' Riddles, then principal assistant to the chief mechanical engineer. The schedule was six hours for the arduous 401.4 miles, including the challenging ascents of Shap, 915 feet above sea level, in Westmorland, with its 1-in-75 northbound gradient, and Beattock, 1,016 feet above sea level, in the southern Scottish lowlands.

On Sunday, 15 November, 6201 *Princess Elizabeth*, fitted with an enlarged superheater, was at Willesden shed being prepared for the following day's exertions. A fitter discovered a leak in one of the joints of the main internal steam-pipe. This would have seriously reduced the performance of the engine. Riddles called Roland Bond, another key member of the Stanier team, who was then assistant works superintendent at Crewe. Bond was entertaining guests for tea. Riddles explained that the spare part needed could only be had at Crewe – could he find it and send it by the 18.40 up express? Yes, of course, came the answer. The one problem was that, this being Sunday afternoon, the works (as opposed to the engine shed) was closed and in the dark. It was also a filthy day, gloomy and tipping down with rain. Bond got one of his guests, a local farmer, to drive him to the works, stopping only to pick up a retired storekeeper named Froggatt who knew the stores backwards. With the help of a box of matches, Froggatt laid his hand on the small part – one of countless thousands in row and after row of racks in the giant works stores. There followed a rush to the station. Bond handed the vital component to the driver of the 18.40 with instructions to hand it to Riddles, who would be waiting at Euston.

Riddles worked through the night fixing 6201. He then rode with the crew on the non-stop run to Glasgow the following morning. Quite what this must have been like is hard to imagine today. There was no corridor tender and so no relief, of any sort, for those on the footplate. Just flasks of cold tea – remarkably few enginemen owned expensive Thermos flasks in the 1930s – and some sandwiches washed down with soot and steam. With a train of seven coaches, including the LMS dynamometer car, weighing 225 tons, *Princess Elizabeth* completed the run, with driver Clarke at the controls, in 353 minutes and 42 seconds, at an average speed of 68.2 mph. Shap had been crested at 57 mph and Beattock at 56 mph. Given that express trains of the day could be down to below 30 mph on these gradients, this was exceptionally good going, although the test train was much lighter than a scheduled west coast express.

Ernest Lemon, now a vice president of the LMS, took Riddles aside at Glasgow and suggested they run faster back to London the following day. Riddles, erring on the side of caution, suggested instead an increase in weight to eight coaches. His instinct seemed to be right when, during the celebratory dinner held in Glasgow on the Monday evening, he was slipped a note informing him that another important component – the left-hand outside crosshead slipper – had run hot and needed re-metalling. Leaving the dinner at 10 o'clock, Riddles took a taxi to the St Rollox works and worked on the locomotive for most of the night. He managed an hour's sleep in the works before *Princess*

Elizabeth steamed out from under the great glass roof of Glasgow Central. With Beattock cleared at 67 mph and Shap at 63 mph, and in squally, unpleasant weather, *Princess Elizabeth* span up to London, cruising wherever possible at 80–95 mph. She pulled into Euston – the terminus then still fronted by Philip Hardwick's monumental Euston Arch, wilfully demolished by the arch-modernizers in 1961 – in 344 minutes and 20 seconds, at an average speed of 70.15 mph. Legally, this time would be impossible by car on the motorways of Britain in 2012 – imagine just how fast it was in 1936.

This was a triumph for the LMS, and for Stanier, although the run did raise key questions. Just how reliable would locomotives need to be if they were to maintain a daily schedule of six hours between London and Glasgow? Given that *Princess Elizabeth* was being fed coal at an average rate of slightly above 3,000 lb per hour – about the maximum a fireman could be expected to sustain over a long run – how could this be repeated in day-to-day running?

The answers were provided in May 1937, when 6220 *Coronation*, the first of Stanier's second-generation Pacifics, made its debut at Crewe. Sheathed in aerodynamically designed casing, shaped not by an industrial artist but by Tom Coleman – if the new Pacifics had to be streamlined, then Coleman would do it himself – *Coronation* was finished in Caledonian blue, lined with silver stripes which appeared to burst from the nose of the casing before shooting along the sides of engine and tender. The most effective streamlining, however, was inside the locomotive. Stanier freely admitted his debt to Chapelon, and Coleman made every effort to ensure that nothing – no cross-sectional restrictions in the steam circuit – could impede the flow of steam. So, although almost exactly the same length and weight as *Princess Elizabeth*, *Coronation* was considerably more powerful. The Princess Royals were timed up to 102 mph, and could produce up to 2,500 ihp; the Coronations were timed up to 114 mph and, when fitted with a double chimney, one produced a maximum of 3,333 ihp on a test run in 1939. In 1985, the preserved 46229 *Duchess of Hamilton* made three runs with special trains where the cylinder horsepower was measured at between 3,500 and 3,700 ihp. With an eleven-coach train of 420 tons, *Duchess of Hamilton* accelerated from 63.5 to 74.5 mph up the 1-in-179 gradient of Saunderton Bank in Buckinghamshire on a run from Marylebone to Stratford. With a twelve-coach train on a trip from Marylebone to York, she increased speed from 44 to 68 mph up the same gradient; and at the head of a twelve-coach load of 460 tons, on a run from Carlisle to York, she fought her way up the 1-in-100 gradient at Mallerstang, at the head of the Eden Valley, her speed rising from 28 to 47 mph.

The press run of the LMS's streamlined Coronation Scot express was made on 29 June 1937. The down journey to Crewe, with an eight-coach load of 275 tons, was scheduled at 135 minutes for the 158 miles. Driver Clarke, hero of the 1936 Glasgow venture with *Princess Elizabeth*, assisted by fireman Lewis, was into Crewe 5 minutes and 15 seconds early. But the last 10.5 miles into Crewe had taken just under seven minutes. In this brief time, *Coronation*, as the dynamometer car revealed, had got up to 114 mph – but that was within two miles of Crewe station. Braking hard, Clarke was a mile away from the platforms and running at just under 105 mph. The train had to negotiate three reverse curves to reach its platform, and the first of these was hit at 57 mph instead of the nominal speed limit of 20 mph. Stanier, Coleman, and co. had done their work on the suspension of the new Pacific very well indeed. She drew to a halt safely.

Cecil J. Allen, who timed the train, recalled the lunch afterwards, at which LMS vice president Lemon addressed the members of the press: 'Commenting on the sudden and violent embraces of standing members of the party [i.e. those at the bar], to an obbligato of crashing crockery, that had preceded the hectic entry into Crewe, he remarked, "Of course, gentlemen, you will realize that we shan't need to do this kind of thing on every trip of the Coronation Scot; we were coming in a little faster than we shall have to do in the ordinary course."'

Driver Clarke was allowed to make his own pace back to Euston after lunch. The trip took 119 minutes exactly, an average of 79.7 mph, with *Coronation* steaming comfortably at between 90 and 100 mph between the many restrictions in force at the time.

There was some disappointment later when the schedule for the Coronation Scot was announced at six and a half hours, when a Coronation Pacific locomotive could make the trip in half an hour less. But the LMS management was keen to ensure that the train would run to time against all foreseeable weather conditions and traffic delays. An early afternoon departure at 13.30 from Euston was made in order to avoid operating delays to the west coast main line's heavy late-evening fast freight services. Business passengers needing longer in London could opt for the 16.30 departure of the LNER's Coronation service to Edinburgh, from where there was a fast connection to Glasgow.

Quite how powerful the new Pacifics were was revealed in tests carried out on 26 February 1939 with 6234 *Duchess of Abercorn*, the first Stanier locomotive to be fitted with a double blast-pipe and chimney. *Duchess of Abercorn* was called on to pull a twenty-coach, 610 ton train from Crewe to Glasgow and back, on typical express schedules. It was the return journey that made her the stuff of railway legend. With driver McLean and fireman Smith of Polmadie, Glasgow, on the footplate, 6234 powered its way over Beattock in driving snow at a minimum of 63 mph and, skittling down to the border, was in Carlisle, a distance of 102.25 miles, in 106 minutes and 30 seconds. This was not just nine and a half minutes early, but within ninety seconds of the schedule of the lightweight and streamlined Coronation Scot.

Driver Garrett and fireman Farrington took over at Carlisle and ran the gargantuan train on time to Crewe. When the results from the dynamometer car were revealed, even Tom Coleman could afford to smile. For mile after mile, *Duchess of Abercorn* had been exerting 2,000 dbhp. On the long southbound climb finishing at Beattock on a 1-in-99 gradient, the locomotive produced a peak of 3,333 ihp. This was achieved with full regulator, 245 psi boiler pressure, and a cut-off of 35 per cent. On the climb south of the border from Carlisle to Shap, a maximum 2,511 dbhp was recorded, with cylinder horsepower rising over 3,000 ihp for considerable distances.

In January of the following year, 1940, the LMS gained much further favourable publicity, courtesy of the Coronations, when 6229 *Duchess of Hamilton*, disguised as 6220 *Coronation*, was shipped off to the United States to take part in the New York World's Fair. The railroad exhibit was to occupy seventeen acres, displaying the latest American and European trains. Paired with a new set of Coronation Scot coaches, complete with cocktail bar, the streamlined Pacific, painted red and gold, was dispatched across the Atlantic on board the *Belpamela*, an Oslo-registered ship fitted with railway tracks, which sank six years later in an Atlantic storm with a cargo of seventeen American-built 141R class 2-8-2s bound for the French SNCF. 'Robin' Riddles, who was in charge of the trip, made the crossing in rather less time and considerably greater luxury on the *Queen Mary*. He was, doubtless, a visitor to the Cunard liner's engine room, where he must have gazed admiringly at the smooth-working 160,000 shaft horsepower Parsons steam turbines which powered the 81,327 ton palace on the waves at a cruising speed of 30 knots.

Accompanied by glowing reviews in the US press – 'This Coronation Scot is a splendid train, neat, compact as a watch' (*Chicago Tribune*); 'A cunning little item . . . Britain's newest and ritziest train' (*Detroit News*) – Riddles, the LMS team, and the brand-new Pacific visited thirty-eight towns and cities across fifteen states as they steamed 3,121 miles from Baltimore to New York, on a trip that took them to Washington, DC, Pittsburgh, St. Louis, Chicago, Detroit, and Schenectady, home of the Alco steam locomotive works. By the time the train reached New York, it had received 425,000 visitors.

Driver Bishop had contracted pneumonia soon after the train arrived at Baltimore on 20 February, after a stormy voyage, so, until he was back in action on 9 April, fireman Carswell did the driving while

Riddles wielded the shovel. American newspapers were astonished to witness a 'top executive' in the role of fireman, and a very hard-working one at that, especially as many large American express passenger steam locomotives were fired by mechanical stokers. Few British working men of the time got to go to the United States, but Bishop and Carswell proved to be good ambassadors for their country and for the LMS, despite their complaints that the Americans were unable to make a decent cup of tea. Some things, at least, never change.

At the exhibition, Britain's most powerful passenger locomotive was displayed alongside the Brobdingnagian Pennsylvania Railroad S1 class 6-4-4-6. With cinematic styling by Raymond Loewy, the industrial designer, the S1 was twice as powerful as the Coronation and, it was said, had galloped up to 140 mph (the claim was never proved, although the S1's speedometer might well have indicated such a prodigious rate). *Duchess of Hamilton* returned, via an Atlantic convoy threatened by German U-boats, to Cardiff Docks and then to Crewe, in February 1942, and was back in wartime service a month later.

If the Pacifics stole the limelight, Stanier's ever-growing fleet of standard locomotives was changing the face of the LMS. For die-hard enthusiasts it was sad to see so many characterful Victorian and Edwardian locomotives fall to an invasion led chiefly by the all-conquering class 5 4-6-0s. For Stanier and the LMS management, here was the outward sign of a modern, integrated railway. While Stanier was all for standardization and clarity in design and engineering, he was also happy to experiment. The story of his Turbomotive, the most successful of British steam-turbine locomotives, is told in Chapter 6, while a streamlined, 75 mph, three-car diesel-hydraulic multiple unit was put into service between Oxford and Cambridge in 1939. This smoothly good-looking train was designed by Thomas Hornbuckle of the LMS. His assistant was Ron Jarvis, who went on to rebuild Bulleid's Pacifics in British Railways days. Diesel shunters were developed with operating costs about a third of those of steam, leading to the many hundreds of simple 350 hp 0-6-0 machines built by British

Railways, including the 996-strong 08 class of 1953–62 – making it the most numerous class of British locomotive, some of which are still in service. Undeniably useful as heavy yard shunters, they were, however, no match for steam tank engines in terms of speed. Where a tiny Collett 1400 class 0-4-2 tank engine could hurtle through the Gloucestershire countryside at recorded speeds of up to 83 mph downhill, these diesel shunters were geared for a maximum speed of 20 mph to give the high tractive effort necessary to move heavy trains.

Stanier, though, was an unrepentant steam man. While he did not stand in the way of assistants keen to investigate diesels – like his successor, the Oxford-educated, steam-trained C. E. Fairburn, and H. G. Ivatt – he made his preferences clear. After sitting through a paper given by Fairburn, Stanier commented: 'I feel that to devote a whole evening to diesel traction in a country like Britain is rank heresy.' Why? An abiding love of steam aside, Stanier cited coal. Britain had plenty of the stuff. Why go to the bother, and uncertain politics, of sourcing oil from abroad when the country had more than enough indigenous fuel to power its railways for a very long time to come?

Stanier was not a specialist detail designer but a very fine mechanical engineer with a great gift for organization. He chose the right people to realize his standardization programme on the LMS, and he achieved this quickly and, for the most part, good-humouredly. By any standards, it was an impressive transformation. By 1939, the Midland Railway's small engine policy which had obstructed Hughes and Fowler seemed a very distant memory. With the outbreak of war, it was not surprising that the government was keen to get hold of Stanier. Bit by bit, he was drawn into national service. In 1942, he became a full-time scientific advisor to the Ministry of Production, and the following year he was appointed a member of the Aeronautical Research Council. Knighted in the 1943 New Year honours, he eventually had to resign from the LMS, doing so, on the very best of terms, in 1944.

Not, though, before he had supervised designs, at the wartime LMS drawing office in Watford, for a streamlined 4-6-4 for express passenger work and a 4-8-4 version for heavy fast goods services over the west coast main line. With its four 17.5 × 28 in cylinders, 300 psi boiler pressure, and 6 ft 6 in driving wheels, the 4-6-4 had a nominal tractive effort of 56,070 lb. Its 70 sq ft grate would have been fired by an American-style mechanical stoker – try to imagine shovelling coal into a white-hot room with a floor measuring 10 x 7 feet and the reason for a mechanical stoker becomes clear. The sustained maximum power of the Coronations, with their 50 sq ft grates, would have been increased significantly if they had been fitted with mechanical stokers. The case against, however, was that they were often less economical than hand-fired grates at medium rates of work, and that the screw feed that carried the coal from tender to fire-grate could become blocked with large lumps of coal. Some American firemen must have been extraordinarily strong and fit as express passenger locomotives like the Pennsylvania Railroad's K4 Pacifics were hand-fired and they had 69.9 sq ft grates – conveniently just within the Association of American Railroads regulations, which stipulated that any locomotive with a fire-grate of 70 sq ft or more had to be stoked mechanically.

There was another reason, never apparently discussed at the time: labour before the Second World War was cheap. When I spent a misty early morning one day in 1990 helping to oil the motion of *Duchess of Hamilton*, I was surprised by the sheer number of lubrication points from which a cork plug had to be extracted before oil could be poured in, through the spout of the kind of venerable hand-held oil can Trevithick might have used when servicing the Pen-y-Darren engine. Given that Stanier was an expert in lubrication, why, one might ask, the need for this awkward, dirty, and even dangerous task beneath the boiler of a 105 ton steam locomotive built in 1938, just a year before the first jet aircraft flew under its own power? In the USA, in contrast, every attempt was being made by progressive railroads to mechanize the firing, oiling, fuelling, and even the cleaning of steam locomotives.

The 4-6-4 was to have raced 500 ton trains from Euston to Glasgow in six hours. It would have been more powerful than any British diesel locomotive built to date. The 4-8-4 would have introduced a type of locomotive best known in the United States – evidence of the increasing attraction American design had for British engineers attempting to boost the power, reliability, and utilization of steam locomotives to new levels. At the same time, the influence of Chapelon was equally important. While the design of the 4-6-4 was being worked up, so a Super-Coronation was also on the drawing boards. Two, with 300 psi boiler pressure, double Kylchap exhausts, a French Houlet superheater, and other modifications, were to have been built at Crewe in 1940. If they had been, they would surely have approached Chapelon's Pacifics in terms of power-to-weight ratio and overall efficiency, while being as easy to maintain as contemporary American locomotives. The war put a stop to these enticing developments.

Other plans had included smaller engines which would have been excellent additions to the Stanier fleet, notably a well-proportioned three-cylinder mixed-traffic 2-6-2, with 6 ft 0 in wheels and a tractive effort of 35,250 lb, designed by Coleman in 1942. This would have been a rival to Gresley's justly feted V2 class 2-6-2s. Timed at 93 mph on the Yorkshire Pullman, these locomotives could sustain 2,000 ihp, and they were equally at home on fast goods trains and proved invaluable during the Second World War, when they could turn their 6 ft 2 in wheels to pretty much any task. Wartime strictures, though, meant that Coleman's 2-6-2 was left on the drawing board. Meanwhile, it was the class 5 4-6-0s, as much Coleman's as Stanier's, that ruled the roost in their place.

As Stanier took on various new roles between 1942 and 1945, he rose to become the Grand Old Man of British mechanical engineering. He was made chairman of Power Jets, helping to develop Frank Whittle's gas turbine for jet propulsion (Stanier said that he had hoped to build a class of fifty turbine-driven LMS Pacifics), a member of the Athenaeum Club, and a fellow of the Royal Society – only the second locomotive engineer to be so honoured, the first having been George Stephenson. In December 1947 he was invited to Euston, where one of the latest Coronation Pacifics was named *Sir William A. Stanier FRS*. He continued to advise several engineering companies and, despite his fondness for steam, helped pioneer the development of gas-turbine engines in railway locomotives. In 1963 he made the snowy journey from his Rickmansworth home – named 'Newburn', the same name as Churchward's house in Swindon – to receive the James Watt International Medal of the Institution of Mechanical Engineers. It was a fitting honour for an engineer who had done as much to increase the workaday efficiency and reliability of the steam engine as Watt had done before him.

At the memorial service held after his funeral at St Margaret's, Westminster, in September 1965, Sir Frank Mason, a fellow council member of the Institution of Mechanical Engineers, said: 'William Stanier is an outstanding example of someone who remained young at heart all his days, and one of his secrets was that he always had time for the younger man. He was able, therefore, to guide and influence younger people. I know because I am one.' As were 'Robin' Riddles, Stewart Cox, and Roland Bond, who were to carry the Stanier torch into the era of nationalization.

*

That came in 1948, when the Big Four were taken over by the state. For some engineers devoted to the ways of their old companies, this meant a parting of ways. Men like Tom Coleman took early retirement, not wishing to become part of some vast bureaucracy weighed down with committees and interminable meetings. Others, like the dynamic Riddles, saw it as a fresh challenge and, all importantly, an opportunity to bring standardization to Britain's steam railway locomotive stock as never before. As it was, on 1 January of that year, the Railway Executive of the new British Transport Commission took over 20,030 locomotives, including diesels and electrics, of 448 different types, some dating back to the 1870s. Riddles was appointed Railway Executive member for mechanical and electrical engineering, with Bond in charge of locomotive construction and maintenance, and Cox becoming executive officer, design.

From the outset of what was to become British Railways, Stanier's young men – now middle-aged – were in charge. Riddles could have proposed changes in traction policy, yet plumped for the continuation of steam. Existing designs from the Big Four were continued in production until 1956, with a total of 1,538 being built. This was considerably more than the 999 British Railways Standard locomotives built between 1951 and 1960. The decision to continue with steam as the main form of traction for the foreseeable future was made on a number of simple assumptions. There was little capital available to be spent on electrification and main-line diesel programmes in the age of austerity. Steam was cheap, and the country had plenty of coal and water, even if the price of coal did rise by 157 per cent between 1939 and 1945.

Before announcing designs for the new British Railways Standard fleet, Riddles outlined his case for steam during his presidential address to the Institution of Locomotive Engineers in November 1950. 'At present,' he said, 'there is undoubtedly a field for steam, for the internal combustion engine, and for electric traction. All are in active use, and the three are likely to exist side by side for a very considerable number of years ahead. The case for electrification and the internal combustion locomotive is often and very clearly stated. There is also a case for steam, and it is that at present, in a considerable range of circumstances, a pound will buy more tractive effort than in the case of any other form of traction.'

A new British Railways Standard class 5 4-6-0, with a starting tractive effort of 26,120 lb and a sustained output of 1,200 dbhp, explained Riddles, would cost £16,000 to build. This equates to a cost of £0.61 per pound of tractive effort, or £0.13 per drawbar horsepower. A 1,600 hp diesel-electric, with a starting tractive effort of 41,400 lb and a sustained output of 1,200 dbhp, would cost £78,200, equating to a cost of £1.89 per pound of tractive effort, or £0.65 per dbhp. The figures for the latest 1,500 volt electric locomotive were, respectively, £37,400, 45,000 lb, 2,120 dbhp, £0.83, and £0.18 pence, and these did not include any allowance for the cost of the overhead catenary system. On this basis, steam was by far the cheapest form of traction, giving what the Americans like to call 'the biggest bang for your buck'.

But what about running costs? Experience, up until the late 1950s, appears to have supported Riddles. A comparison of the operating costs between the last two Coronation Pacifics and the first two LMS 1,600 hp diesel-electrics reveals that over the period 1949–57, the steam locomotives ran a slightly higher mileage than the diesels and their total repair costs were £39,823, compared with £111,347 for the diesels. These were early days for British diesels, and yet such costs were to be compounded by the poor reliability of many of the wide variety of largely untried and untested diesels ordered after the announcement of British Railways' Modernization Plan for 1955. At the time, British Railways had 18,000 steam locomotives on its books.

Plans had been drawn up, late in the day, by some members of the LNER management to dieselize the east coast main line immediately after the war, but they were dropped, with little complaint. It was not the case that Riddles and his team were against new forms of traction. In fact, they believed that ultimately conventional steam locomotives should give way to electric traction. What they were unsure about was the rate of transition from steam to electric. Bond's view, as expressed in a memorandum written in September 1954, was that the steam fleet should slowly be reduced and that a core of five thousand of the most efficient engines should be improved and serviced in motive power depots, being brought right up to date with mechanized lubrication and ash disposal. There was also a case for building new steam freight locomotives as electrification progressed. Bond expected main-line steam to be extinct by 1985, or 1995 at the very latest.

Steam, though, was under attack from research into what became the Clean Air Act of 1956, and from the Federation of British Industries which, in a 1952 report, criticized the very low thermal efficiency of the average steam locomotive (about 4 per cent at the drawbar), and the railways' consumption of 14 million tons of coal per year. This fuel could be put to better uses. If that meant electricity generation in power stations, steam locomotive engineers were not against the idea. What they were hoping for was an orderly and rational shift from steam to electric. This was not to be the case, however, due to external government pressure on the British Railways board.

Meanwhile, Sir John Elliot, the perceptive chairman of the Railway Executive, asked the SNCF's André Chapelon if he would visit Britain to offer his comments and suggestions on steam locomotive design. Chapelon declined the invitation because he knew the new British Railways Standard Britannia Pacifics were suffering from teething problems – problems that British engineers could solve for themselves – and he felt that his visit might embarrass his hosts. Only a year later, Elliot and the Railway Executive had gone and the opportunity to benefit from the Frenchman's technical wisdom had been missed.

Riddles, Bond, and Cox had been brought up to believe that the steam railway locomotive should be a simple machine. When the Standard types were unveiled in 1951, Cox said: 'This is the steam locomotive of today and tomorrow, and this is the form in which it will fight for survival against the diesel and the electric. As a cheap, rugged tractor, it can still have a part to play, a part which it cannot sustain should it leave its vantage ground and once more descend to the complexities of the compound, the turbine and the condenser.'

Was this disingenuous? Perhaps. The 999 Standard locomotives were certainly not an adventure in steam. For the most part, they were neatly designed, well proportioned, simple, spritely, and competent. What they were not is an advance in any particular way or form on what had gone before, apart from labour-saving devices including rocking grates and hopper ashpans. The class 5 4-6-0 was Stanier and Coleman's Black 5 of 1934 brought up to date. The class 4 2-6-4 tank engine was a slightly modified version of Stanier's 2-6-4 tank engine of 1934. The Britannia class 7MT two-cylinder Pacific could be an impressive performer – it revolutionized services from Liverpool

Street to Norwich – but it was no more efficient than Coleman and Ivatt's rebuilds of the Royal Scot 4-6-0s from 1943.

Only the class 9F 2-10-0 offered something new, a freight engine with 5 ft 0 in driving wheels and a real turn of speed as well as high tractive capacity. A slightly shortened Britannia Pacific, it proved to be a good steam producer. Although designed to run heavy mineral trains composed of long, rattling strings of four-wheeled wagons, mostly without fitted brakes, at a maximum of 25 mph, and fast, fully fitted, express goods trains at 60 mph, the 9Fs proved to be exceptionally able mixed-traffic locomotives, with a remarkable turn of speed. The fact that unfitted goods trains of up to 1,000 tons in weight were at work on Britain's main lines in the 1960s was a handicap to efficient operation, although power braking was a priority of the Modernization Plan. It was instructive, to say the least, to see gleaming German 2-10-0s working hard at the head of massive, modern, air-braked freight trains, with sections of their routes on electric main lines, in the late 1970s.

If one single performance can illustrate the operating flexibility of the 9F, of which 251 were built, perhaps it is a run made by the double-chimneyed 92000 on 14 July 1961 at the head of the southbound Pines Express on its final leg from Manchester to Bournemouth. The twelve-coach train, bringing its packed summer load of holidaymakers from the industrial and manufacturing North and Midlands, reached Bournemouth from Bath over the Mendip Hills. This was the main line of the old Somerset & Dorset Joint Railway; it was as picturesque and as challenging as any British railway. From Georgian Bath, the line (which was closed in 1966) climbed immediately up a 1-in-50 gradient with S-bends, and other challenging gradients followed. The Somerset & Dorset passed through idyllic English countryside, innocent of speculative housing, supermarkets, and roads roaring with tailgating traffic. The line was steam-powered to the end.

That day, Baron Gérard Vuillet, the French expert train-timer, polymath technologist, business administrator, and author of *Railway*

Reminiscences of Three Continents (1968), was on the footplate with driver Beale and fireman Smith of Branksome shed. Leaving Bath Green Park (now a supermarket) twelve and a half minutes late, in a fierce summer rainstorm, 92000 was very nearly on time at the first wayside stop, Evercreech Junction, 26.4 miles across the Mendips covered in exactly 46 minutes, against a schedule of 56 minutes. Attaining 2,240 ihp, the 9F climbed the 1-in-50 gradients at up to 36 mph. With speeds up to 65 mph where possible on this curving line, Beale and Smith rapidly won back more lost time. On the last big climb, between Blandford and Broadstone, 92000, regulator fully open and cutting off at 45 per cent, was over the 2 mile 1-in-80 climb, after a 50 mph speed restriction, at 43 mph. The Baron calculated that the big black goods engine had maintained 2,700 ihp up the bank.

As if to crown this noble performance, 92000 rushed away from Parkstone on the 4.4 mile thrash to Bournemouth West – the beach, the sea, Punch and Judy, and kiss-me-quick hats – at full regulator and 49 per cent cut-off. A mile of level track saw her up to 47 mph, dropping to no less than 41 mph up the 1.5 mile 1-in-60 climb ahead. 'It is difficult to assess the horsepower output because of the shortness of the run and the helping wind,' wrote Vuillet to O. S. Nock, who lived just outside of Bath, 'but calculations point to a cylinder horsepower in the region of 2,800 to 3,000 for one minute.' For an 86 ton engine, that was quite some minute. Taking the lower of Vuillet's figures, it works out as more than 32 hp per ton – as good as a Stanier Coronation, if not quite in the league of Chapelon's rebuilt Pacifics, 2-8-2s, 4-8-0s, and 4-8-4s in France. What mattered, though, is that the 9F had performed so very well throughout the run and was never remotely short of steam or in any other way winded. The train gained fifteen minutes on its schedule. It seems idiotic that some of these locomotives were taken out of service when they were just five years old – but such was the pressure for eliminating steam, no matter how effective, in the 1960s.

The 9F was a very good, if straightforward, locomotive. Its basic robustness was its strength. The class had cost between £23,975 (the first batch, built at Crewe in 1953–4) and £30,200 (the last batch, completed at Swindon in 1960). In line with the cost of the Britannia Pacifics, this was very good value, and perhaps the low cost was an added reason why the modernizers were able to sign off such young locomotives to the breakers' yards. Management wanted to see the back of steam quickly, and writing them off prematurely might not have seemed the wasteful extravagance it would have done had they cost as much as new diesels.

In contrast, the solitary British Railways express passenger locomotive, 71000 *Duke of Gloucester*, built in 1954 had promised real technical and thermodynamic progress. Designed largely under J. F. 'Freddie' Harrison, one of Gresley's young men, this was a replacement for the short-lived Stanier-style Pacific 46202 *Princess Anne*, itself a rebuild of the Stanier Turbomotive. (*Princess Anne* was involved in a horrific crash at Harrow and Wealdstone in 1952, just eight weeks after she had emerged from the Crewe works.) Harrison's handsome, three-cylinder *Duke of Gloucester* was completed in 1954. With improved Caprotti poppet valve gear, the locomotive's cylinder performance was exceptionally efficient, but the engine was often let down by generally poor steaming and was never liked in service by west coast crews accustomed to the Coronations. In preservation, a number of manufacturing faults were discovered, and since these have been put right *Duke of Gloucester* has put up performances good enough to challenge the might of the Stanier Coronations.

Harrison, who went on to become chief mechanical engineer of British Railways in the diesel and electric era, had wanted ideally to build a three-cylinder compound 4-8-2 and so increase the power and efficiency of the British steam locomotive to radical new heights. But such thinking was out of step with the Bond–Cox line, and by the time *Duke of Gloucester* emerged from Crewe, the Modernization Plan was being drafted. As for Riddles, he was very interested in Chapelon's work with compounding. Not only was he happily photographed in front of Chapelon's magnificent 242A1 at Paris Gare du Nord in 1949, but he also adopted the French engineer's suggestion, made in 1957, on reading the British Railways test report on *Duke of Gloucester*, that the exhaust cam profile should be changed to enable more work to be done in the cylinders. Indeed, Tom Daniels, a veteran GWR-trained engineer, has designed new exhaust cams following Chapelon's advice and these, along with double Kylchap exhausts, have made the restored *Duke of Gloucester* a more powerful and efficient machine.

One engineer who tried heroically – though some would argue over-ambitiously – to advance the British steam locomotive was Oliver Bulleid. Possibly the most controversial of British steam locomotive engineers, Bulleid created machines that were as impressive and fascinating as they were, sometimes, temperamental. From the moment he arrived at Waterloo as chief mechanical engineer of the Southern Railway in 1937, Bulleid was determined to do things differently. Finally, he went so far as to build one of the most radical of all steam railway locomotives, the diesel-lookalike, six-cylinder Leader 0-6-6-0 (see Chapter 6) – a story that ended in failure and yet raised fundamental questions about what a modern steam locomotive, if such a thing was still desirable, should be.

What was astonishing – both at the time and in retrospect – is that the Southern, of all railways, was Bulleid's vehicle for the design and production of one of Britain's most radical main-line steam locomotives. For the Southern Railway, carrying very heavy commuter traffic, had been electrifying steadily throughout the 1920s and 1930s. By 1936 its electric trains ran a greater total annual mileage than its steam trains. Sir Herbert Walker, the Southern's dynamic general manager from 1923 to 1937, took good care to employ a brilliant public relations officer in John Elliot (who, as Sir John Elliot, was later to become chairman of the Railway Executive and, in 1953, chairman of London Transport) and, less affected than other railways by the loss of goods traffic at the time of the Great Depression, paid his shareholders an annual dividend of 5 per cent, something the other companies found it impossible to match.

Nevertheless, there was still a substantial place for steam on the Southern Railway, the smallest of the Big Four in route mileage. Trains over the former London & South-Western Railway lines from Waterloo to Salisbury, Exeter, Plymouth, and Padstow were steam-hauled, as were those to Southampton, Bournemouth, and Weymouth. The Golden Arrow from Victoria to Dover was steam-hauled, as were services along the north Kent coast to Margate, Broadstairs, and Ramsgate, together with those running over branch lines and cross-country routes. Goods trains were too. But because the Southern Railway had concentrated investment in electrification, Bulleid inherited a very mixed bag of 1,847 steam locomotives, of eighty different classes, many of them housed in depots unchanged since the turn of the century.

Some of the main-line engines, like the forty Schools class, three-cylinder 4-4-0s from 1930–5, designed under the direction of Bulleid's predecessor Richard Maunsell, were excellent machines, yet none were fast or powerful enough to meet Bulleid's requirements, although he did clothe one of the Schools, 935 *Sevenoaks*, in wooden streamlining for publicity purposes – fortunately, the idea was dropped. What Bulleid really needed were locomotives that could accelerate as quickly as possible, given that many steam services had to thread their way through electric commuter trains out of London. He wanted locomotives that could run 600 ton trains to Exeter, Southampton, and Dover at average speeds of 70 mph. And he wanted new, modern coaches to match the design and image of what were to become some of the most charismatic and controversial of all main-line British steam engines: the Merchant Navy, West Country, and Battle of Britain Pacifics.

Most of all, Bulleid wanted to go his own way, based on his wide experience and exhaustive studies of locomotive engineering. A fierce individualist, he had met his match only in Gresley, six years his senior, with whom he enjoyed a working partnership that endured for the best part of a quarter of a century. Both men were energetic, inventive, and keen to explore new ideas from wherever they originated. They thought big, had great respect for French locomotive technology, and, above all, were inspired by the potential remaining for steam. If Gresley developed express passenger locomotives that could run at sustained high speeds, and thus may have held back the development of rival forms of traction for a number of years, Bulleid was determined to ensure a long-term place for steam.

Born at Invercargill, New Zealand, on 19 September 1882, Oliver Vaughan Snell Bulleid was the eldest son of William Bulleid, a Devonian who had emigrated in 1875, and Marian Vaughan Pugh, a childhood sweetheart whom he met again on a business trip to London. In 1889, William contracted pleurisy and died, at the age of forty-three. Mrs Bulleid brought her children to her mother's home in Wales. The clever, charming Oliver grew up into an imaginative young man, academically gifted, but fascinated, from as early as anyone could recall, with craftsmanship and the making of things. His village of Llanfyllin in mid-Wales (its railway station, on the line to Oswestry, was closed in 1960) boasted a blacksmith as well as a cooper, a coppersmith, and a tinsmith. Oliver helped them all. And if he was not in the smithy, he would be finding something useful to do in the local sawmill or gasworks. Here was a child with his head in the clouds of imagination but with his feet firmly on the ground.

At first, it seemed that he was destined to become a lawyer, and there was a moment when he was nearly shipped off to New Zealand. With help from his cousin, the Rev. Edgar Lee, vicar of Christ Church, Doncaster (an early Gothic Revival foundation of 1829), Bulleid was apprenticed to the GNR; one of the Rev. Lee's devoted parishioners and a close friend was H. A. Ivatt, the GNR's locomotive superintendent. In 1908, Bulleid married Ivatt's youngest daughter, Marjorie, the wedding taking place in Christ Church, Doncaster.

Bulleid's career did not progress along obvious lines. Far from it. Just before getting married, he accepted the post of chief draughtsman and assistant works manager for the Westinghouse company at Freinville, near Paris – makers of steam pumps, electric compressors, and other brake equipment for railways. He learned to speak excellent French. After a year, he took on a job as mechanical and electrical engineer for the Board of Trade, working on big British trade exhibitions in Brussels and Turin. He learned Italian too. And then, in 1912, he came back to Doncaster as personal assistant to the GNR's newly appointed locomotive superintendent, H. N. Gresley.

Bulleid had hardly settled in when the war with Germany broke out. As part of a volunteer unit of railway engineers attached to the Army Service Corps, Bulleid was commissioned with the rank of lieutenant and went off to France for a second time. He was nearly killed twice by German artillery shelling the trains he was working with, and was witness to the unspeakable carnage of the front lines. It was partly because of this that he turned to Rome and was received into the Catholic faith. By the end of the war, Major Bulleid was deputy assistant director of railway transport, although he was deeply irked when posted back to England in July 1918; he had no intention, he said, of joining 'a collection of war evaders'.

A free-thinking and independently minded conservative Roman Catholic, Bulleid was a bundle of contradictions. Somehow, these opposing traits showed in the design of his locomotives for the Southern Railway – a marriage of deep-rooted common sense and audacious experimentation. Bulleid, however, was a remarkably persuasive man – and he needed every ounce of his charm and keen intelligence to persuade both the Southern Railway and the government to approve the first of his designs to be built at Eastleigh: the three-cylinder Merchant Navy Pacifics of 1941. He had originally wanted 4-8-2s, but these would have been too heavy for some of the Southern Railway's bridges. He scaled down to 2-8-2, but the Southern's civil engineer turned that down on the same grounds. A Pacific it had to be.

Britain was at war with Germany again by the time drawings for the new Pacific had been agreed. The state took effective overall control of the railways, although they were run day to day by the Big Four. Capital expenditure on major projects, including the construction of new locomotives, needed government approval, and no express passenger locomotives were to be sanctioned. Bulleid, though, now nearing sixty, was determined to design and build his very own high-powered express locomotives. He got the Merchant Navy class accepted by claiming that it was for mixed-traffic use. This was credible because the dramatic new Pacifics were to run on 6 ft 2 in driving wheels – the same diameter as the mixed-traffic Gresley V2s – rather than the 6 ft 6 in to 6 ft 9 in of all the strictly express passenger engines built by the Big Four. And, during the war, the new Pacifics did a good deal of main-line freight work.

The first of the Merchant Navy Pacifics, 21C-1 (the unusual number was Bulleid's variation on the French numbering system), steamed for the first time on the same day that Generalleutnant Erwin Rommel arrived in North Africa to take command of the Afrika Korps. On 22 February 1941, 21C-1 ran a twenty-coach test train to Bournemouth and back; that same day, the German battleships *Scharnhorst* and *Gneisenau* sank five ships in an Atlantic convoy. On 10 March, 21C-1 was named *Channel Packet* by the minister of transport, Lieutenant Colonel J. T. C. Moore-Brabazon, at Eastleigh; this was the week the German extermination camps, including Auschwitz, Buchenwald, Sobibor, and Treblinka, went into full operation. It was indeed no time for frivolity, much less for the kind of glamorous streamlined express passenger locomotives that had regularly made newspaper headlines before the German invasion of Poland on 1 September 1939.

The newly named mixed-traffic locomotive was not exactly a Stanier Black 5 or a Gresley V2. Sheathed entirely in an 'air-smoothed casing' – panels of sheet steel – and appearing to have no chimney, dome, or safety valves, let alone sand and oil boxes, or a running board of any kind, *Channel Packet* was a Buck Rogers among contemporary steam locomotives – futuristic, almost otherworldly. Her leading and driving wheels eschewed spokes in favour of discs and ellipses, as were widely used in America. Her valve gear, for anyone who cared to look beneath the casing, was wholly enclosed in an oil bath. Drive was by chains. Lamps and cab lighting were electric, powered by a 0.75 hp steam turbine. New welding techniques had been used wherever possible, rather than bolted construction. Her reversing gear was steam-powered. So much seemed so very new: this was evidently an attempt to perfect the traditional Stephensonian locomotive.

But would it work? Away from Gresley, who applied mature judgement to new ideas, Bulleid knew that he had limited time to put his ideas into practice and so introduced them into production locomotives without lengthy prototyping. The oil bath and chain drive, however, which were to dog Bulleid's Pacifics before they were rebuilt in the 1950s, were a consequence of the Southern Railway's stores department refusing to allow the chief mechanical engineer to buy the Caprotti poppet valve gear he had wanted for the Merchant Navy class from an outside supplier. The strength of the class, however, was clear. Its all-welded boiler, with steel fire-box, was one of the very best designed in Britain. Its very high evaporative capacity supplied steam through well-designed and generously dimensioned pipes to free-flowing valves and cylinders.

On 5 May 1941, *The Times* ran a report on the new sixteen-coach wartime Atlantic Coast Express from Waterloo to Plymouth and points west:

> The Merchant Navy engines are an example of
> engineering skill aimed at the concentration of energy in
> the smallest possible space, and their introduction has
> enabled parts of long routes which formerly needed two
> engines to be covered by one. There are sections of the
> West Country journey, for instance, where the rise in
> gradient is so exceptional that no ordinary engine could
> climb them, but to the new type they offer no difficulty.

This was a slight exaggeration, as older engines like Maunsell's two-cylinder King Arthur class 4-6-0s were in fact rarely piloted over the steep hills between Salisbury and Exeter. The Bulleid Pacifics, however, would charge up 1-in-80 gradients at unprecedented speeds, with boiler pressure rising. Fully able to generate 3,000 ihp and to run occasionally at 100 mph and more, the new Pacifics weighed less than 95 tons. Sadly, they were also beleaguered by teething problems. The idea of encasing the valve motion in an oil bath was perfectly logical and desirable, as this was commonplace with internal combustion engines and avoided the need for multiple lubrication points. In practice, however, the oil baths of the Bulleid Pacifics tended to leak. These leakages often caused the locomotives to slip badly, something they were prone to do anyway, if not handled carefully. The locomotives were also fitted with lightly built steam-reversers which tended to creep, due to steam leakage, and could move without warning from, for example, 25 per cent cut-off to a full 75 per cent.

When, years later, he was sent a copy of *Bulleid Pacifics*, Peter Handford's latest recording of the sound of steam locomotives at work for the Argo Transacord label, Bulleid sent out for a record player. Sean Day-Lewis, Bulleid's first biographer, described what ensued:

> When the machine was installed in his office, silence was
> called for and the record started. Bulleid's bright and
> expectant face soon became cloudy and pensive. The first
> soloist was a Merchant Navy starting out of Salisbury in
> the up direction with multiple slipping, steam escaping
> in all the wrong places and a great deal of wheezing.
> The engine was clearly in bad condition . . . After a few
> moments the designer could stand it no longer: 'Take it
> off, take it off,' he cried. 'They aren't my engines.'

As Day-Lewis pointed out, this was a pity because 'other aspects of the record demonstrated the engines at their best, notably when an express is heard climbing with magnificent power through Templecombe'.

I was given that record when I was very young. I dug in a trunk when writing this book and – with a mixture of nostalgia and quiet joy – found Peter Handford's recording of Bulleid Pacifics at work. The opening track of side two must have been the one that so upset Bulleid. Here, 35023 *Holland Afrika Line*, according to the sleeve notes, 'sets out in pouring rain with the up Atlantic Coast Express. Slipping heavily at first, on the wet greasy rails, the Merchant Navy finally gains adhesion to take the train steadily past on the 1-in-305 rising gradient towards London.' The effects remain operatic more than half a century on. The Merchant Navy tearing down through Templecombe at high speed was the newly rebuilt 35020 *Bibby Line*, one summer's afternoon in 1956; the sound is like a cross between a heavy machine gun and rolling thunder. And yet, it is the sound of *Holland Afrika Line* slipping, as if trying to find her feet on ice, that lingers in the mind.

There were other problems. The drive-chain pins tended to develop wear, resulting in slack chains which were difficult to tighten. The engines were heavy on coal. Fires occasionally erupted between the boiler and cladding as soot and oil gathered into a combustible mixture in the space between them. The driver's view ahead was limited both by the width of the air-smoothed outer casing and by exhaust steam tending to cling to it.

Despite these criticisms, thirty Merchant Navys were built between 1941 and 1949. This, though, was just the beginning. Between 1945 and 1951, no fewer than 110 West Country and Battle of Britain light Pacifics were built. Scaled-down versions of the Merchant Navys, these potent machines weighed just 86 tons and were put into service throughout the non-electrified parts of the Southern Railway system, one day in charge of the fast and heavily loaded Atlantic Coast Express, another pottering along one of the north Cornwall branch lines with two coaches, weighing much less than the locomotive, in tow. On most days, the light Pacifics (the two classes were identical) performed admirably. Sadly, there were also bad days. Nonetheless, during the

1948 Locomotive Exchanges, organized to compare the performance capacity and efficiency of the principal existing British locomotive types, 34006 *Bude* produced outstanding efforts on the difficult Marylebone to Manchester main line, sustaining around 2,000 ihp on several occasions, while another West Country climbed the severe gradients of the Perth to Inverness line at speeds previously quite unknown.

Bulleid did not like to hear his Pacifics criticized. He did, however, make the point that features like the valve-gear oil baths and chain-driven motion were in their infancy. Just as it had taken a while to iron out problems with the internal combustion engine, so time was needed to overcome initial problems with this new generation of steam locomotives. Time, however, was something the steam engine of the 1940s did not have on its side, especially in wartime, when rugged simplicity was a virtue and, for the most part, a necessity. While it was true that many contemporary diesel engines were far from being oil-tight between their crankcases and cylinder blocks, Bulleid's claim could only sound like special pleading.

Finally, in February 1956, Merchant Navy 35018 *British India Line* emerged from Eastleigh for a second time after being rebuilt under the supervision of Ron Jarvis, chief technical assistant at the Southern Region's Brighton works. Bulleid, now in Ireland, was aghast, yet Jarvis had produced an elegant and functionally more reliable machine, and had worked Bulleid's tour-de-force into an exceptionally fine locomotive. A former LMS engineer, who had been involved with the design of the British Railways class 9F 2-10-0, Jarvis removed the 'air-smoothed casing', chain drive, oil bath, steam-reverser, and others of what were seen as Bulleid's idiosyncrasies. By October 1959, all thirty Merchant Navy Pacifics had been rebuilt. The light Pacifics followed, with 34005 *Barnstaple* being the first, in June 1957. However, by the time the rebuilding of 34098 *Templecombe* had been completed, in June 1961, British Railways was in no mood for further investment in steam. Fifty of the 110 West Country and Battle of Britain

Pacifics remained in more or less original condition until the last was withdrawn from service in July 1967, when steam operation on the Southern Region ceased. The contemporary statistics are interesting, however. The rebuilding programme was to have been extended to all 140 Bulleid Pacifics, at a cost of £760,000, which would, said the report issued by H. H. Swift, the Southern Region's chief mechanical and electrical engineer, have saved £2,051,400 on repair and running costs by 1987, the year the locomotives were expected to be scrapped.

The reliability of the short-lived rebuilt locomotives was exemplary and performances equalled those of the originals at their best. It was not just their ability to sprint at up to 105 mph and perhaps a little more – despite a nominal speed limit of 90 mph over British Railways track – and flatten the hills west of Salisbury with the heaviest trains; the sheer consistency of their running, something that matters to passengers and management alike, was also compelling. The Atlantic Coast Express – a crack train, always in tip-top condition, which linked London with nine separate destinations in Devon and Cornwall after mile-a-minute runs to Salisbury and Sidmouth Junction – last ran in 1964, and D. W. Winkworth, author of *Southern Titled Trains* and *Bulleid's Pacifics*, spent a week's leave riding the up 'ACE' every day, except Sunday, from Exeter to Waterloo.

Every log made by Winkworth revealed a net gain in time to the Merchant Navy Pacifics, with average speeds of between 62 and 66.8 mph over the saw-tooth route from Sidmouth Junction to Salisbury, and from 64.5 mph to 66.7 mph between Salisbury and Waterloo. Even in their last year of regular service, 1967, when the Pacifics were becoming run down and were usually spectacularly dirty – their Brunswick green paintwork now a rusty brownish grey, and their name and number plates missing – they proved able to run at 100 to 105 mph as drivers let rip for the last time.

If the Pacifics were controversial, so, too, was Bulleid's inside cylinder 0-6-0. The simple 0-6-0 goods locomotive had been a staple of Britain's railways since the 1850s. A penny-plain machine, it was pushed into service as a mixed-traffic engine before the arrival of locomotives like the Stanier Black 5 4-6-0s of 1934 and the Ivatt class 4 2-6-0s of 1947 which were ideally suited to such work. Even then, the type continued to be a useful maid-of-all-work, especially on secondary and cross-country lines. But Bulleid's Q1 class of 1942 drew attention to itself like no 0-6-0 ever had.

'Where's the key?' asked Stanier, jokingly, when he saw a photograph of this new wartime design. Externally, the Q1 was the locomotive equivalent of the Nissen hut and the Sten gun. Stripped to the essentials, it eschewed such polite details as smooth boiler cladding, running board and splashers running over the driving wheels, or a flared chimney, a feature of the vast majority of British locomotives. The aim was to build as powerful and as robust an 0-6-0 as possible with a maximum weight of just 51 tons. Weighing 51.75 tons in fact, the Q1 made its debut in March 1942. Bulleid rode C1, the first of the class, at 75 mph, tender-first, although in normal practice the Q1s were restricted to 55 mph. These were the most powerful British 0-6-0s and Bulleid was justly proud of them. His Christmas card for 1942 showed C8 at the head of forty covered wagons, weighing 420 tons, with the message 'May "Austerity" bring you loads of good times this Christmas and in the New Year'.

Although they looked different from any other locomotive, the Q1s were essentially conventional, two-cylinder locomotives, and worked without fuss until the class was ousted in 1966. Bulleid, though, seemed incapable of skirting controversy. Just before his retirement at the age of sixty-seven in 1949 – he was no fan of nationalization – he designed double-deck electric multiple units to provide greater passenger capacity for service on the north Kent commuter services to and from London; buffet cars disguised as mock-Tudor pubs, complete with leaded lights and fake oak beams; and the Leader class 0-6-6-0, one of the most unconventional of all steam locomotives and a machine that seemed the polar opposite of what Riddles, Bond, and Cox were aiming to do with the Standard series of steam locomotives for British Railways. Riddles, however, was a friend of Bulleid's and was keen on innovation if it was combined with reliability in service.

Perhaps Bulleid might be likened to a Cavalier general charging solo into the unified ranks of a Puritan army. As late as 1967, it was a special delight to ride in Bulleid's stylish and elegant malachite-green coaches – mock-Tudor bars aside, he had been good at carriage design since his earliest days on the GNR – behind an unmodified Pacific. And what a poignant sight it was on 30 January 1965 when the (un-rebuilt) Battle of Britain 34051 *Winston Churchill* pulled out of Waterloo at the head of Sir Winston Churchill's funeral train.

After his retirement from the Southern Railway in 1949, Bulleid was offered the post of consulting mechanical engineer to the CIE (Córas Iompair Éireann), based at the Inchicore works, Dublin, starting work on 1 October. He was raring for a fresh opportunity. Formally appointed chief mechanical engineer in February 1951, he pursued a remarkably level-headed course, and, when he retired seven years later, the railway was genuinely sorry to see him go.

When Bulleid arrived in Dublin, there had been much talk in the press of how desperate the CIE must have been to have imported a retired engineer from England. In his satirical column for the *Irish Times*, written under the pseudonym Myles na gCopaleen, Brian O'Nolan, the Irish journalist and novelist, perhaps better known by his pen name Flann O'Brien, wrote: 'Mr O. V. Bulleid – or "John" Bulleid as I prefer to think of him – is too old to work for BR . . . and therefore qualifies to be the big boss at Inchicore. When Sean T. [Sean O'Kelly, president of Ireland] retires we may also manage to get Churchill into the Vice-regal lodge . . . Do I sound bitter? Perhaps. Do I speak for Ireland? I think I do . . . I refuse to be Bulleid.'

Yet when it was discovered that 'John' Bulleid was a Catholic and that he worked at his desk at Inchicore under a crucifix, much was forgiven. Besides, Bulleid had lost none of his charm over the years and was just as happy – as Gresley and Stanier had been – talking with engine drivers and apprentices on the shop floor as with senior management and politicians. His proved to be a popular appointment. He was happy in Ireland.

Given that the CIE had already agreed on dieselization, much of Bulleid's time was taken up with ensuring that the right decisions were made in terms of buying in new diesels and building lightweight coaching stock to go with them. In the event, he chose well. He might not have been fond of them, but he had experience with main-line diesels, having overseen the design of a pair of 1,750 hp diesels which were built by British Railways' Ashford works with English Electric in 1950–1. The first of these, 10201, was displayed at the Festival of Britain. A third, fitted with a 2,000 hp engine, was built in 1954 and formed the basis of the English Electric type 4 2,000 hp diesels which nosed Stanier's Coronation Pacifics aside from the late 1950s. Rather ironically, it was Roland Bond, now chief mechanical engineer of British Railways and one of the engineers critical of Bulleid's steam engines, especially the revolutionary Leader, who oversaw development of the English Electric type 4s.

The Leader design that had led Bulleid – and his successors at British Railways – into major problems continued to intrigue him. Even while dieselizing the CIE, he used his new job in Ireland to pursue the design of a double-cabbed, turf-burning 0-6-6-0 which was very nearly a success. Just as Ireland was going 100 per cent diesel, a prototype main-line steam locomotive was being nurtured at the Inchicore works. Bulleid eventually retired, with his wife Marjorie, to Malta – he had always felt the cold – where he died in April 1970. A gifted and inventive engineer, he had been willing to experiment boldly, and yet his timing could often seem very wrong indeed. Wartime and austerity Britain had been no places for costly experiments with steam when what was needed, above all, was a fleet of sturdy and wholly reliable locomotives. He had, however, lived long enough to witness the end of main-line steam in Britain and the beginnings, with the founding of the Bulleid Pacific Preservation Society in 1965, of an eventual return to steam, on special workings, which began in 1971, just a year after his death.

*

The first steam locomotive to run back on the main line was 6000 *King George V*, one of the Collett locomotives that Stanier had worked on and the design legacy of which stretched back through Churchward and Gooch to the Stephensons and *Rocket*. Bulleid would have been delighted to see his Pacifics back in action, although he would never have expected that no fewer than thirty-one of them would survive into the twenty-first century (eleven Merchant Navys and twenty West Countrys and Battle of Britains). And much as it was a personal thrill for me to steam out from the newly rebuilt St Pancras station in May 2011 on a special to Canterbury and the Kent coast behind 34067 *Tangmere*, an un-rebuilt Battle of Britain (and with only a slight slip as we left), Bulleid himself might have wanted this train to have been headed by a very different type of steam locomotive.

Development of main-line British steam, however, had effectively come to an end with Bulleid's retirement in 1949. Even then, most new locomotives were reiterations of a technology that dated back to Churchward and into the nineteenth century. Dedicated British Railways engineers, shed masters, maintenance staff, and crews performed quiet miracles with the stock of essentially 1920s and 1930s locomotives that they ran so very well, for the most part, into the 1960s. With their German-style smoke deflectors, double Kylchap exhausts and chimneys, and other modifications, Gresley's A3s were kept up to, and even well above, the mark, happily keeping pace with diesel schedules until they disappeared from King's Cross forty-one years after Cecil J. Allen first set eyes there on *Great Northern*.

What, though, if British steam had been developed further? If it had been, the first generation of diesels would have seemed to be lacking in power and performance capacity, and perhaps they would have been unnecessary. A new generation of powerful, high-speed steam might have given way only to electric traction. This, though, was not what happened. And anyway, the Second World War intervened, doing much to stop new steam development. Afterwards, fuel shortages, miners' strikes, a lack of skilled labour, and an obsession with modernization further damped the fires.

Other contributory factors were the overriding conservatism of mainstream steam locomotive engineers – something that had its roots in their intensely practical knowledge of running sheds, servicing, and maintenance conditions – and, to an extent, a degree of nationalistic chauvinism. Although Chapelon was taken seriously in terms of his ideas on the internal streamlining of steam flow within the locomotive, his belief in compound drive was seen by many as a little too complicated to be successful, given existing standards of driver training and shed maintenance – too intellectual and, perhaps, a little too French. There was a feeling among most British Railways steam men that home-grown was best. Stewart Cox once said that it was engraved on his heart that 'we wouldn't have compounds here', although perhaps his attitude, and that of many British steam men like him, was influenced by the poor or at best average performance of some of the British compounds of the late nineteenth and early twentieth centuries.

Despite its flashes of undoubted brilliance and occasional adventures into the more exotic realms of engineering, British steam locomotive design had been a cautious affair. *Evening Star*, the last locomotive to be built in Britain for regular main-line service, was very much a descendant of the Stephensons' *Rocket*. But if British engineers erred on the side of pragmatism and tradition, what superb machines they created when they really tried, or when they were given their head: Gresley's A4s, Stanier's Coronations, and Riddles's class 9F 2-10-0s were truly excellent designs. There was, though, something almost bizarre in the fact that such locomotives worked alongside venerable inside-cylinder 0-6-0s and other essentially Victorian locomotives into the late 1960s. Steam locomotive development could have been pushed much further in Britain, but since the machines that were built did the jobs they were asked to do, often very well indeed, ultimately there was little reason to push the boundaries.

The passion for steam itself remains. It is proved by the popularity of special trains which run both on preserved railways and on the main line in Britain today, with Gresley, Stanier, Collett, and Bulleid locomotives very much to the fore – and it has, in fact, never really gone away. Colonel Hugh Rogers, a former signals officer with a distinguished military career, once told a delightful story of 'Robin' Riddles's first ride in the cab of a new class 87 5,000 hp electric up the west coast main line to Crewe in the mid-1970s. Rogers asked him what it was like. 'I didn't really notice,' Riddles replied, 'the driver was an old steam man and we talked about steam engines all the time.'

CHAPTER 2

GERMANY
Strength through Standardization

One logical end of the Deutsche Reichsbahn *Einheitloks* (unified locomotive types) programme of 1923 was the class 52 2-10-0s, first steamed at Borsig works on 12 September 1942 in the presence of Albert Speer, Hitler's minister for armaments and production. The class 52 *Kriegslok* (war locomotive) was designed for mass production in factories in Germany and in territories conquered through *Blitzkrieg*, the 'lightning war' of 1939–41 which brought much of Europe under the Nazi yoke. Between 1942 and 1945, a total of 6,239 class 52s were built, in twenty factories across Europe. This side of the Russian 0-10-0 standard freight locomotives, it was the biggest class of steam locomotives ever built.

The principal purpose of these brutally functional locomotives was to work freight and troop trains through the eastern front. Until the headlong German retreat of 1944, the Deutsche Reichsbahn's track mileage had increased by 16,000 miles during the war. The class 52s were also used for the transportation, at a stipulated 45 kph (28 mph), of three million Jews, and others who fell foul of the Nazi regime, to concentration and extermination camps. Perhaps no other class of locomotive has been built for such savage purposes.

Such was the efficiency of the Borsig works that the first of the class was completed three months ahead of schedule. Speed was, of course, of the essence in wartime, yet the drive and ability to build so quickly was the result not just of the *Einheitslok* programme, whch made locomotive building in Weimar and Nazi Germany a model of efficiency, but also of the creation of the Gemeinschaft Grossdeutscher Lokomotivfabriken (GGL) in 1942, as part of Speer's new ministry founded earlier that year. The Nazi regime had taken absolute control of the Deutsche Reichsbahn, which had been established in 1922 as an independently run state business, able to raise its own finances. Now the GGL was to determine locomotive design and production. Perhaps it is not surprising that, in the wartime imagination, the class 52 had more than something of the look of a Nazi stormtrooper about it.

Detailed design work on the class 52s was led by Friedrich Witte. His predecessor, Richard Paul Wagner, architect of the *Einheitloks* programme, was forced to resign his responsibility for centralized Deutsche Reichsbahn locomotive design and production in the summer of 1942, as the Nazis tightened their grip on the railways. Hitler and Speer believed that the Deutsche Reichsbahn had been slack in its response to war demands, the Führer calling for steam locomotive production to be upped to 7,500 per year. This was an impossible figure, although production did increase from 660 in 1939 to a peak of 4,533 in 1943. Wagner, who had the responsibility of building up the Deutsche Reichsbahn fleet after some five thousand German locomotives had been packed off to the country's former enemies as part of the war reparations demanded by the Treaty of Versailles, had been happy with an annual production of 800 new steam locomotives. Even so, that was only possible because of the standardization of design and construction. Significantly, perhaps, Germany built more steam locomotives in total – approximately 155,000 – than any other country except the USA, which produced around 177,000. Britain, a small country with a big empire, built 110,150, Russia around 50,000, and France 39,000. No other country came anywhere near these figures. According to Philip Atkins, former librarian at the National

Railway Museum, York, 205 were built in South America, thirty-one in Africa, and, rather charmingly, just one in Portugal.

E. S. Cox, who visited Germany in the 1930s to inspect Wagner's latest locomotives, said that he 'seemed a very perfunctory adherent of the Nazi party . . . and unlike some of his henchmen, his "Heil Hitler" greeting to colleagues and subordinates, then obligatory, lacked a good deal in precision and zest'. Cecil J. Allen accompanied other members of the Institution of Locomotive Engineers on their trip to Germany in 1936 – during which Stanier rode on the footplate of a streamlined 05 class 4-6-4 at 118 mph – and had the same recollection of the cigar-smoking Wagner, whom Cox also described as a big, friendly, bear of a man. The British party, said Allen, were quite unsure how to behave when railway officials and party functionaries greeted them with Heil Hitler salutes and tiresome renditions of '*Deutschland über Alles*' and the '*Horst-Wessel-Lied*'; the embarrassed British engineers returned the salutes in 'willy-nilly' fashion. Their feeling, shared by Wagner and many of his team, was that the railways were an apolitical service and that politics was at best an unavoidable nuisance. Neither the British nor Wagner could have imagined the ends to which the Deutsche Reichsbahn and its locomotives would be put in the following decade. As it was, Wagner would be invited by the Allied authorities in 1946 to help with the reconstruction of the railways, while Witte, despite his close association with Speer and the regime, would become responsible for the development of post-war steam locomotives.

It seems a shame, however, to begin a chapter on late German steam design with Hitler, Speer, the Nazis, the Second World War, and the Holocaust – and not least because Hitler himself had no real interest in railways. He was to become excited about them, but only after the German invasion of the Soviet Union in June 1941, when the movement of men and materiel began to stretch across Poland and the vast plains to the east. And yet, Hitler and Speer, despite their criticisms, were well served by a locomotive industry which had gone from strength to strength since the founding of the Deutsche

Reichsbahn in 1922 and the appointment of Wagner the following year as the instigator of German locomotive design policy.

The idea behind Wagner's 1923 programme was technocratic and politically innocent. Perhaps politicians and soldiers had already seen potential advantages for future struggles in the design of highly standardized machines; and, indeed, there was a military-like precision in the way that Wagner pushed ahead with a policy that had no counterpart in any other country. A part of this was down to that old cliché, German efficiency. Born in Berlin in August 1882, Wagner was educated at the Charlottenhof Technical High School, before joining the Prussian State Railways. There he would have witnessed the development of the legendary P8 class two-cylinder 4-6-0, a notable general purpose passenger locomotive of which 3,948 were built between 1908 and 1924. Its original design was by Robert Garbe, and some P8s were still in service as late as 1974.

But his experience as a transport officer during the First World War had showed Wagner the limitations of many indigenous designs. At the time, various German states and the Kingdom of Bavaria had built an array of locomotives as varied as that found in Britain. So, when the Deutsche Reichsbahn was created and he was made national head of design (Bavaria became a part of Germany in 1918), Wagner was intent on shaping a unified fleet of passenger and freight locomotives with standardized components, which could be serviced and repaired locally. Interchangeable parts – boilers, cylinders, driving wheels – would mean optimum manufacturing efficiency. He was not a revolutionary – far from it. Wagner built steadily on the work of his predecessors, whose standard Prussian State Railways designs were built in huge numbers. The basis of those designs was two-cylinder simple-expansion drive, relatively low boiler pressure, and outside Walschaerts valve gear, combined with relatively high superheating. They included the G8 class 0-8-0, of which 5,155 were built between 1913 and 1921, and the G10 class 0-10-0, of which 2,677 were produced between 1910 and 1925 – two freight locomotives that were worth far more than their weights in coal.

Wagner's ideal, then, was for simple, two-cylinder locomotives that, while neither notably powerful nor particularly fast, would provide an overall high standard of performance, economy, and reliability throughout Germany. Prussian efficiency remained the key, not publicity or record-breaking. In any case, unlike in Britain where speed limits were set by the civil engineers of each railway according to the specification or state of the tracks, in Germany, as in France, strictly imposed maximum speeds were set by both the government and the railway authorities for each class of locomotive, up to a general limit of 120 kph (74.5 mph). So, while in Britain trains could sometimes be found whistling downhill at 90 mph a quarter of a century before the First World War – and often climbing hills painfully slowly – in Germany, the fastest trains were timed so that the locomotives ran at moderate, but as far as possible uniform, speeds uphill and down.

In Prussia in particular, there was no call for very high power outputs because the railways ran mainly across the great plain that stretches across northern Europe from the Urals to the English Channel. Here there were no Shaps or Beattocks. The idea of a kind of steady-state locomotive emerged, although Wagner was forced to accept that something more powerful was needed further south in Germany, especially in Bavaria where the landscape erupts into magnificent hills, mountains, and valleys.

Thus Wagner continued the production of proven, non-standard, Bavarian locomotives, including the four-cylinder S3/6 compound Pacific, designed at Maffei by a team led by Anton Hammel. The first of these engines, with their distinctive conical smoke-box doors, suggesting great speed even though they were in fact limited to 120 kph, emerged from Maffei's Munich works in 1908, the same year as Churchward's *The Great Bear*. These strong (1,800 dbhp on test) and efficient compounds were made by Maffei until 1931. Some were rebuilt in 1953 with combustion chambers giving more power and were able to match the performance of Wagner's larger-boilered, two-cylinder 01 class Pacific of 1925. Although keen on uniformity, Wagner could see the merit of purpose-built machines designed for specific lines.

As Garbe and Lubkens's P8 had been the basis for a number of Prussian standard designs, so Wagner's 01 was the building block for many of the larger passenger and freight locomotives made throughout Germany between the two world wars. Although heavier than a contemporary Gresley Pacific, the German 01s were generally worked at lower power outputs than the LNER engines and were never asked to run as fast. Built between 1925 and 1938, these rugged, functional locomotives were designed for optimum efficiency at moderate rates of working. With a large boiler pressed to 235 psi, a high degree of superheating, long-lap, long-travel valves, and two big 650 × 660 mm (25⅝ × 26 in) cylinders, the 107 ton 01s were able to deliver a tractive effort of 43,000 lb, coping well with moderately timed 600 ton express trains, and lighter, faster ones, yet restricted to a maximum of 120 kph – raised to 130 kph (81 mph) in 1934. They were rated at 2,210 ihp; this was an official figure, intended as a guide to the operating management as to what these locomotives were capable of on a regular basis. Again, Wagner was more concerned with consistency of performance than with high power output. With running boards set clear of the 2 m (6 ft 6 in) driving wheels, all-enclosed cabs, and clear lines, the 01s aged very slowly in terms of both looks and performance. Immaculately clean 01s could still be seen at work at the head of express trains in East Germany until 1982.

Not that the 01s dominated express passenger services in the 1920s, as Gresley's A1s had. Wagner had to wait until the main lines were rebuilt in the early 1930s, to withstand greater axle-loading weights, before the 01 with its 20 ton axle load became a universal type. Concurrently with the first 01s, Wagner experimented with a four-cylinder compound variant, classified as 02, before 01 production got into its stride. In fact, he built ten two-cylinder and ten four-cylinder compounds in 1925–6, pitting the two variants against one another. However, detailed design of the compound 02s was out of his hands, and their valve gear and design of the steam-flow circuit were poor, resulting in severe throttling of steam at speeds higher than 75 kph, while the 01 was more economical. The compound 02s were converted to 01s in 1941–2.

On the basis of this comparison, Wagner seemed to have proven that a well-designed, two-cylinder Pacific could do the job of a more complex and more expensive compound. (This 'evidence' had a marked effect on British engineers like Cox and Bond when they were considering standard British post-war designs.) And yet, back in the 1920s, Deutsche Reichsbahn chief mechanical engineer Friedrich Fuchs and chief testing engineer Professor Hans Nordmann continued to investigate the potential of compound drive, no doubt inspired both by the performance of the French Nord railway Super Pacifics, which were appreciably smaller than the 01s but exerted power outputs in daily service well above the rated power of the 01, and, from 1929, by the remarkable work of the Chapelon rebuilds.

In 1932, four separate experimental high-pressure compound types were introduced, while in 1935, at Fuchs's instigation, Adolf Wolff at Borsig prepared project drawings for a four-cylinder compound 4-8-0 derived directly from Chapelon's design, but substantive work on this was prevented by the Second World War. Eventually, 231 standard 01s were built. Between 1950 and 1957, and again from 1957 to 1961, two batches of 01s were rebuilt with combustion-chamber boilers under Witte's direction for the Deutsche Bundesbahn, the West German state railway, and rated up to 2,417 ihp. It was a delight to see these and other 01s hard at work, and in spotless condition, on expresses in the early 1970s. From 1962 to 1965, the Deutsche Reichsbahn, the East German state railway, rebuilt thirty-five 01s at Meiningen works in a more radical fashion. With new, larger fire-boxes and higher-set, combustion-chamber boilers, a continuous, Soviet-style dome cover running the length of the boiler, clipped Witte smoke deflectors, new cabs, and more powerful brakes, these 01.5s were superb and highly distinctive machines. Rated at 2,500 ihp, these red and black Pacifics – half of them oil-fired – were kept busy on the Berlin to Dresden route until 1977, and the class survived for a further five years on express duties before finally being replaced by Soviet diesels.

The 03 class, a lighter version of the 01, appeared in 1930, with 570 × 660 mm (22½ × 26 in) cylinders and rated at 1,943 ihp. With an axle loading of 18 tons, compared to 20 tons for the 01s, these light Pacifics were able to operate many of the secondary main lines from which the earlier Wagner Pacifics had been banned. A total of 298 engines was built, up until 1938, by Borsig, Krupp, Henschel, and Schwartzkopff. Unlike in Britain, where locomotives were built mostly by railways in their own works, German engines of the 1920s and 1930s were the product of commercial manufacturers working in collaboration with Wagner's design team. In fact, it was the British way of building steam locomotives that was unusual – a product, perhaps, of the craft-based engineering culture that emerged with the Industrial Revolution, which took hold in Britain quite some while before it shook up Germany.

The sheer power demanded by heavy freight duties saw Wagner turn to three cylinders for his first 2-10-0s, the class 44 of 1926. Only ten of these giants, known as 'Jumbos' to German crews, were built that year. Production resumed in 1937, with more robust frames, when the demand for very powerful freight locomotives was clear, and continued through the Second World War until 1949, by which time there were 1,989 class 44s at work in East and West Germany. The last scheduled steam service on the Deutsche Bundesbahn, on 26 October 1977, was worked by 043 903-4, one of thirty-five two-cylinder derivatives of the class 44s that were built in 1927–8. Mass production of 2-10-0s, as characteristic of German steam in the mid-twentieth century as Wagner's Pacifics, really began with the two-cylinder class 50s in 1939. These machines, adopted by the Nazi government as *Kriegslok* war locomotives, were built throughout the war, with production continuing in West Germany until 1948, by which time 3,164 class 50s had been built. Many, however, had been destroyed by allied bombing.

So successful were the class 50s that a new batch with all-welded boilers, designated 50.40, was built at the Lokomotivbau Karl Marx in Babelsberg for the East German Deutsche Reichsbahn between 1956 and 1960. These were the last brand-new German steam locomotives. They were withdrawn in 1980, seven years before a number of the original 50s that remained in service in East Germany.

Locomotive developments in Germany had been steady and rational, yet in the 1930s the quest for speed was to make Wagner think anew. From designing 120 kph locomotives, the Deutsche Reichsbahn was now set on creating the world's fastest trains. This development had begun in the late days of the Weimar Republic, with the launch of high-speed diesel services, beginning with the *Fliegender Hamburger* in 1932. The need for heavier trains able to run at speeds of 150 kph (93 mph), and even above, led to a new generation of streamlined steam locomotives which, superficially at least, were everything that Wagner seemed to have stood against.

The genius of the high-speed German steam locomotives of the 1930s was that, despite a few experiments along the way (see Chapter 6), they were basically simple, if meticulously built, machines beneath their wind-cheating skirts. The first of the high-speed German locomotives was 05 001, built at the Borsig works in 1935. Nothing quite like this stunning three-cylinder machine had been seen on rails before. Painted a deep red, all moving parts were hidden, with side-skirts falling to barely inches above the track. Only the whistle and chimney rising from the sloping front of the engine, set above a large, faired-in headlamp, made it in any way evident that this was a steam locomotive. The ten-wheeled tender was all of a piece with the engine. In fact, 05 001 looked more like a submarine than a machine that ran on rails.

Beneath the voluptuous cladding was a beautifully proportioned and exquisitely crafted 4-6-4, all but guaranteed to be a record-breaker.

The design was by Adolf Wolff, chief locomotive design engineer at Borsig. Born in Goslar, in Lower Saxony, Wolff was educated at the Technical University of Hanover and worked for Hanomag, where he designed some impressive and long-lasting compound 4-8-2s for the Norte railway in Spain. Some 40 per cent of Hanomag's locomotive production – it was well known for its cars and tractors too – was exported. Precociously talented but modest, 'kleine Wolff', as he was known, moved to Borsig in 1929. After the Second World War he was employed by Krauss Maffei as technical director, where, among other projects, he rebuilt the 05s into non-streamlined 4-6-4s. This, though, is jumping the gun.

There was nothing complex in the specification of 05 001 or its one sibling, 05 002. Everything, however, was done (this side of fitting a combustion-chamber boiler, which was rejected by Wagner) to give these engines the best possible steam-flow circuit, with piston valves 30 per cent greater in diameter than those of Gresley's A4s. The large boiler was pressed to the then high figure of 294 psi, heated by a fire-box with a 50.6 sq ft grate. Superheated steam flowed, at speeds of up to 200 mph, to three 450 × 660 mm (17¾ × 26 in) cylinders, driving 2.3 m (7 ft 6½ in) coupled wheels. The design speed was 175 kph (109 mph) and nominal power rating was 2,360 ihp, although a maximum of 3,400 ihp was attained on test.

Wolff's masterpiece made its debut in March 1935, six months ahead of Gresley's A4 for the LNER and six weeks before the Chicago, Milwaukee, St. Paul and Pacific Railroad's streamlined Atlantic, specified by Charles H. Bilty, broke through a ribbon at the Alco works in Schenectady, New York. Wolff's 05 001, with its advanced technology and aerodynamic cladding, was proof – if proof were needed – that the speed bug had infected railways around the world.

Streamlining could certainly help locomotives to run faster, as a smooth casing reduced wind resistance, but it was often as much a styling fashion, introduced to make steam engines look as futuristic as the latest monocoque aircraft, speedboats, and racing cars. Indeed, a year before 05 001 steamed for the first time in Berlin, the South Manchuria Railway had introduced its streamlined and air-conditioned Asia Express between the port of Darien and Hsinking, the capital of the Japanese puppet state of Manchukuo, carved in 1932 out of Manchuria and Inner Mongolia – where the last great Chinese steam locomotives, the QJ class 2-10-2s, were to rule the great passes of the newly built Jitong Railway until 2005. To haul the train, the South Manchuria Railway commissioned twelve streamlined two-cylinder Pacifics, following American design practice, from Kawasaki and the railway's own Shahekou works. Complete with observation cars and cocktail car, the Asia Express, a symbol of presumed Japanese technological superiority, had beaten the Americans and Europeans at a game that should have been theirs. The Pashina class locomotives, however, were not as fast nor as powerful as they looked. Their highest recorded speed was 83 mph. Nevertheless, this was a revolution in China. The locomotives survived war and revolution and were still at work in the 1980s. At least one has been preserved.

By the time of the Second World War, streamlined locomotives could be found on the least promising lines. In 1941, a new railway connection between Iraq and Syria meant that the Taurus Express could run direct from Istanbul to Baghdad. This was the route – much of it built to the highest specification by German engineers of the Second Reich – that was supposed to have linked Berlin with Baghdad. To celebrate the new through service, in 1941 Iraqi State Railways took possession of four streamlined two-cylinder oil-burning Pacifics, designed by the railway's own William Ikeson and built by Robert Stephenson and Hawthorn's. One was lost in a convoy on the way, but three made it to Iraq, where they ran until 1960. From a distance, they might have looked a bit like a Stanier Coronation crossed with a Gresley A4 – but did they ever get above 60 mph?

Wolff's 05s, however, were in a different camp altogether. Their streamlining was scientifically researched. Wolff claimed, not without justification, that the streamlined casing of engine and train lessened air resistance to achieve a 20 per cent reduction in the power needed to work a 250 ton train on the level at 150 kph (93 mph). The 05s proved to be very fast engines indeed. German and other enthusiasts describe them as the fastest steam locomotives in the world, despite *Mallard's* 126 mph. The claim is an interesting one, and, in certain ways, justified. On 7 June 1935, 05 002 sprinted up to 191.7 kph (119.1 mph) on the line between Berlin and Hamburg. It went on to make six further runs with speeds above 177 kph (110 mph). On 11 May 1936, pulling a 197 ton train, it soared to just over 200 kph – 200.4 kph to be exact (124.5 mph) – not downhill but on level track, near Friesack. The speed was maintained for long enough to be measured precisely; it required an output of 3,400 ihp. *Mallard* travelled at 125 mph for just 305 yards; if it really did get above that speed, the last 1 mph must have been over a very few yards indeed. Gresley himself never claimed 126 mph, and, in railway enthusiast circles, the debate continues today. It is also possible that 05 002's 124.5 mph was an average speed over between 1 and 2.5 kilometres, in which case it might have beaten *Mallard's* 126 mph anyway. In charge of testing on the Deutsche Reichsbahn, Professor Nordmann erred on the side of scientific caution.

A letter in *Railway World* in April 1969 from John F. Clay, a member of the Stephenson Society, argued the case for *Mallard*: 'The difference between the maximum speeds for *Mallard* and 05.002 is so small as to be in the range of uncertainty present even with the most sophisticated of dynamometer car equipment.' Clay went on to help gauge the particular merit of *Mallard's* record run:

> An A4 was built to a much more restricted loading gauge than the larger and more specialised 05. It would be impossible in this country [Great Britain] to build an engine with 7 ft 6 in driving wheels and an adequate boiler. *Mallard's* load of 240 tons, light at it seems, was heavier in proportion to the size of the engine than the 200 tons behind the 05. Although Stoke Bank

is downhill the initial acceleration from 24 mph at
Grantham to 74 mph at Stoke Box up 1-in-200 would, in
itself, have winded a lesser engine even before the high-
speed attempt could begin. The smaller wheels of the
A4 had to reach a higher rotational speed to equal the
road speeds of the German engine. Although we must be
sensible about *Mallard*, we still have every justification
for a little national pride.

Quite what it was like to ride on the footplate of the German 4-6-4 at
2 miles per minute was vividly described by Paul Roth of the Deutsche
Reichsbahn's locomotive testing department at Grunewald. In an
article published a year after his death in *Lok* (*Locomotive*) magazine,
Roth explained that Wagner had been hoping to break the 200 kph
barrier with the 05s. Despite 05 002's free running and reserves of
power, whenever the engine was worked up to a tantalizing 195 kph
problems arose, now with broken springs, now with loose tyres due to
the high lateral forces between tyre and wheel rim at very high speed.

On 11 May, 05 002, pulling one coach less than on previous runs, had
been delayed by signals and speed restrictions. Leaving Wittenberge
for Berlin, every attempt was made to regain time, meaning that long
stretches would have to be run at 180 kph (112 mph). Roth recalled:

As a result of the reduction in weight by fifty tons,
the lack of a side wind and with wet rails, the train
resistance was significantly reduced and the 05 reached
195 kph much faster than usual. At this speed a howling
at the chimney started up. It sounded like a ship's
hooter and indicated a very high boiler performance. An
additional circumstance egged our crew on. In Hamburg,
they had learned from our passengers that one of the
diesel-electric railcars had reached the 200 kph barrier
between Stendal and Hanover. Till then, no diesel had

run as fast as the 05, so our crew was rather displeased.

The 05 was now racing faster and faster; no one was thinking about broken springs and tyres. The pressure gauge read 20 atmospheres [294 psi]. There was sufficient water in the boiler. The driver, Oscar Langhans, asked if he could link up a few cogs. After a short while, the speedometer needle touched its stop [200 kph]. Everything went much faster than usual. In the train, meanwhile, people had also recognized that something special was going on. When the speed of 200 kph was reached, the dynamometer car gave a long honk, a signal to the crew up front. Since speedometer readings are never fully accurate, the crew maintained the speed for a while. Not at any price did we want to stand there at 199.5 kph.

Being in the cab of a 200 ton steam engine [the weight with tender] racing at 200 kph is not comfortable . . . the crew's nerves were on edge. Even so, or perhaps because of this reason, our fireman, Ernst Hohne, performed an Indian dance with his broom in the cab.

The driver would have been mostly concerned with the view of the road ahead. German main-line signals at the time were spaced at three-quarter-mile intervals, but even with an emergency brake application, 05 002 needed 0.85 miles to stop from 180 kph (112 mph). But the test runs with the streamlined 4-6-4 were useful, not least because they prompted significant improvements in locomotive, and train, brakes. *Mallard*'s own record run down Stoke Bank on 3 July 1938 was described by the LNER as the result of a high-speed brake test using quick-service application valves, combined with an attempt on the world record.

That 05 002's world-record run was an exercise in propaganda is made clear by the fact that senior members of the government, including Heinrich Himmler, head of the SS, and his deputy, Reinhard Heydrich, were on board, along with Wolff, Wagner, and the Deutsche Reichsbahn's head of testing, Professor Hans Nordmann. A trip two days earlier – one of four very high-speed return journeys made between Berlin and Hamburg with 05 002 that week – was laid on specially for senior German military officers. However hard the Deutsche Reichsbahn tried before the war to maintain a strictly technocratic stance in its dealings with the Nazi state, it was impossible to remain anything like detached.

None of the high-speed runs affected 05 002's performance. On 30 May, the record-breaker took the British party from the Institution of Locomotive Engineers, including Stanier and Cecil J. Allen, on a run from Berlin to Hamburg and back with a three-coach, 150 ton train. Allen reported that 250 miles of the journey had been reeled off at a mean speed of 91 mph, with much ground covered at three-figure speeds, including a maximum of 118 mph. On the return journey, 05 002 sprinted away from Wittenberge with the alacrity of a modern electric – the train was very light – covering the 70.1 miles to a signal stop fourteen miles west of Berlin in 48 minutes and 32 seconds, at an average of 86.7 mph. There was no doubt, Allen wrote, that 'the engine could travel for indefinite distances at 100 mph and could obtain considerably higher speeds when necessary'. It certainly could. Given the sheer number of times 05 002 reached 110 mph and more on level track and went on to average 124.5 mph over some distance, it might well be right to call Wolff's locomotive the fastest steam engine in the world.

What was equally impressive is that on regular services between Hamburg and Berlin, with up to six coaches, the 05s could very nearly equal the timing of the lightweight, two-car *Fliegender Hamburger*. A third 05 was commissioned from Borsig, but this was an experimental cab-forward locomotive designed to burn pulverized coal (see Chapter 6). To increase the maximum speed of express trains generally from 120 to 140 kph (74.5 to 87 mph), and even 150 kph (93 mph),

Wagner had fifty-five streamlined, three-cylinder 01s built from 1939. Classified 01.10, these looked like smaller versions of the 05s; while sixty 03.10s – streamlined, three-cylinder light Pacifics – followed closely on their heels. Three cylinders promised smoother running at speed and lower track 'hammer blow', while the streamlining saved power, and hence fuel, at speed. More of both classes were to have been built, but by then Germany had plunged Europe into the most destructive war the world has ever known.

When Germany emerged from the war, those 01.10s and 03.10s that had survived were stripped of their streamlined casing and, looking much like their unadorned, two-cylinder siblings, and working on identical passenger duties, could still be seen hard at work until the mid-1970s. As for the 05s, they were de-streamlined in 1950 at the Krauss Maffei works by Adolf Wolff himself. With boiler pressure reduced to 235 psi, these handsome 4-6-4s lost some of their edge and were, in any case, limited to a modest 140 kph. They did, however, work the longest regular express services on the new Deutsche Bundesbahn, the 703 kilometre route from Hamburg via Cologne and Frankfurt. But as they were not standard locomotives – the blessing or curse of Richard Wagner – the 05s were withdrawn in 1958, despite having a good many years left in them. Very sadly, 05 002 was scrapped, although her sister, 05 001, was fully restored to her original condition in 1963 – Adolf Wolff witnessed the work – and is now on display in the Nuremberg transport museum. In 2011, *Mallard* was shipped from her home at the Railway Museum in York to meet 05 001 at Nuremberg as part of a seventy-fifth anniversary celebration of 05 002's world-record run.

There had been one other successful attempt at a steam rival to the latest high-speed German diesels. This was the remarkable Henschel-Wegmann Train, produced by the Henschel works in Kassel and the local coachbuilders, Wegmann, a firm that also made tanks for the military in both world wars (and once again when production of the Leopard 1 began in 1965). The idea of a two-car, push-pull, high-speed, streamlined steam express train, which was, in essence, a steam multiple-unit, had been proposed to Wagner and the Deutsche Reichsbahn by Henschel's manager, Karl Imfeld, in April 1933. The following February, Dr Friedrich Fuchs, the Deutsche Reichsbahn's chief mechanical engineer, went to visit Imfeld. The answer was yes, but Fuchs insisted on a four-coach train.

The result, unveiled in May 1935, was a streamlined, if slightly bulbous, 4-6-4 tank engine blurred into the four coaches, including an observation car, fitted with roller bearings and disc brakes, trailing behind it. First shown to the public during the centenary celebrations held for the German railways between July and October 1935 – Hitler was one of the many visitors – the train began service on a very tight 65 mph schedule over the 176 kilometres between Berlin and Dresden the following summer. The 1 hour and 40 minute timing cut 28 minutes from the fastest existing schedule; in 2012, the fastest train between the two cities took 2 hours and 4 minutes.

Even more impressive was the fact that the train made two return journeys each day. The solitary two-cylinder class 61 4-6-4T was well up to the job. Beneath its voluminous dress, it was a well-proportioned, free-steaming locomotive, with a boiler pressure of 294 psi, which ran at 160 kph (99.5 mph) in everyday service and up to 175 kph (109 mph) when required; on test, 61 001 reached 185 kph, or approximately 115 mph, a world record for a tank engine. This was no Thomas. When the locomotive returned to Henschel for a major overhaul, it was replaced by 01 and 03 Pacifics. Although the streamlined Dresden service ceased to run in August 1939 as Germany prepared for war, 61 001 was returned to traffic in 1948, based at Bebra, close to Kassel. Badly damaged in an accident at Munster in November 1951, she was taken out of service and scrapped six years later.

A second and sleeker class 61 joined 61 001 in 1939. With three-cylinders and a bigger water tank and coal bunker, 61 002 only just made it into passenger service in the summer of 1939. Fate, however, was kinder to 61 002. In 1961, she was converted at Meiningen works by the Deutsches Reichsbahn into a semi-streamlined, three-cylinder tender locomotive, with larger cylinders and a combustion-chamber boiler, while retaining her 2.3 m (7 ft 6½ in) driving wheels (the largest fitted to a Pacific), designed to test new coaching stock at high speeds. Fitted with a highly efficient Giesl ejector exhaust, 18 201, as she was now numbered, was rated at 2,120 ihp, with a maximum speed of 180 kph. On test in 1972, this elegant green engine steamed up to 182.4 kph, or about 113 mph, making her the fastest post-war steam locomotive on record, beating the record set by A4 60007 *Sir Nigel Gresley* in 1959 by just 1 mph. Since 1980, 18 201 has worked special trains and in 2012, owned by Dampf-Plus, she is still very much in action and, on occasion, runs at very high speed.

High-speed trains were glamorous, much feted, and greatly admired. But, as trains grew heavier throughout the 1930s, what operating departments required most of all was power: reliable, consistent, readily available power. So, the Deutsche Reichsbahn's final streamliners were a pair of mighty three-cylinder 4-8-4s, the 06 class, crafted by Krupp in 1939. No other 4-8-4s were built in Germany. The locomotives were 26.5 m (87 feet) long and weighed 142 tons (a Stanier LMS Coronation was 70 feet long and weighed 105 tons). Rated at 2,761 ihp, they were designed to pull 650 ton trains on the level at 120 kph (74.5 mph), with a maximum of 140 kph (87 mph). Hugely impressive to look at, the 06s, with their long wheelbase, tended to derail on sharp curves. The boilers, meanwhile, developed cracks. Doubtless, Krupp and Wagner would have improved the engines if more had been built, but by summer 1939 sheer power was needed, mostly to pull freight trains. The fleet of Pacifics that Wagner and the German manufacturers had built up since 1925 was perfectly adequate to the tasks asked of them by railway management. The 06s survived the war, but were scrapped by the Deutsche Bundesbahn in 1951.

The 06s used the same boiler as the class 45 2-10-2s which, by rights, should have been the mainstay of Deutsche Reichsbahn heavy freight operations from their inception in 1936 and for the next forty years. And yet, just twenty-eight of these impressive-looking, three-cylinder machines were built, an order for 103 being cancelled in 1941. Faster than previous Deutsche Reichsbahn freight locomotives – 90 kph (56 mph) as opposed to 80 kph (50 mph) – and far more powerful, the 45s promised a great deal, but, like the 06s, they suffered from boiler problems, and there was no time, or will, after the invasion of Poland in September 1939 to develop them further. When equipped with new combustion-chamber boilers and mechanical stokers from 1950, the 45s finally showed what they could do. Only five were rebuilt, however, and in 1968 the last three members of the class were made redundant.

As German troops swept across Poland and Hitler began to prepare for Operation Barbarossa, the invasion of the Soviet Union, the Deutsche Reichsbahn was extended ever further east, while more troop trains, trains ferrying tanks and artillery pieces, trains fetching fuel, and trains supplying factories across the newly conquered territories pushed what was a well-run railway to unprecedented limits. With new lines laid quickly, the cry from operators in the east was for simple, strong engines with light axle loads. Fitness for purpose and simplicity truly were the keys to good wartime design. Even Wagner's powerful and dependable class 44 2-10-0s were too heavy in axle loading and too complex for the rigours of wartime assignments.

Wagner responded with the class 50 2-10-0s, first built in 1939, rugged, two-cylinder machines with an axle loading of just 15.2 tons (anything under 18 tons is light). Weighing 87 tons and allowed to run at 80 kph (50 mph) in both directions, the class 50s were as popular as they were reliable. They were designated *Kriegsloks* and were among some seven thousand steam locomotives produced in Germany during just two and a half years of brutal conflict. Even so, the first class 50s were considered too complex for the kind of mass production that men like Wagner could never have envisaged in the 1920s. The revised class 50UK (*Übergangskriegslokomotive*, or transitional war locomotive), with fabricated welded construction replacing steel castings, was the result – yet even this was seen as too complex for the rapid production the government and military demanded. Cue the class 52, an austerity version of the class 50 and the archetypal *Kriegslok*, a steam locomotive prepared for all-out war as never before.

The class 50, however, continued to be built, with gaps, not just throughout the Second World War, but for a long time afterwards. The final members of the class were built, with modifications to the original design, by the East German Deutsche Reichsbahn at the Lokomotivbau Karl Marx in Babelsberg in 1960, by which time 3,164 had been produced. Class 50s continued in front-line service on the Deutsche Bundesbahn until the end of steam in 1977, and on the Deutsche Reichsbahn until 1987, two years before the fall of the Berlin Wall.

These engines were great travellers. Either seized by allied railway engineers or made over as war reparations, the class 50s could be found at work between the 1950s and 1970s in, among other countries, Austria, Poland, Denmark, France, Turkey, the USSR, and Norway, as well as throughout the Balkans. They may have been used for evil ends in the early and mid-1940s, but the steam locomotive is in itself an innocent machine, and the class 50 was much needed and much liked wherever it went.

The class 52 began service just as German expansion eastwards was grinding to a halt. In this sense, they were too late; yet few can doubt that, whatever the job they were asked to do, the locomotives themselves performed reliably and well. Brutes to look at, the class 52s were among the quickest of all steam locomotives to build. Records of exactly how many man-hours were needed to build a complete 52 are uncertain, but the production figures speak for themselves. Between September 1942 and May 1945, more than 6,300 had been put into service. More were built between 1945 and 1950, bringing the total up to what seems to have been 6,719. From 1960, the Deutsche Reichsbahn rebuilt 200 with new boilers, and a total of 290 with Giesl ejector draughting to enable low-grade coal to be burned efficiently.

After the war, the class 52s were dispersed throughout various parts of Europe, although it was somehow strange to see some of the very last of them working for the Polish railways. It was the invasion of Poland that had signalled the start of the Second World War and it was in Poland that the worst of the Nazi extermination camps were sited – and it was the 52s that had brought so many to their deaths there. But as an example of how a machine that was essentially the product of a long craft tradition could be transformed into a unit of mass production, the 52 remains a fascinating locomotive.

A heavier *Kriegslok*, the two-cylinder class 42, was built in much smaller numbers – 837 in 1943 and 1944, with further examples produced between 1945 and 1949 – to be used where limitations on axle loads were less demanding than on the eastern front. There was, however, a design for a much larger *Kriegslok* altogether. This was Adolf Wolff's 1943 proposal for a 2-6-8-0 compound Mallet, a form of articulated locomotive with two engine units beneath the boiler, devised by the Swiss engineer Anatole Mallet. At 27.4 m (90 feet) long and weighing 140 tons, this impressive locomotive would have been a formidable performer, but by the time Wolff was drawing up outline designs the Borsig works had been severely damaged by allied air raids, and as 1944 dawned it was clear to most steam men – if not to Adolf Hitler – that the war was lost and that, as Germany fought an increasingly desperate rearguard action on two fronts, the production of weapons and ammunition would have to take over from that of locomotives.

*

Production of steam locomotives recommenced in 1950, by which time Germany was divided. In both halves of the country, however, it was essential to get the railways running as efficiently as possible once again. The need for new steam production seemed clear enough at the time. Steam locomotives were cheap, the know-how was there, and coal was plentiful. In those first few years, though, examples of Wagner's and Wolff's superb streamliners could be seen wheezing

along in filthy condition with great chunks of their cladding missing –
it could have been Britain in the 1960s. And yet, such had been the rate
of production of wartime 2-10-0s, there was a surplus of heavy freight
locomotives in 1945. Then it was found that there were sufficient
Wagner Pacifics to maintain a decent main-line passenger service. So,
initially under Friedrich Witte, new steam locomotives returned in the
guise of mixed-traffic tender and tank engines, efficient, reliable, and
modern, but far from fast or powerful.

The only new type of locomotives built in any number in West
Germany before the decision to abandon steam production were the
class 23 2-6-2s, of which 105 were built between 1950 and 1959.
Completed by Arnold Jung Locomotivfabrik of Kirchen in December
1959, 23 105 was the last steam locomotive built for the Deutsche
Bundesbahn. Much of the engine – boiler, frames, tender – was
welded, while the locomotive was mechanically lubricated and very
easy to maintain. It was neither very fast – its top speed was limited to
110 kph (68 mph) – nor especially powerful. The class 23 was, though,
a quiet culmination of the work that Wagner had started in 1923 with
his standardization programme. Things might have stood there, had
not a glamorous new express passenger locomotive emerged in 1957
from Krupp, as if it were the 1930s all over again – but without the
Nazis.

Known as the *Schwarze Schwäne*, the Black Swans, 10 001 and 10
002 were fated to be the only two members of a class – the oil-fired
class 10 – intended to replace the veteran, if still decidedly game, 01
and 01.10 Wagner Pacifics. These striking, semi-streamlined, three-
cylinder machines, with 265 psi boiler pressure and double blast-pipe
and chimney, were an intriguing mix of the latest German, French,
and American practices, complete with haunting chime whistle.
They were well engineered and easy to maintain, and they went on
to perform very reliably indeed, clocking up 150,000 miles between
major servicing (even the latest British Pacifics struggled to get to
100,000 miles). But the Black Swans had arrived too late in the day.

They had short working lives – ten and eleven years – although 10 001 can be seen at the German steam locomotive museum in Neuenmarkt-Wirsberg, in Bavaria, housed in a retired engine shed. It seems a shame that one cannot see this exquisite machine in steam.

In East Germany, steam locomotive construction on the Deutsche Reichsbahn began in 1954, later than on the Deutsche Bundesbahn. Here, great efforts were made to improve existing types rather than to build new ones. Max Baumberg was the key figure in the development of several classes of pre-war Deutsche Reichsbahn locomotives, including the 01 Pacifics.

To visit East Berlin in the 1970s and 1980s was an extraordinary experience. Once through Checkpoint Charlie, it was as if the clock had been turned back. Shell-damaged buildings – among them many of the city's great Neo-Classical masterpieces – appeared seemingly unchanged since Marshal Zhukov's Red Army troops hammered their way into Berlin in the spring of 1945. Blackened columns, capitals, and balustrades were still riddled with holes made by machine guns, pock-marked by artillery fire. There was little of the consumer economy that was glistening and winking on the western side of the Wall. And yet, for the transport enthusiast, the eastern half of the city was an Aladdin's Cave: veteran trams, vintage U-Bahn trains, and, best and most unforgettable of all, the truly magnificent sight of Baumberg's distinguished and haughty 01.5 Pacifics drawing in from Dresden.

They were impressive in terms of both performance and looks. With new combustion-chamber boilers, stylish, clipped, Witte-style smoke deflectors, and a skyline dome cover running from chimney to cab, the 01.5s had a gloriously purposeful appearance. They were, essentially, new locomotives, thirty-five of them rebuilt from donor 01s at Meiningen works between 1962 and 1965. They were rated at 2,500 ihp, with a speed limit of either 130 or 150 kph (81 or 94 mph); they were fitted with more powerful brakes than the original 01s, and their new cabs were more comfortable to work in. In 2012, two preserved 01.5s – 01.509 (1963) and 01.533 (1964) – were operational. The east of Berlin has changed greatly since the fall of the Wall in 1989 and German unification two years later, and yet, if you scan the timetables of special trains carefully, you will still be able to steam out of the city behind one of a number of preserved German Pacifics.

There were economic reasons to stay with steam in the German Democratic Republic, even after the announcement, made in 1956, ordering an end to steam development in the Soviet Union. While East Germany was a Soviet satellite state, its railways managed to plough their own course. The country remained one of the great steam centres into the 1980s, not least because of the intelligent work of Max Baumberg and his colleague Hans Schultz.

Baumberg was born in Arnstadt, in Thuringia, in June 1906. He studied mechanical engineering in Munich before working at Meiningen, where he learned to drive steam locomotives as well as to get to grips with their mechanics. Still very much in action today, the Dampflokwerk Meiningen (Meiningen Steam Locomotive Works) was built in its present form by the Prussian State Railways in 1914 as a repair and maintenance centre for all Prussian locomotive types. It continued in this role under the new Deutsche Reichsbahn, and even during its occupation by the US military, which captured the works in April 1945. Now owned by Deutsche Bahn AG, Meiningen remains a 'holy city' for steam owners, operators, and enthusiasts worldwide. With a staff down from 2,200 in its heyday to 120 in 2012, Dampflokwerk Meiningen is able to repair and overhaul steam locomotives shipped here from around the world, and to build new components and even entire new engines. This is where, in 1961, Baumberg converted the streamlined class 61 tank engine into the high-speed Pacific 18 201, and where the locomotive was completely restored for main-line service in 2002. Here the 01 class Pacific 01 1102 was re-streamlined between 1994 and 1996 and brought back to steam. In 2006, the works completed a boiler for the brand new A1 Pacific 60163 *Tornado* (see Chapter 7), and in 2009 it delivered a brand-new narrow-gauge 2-8-2T locomotive, 99 234.4, to the narrow-gauge

Molli railway which runs between Bad Doberan and Kühlungsborn on the Baltic coast. The Molli remains a joy. Trains leave the terminus at Bad Doberan and then run right through the town's high street before heading up to the coast, where they sprint beside the sandy beaches to Kühlungsborn, stopping at Heiligendamm, the newly restored Neo-Classical spa town founded by Friedrich Franz I, Grand Duke of Mecklenburg, in 1793.

Baumberg moved on to the works at Glückstadt, in Schleswig-Holstein, where locomotives running on the 'Marsh Railway' were serviced. This was the line that saw some of the very last regular express passenger steam trains in Europe; a journey from Hamburg to Westerland on Sylt island, reached across a spectacular bridge spanning the Rhine Canal, was one of the great railway trips of the early 1970s. The Wagner Pacifics were often well polished and ran the 277 kilometre trip from Hamburg across misty flatlands at consistent speed. For mile after mile, the crisp beat – slightly jazzy in the case of the three-cylinder engines – of Wagner's locomotives was accompanied, in winter, by plumes of white steam trailing across marshland and sea. In the years after regular steam had gone on so many of the world's railways, anyone with steam in their soul, seated by a window in the warm compartment of a deep-green carriage, would discover that the Marsh Railway was a veritable heaven.

During the Second World War, after the 1940 armistice, Baumberg was sent to France. Working as a technical liaison engineer with the SNCF at Tours, he studied and learned to admire Chapelon's four-cylinder compound Pacifics and 4-8-0s shedded there and the ways in which the great French engineer had made such significant improvements to the steam circuit of the many locomotives he had rebuilt. After some trouble adjusting to the new political system in East Germany, Baumberg rose to become director of VES-M Halle in 1960. This was the Deutsche Reichsbahn's national research, development, and testing department; it was closed in 1996.

Pressure to rebuild the Deutsche Reichsbahn's steam fleet had grown throughout the 1950s. Many of the pre-war engines had been hard pressed both during and immediately after the war, as a divided Germany clambered back on to its feet. Some of the boilers fitted to certain classes in the years just before the war suffered a number of technical problems, including metal fatigue. It was said that they were becoming dangerous. In 1956 alone, 300 Deutsche Reichsbahn steam locomotives were taken out of service because of concerns over the safety of their boilers. In 1958, the boiler of the Pacific 03 1046 exploded at Wünsdorf. Transport minister Erwin Kramer called on the railways to push ahead smartly with the reconstruction programme.

As a result, Baumberg set about improving not just the Wagner 01s but also the class 41 two-cylinder fast freight 2-8-2s of 1937–41. These and other Baumberg rebuilds were known as *Rekloks*, or reconstructed locomotives. Designed by a team led by Friedrich Wilhem Eckhardt at Schwartzkopf, in Berlin, the 102 ton class 41s had been excellent machines, before flaws in their boilers showed up, noted for their rapid acceleration. The war had put a stop to production after a total of 366 had been built. Between 1957 and 1961, 107 surviving class 41s were rebuilt for the Deutsche Bundesbahn, with new welded combustion-chamber boilers, and worked till the end of steam in 1977. Eighty Deutsche Reichsbahn class 41s were similarly rebuilt, with new boilers and slightly larger fire-grates, capable of generating more steam than their Deutsche Bundesbahn counterparts. Rated at 1,950 ihp, the Deutsche Reichsbahn 41s were well-liked, mixed-traffic engines, working hard until the end of East German steam in 1988.

Baumberg continued to work on the *Rekloks* and other new steam engines for the Deutsche Reichsbahn, although sadly he was unable to obtain authority to build the proposed 01.20 four-cylinder compound Pacifics embodying Chapelon design principles. Nevertheless, more than six hundred locomotives, of a variety of classes, were fitted with Giesl ejectors, and there was never a time when Deutsche Reichsbahn steam engines were neglected or downgraded. They were thoroughly maintained until replaced by diesel or electric services.

*

Wagner's influence, meanwhile, had spread beyond Germany. This was not just because the German engineer was well travelled and well liked, giving talks to technical institutions abroad, but because German political and economic influence had spread across much of Eastern Europe, the Balkans, and even parts of the Middle East by the end of the nineteenth century. Much of Prussia was in what is Poland today, so it is not surprising that Polish steam locomotives have always looked German even if they have been built at home.

Prussian State Railways class P8 4-6-0s could be found at work in Belgium, Czechoslovakia, France, Greece, Latvia, Lithuania, Poland, Romania, Russia, and Yugoslavia. The Deutsche Reichsbahn *Kriegslok* 2-10-0s made their way across even greater stretches of Europe during and after the Second World War. Indigenous designs were few and far between in most of the countries within Germany's orbit. While Czechoslovakia had a proud engineering tradition of her own, and built some seven thousand steam locomotives, Romania built 1,610, and Bulgaria managed just three.

In fact, despite fuel crises and the sheer expense of importing oil, Bulgaria was the first Eastern bloc country to rid itself of steam. This is interesting not only for what it tells us about the politics of modernization in both communist and capitalist countries – the image of the railways was all-important and steam was considered to look old-fashioned – but also because some of the finest Wagner-influenced engines never to run in Germany performed brilliantly throughout the challenging landscape of this particularly secretive Soviet satellite up until 1980.

Few foreign engineers, however, let alone steam enthusiasts, saw this extraordinary outpost of high Wagnerian steam in action. Which was a pity, because there must have been few sights more stirring than a 155 ton, two-cylinder 2-12-4T shouting up a mountainous hillside in charge of a formidably heavy coal train. These particular engines, the heaviest of all non-articulated tank engines and with a tractive effort of 65,980 lb, were built in Germany in two batches – twelve two-cylinder machines in 1931 and eight three-cylinder variants in 1943 (Bulgaria having been allied to the Axis powers between 1941 and 1944). These were very much Wagner-derived locomotives, but stretched and filled out to cope with the onerous operating conditions of Bulgaria. Bulgarian State Railways also operated the only 4-10-0s in Europe, and some of the only examples of this wheel arrangement worldwide. Built by Henschel in 1941, these forceful, three-cylinder engines could only have been German and would have readily fitted into the standard German fleet. Is there a recording of these Bulgarian giants – the 2-12-4Ts and the 4-10-0s – in action? That would be a heavy metal thrash with a vengeance. What was even more remarkable about the Bulgarian steam locomotive stock in its latter days is the fact that it was, if such a thing were possible, even more standardized than its German counterpart. Most larger locomotives of whatever purpose or wheel arrangement shared the same boilers, as well as other components.

What was evident, too, traveling in the post-war period, whether through Poland, Bulgaria, or Turkey, is that the aesthetic of the steam locomotive in those diverse countries was not simply German, but largely derived from Wagner and his 01 Pacifics of 1925. Perhaps their last true descendants were two impressive, two-cylinder 56 class 2-10-0s built by the Turkish State Railways at Sivas and Eskişehir in 1961. These were Wagner Deutsche Reichsbahn class 50s in all but name. They were the last brand-new main-line steam locomotives built in Europe until *Tornado* (see Chapter 7). They were also the first two steam locomotives built in Turkey. The 56 class was designed by Henschel. Delivery began in 1937, but was interrupted by war; in the late 1940s, further examples were built by Škoda in Czechoslovakia, and by Beyer Peacock in Manchester.

In Britain, too, Stewart Cox, in charge of design of the British Railways Standard fleet, admitted to owing much to Wagner. He and his colleagues had met their fellow German engineers, especially

Wagner and Nordmann, and had followed their research papers diligently. 'In particular,' wrote Cox, 'the work of these two engineers went deeply into the question of boiler and tube proportions. On this subject, for long years opinion had taken the place of exact measurement and there was a wide band of tolerance as to what was considered acceptable practice or indeed acceptable steaming capacity. With the assistance of the Grunewald testing station, Wagner was able to arrive at sufficiently exact dimensional relationships to eliminate much of the need for inspired guesswork.' The result was the development of boilers for British Railways locomotives, including the Britannia Pacifics, the class 9F 2-10-0s, and the solitary three-cylinder 71000 *Duke of Gloucester*, that were evaporatively efficient.

In terms of overall and absolute efficiency the use they made of steam and hence fuel – that is, their thermal efficiency – Wagner's and Witte's engines ranked in between the high efficiency of modern French compounds and the greater specific consumption of steam in most American locomotives. They were on a par with the very best British engines. What they offered that was truly special was a degree of standardization that was approached nowhere else in the world. It would be wrong to put this down to some genetic German need or desire for order or pure reason, for Germany is as much the country of the operatic music of another Richard Wagner as it is a nation of highly skilled engineers. There was, though, something indefinably militaristic about the appearance and the efficient, clipped performance of the majority of steam locomotives designed and built by the Prussian State Railways and the Deustsche Reichsbahn. And something very special indeed in watching these black, no-nonsense engines set about their work, whether at the head of a mile-a-minute express train or of a vast freight train going into the diesel and electric age.

CHAPTER 3

FRANCE

'Chapelon, vous avez fait quelque chose'

Trained as an architect, Graham Laidler was a brilliant English cartoonist who drew a delightful and telling series for *Punch* magazine in the 1930s under the title 'The British Character'. One of these, dating from October 1934, shows a pukka English gent – a retired colonel by the look of it – sitting on his luggage at what looks like Paris Gare du Nord. Unflappable, he looks on without so much as batting an eyelid as an assortment of jabbering French policemen and railway officials gesticulate wildly. Clearly the gentleman has fallen foul of some Napoleonic law or other, but equally clearly he is unable to understand a word of what is being said and, even if he did, you know that he would be wholly uninterested. The caption reads: 'Skill at Foreign Languages'. Another cartoon from the same series, published in January 1937, depicts a crowd of smartly dressed men and women at a grand party rushing away from a lone bearded figure in a shabby suit holding forth in the centre of the room. The caption reads: 'Fear of Intellectuals'.

What on earth have these deliciously funny and beautifully observed cartoons got to do with the French steam locomotive in the twentieth century? The answer is nothing, and everything. French steam locomotive development was a thing apart. It was the product of skill, common sense, and know-how, as all steam locomotive design has been; but, at its best, it was also the stuff of deeply researched theory into thermodynamics and a level of intellectual engagement that most engineers in other parts of the world – notably Great Britain and the United States – seemed to shy away from. In particular, the reluctance that so many British locomotive engineers showed towards compounding and its alleged intricacies was wrapped up in a notable inability to speak foreign languages and a wish not to be thought of as intellectual. Down to earth, yes; feet on the ground, certainly.

And yet, the three British steam engineers I have singled out in Chapter 1 as Britain's very best or most inspired – Gresley, Stanier, and Bulleid – were all well aware of the remarkable French contribution to locomotive design. Two of them, Bulleid and Gresley, were Francophiles who spoke the language well. They were also proud to be called friends of, arguably, the greatest steam locomotive engineer of all, André Chapelon. Chapelon could claim English engineering ancestry on his father's side of the family. He did not write in English but he could read it well. The 1952 revised edition of his magisterial book, *La Locomotive à Vapeur* (*The Steam Locomotive*), first published in 1938, was eventually translated into English and updated by his friend and collaborator, George Carpenter, in 2000.

Chapelon, a straightforward and modest man, just happened to be both very gifted and – I think it can be said without sounding ridiculous – passionately in love with steam. Possessed of a very keen intellect and great determination, he was no impractical theorist. The principles he evolved to improve the steam locomotive were put into practice, and they worked. He said these principles were inspired by the work of eminent predecessors, notably Anatole Mallet, Gaston du Bousquet, Wilhelm Schmidt, and G. J. Churchward. They worked so well that many engineers found it hard to believe the results he achieved until they actually visited France and, like Thomas placing his fingers into the wound in Christ's side, witnessed Chapelon's extraordinary engines for themselves. Chapelon was not exactly a prophet without honour in his own country, yet some rival engineers and modernizers among the French railway management proved keen to denigrate his genius.

Indeed, in 1946 Chapelon created what is perhaps the greatest of all steam locomotives to date, the SNCF's 242A1, a three-cylinder compound which could produce 5,500 ihp, almost double that of the three-cylinder simple-expansion 4-8-2 from which it had been rebuilt, and a level of power that had been unimaginable before then outside of the United States, where the last generation of steam engines were truly vast machines. As a result, the 242A1's maximum performance could equal the schedules drawn up for the electrically hauled trains which had yet to begin service but were intended to replace French express passenger steam on the Paris to Lyons route. Sadly, this superb locomotive was to be unceremoniously scrapped in 1960, a loss that might be compared to a decision to demolish Andrea Palladio's Villa Capra at Vicenza, one of the finest of all Italian Renaissance houses, or, closer to home, the wanton scrapping of Cugnot's preserved steam tractor, which is thankfully safe in the halls of the Musée des Arts et Métiers.

The British view, as expressed shortly before and after the Second World War, recognized the value of Chapelon's work in enlarging steam flow circuits to maximize throttling losses but was politely dismissive of his achievements with compounding. Several key members of the ex-LMS British Railways design team from 1948 considered that compounding – a part of the essence and puissance of 242A1 – was too complex: a little too intellectual, and perhaps a little too French into the bargain. Doubtless chauvinism played its part. While Chapelon was being undermined by fellow engineers and a spirit of increasingly dogmatic modernization at home, in Britain locomotive engineers were refusing to recognize the potential for increasing the performance and efficiency of new and existing locomotives if this involved compounding. Furthermore, some, rather insultingly, argued that the great British workman would be quite unable to cope with, much less understand, the technical complexities of compound operation.

There is no great mystery to the compound steam engine. The idea is simple. Instead of using steam once to move pistons backwards and forwards in cylinders before it is exhausted to the atmosphere, compound engines use the same steam twice – or even three times, in triple expansion – through the use of high- and low-pressure cylinders. Steam is admitted first to high-pressure cylinders and then, through receiver pipes, to low-pressure cylinders, before being exhausted through blast-pipe and chimney. The object of compounding is to get more work from the steam and to reduce the amount of fuel required, because the steam is passed through two stages and thus used more expansively and economically than in a simple-expansion engine using steam at equal pressure. Thus a well-designed compound will be more powerful than a simple-expansion engine of the same overall dimensions. From early on, however, while the French made increasingly effective use of compounding, the British experience of it was varied and sometimes unsatisfactory.

This was not the fault of compounding itself, but a consequence of the way it was employed by a number of British locomotive engineers, notably Francis Webb. A rector's son from Staffordshire, Webb was – for all too many years, as far as some of his colleagues were concerned – locomotive superintendent and then chief mechanical engineer of the LNWR. Webb went for compounding early on, yet none of the various 2-2-2-0, 2-2-2-2, 4-4-0, and 0-8-0 three-cylinder compounds he designed gave a particularly good account of themselves. This was partly because he insisted on using two small high-pressure cylinders set outside the frames to feed one exceptionally large low-pressure cylinder between the frames. The other way round – a single high-pressure cylinder feeding two low-pressure cylinders outside the frames – would have been a far better proposal, although the limitations of the British loading gauge (British trains have to fit inside a very tight envelope of space compared with their continental or American cousins) meant that outside cylinders could never be as big as engineers might have liked. Webb's low-pressure cylinders were often short of steam. Moreover, because of the peculiarities of his valve gear as well as the lack of power as steam was applied to the tiny high-pressure cylinders, not only did some of his compounds find it hard to produce the necessary oomph to get express trains bound for Scotland out of Euston and up the steep Camden Bank immediately beyond the platform ends, but they could even find their front driving wheels slipping in one direction and their rear driving wheels (the two were not connected on Webb's 2-2-2-0s) spinning in another, with the result that there was much sound and fury but no forward motion. Edward Talbot explains the situation as follows, in *The LNWR Recalled*:

> The problem was that when the low-pressure cylinder was equipped with a slip eccentric – as was done not initially but later to ensure the low-pressure cylinder was in effect always in full gear – the driver had no means of reversing it. So when an engine backed into a terminal station like Euston and coupled on to its train, and the driver then wound the gear to go forwards, the low-pressure cylinder slip eccentric remained in whatever position it was in when the engine stopped. For it then to be reversed, the high-pressure cylinder had to move the engine and train (i.e. one pair of driving wheels had to do that) until the slip eccentric changed direction and the low-pressure cylinder got steam and helped to move the train forward. So if the high-pressure cylinder slipped without the engine moving very much – as was common if trying to move the whole train – steam reached the low-pressure cylinder when its slip eccentric was in the position for going backwards. Then bingo

> – high-pressure driving wheels going one way, low-
> pressure the other.

Got that? Although such complex and frustrating episodes were rare, they soon became the stuff of railway lore. Webb, although in many ways a great engineer, never got his many compounds – Experiments, Dreadnoughts, and Teutonics – to run half as well as his lighter and older simple-expansion engines. The legendary performance of 790 *Hardwicke*, Webb's bantamweight Precedent class two-cylinder 2-4-0, in the 1895 railway races from London to Aberdeen was quite outstanding. On 22 August 1895, *Hardwicke* sprinted the 141 miles over Shap from Crewe to Carlisle in 126 minutes, at an unprecedented average speed of 67.1 mph, a record that stood throughout the steam era. *Hardwicke*'s three-coach train might have been light, but so was the locomotive, at 35 tons. Its tractive effort was 10,918 lb. One also has to imagine what it must have been like for the crew on the flimsily protected footplate of this fiery machine as it rode down Shap at up to 90 mph.

Webb's compounds, although not as fast, could in fact be very reliable. The Teutonic 1304 *Jeanie Deans* worked the heavy 14.00 Glasgow 'corridor' dining-car express from Euston as far as Crewe, and the corresponding train back, almost every day for eight years. They were controversial, however, providing grist to the anti-compound mill and giving compounding a bad name in Britain from which it never quite recovered. Although the forty-five Midland Railway compounds built from 1902 to 1909, and the 195 built by the LMS from 1924 to 1932, were successful and economical engines, they were not sufficiently powerful to make significant improvements to heavy main-line services on the west coast route to Scotland. They were relatively old-fashioned in front-end design for machines built in the mid-1920s, by which time the Collett Castle class and Gresley A1s were in service.

In France, the first compound locomotive, a two-cylinder 0-4-2 tank engine – a slip of a thing – was built by Anatole Mallet for the Bayonne–Biarritz railway in 1876. Two key factors were at work to make the compound a success. The first was coal. France was not endowed with such huge reserves of coal as was Britain, and much of the coal that was mined, mostly in the north of the country, was small, dusty stuff, sometimes with a low calorific value. This meant that coal had to be imported, at great expense. One way of reducing consumption on the railways was to adopt compounding, where the softer exhaust beat enabled small coal to be burned more efficiently. To the GWR fireman brought up on glistening lumps of high-grade Welsh coal, the French offering would have seemed very poor. If the supply of decent-sized coal for locomotive use was one problem the French railways faced, the other was the way in which most of the main lines had been laid with relatively light rails, compared with many in Britain. This meant that locomotives had to be relatively light too, putting as little stress on the track bed as possible. Partly because of this, a national speed limit of 120 kph (74.5 mph) was ordained for the railways during the reign of Napoleon III. When it was revoked in the 1930s, the new limit was just 130 kph (81 mph).

If, then, an express train was going to live up to its name and average a mile-a-minute between the two world wars, it had to be able to accelerate rapidly, and it had to maintain high speeds uphill because there was little opportunity for racing downhill. The express locomotive would also have to run as smoothly as possible in order to spare the track and to burn as little costly coal as possible. Once these conditions are understood, the rise and rise of the compound steam locomotive in France becomes not just comprehensible, but almost a matter of principle. For many French steam locomotive designers, compounding was as much a national religion as it was a form of engineering.

Because many early compounds required two sets of valve gear and controls to regulate steam supply to the high- and low-pressure cylinders, they were often more complex machines to drive than their simple-expansion counterparts. In France, drivers – *mécaniciens* – spent two years in the workshops as a part of their training and were instructed in the theory and practice of working steam locomotives. In this regard, they were a breed apart from drivers in other countries, whose job was primarily to drive or fire locomotives and not to be overly concerned with the niceties of thermodynamics and the intricacies of mechanical engineering. There are many stories – some apocryphal, others true – of *mécaniciens* spending their holidays at locomotive works to see their compound Pacific through its annual general overhaul, while for many years in France individual main-line express locomotives were allocated to specific crews.

This devotion to duty, or obsession, is well caught both in Émile Zola's 1890 novel *La Bête Humaine* and in Jean Renoir's classic adaptation of this disturbing psychological thriller for the cinema in 1938. In the story, Jacques Lantier, a *mécanicien* on the Paris–Le Havre line, is as obsessed with his locomotive as he is with the femme fatale and stationmaster's wife, Severine. The sequences on the footplate of a compound Pacific are as compelling as the story itself.

Equally, *Pacific Senator: A Train Driver's Life* (1984), by the Pacific *mécanicien* Marcel Péroche, is an extraordinary book which helps one to understand the French love affair with a form of locomotive that could belong to no other country. Speaking of Pacifics that were pooled and not assigned to individual crews, Péroche writes: '*On les appelait les "putains" parce qu'elles n'avaient pas de mécaniciens titulaires*' ('They were called "whores" because they didn't have regularly assigned drivers'). This compelling book, which is particularly good on how French railway workers coped with the German occupation during the Second World War, captures the bloody-minded yet critically intelligent spirit of the men who helped to make André Chapelon's and other outstanding compound locomotives so very effective.

'When I took leave,' Péroche writes, 'I made sure my engine was in the hands of a conscientious driver so as to be sure to find her in good shape when I got back. With today's way of thinking, no doubt I'd be classed as a fool, but I can tell you that I often spent my rest day tinkering about on my engine. I used to get to the depot around nine and wash down the wheels and connecting rods with boiling water. Then I'd clean out the axle boxes and clear the grease nipples so that the oil could get through. It was the old school. Time was of no matter since we lived for the railway. For us, looking after our locomotive was a pleasure in itself.'

To watch a highly polished, dark-green Chapelon Pacific start a boat train for Paris away from Calais Maritime was a wonder. Almost silently, save for a piercing high-pitched screech from its whistle, the complex engine would move its heavy train out of the station in one smooth movement. Even at speed, with little variation uphill and down, the exhaust was silent and, in warm months, no more than a heat haze from the chimney. These locomotives ran like silent sewing machines and it was hard to gauge just how very hard they might be working. They were the product of a designer who was little short of a genius and was backed up by highly trained engine crews and maintenance staff.

André Chapelon was born on 26 October 1892 in Saint-Paul-en-Cornillon, a small village, of which his father was mayor, dominated by a medieval castle and set high above the Loire in the Massif Central, some forty miles south-west of Lyon. His great-great-grandfather, James Jackson, pioneered the crucible-melting process for steel making when he came to France from England in 1814, establishing a steelworks in Saint-Étienne. By 1850, the Jackson family steelworks produced half of all the steel in the Saint-Étienne valley. In 1857, Jackson's granddaughter, Elizabeth Esther, married Antoine Chapelon.

As if the landscape were not sufficient distraction, the young Chapelon would spend as much time as possible watching the trains of the PLM, the Paris–Lyon–Mediterranean railway, running close by between Le Puy and Saint-Étienne. His first footplate ride, in 1903, at the age of eleven, was on board a venerable 4000 class PLM 0-8-0, with its tall chimney, huge dome, and weatherboard cab. Chapelon was in love with steam from as far back as he could possibly remember. A woman he had fallen in love with married another man while he was away on service during the First World War. After that, he appears to have given himself over wholly to a lifelong passion for steam.

What is regrettable is the fact that Chapelon's life's work was badly interrupted when he was in full creative flow by the Second World War, and then by the SNCF's decision to put a stop to steam development in 1951. Chapelon hoped to continue building main-line French steam until 1970, by which time, he believed, electric traction would be able to make a quantum leap over steam in terms of high-powered performance. Was he wrong? The TGV, an electric train that has truly revolutionized travel by rail, started running in regular service in 1981. One of these striking, prognathous machines has reached 574.8 kph (357.2 mph), while regular services have been scheduled, from Lorraine to Champagne-Ardenne, at average speeds of 279.4 kph (173.6 mph), or very nearly 3 miles per minute. This is just what Chapelon, still very much alive when TGV development began in the early 1970s, had wanted. Before French steam development came to what must have felt like an emergency stop, he had designed express passenger locomotives that would have run comfortably over long distances at 200 kph (125 mph), and he was thinking ahead to locomotives capable of 250 kph (155 mph). These were not idealistic pipe dreams; they could have been realized.

When Chapelon was eight years old, one of a pair of highly successful four-cylinder compound locomotives was put on show at the 1900 Paris World Fair. These Atlantics had been built at Mulhouse the previous year to the designs of Alfred de Glehn, the English-born chief engineer of the Société Alsacienne de Constructions Mécaniques, then in German Alsace, and Gaston du Bousquet, chief mechanical engineer of the Nord railway. They were impressive machines, light on the track and yet fast and powerful for the day; trains of 350 tons could be run over considerable distances at 120 kph (74.5 mph) and, on test, these non-superheated Atlantics achieved up to 1,444 ihp. It was one of these Atlantics that Churchward bought for testing on the GWR, followed by two more of the slightly larger Paris–Orléans version. One other small, if hugely significant, exhibit on show in Paris in 1900 was a revolutionary form of engine running on peanut oil; its inventor was the French-born Rudolf Diesel.

While du Bousquet was making a great success with compounding on the Nord railway, in Germany Wilhelm 'Hot Steam Willy' Schmidt, a mechanical engineer working in Kassel, was developing a practical superheater for steam locomotives. This device reheated saturated steam produced in the boiler until it was all but dry and very hot – upwards of 350 °C (662 °F). Superheated steam was so effective that it substantially raised the thermal efficiency and power output – by up to 25 per cent – of many of the early locomotives to which it was applied. The first, in 1898, was a Prussian State Railways two-cylinder 4-4-0. With compounding and superheating, twentieth-century steam locomotive engineers had two very powerful tools to hand, and Chapelon was to make highly effective use of both.

Chapelon himself took great interest in the work of both du Bousquet on the Nord railway and Churchward on the GWR, even before he had passed the necessary exams to enter the École Centrale des Arts et Manufactures. Founded in 1829, this was the leading French university in the field of practical engineering. But, with the outbreak of the First World War, on 28 July 1914, Chapelon, an artillery officer cadet, was soon in action at the front, observing artillery fire. During the Somme offensive of June and July 1916, he was an aerial observer, spending up to sixteen hours a day high over the battlefields in the basket of a hot-air balloon. This was a perilous position and on a single day five French balloons, with his friends aboard, were destroyed around Chapelon's – his was the only one to survive unscathed.

Chapelon went on to become a staff officer with the 106th Heavy Artillery Section, based in the fortress at Verdun. His biographer, Colonel Hugh Rogers, recalls Chapelon's great gift of accurate range prediction, achieved through a mixture of imagination and meticulous research:

Here Chapelon used his off-duty time in writing a
paper setting out, with examples, his method of fire
... His Colonel submitted his treatise to the Artillery
Improvement Centre. It was examined there by the
mathematician Émile Borel, who could find no fault in
the system. A practical demonstration was then given by
the Artillery Training Centre at Mailly camp. During a
practice carried out with 75 mm guns the average point
of impact with fifty shots practically coincided with the
target. As a result, Chapelon's new system was embodied
in Artillery Regulations.

In April 1919, a decorated Chapelon returned to the École Centrale
and on graduating in 1921 he joined the PLM. (It was, as we will see,
some of those in the engineering department of the PLM component
of the future SNCF who later did much to undermine Chapelon, and
even attempted to destroy his legacy.) In 1921, the PLM was one
of six major French railways; the others were the Nord, Midi, Est,
Ouest, and Paris–Orléans railways. They had been formed through
the government-led merger of the nation's railways in 1852. The state
took control of the Ouest railway in 1908, and had overall control
of the railways during the First World War. Suffering immense
reconstruction problems in the wake of the war, and then the Great
Depression, the SNCF was formed on 1 January 1938, two years
after the return of the leftist Popular Front government in 1936. The
government owned 51 per cent of this new national corporation, and
the railway shareholders 49 per cent. The six major pre-SNCF railways
became regions, and continued to develop along lines of their own,
although locomotive and rolling stock policy was now to be centrally
controlled. The state finally took full control of the SNCF in 1983,
when the last private shareholdings were bought out.

In the early 1920s there was little locomotive development going
on at the PLM to stretch a young man of Chapelon's abilities, nor, in

the conservative engineering climate that prevailed there, were his theories on how to improve the flow and use of steam in locomotives likely to be well received – so he left to work with the Société Industrielle des Téléphones in the autumn of 1924. The realization, however, that he might now be separated from working with steam forever hit him quickly and hard. With the help of Louis Lacoin, his professor of thermodynamics at the École Centrale, Chapelon was back with the railways in January 1925, now in the research and development section of the Paris–Orléans railway.

This was the challenge Chapelon needed. In 1923, the Paris–Orléans had decided to electrify its main line from Paris to Bordeaux and Toulouse, and not to order any further steam locomotives. However, with the widespread introduction of heavier, all-steel coaches, the performance capacity of the railway's 189 compound Pacifics was becoming inadequate, and the solution was clearly to increase the performance of the existing steam stock. The Paris–Orléans railway was also interested in fuel economy. The upshot was that Chapelon's design chief, Paul Billet, gave the young man his head. Chapelon took 3566, one of the Paris–Orléans's Pacifics, built in 1913 and known by shed staff as 'Le Choléra', and transformed it, after careful analysis, from an adequate, if unloved, 1,450 dbhp express engine into a 2,700 dbhp machine. Perhaps not surprisingly, news of Chapelon's remarkable achievement was met, at first, with disbelief on both sides of the Atlantic.

It was only when trials began in November 1929 between Orleans and Bordeaux on the main line from Paris, almost exactly a century after *Rocket*'s winning performance at Rainhill, that the apparent miracle that Chapelon had performed was proved to be no illusion. On 4 April 1930, 3566 ran the 70.1 miles start to stop from Poitiers to Angoulême with a train of 362 tons at an average speed of 70 mph. Once up to the line limit of 120 kph (74.5 mph) the compound remained at that speed uphill and down, the speedometer needle only moving when the train had to slow down to stop – it was almost as if the engine were being supplied by a constant electric current.

Shortly afterwards, 3566 worked a 567 ton train between Poitiers and Angoulême at an all but incredible average speed of 67 mph, again without exceeding the 75 mph line limit.

What Chapelon had given 3566 was an unrestricted flow of high-temperature steam. His great achievement was in the application of holistic thermodynamics to the steam locomotive. Intuitively, he saw the steam engine as an organism, and even before techniques existed to see inside the steam locomotive under power, Chapelon had thought through the best way for steam to flow through the circuit of boiler, superheater, cylinders, and exhaust for optimum effect. Every attempt was made to create a steady flow of steam superheated to a very high temperature. Eddies and vortices of boiler gas flow needed to be stabilized and controlled. The whole cycle had to be as seamless as possible.

To achieve this, and to produce such spectacular results, Chapelon made the following improvements to 3566. The cross-sectional area through the steam-flow circuit, from regulator through to superheater, was doubled, reducing pressure drop and power loss by 75 per cent. The steam-chest volume was quadrupled, as was the steam-port area through the large-diameter poppet valves. Steam temperature was raised from 300 °C to 400 °C. A Kylchap exhaust, patented in 1926, provided a strong and uniform exhaust across all of the boiler tubes in the smoke-box, greatly improving combustion efficiency while decreasing back-pressure in the cylinders. The Kylchap exhaust system was based on the Kylala mixing device invented by the Finnish locomotive inspector Kyösti Kylälä. Kylälä had been looking, primarily, for an effective form of spark arrester – Finnish locomotives often burned wood – but found that his invention also saved fuel. Chapelon's eye fell on research from anywhere in the world that would help him improve the steam locomotive. Eventually some four thousand locomotives worldwide – including two thousand in France and two hundred in Britain – were fitted with Kylchap exhausts, greatly improving power while reducing fuel consumption.

A test run on 24 March 1931 with 3566 and a train with guests drawn from the rival French companies showed the locomotive averaging 65 mph between stops and gaining many minutes of lost time in the process, without exceeding 75 mph. When the special drew in to Bordeaux, Marcel Bloch, the Paris–Orléans's chief engineer for rolling stock and workshops, turned to his young locomotive engineer and said, *'Chapelon, vous avez fait quelque chose'* ('You have certainly done something').

He had. Chapelon had made a great leap forward in the design of the steam locomotive. On a power-to-weight basis, 3566 was the world's most powerful steam locomotive. Its performance was no flash in the pan: the engine could be worked hard, when necessary, for mile after mile, day after day. And this was just the beginning. The other French railways began following Chapelon's principles and rebuilding their Pacifics and other passenger locomotives, especially after trials held on the Nord railway in the winter of 1932–3 which set Chapelon's 3566 against a Nord railway Super Pacific of 1931, an Est railway 4-8-2 of 1925, and the PLM's latest 4-8-2, also of 1931. Regular trains worked included the heavy Pullman *Flèche d'Or* on its Calais Maritime to Paris Gare du Nord run. The Nord railway inspectors were suitably impressed when 3566 hauled the 650 ton Pullman up the 24.9 miles of the Gannes bank, a gradient of between 1-in-333 and 1-in-250, at an unflinching 120 kph (74.5 mph).

The Nord railway ordered twenty Paris–Orléans rebuilds, as well as twenty-eight brand-new Chapelon Pacifics built by private industry. These became the 3,400 ihp 231E class and could still be seen at the head of the *Flèche d'Or* in the mid 1960s, still turning in the same precise performances as had been expected of them three decades earlier. The last was withdrawn in 1967. Weighing just 91 tons, or 160 tons with tender, the new Chapelon Pacifics had a power-to-weight ratio not just higher than that of any other steam locomotive of the time, but higher than that of some much-vaunted diesels, like the English Electric Deltics, the class of diesel-electrics designed to take over from Gresley Pacifics on the east coast main line in the early 1960s. The Deltics had a maximum power output of 3,300 ihp – and while this could be produced at the turn of a handle, much the same was true for the French Pacifics.

The new Nord Pacifics could have been more powerful still. In 1932, Chapelon converted one of the smaller-wheeled saturated Paris–Orléans 4500 class Pacifics of 1907 into a four-cylinder compound 4-8-0. This was done to improve performance on the southern stretch of the 443 mile main line from Paris to Toulouse. The last 250 miles were characterized by steep gradients and continuous reverse curves. Many trains had to be double-headed, a policy that was largely anathema in cost-conscious France. What is more, the Paris–Orléans railway wanted to accelerate passenger trains on this route, especially during the popular skiing season in the Pyrenees, and to increase their maximum weight from 500 tons, to which the Pacifics were limited by considerations of adhesion, to eighteen-coach loads of 700 tons. The result was 4521. Again, this was a rebuild of an earlier Pacific, one of the 4500 class of 1907, the very first European Pacifics.

With extended mainframes, a new long, narrow fire-box with a 40.5 sq ft grate, a boiler pressure of 290 psi, and Chapelon's thermodynamic elixir, the reborn 4-8-0 was the prototype for one of the greatest of all classes of locomotives at work anywhere in the world, the 240P of 1940. The eight-coupled, four-cylinder compound 4521 emerged in steam from the Tours works on 16 August 1932. The 104.5 ton locomotive's performance was truly sensational. She soon proved capable of maintaining 3,450 ihp continuously, with a maximum of 4,000 ihp, and a maximum recorded speed of 94 mph, considered very fast indeed at the time for a locomotive with 1.85 m (6 ft 0¾ in) driving wheels. On one test, 3,030 dbhp was sustained for one hour at 62 mph, during which time the fireman, chauffeur Marty, fired four tons of coal. He had previously been a torpedo-boat stoker, but said that he preferred working in the open air.

Equally at home at the head of heavy freight and express passenger trains, 4521 created the greatest interest among train operators throughout France. Twelve of these Chapelon 4-8-0s were built. Two were loaned to different French railways, and their performance on test never failed to impress. On 18 February 1935, 4707, now renumbered 240.707, ran a 650 ton test train over the 183 miles from Calais to Paris, with a water stop at Amiens, at an average running speed of 71.2 mph, and averaging 87 mph over 20 miles of level track. On 21 March, the Deutsche Reichsbahn engineers Drs Fuchs and Nordmann rode a fourteen-coach, 607 ton test train on the État railway between Paris and Cherbourg – 230 miles over heavy inclines – behind the same engine. Both men were deeply impressed as they saw it achieve 2,800 dbhp on the banks, equivalent to 3,200 dbhp on level track, something they had thought impossible from such a compact and – to German eyes – complex-looking machine. Back in Berlin, a proposal for a Deutsche Reichsbahn 4-8-0 derived from the Paris–Orléans machine was prepared at the Borsig works, although the war put a stop to this Franco-German design.

On loan to the PLM – by now the SNCF's south-east region – in 1938, 240.705 worked the fastest expresses over the 317.5 miles from Paris to Lyons, gaining up to half an hour on schedules booked at more than a mile-a-minute. Marcel Japiot, the PLM's new chief mechanical engineer, was suitably impressed – and even more so when, on 18 July, 240.705 was put at the head of a fifteen-coach express weighing 672 tons, more than double the normal 320 tons of the Côte d'Azur Pullman. Ten minutes late away from Laroche, through no fault of its own, the Chapelon 4-8-0 was on time at Ancy le Franc forty miles on, and five minutes ahead of time at Blaisy summit, having gained 15 minutes in 83 miles.

This was in 1938, the year the French railways were nationalized. Japiot, who was now chief mechanical engineer of the south-east region, had little hesitation in ordering twenty-five 4-8-0 rebuilds of the Paris–Orléans 4500 class Pacifics. Significantly, Japiot had succeeded René Vallentin, who resented Chapelon's achievements, especially when, in 1936, 240.705 outperformed 241.C1, the PLM's prototype large-wheeled 4-8-2, in terms of both greater power output and lower fuel and water consumption.

Chapelon took the opportunity further to strengthen the frames at the rear of the locomotives, slightly to enlarge the inside low-pressure cylinders, and to install mechanical stokers. Justly proud of the new engines – the 240P class – Chapelon wanted to improve their appearance over the dozen Paris–Orléans 4700 class 4-8-0s. He asked his friend, the artist Émile André Schefer, to help with their styling. Schefer's inspired paintings of French railway locomotives and posters for the railway companies, capturing and framing images of speed, grace, and power, were well known and very popular. The result was the raising of the running board clear of the driving wheels, for greater accessibility, a larger boiler casing, under which most of the external pipework of the earlier 4-8-0s was concealed, a PLM-style 'windcutter' cab, and a conical smoke-box door, complete with Schefer's version of the SNCF's famous circular badge. The result was one of the best-looking of all French locomotives, as well as the steam locomotive with the highest power-to-weight ratio anywhere in the world. The fact that no 240P has survived into preservation is little short of a tragedy.

The 240Ps were rebuilt from Paris–Orléans un-superheated Pacifics at Tours and Périgueux between May 1940 and October 1941. In June 1940, the French had surrendered to the Germans. The armistice was signed in the Compiègne forest inside carriage 2419 of the Orient Express, a handsome restaurant car brought from a museum in Paris for the occasion – the Germans had been forced to sign the armistice in the very same coach in the exact same location on 11 November 1918. The Germans imposed a national railway speed limit of 100 kph (62 mph), although speeds had already been cut by the SNCF after the declaration of war in order to minimize wear on track and rolling stock, so the new 240Ps were not required to run fast. Their power, however, proved to be prodigious.

Testing began in spring 1941. On 31 May 1941, 240P.5, with driver Chartier and fireman Jarry of Laroche on the footplate, set a new world record for steam power. From Laroche, and with seventeen cars weighing 800 tons behind the tender, the compound climbed the 19.4 mile gradient, averaging 1-in-187 and peaking at 1-in-125, between Les Laumes and Blaisy without the speed falling below 60 mph. Power increased steadily as the gradient steepened, with 240P.5 maintaining full boiler pressure, reaching 4,400 ihp, equivalent to 3,600 dbhp – very nearly 40 ihp per ton of locomotive weight. This was greater than the power-to-weight ratio not only of any other steam locomotive but also of any diesel locomotive of the next decade. Given that 240P.5 was mechanically fired, there had been no need for the heroics of chauffeur Marty. If Chapelon had 'done something' with his first Pacific, he had done something else again with the 240Ps.

The 240Ps were mainly shedded at Laroche, working to Dijon, Lyon, and through to Paris. At the end of the Second World War, they headed the sole main-line day passenger train from Paris to the south of France, loaded with up to twenty-eight coaches, or 1,400 tons. And yet, these herculean 4-8-0s were broken up by the end of 1953. This seems extraordinary, as surely these young, immensely powerful, and hugely competent locomotives – Chapelon's favourites among his own engines – should have been transferred elsewhere on the SNCF. But unfortunately, Chapelon – a kind and profoundly religious man with no ego and no side to him – was resented by some in management for continuing to argue that there was still a place for steam in the SNCF's post-war motive power policy. He was increasingly regarded by these people as a *passéiste*, a man of the past. His steam locomotives were resented too. Even so, there were plans to move the 240Ps to the south of France, where they would have radically improved services over the difficult, if often beautiful, coastal route to Nice. However, this would have required conversion to oil-firing because of the threat of line-side fires posed by coal-fired locomotives in this hot, dry, inflammable region, and the 240Ps were rejected because the SNCF had ruled that no further development could be made to steam locomotives after 1951.

Chapelon believed that there was always considerable resistance to his proposals for new and rebuilt locomotives from forces within the motive power running departments on the Paris–Orléans railway. (In France such departments came under the aegis of the chief mechanical engineer until 1970.) This was overcome by the determination of the Paris–Orléans's chief mechanical engineer Édouard Épinay and his chief engineer for rolling stock and works, Marcel Bloch. On the Est and within the SNCF, there was similar resistance.

Chapelon was appointed a *chevalier* of the *Légion d'honneur* in 1934 for his work in locomotive development and won increasing fame outside of France, especially after the publication of *La Locomotive à Vapeur* in 1938. But he rose only slowly up the railway hierarchy. A dedicated design engineer and not a management man, he was eventually appointed the SNCF's chief steam locomotive design engineer, although he was never, like so many of his disciples around the world, a chief mechanical engineer. He did, though, have a remit to produce new designs both during and after the Second World War, including designs for an altogether new generation of high-power steam locomotives which would make even the 240Ps seem underpowered.

Chapelon's most innovative design was a prototype six-cylinder compound 2-12-0. Built at Tours in 1940, 160.A1 was kept hidden from the Germans and was only fully tested from 1948. The idea was to shape a locomotive capable of hauling heavy freight trains at slow to moderate speeds over extremely hilly routes with the thermal efficiency of an express passenger engine working at speed. The idea had originated as early as 1933, when the operating department of the Paris–Orléans had been looking for a locomotive to haul 1,200 ton freight trains over the long 1-in-100 gradients of the steam-operated section of the Toulouse line. Chapelon believed he could produce a 2-12-0 with half as much power again as the existing four-cylinder compound 2-10-0s working these trains. Although commissioned in 1935, it was five years before 160.A1 was first steamed and another year before she was able to prove her remarkable power and efficiency. At the time of the German invasion, the brand new locomotive was returned to her home depot, Brive, at the head of a 1,200 ton freight train, without having been run in; she climbed the heavy gradients from Limoges at a steady 40 kph (25 mph), producing a sustained 2,700 dhp in the process.

Steam locomotives are generally more efficient the higher their rotational speed, measured in rpm. At lower rpm and piston speeds, more heat is lost through the cylinder walls, condensation, and leakages. To minimize these, Chapelon used steam-jackets surrounding the cylinders between the high-pressure and low-pressure stages. Four low-pressure cylinders gave the increased cylinder volume required to enable steam to be used expansively at low speeds, employing relatively short low-pressure cut-offs.

Tests conducted after the war, in May and June 1948, vindicated Chapelon's ideas. The engine was easy on coal and water and was powerful throughout its speed range, peaking at 2,750 dbhp – sustained on test over three hours without a break – at 60 kph (37 mph) with a train of 1,650 tons. She used 40 per cent less coal than a three-cylinder 150X class 2-10-0 (German class 44s of the SNCF) when both locomotives were worked at 1,600 dbhp.

Further tests demonstrated that steam-jackets eliminated the need for superheating the high-pressure cylinder and for very high initial steam temperatures, superheating being provided only between the high-pressure and low-pressure stages. Sadly, the 2-12-0 was taken over by events as the Brive to Montauban section of the Toulouse line for which it had first been planned, fifteen years earlier, had been electrified in 1943. It was also too late to affect the design of the last compounds built for the SNCF, although its principles were to have been applied to Chapelon's proposed, if ill-fated, high-power designs. Although it should have been preserved, 160.A1 was scrapped in 1955.

During the war, Chapelon not only pushed on with wholly new designs but was also partly responsible for 318 mixed-traffic 2-8-2s.

These were the 141P class four-cylinder compounds of 1941, designed in collaboration with Georges Chan, an outstandingly powerful and reliable type, with 1.7 m (5 ft 5 in) driving wheels, which could run up to 110 kph (68 mph) on test and could sustain 3,330 dbhp at 80 kph (50 mph). The maximum power of the 141Ps, at 4,000 ihp, was almost equal to that of the Chapelon 4-8-0s at speeds up to 100 kph, and double that of the PLM Mikados they replaced.

At the end of the war, SNCF ordered 1,340 simple-expansion two-cylinder 2-8-2s from the United States as a matter of urgency to help replace the thousands of locomotives destroyed between 1939 and 1945. When the SNCF was formed in 1938, it had a fleet of approximately 17,800 steam locomotives; by May 1945, this had been cut by German appropriation to 12,000, of which only about 3,000 were in running order. The new 141R class, of which 1,323 went into service, the other seventeen being lost off the coast of Newfoundland on the way to France in April 1947, were very different from the 141Ps.

Featuring robust frames, roller bearings, Boxpok disc wheels, and much larger cabs than French crews were used to, these rugged Jeeps of the French railways were based on a 1937 Alco design for the Green Bay and Western Railroad and were put into common-user service, meaning that, unlike their more evolved French cousins, they were driven and fired by any number of crews. Extremely reliable – they ran up to 125,000 miles between general overhauls – they were popular and remained at work up until the end of steam on the SNCF in 1974. They were neither as fast – limited to 100 kph – nor as powerful – 2,633 dbhp at 50 mph – as the 141Ps, but they did show the value of rugged American engineering, and the strides that had been made across the Atlantic in terms of new manufacturing techniques which made engines easier and quicker to build than in much of Europe, as well as inherently more robust.

The second batch of 141Rs consisted of 640 locomotives fitted with single Kylchap exhausts, boosting their maximum sustained power output to 2,928 dbhp at 50 mph. The first batch used 40 per cent more coal and water than the ex-PLM Mikados but were cheaper to maintain. Before the end of SNCF steam development in 1951, Chapelon was able to modify 100 141Rs with improved valves and steam passages and higher superheating, improving fuel economy by 15 per cent and raising their maximum power to 3,300 dbhp. For many holidaymakers to the south of France into the early 1970s, the 141Rs were their first and abiding impression of French steam, as they worked smartly timed passenger trains along the Côte d'Azur from Marseilles to the Italian border.

Another of Chapelon's wartime designs had been for modular utility locomotives. These were based on a two-cylinder simple-expansion engine which could be stretched from a 2-6-0 to a 2-8-0 or even a 2-10-0. With 1.7 m (5 ft 5 in) driving wheels, all three classes would have been able to run at up to 110 kph (68 mph). These would have been successful machines, but they proved unnecessary since by the time they would have been ready for production, North American locomotive works were already making 141Rs at a rate quite beyond the capacity of the domestic French industry.

Like so many French people at the time, Chapelon coped with the Nazi occupation as best he could. Soon after the war's end, however, he was one of those disgracefully arraigned by an SNCF 'purification' committee, which accused him of demonstrating a 'passive attitude towards the enemy'. He was to be questioned immediately after Marc de Caso, who, like Chapelon, was a decorated First World War artillery officer and former student of the École Centrale, and had gone on to join the Nord railway and to design a number of impressive, efficient, and beautiful 4-6-4s at the beginning of the war.

Born in Montepellier to a family with Italian and French ancestry, de Caso was an ebulliently outspoken and passionate man, and also a great admirer of Chapelon. He liked to say: 'I don't leave my tongue in my pocket.' As he lambasted the committee, one of whom was a railway engineer who resented his and Chapelon's eminence, de Caso's tongue was very much in evidence. When he had finished, there was silence and the chairman of the committee said: 'Tell Monsieur Chapelon we don't need to see him.' Nevertheless, both Chapelon and de Caso were downgraded from their rank of *ingénieur principal* for six months, despite considerable protest from colleagues.

As John van Riemsdijk, former keeper of mechanical engineering at the Science Museum in South Kensington, pointed out in *Compound Locomotives* (1994), Chapelon was never more or less during the war than an apolitical technician and he would have kept his thoughts to himself, although after the German defeats in Russia and North Africa in 1942–3 he did contact a Resistance group. As Van Riemsdijk recalled: 'I had some contacts with SNCF personnel when I worked in the Special Operations Executive and followed these up in early 1946, when I formed lasting friendships with railwaymen of various grades. The conclusion to be drawn from all the sources is that, apart from a politically motivated minority, the prime loyalty was to France but some collaboration with the Germans was necessary to protect French lives. Chapelon continued working on post-war locomotive design and advising on motive power matters. He was a backroom boy largely uninvolved in politics. However, both he and Marc de Caso, like numerous others, were investigated after the war.'

Whatever professional and personal jealousies were involved in these purification committees, Louis Armand put a stop to all such witch-hunting when he was appointed assistant general manager of the SNCF in 1949. A railway mechanical engineer and a genuine Resistance hero, Armand had formed the *Resistance-Fer* (Railway Resistance) in February 1943 when he was chief mechanical engineer of the SNCF. Denounced by collaborators, he was about to be sent to a concentration camp in Germany in July 1944, but was saved by the allied bombing of the Paris to Strasbourg line, and then by the Swedish Red Cross and the timely arrival of French and American troops. He, if anyone, would have known who the real collaborators were.

Today, Armand is best known to steam enthusiasts for his *Traitement intégral Armand*, a system of controlled chemical water treatment to eliminate boiler scaling and corrosion, which was applied to all SNCF steam locomotives, reducing boiler maintenance costs by between 85 and 90 per cent and cutting fuel consumption by 7.5 per cent as a result of improved heat transfer within the boiler. In fact, Armand's treatment, together with a preventive maintenance system introduced by Joseph Poissonier of the Nord railway, enabled the SNCF's fleet of 9,000 steam locomotives in 1955 to average 250,000 kilometres (156,000 miles) between failures, a degree of reliability never achieved in Britain with any form of traction.

As for Marc de Caso, he was not only Chapelon's friend and ally but also the one other truly notable French steam locomotive engineer of the super-power steam era. Joining the Nord railway in 1921, his first job was to renovate a fleet of ex-Prussian State Railways P8 class 4-6-0s, locomotives given to France as part of Germany's post-war reparations, and in deplorable condition. He moved on to design all-steel monocoque coaches for the Nord railway – the first to enter quantity production in Europe – before improving the valve mechanism of the Nord railway's Super Pacifics, which he did very successfully.

His first locomotives were the powerful 5.1200 class four-cylinder compound 2-10-0s of 1933 featuring Super Pacific boilers and a very large steam-flow circuit. With an official top speed of 105 kph (65 mph), these heavy freight and mineral train locomotives were also often put to work on heavy passenger trains making frequent stops. Capable of 3,000 ihp, these highly successful machines continued in production in SNCF days, classified as 150Ps.

In 1933, de Caso became locomotive design engineer of the inter-railway central design office, where he continued his design work on his remarkable 4-6-4s for the Nord railway, with 290 psi boilers, 54 sq ft fire-grates, mechanical stokers, robust frames, and large steam-flow circuits. Three three-cylinder simple-expansion 4-6-4s and five four-cylinder compound 4-6-4s were built from 1941, the latter developing a maximum of 4,500 ihp. They were so successful, and impressive, that the SNCF's north region proposed building a further twenty improved de Caso 4-6-4s in 1950, but this was stopped by the ministry of public works and the region was allocated 241Ps instead.

Meanwhile, Chapelon's own masterpiece and, arguably, the finest steam locomotive yet built, was to emerge from the embers of the war. Projected in 1938, authorized in 1942, and finally completed in 1946, this was 242A1, a three-cylinder compound 4-8-4, a prototype for the new standard types the French engineer hoped to build to meet traffic needs up to 1970. This was not the fastest or the biggest or the most powerful steam locomotive in the world; but it was extremely efficient, and one of the very few steam locomotives that forced the design engineers of the latest electric engines to think again.

Chapelon had first proposed this development when he was given the opportunity to rebuild an État railway three-cylinder simple-expansion 4-8-2 which had fractured a cylinder. There was, though, no chance of building a prototype express passenger locomotive during the war. So 242A1 was not revealed until 18 May 1946. Built at the forges of Ateliers de la Marine et d'Homécourt, near Saint-Étienne, this locomotive was the stuff of painstaking research, mechanical inspiration, and – or so it must have seemed to those who experienced the solitary French 4-8-4 in action – something like sorcery. Weighing 148 tons, 242A1 employed three, rather than four, cylinders. This was a major departure for Chapelon. The idea was not so much for simplicity's sake as to create room for much thicker inside driving cranks and wider axle boxes; while these components (in thinner and lighter form) gave satisfactory results in the 240Ps and 141Ps at up to 4,000 ihp, Chapelon believed they would need to be much stronger for the higher power output expected of the 4-8-4.

The appearance of the locomotive was that of a scaled-up 240P. It looked long and racy, especially with its small cab which made the driver seem like the jockey of a particularly strong and lithe racehorse. With its triple Kylchap exhaust and chimney, thrusting conical smoke-box, high running boards, huge 'elephant-ear' smoke deflectors, massive outside low-pressure cylinders, and close-coupled driving wheels, it seemed like one of those futuristic French steam locomotives bursting out of the brilliant 1930s posters by graphic artists like Adolphe Cassandre. It looked every last centimetre the dashing and heroic, if tragically short, part it was to play in the story of the steam locomotive.

The driver's job was certainly not one for the inexperienced. There were two regulator handles, instead of the one found on conventional steam locomotives. On starting, the driver would open the low-pressure regulator to get the train moving, followed by the high-pressure regulator. Full compound working would begin at about 15 mph, when the driver would close the low-pressure regulator, and as 242A1 accelerated he would adjust the two cut-offs for the high- and low-pressure cylinders so as to give equal power. On production engines, the low-pressure regulator would have been retained for starting but the ratio between high- and low-pressure cut-offs would have been achieved automatically.

There was no question, though, that Chapelon had done something truly exceptional with 242A1. Here was a European steam locomotive as powerful as many American engines 50 per cent heavier. Here was a 148 ton 4-8-4 that used approximately 20 per cent less coal than a 105 ton Stanier Coronation – one of Britain's finest – needed to produce a proportionate amount of power. Here was the first European steam locomotive able to maintain a constant 4,000 dbhp. Fire-box and boiler – pressed to 290 psi – produced steam at a continuous rate of 52,240 lb per hour (a Coronation would produce a maximum of 40,000 lb per hour on test). The engine rode well up to its specially permitted maximum of 150 kph (93 mph); it was normally limited to 130 kph (81 mph). With high and reliable power on tap, sure-footed starting with the heaviest trains on the steepest gradients, rapid acceleration, and the ability to run at the normal speed limit uphill and down, except over the most severe gradients, 242A1 was able to equal the performance of existing SNCF electric locomotives.

On trial between 1946 and 1948 on the ex-PLM *Ligne impériale*, 242A1 bettered the performance capacity of the planned 144 ton 2D2.9100 class electrics, which were designed to go into service between Paris and Dijon in 1949. SNCF officials could only gawp in astonishment as, on 14 October 1948, the Chapelon locomotive tackled an eighteen-coach Paris–Lyon–Nice express weighing 861 tons, storming over the steep and curving gradients north-west of Dijon without falling below 101 kph (63 mph). The 31.2 kilometre (19.4 mile) section between Les Laumes and Blaisy was covered in 18 minutes and 17 seconds, despite slowing down for permanent-way works. At 117 kph (73 mph) the engine generated 5,500 ihp, with the single high-pressure cylinder producing 1,920 ihp and the two low-pressure cylinders 3,580 ihp.

An immediate consequence of this was the order to uprate the maximum one-hour rated power of the new *Ligne impériale* electrics from 4,000 hp to 4,950 hp – there was no way that management could allow a steam locomotive to outperform their electrics even before they had gone into service. Here was that very rare case of a steam locomotive influencing the design of electrics. However, due to its much lower frictional resistance, a 2-Do-2 with 4,950 hp at the motor shafts developed 4,500 dbhp at 75 mph; at the same speed, 242A1 gave about 4,400 dbhp from the 5,500 ihp generated in her cylinders.

On 12 September 1952, and with the brilliant Argentine locomotive engineer Livio Dante Porta on the footplate, 242A1 worked a Paris to Brest express under the electric wires to Le Mans. Loaded with twenty cars, weighing 810 tons, Chapelon's three-cylinder compound averaged 116 kph (72 mph), undercutting the new electric schedule. From the first time it turned its eight 1.95 m (6 ft 4¾ in) driving wheels, there had been something quite unparalleled about the performance of this peerless locomotive. Imagine what it must have been like to watch the green giant lift a 742 ton train east from Lisieux, on 23 April 1947, up a snaking 1-in-125 gradient on a blustery day with a 40 kph (25 mph) side-wind, accelerating to 80.5 kph (55 mph) in just under 4 kilometres (2.5 miles). Truly, nothing like this had been seen or experienced before in Europe. And, true to Chapelon form, the 4-8-4 went about its work with great brio.

John van Riemsdijk later summarized the capability of this great machine: 'On those main lines with formidable gradients, such as Blaisy, between Paris and Dijon and the Lisieux bank between Paris and Caen, 100 kph would be sustained. On the well-known climbs to the summit at Survilliers on the Nord main line, this locomotive was able to run freely with 700 or 800 tons at 75 mph, which was the normal speed limit. In fact, gradients almost ceased to exist for practical purposes because the speeds of the trains did not drop appreciably when this locomotive was pulling them.'

Allocated to the west region, 242A1 was based at Le Mans. When it pulled Paris to Brest expresses over the 412 kilometres (256 miles) from Le Mans, where it took over from electrics, the locomotive gained up to forty minutes in recovery time, with trains of up to 850 tons, on schedules designed for the smaller 4,000 ihp 141P class 2-8-2s. As French engine crews were paid bonuses for regaining time, as well as for saving fuel, 242A1 was greatly in demand at Le Mans depot, although there was some degree of rivalry over who should be allowed to drive such a boost to the pay-packet. With the final cancellation of Chapelon's high-powered locomotive designs in 1951, the wholly reliable 242A1 was withdrawn prematurely in 1954, and finally scrapped in 1961 – despite an offer to buy the locomotive made by Dr Armin Glazer, a Swiss enthusiast, who received a reply a year later informing him that the locomotive no longer existed. There have long been dark murmurings to the effect that the engine was not saved for posterity because it was an embarrassment to the SNCF modernizers. Why else would the most powerful steam locomotive ever built outside the United States, and one of the most economical of all steam locomotives, have been cut up? As it is, enthusiasts from around the world would pay the SNCF handsomely to see a reconstruction of the greatest steam locomotive of all in action once again.

With its unsurpassed performance, 242A1 should have been the genesis of a new era of SNCF steam development. On 7 June 1944, the day after D-Day, Louis Armand, then chief mechanical engineer of the west region, attended a meeting to discuss future motive power policy. Assuming – though not lightly – that the Germans were finally on the run, it was time to think ahead once again. While the electrification of key main lines was not in doubt – Paris to Lyon had been agreed in 1942 – there would still be a fairly lengthy period of changeover from steam to electric and a need to improve the speed and frequency of services on routes scheduled for electrification in the more distant future. To meet this need, Chapelon and Chan worked up proposals for a high-powered series of modular locomotives, this time combining the best in modern American construction and practice with the best in French thermodynamics.

Chapelon discussed these designs for the first time at an SNCF-authorized lecture that he gave on 14 December 1945 to members of the Association Française des Amis des Chemins de Fer (AFAC) at the Conservatoire des Arts et Métiers in Paris. I wish I could have been there. Outline drawings revealed four types of three-cylinder compound to be produced from standardized components. These machines, intended to be capable of developing 5,000 ihp continuously, with a maximum of 6,000 ihp, comprised: a 4-8-4 for heavy express duties, designed to haul 950 ton *rapides* up 1-in-200 gradients at 120 kph (74.5 mph), with a maximum speed of 140 kph (87mph); a 4-6-4 for *ultra-rapides*, capable of 140 kph (87 mph) up 1-in-200, and a maximum speed of 200 kph (124.5 mph); a 2-8-4 for heavy mixed-traffic use, capable of 90 kph (56 mph) up 1-in-200 pulling 1,200 tons, with a maximum speed of 120 kph (74.5 mph); and a 2-10-4 for heavy freight, capable of 70 kph (43.5 mph) up 1-in-200 with 2,000 tons, and a maximum speed of 110 kph (68 mph).

Artists' impressions reveal a good-looking, modern group of engines, of elegant outline, with generous and fully enclosed cabs, and a fine sense of artistry as well as technical excellence. The locomotives would feature single-piece integral frames, roller bearings fitted throughout, and automatic lubrication. The large boilers, similar to that of 242A1, would be pressed to 320 psi, but with longer, mechanically fired, 64.5 sq ft grates. Willoteaux double admission and exhaust piston valves would ensure an unrestricted flow of steam in and out of the three cylinders.

Chapelon also showed designs for two complementary projects. One was for a one-man-operated, oil-fired, four-cylinder compound 4-6-4 tender-fourgon, a streamlined tank engine with built-in luggage and guard's compartments. All four cylinders were to have been mounted externally in side-by-side pairs. This intriguing machine, derived from a Paris–Orléans project of 1936, would have provided fast services on main-line stopping trains and on secondary and tertiary cross-country lines. The tank locomotives would have replaced what were, at the time, rather noisy and uncomfortable diesel-railcars. A 2,000 ihp engine, with a top speed of 130 kph (81 mph), it would have accelerated a 100 ton, three-car train from rest to 120 kph (74.5 mph) in two minutes, revolutionizing the kind of service provided by slower diesel-railcars. The proposal was strongly supported by the south-east region's chief mechanical engineer, Marcel Japiot. Chapelon's figures, always erring on the side of caution, can be accepted as fact. Throughout his career, he calculated to remarkably small margins of error; figures that appeared on paper were equalled, and usually bettered, when the locomotives were completed and out on the track.

The other project was for a streamlined, 3500 ihp, mechanically fired, four-cylinder compound 4-6-0, using a slightly shortened 240P boiler at 290 psi, which was to have rocketed 350 ton *trains-drapeaux* (prestige trains) from Paris to Marseilles and Paris to Strasbourg at an average speed of up to 144 kph (89 mph), with a maximum speed of 200 kph (124.5 mph). Unfortunately, post-war track conditions ruled out such maximum speeds and the 230P, as it was classified, was cancelled. This dashing machine was, however, to influence the design by David Wardale, a modern British steam locomotive engineer, of the proposed 200 kph 5AT class 4-6-0 (see Chapter 7) half a century later. The dream – far from idle – of a steam locomotive that can cruise at 200 kph was ignited by Chapelon; it has yet to dissipate. Chapelon himself believed in higher speeds still for steam traction, outlining proposals for a possible further generation of three-cylinder triple-expansion locomotives designed for up to 250 kph (156 mph).

A start was made at the Compagnie des Ateliers et Forges de la Loire, Saint-Chamond, on the frames and cylinders of what was to be the first of a hundred 152P class 2-10-4s, but in 1947 SNCF management, following government instructions to reduce consumption of coking coal in order to conserve supplies for the steel industry, declared the suspension of new steam development in favour of electrification. Four years later, electrification of the trunk route between Valenciennes and Thionville, for which the 152Ps had been intended, prompted their final cancellation. Substantial compensation had to be paid to the builders.

Chapelon succeeded Georges Chan as chief locomotive design engineer of the SNCF in 1949. While construction of new steam locomotives was ruled out from 1951, Chapelon was able to make major improvements to a number of locomotives, including the 141Rs and 241Ps. The latter were a class of express passenger four-cylinder compound 4-8-2s, of which thirty-five were built between 1948 and 1952 for service on the former PLM main line from Paris to Lyon and Marseilles, and the Nord railway line from Paris to Lille and the Belgian border. Developed from the rebuilt 241.C1, the PLM prototype four-cylinder compound 4-8-2, the 241Ps, once given the Chapelon treatment, were capable of producing a maximum 4,300 ihp. When displaced by electrics on the PLM main line, they worked on the État main lines from Paris to Le Mans, Brest, and Nantes, where they powered expresses of 800 to 900 tons at average speeds of 100 kph (62 mph) until 1969. In 1956, two pooled 241Ps from Lyon Mouche depot each averaged 19,250 miles in thirty-one days pulling the heaviest and fastest expresses to Marseilles, without incident. These were the highest monthly mileages recorded by European steam locomotives.

Chapelon retired from the SNCF in 1953. He had already taken up an appointment as consulting engineer for GELSA (Groupement d'Exportation de Locomotives en Sud-Amérique), for which he had designed twenty-four simple-expansion 4-8-4s and sixty-six 2-8-4s for service on metre-gauge railways in Brazil, built between 1950 and 1953. In spring 1951, Chapelon led a mission to Brazil to see the first of the new locomotives in action; he journeyed on to Argentina where he met his most fervent disciple, the engineer Livio Dante Porta, who was described by Chapelon as 'eminent amongst those who believe in the further development of the steam locomotive'.

If he had been able to continue with the development of steam on the SNCF, Chapelon would have pushed ahead with designs for triple-expansion four-cylinder versions of his 6,000 ihp, three-cylinder compound locomotives. The 4-8-4 would have been more powerful than any locomotives of this wheel arrangement built in the United States. A very high pressure – 584 psi – boiler with water-tube fire-box would generate saturated steam passed to an inside steam-jacketed high-pressure cylinder driving the third coupled axle. This would feed the medium-pressure cylinder set between two low-pressure cylinders driving the second coupled axle. Steam would be superheated between the high- and medium-pressure cylinders, and re-superheated between the single medium and twin low-pressure cylinders. This might sound complex, but it would have remained a simpler machine than a diesel locomotive; basically, any steam engine is a relatively straightforward device, with remarkably few moving parts. The result was to have been an express engine, and other types, capable of exerting a sustained 6,000 dbhp and around 7,500 ihp. This design, Chapelon said in 1970: 'shows the development of the classic steam locomotive that was still possible if work had continued since 1945 during these twenty-five years that have been wasted on the Diesel'.

It seems sad that in his lifetime Chapelon should have come under attack from rivals jealous of his success, as well as from those who insisted, in the face of the evidence, that compounds were undesirable simply because they seemed to be complex in comparison with the ideal of simple and rugged locomotives favoured in the English-speaking world. In his *World Steam in the Twentieth Century*, Stewart Cox noted: 'In the case of the engines having the highest power-to-weight ratio of all, the Chapelon 4-8-0s of class 240P, turned out in 1940, and set to work on the PLM main line, a remarkably short life ensued before the engines had to be taken out of service due to mechanical deterioration.' This was untrue and clearly a case of wish-fulfilment on the part of a British engineer who, although probably misinformed by SNCF engineers, believed in simplicity at all times. Nevertheless, to his credit, Cox did add: 'It is sufficiently clear that in relation to the size of the machines concerned, they [Chapelon's compounds] were unmatched anywhere else in the world both in their contribution to brilliant running and in the elegance with which it was achieved.'

It was Chapelon, a touch ironically, who ultimately helped rescue the underperforming British Railways Standard Pacific 71000 *Duke of Gloucester*. On a visit to the Rugby testing plant in 1957, he analysed the report on the tests made with the *Duke* and advised a change in the profile of the exhaust cams to increase the power developed in the cylinders. Nothing happened at the time, but when *Duke of Gloucester* was rebuilt for main-line running in the 1990s, the opportunity was taken by Tom Daniels, the 78-year-old engineering adviser to the restoration project, to follow Chapelon's advice; as always, this proved to be highly effective. Daniels was also able to fit 71000 with double Kylchap exhausts, just as Chapelon had recommended forty years earlier, and this has significantly boosted *Duke of Gloucester*'s performance. In any case, every British steam locomotive engineer worth his weight in coal and water had adopted Chapelon's ideas on 'internal streamlining', or the unrestricted flow of steam from regulator to cylinders, while his Kylchap exhaust was second to none in raising the performance of locomotives that had yet to reach their potential.

Chapelon's passion for steam and his overriding belief that there was a future for the steam locomotive, if only it were developed to anything like its full potential, remained with him until his death in 1978. In the 1970s he worked, with assistance from George Carpenter, on designs for new steam locomotives for American railroads. This collaboration was in response to the oil crisis of the time when, for a while, it really did look as if some railroads might consider returning to steam locomotives burning indigenous coal. That crisis has never really passed; the USA has been plunged into wars triggered by the struggle over the production and supply of oil. The steam locomotive still has its place. There was also a discussion in 1974, agreed to by Chapelon, with the Chinese National Railways, led by Kenneth Cantlie, former consultant engineer to the Chinese National Railways, over the possible construction of 152Ps. The Chinese showed great interest in locomotives 30 per cent more powerful than their robust, 3,500 ihp, QJ class 2-10-2, still very much in production at the time. However, the ministry of heavy machine production, which controlled Datong works where the QJs were built, stated that retooling for the 152P would cost a year's delay in production, or three thousand new locomotives, a figure the railway was unable to contemplate. It is fascinating, however, to see that Chapelon's design was still being considered for production twenty years after his retirement; had it happened, it would have given him great satisfaction.

Chapelon was not the only French locomotive engineer of merit in the age of super-power steam. His friend Marc de Caso designed some very fine engines, not least the seventy-two powerful 2-8-2 TC class tank engines built from 1932, which many of us can remember from our first trips to Paris, busy at work on the push-pull suburban trains running in and out of the Gare du Nord. These had remarkable powers of acceleration. Chapelon, however, had taken the steam railway locomotive to new heights; and he demonstrated that, as the politics of fuel become ever more important, steam is far from being finished.

Sentimental *passéiste* or painstaking and passionate innovator? André Chapelon was quite clearly the latter, and over his long career he was to gain many more admirers than detractors. This heart-felt appreciation, offered by the SNCF steam locomotive engineer Jean Gillot, who had taken Chapelon's traction course at the École Centrale, seems as fitting a tribute as any: 'Whilst his work was immortal, one realizes that the man himself was not. When one met him and until the end of his life he was always straightforward and modest, with his lively mind and wonderful memory, his clear and vivid speech and the little flame that seemed to light up in his eyes when he spoke of "the locomotive" . . . his departure marked the end of a glorious epoch of the steam locomotive which reached its ultimate development thanks to him because he was its greatest worldwide craftsman.'

CHAPTER 4

THE UNITED STATES

Big Boys, Bright Lights, and Dream Tickets

It was someone in the Schenectady erecting shops who chalked the legend 'Big Boy' across the frames of the biggest locomotive Alco had ever been asked to build. Alco was the American Locomotive Company, Schenectady the upstate New York town where steam trains had first run, to nearby Albany, in 1831. Over the ensuing 110 years, railroads had spread their steel web the length and breadth of the United States. The most extensive of all, now as then, was the Union Pacific Railroad. By the outbreak of the Second World War, the Union Pacific ran trains west of the Mississippi and out in a great fork as far as Seattle and Los Angeles on the Pacific coast.

In shifting prodigious quantities of freight from west to east and east to west, Union Pacific trains had no alternative but to climb some of the steepest gills between the Rockies and the Appalachians. The most notorious sections of its tracks were between Ogden, Utah, and Cheyenne, Wyoming. Running east from Ogden (elevation 4,355 feet), trains were faced with a 62 mile climb to a summit at 6,799 feet.

Heading west from Cheyenne (elevation 6,060 feet) they faced a 30 mile climb to the top of Sherman Hill (8,013 feet). This would have been tough going for a lightweight streamlined express in the years immediately before the Second World War, but for the massive freight trains needed to fuel the American war effort, these climbs demanded a herculean effort on the part of Union Pacific locomotives. And imagine these great mountainous plains in the white depths of winter: the challenge they posed to railroad engineers was formidable.

But this was where, late in the day, the American steam locomotive came to the rescue, making one of its last supreme efforts before the oil and diesel lobby forced it into retirement. Big Boy would be a veritable wonder – not the biggest, or the heaviest, or even the most powerful of steam locomotives, but in terms of speed, usable power, availability and flexibility, one of the mightiest of them all.

Throughout the 1920s and 1930s, the Union Pacific had specified ever bigger locomotives to deal with the Wahsatch and Sherman Hills. Its three-cylinder 4-12-2 class, built between 1926 and 1930, was a good slogger but not particularly fast, and it was unable to cope single-handedly with the loads expected in wartime. The Challenger class 4-6-6-4 of 1936–44 was a maid-of-all-work, able to run at 70 mph and to manage both passenger and heavy freight trains; yet even these bravura machines had to be assisted by a second locomotive over the formidable Utah and Wyoming peaks.

The Union Pacific wanted freight trains of at least 3,600 tons (something like 110 fully laden modern British railway carriages) worked by a single locomotive and crew over the gradients that challenged their Challengers. This made economic sense, especially in wartime when manpower was inevitably going to be in short supply. This was why, in just three short and very intensive months in 1940, the company vice president in charge of research, Otto Jabelmann, working with Robert Ennis and A. I. Lipetz at Alco, drew up the specification and design for the 4000 class, the one and only 4-8-8-4 type ever built. To ensure a rapid turnaround of locomotives, freight cars, and crews, these giant new locomotives would need to run fast. In fact, the 345 ton engines (535 tons with tender) could top 80 mph when pressed or on test, although 60 mph was a more normal maximum.

In Big Boy – and this was the key to its success – the Union Pacific had produced not some muscle-bound monster, but a remarkably lithe machine, rather like a sixteen-stone marathon runner, or a heavyweight boxer able to dance around the ring for an entire match. Twenty-five were built, in two batches – in 1941 and 1944 – at a cost of $256,000 each. To put the sheer scale of Big Boy into international perspective, consider the dimensions of the largest, latest, and most powerful British freight engine, the British Railways class 9F 2-10-0 built between 1954 and 1960. A Big Boy weighed 345 tons, a 9F 86 tons. Big Boy had a nominal tractive effort of 135,375 lb, compared with the 9F's 39,670 lb. Big Boy could sustain 6,290 dbhp at 35 mph, or around 7,500 ihp; the figures for a 9F were about one third of those. At 132 ft 9¼ in, Big Boy was twice as long as its British cousin. It was also much wider and far taller than a 9F.

Inside Big Boy's enormous boiler, pressed to 300 psi, there was over a mile of tubes and flues to heat. The fire-box measured 150 sq ft. If you had been able to endure the intense heat (2,500 °F), you could have held a cocktail party inside. The vast grate swallowed low-grade Wyoming coal, mined close to Union Pacific tracks, shovelled automatically through two steam-powered stokers from Big Boy's fourteen-wheeled tender. The tender was loaded with 28 tons of coal and 24,000 gallons of water; at full blast, a Big Boy had a huge appetite, working its way through this seemingly generous supply in just 55 miles.

In full cry, the 4-8-8-4s – and you can hear this in Union Pacific's own homage to the articulated locomotives, the handsome black-and-white film *Big Boy*, made in 1958 – sounded like a fast-moving thunderstorm or a continuous broadside from a battleship, as, with exhaust roaring from triple blast-pipes and chimneys, they took 4,200 ton loads (well above their design specification) east and west over the hills they were built to flatten. Built for this single purpose, the black and silver 4000 class did exactly what it was mean to do, reliably and poetically, until the summer of 1959, when diesels took over. No individual diesel could possibly match the power of a Big Boy, especially at speed, but several easy-to-service diesels could be coupled together in series and manned by a single crew – a gang of Davids to the steam engine's Goliath. A number of Big Boys were kept steaming until 1962, by which time each of the original batch had run more than one million trouble-free miles and the US railroads were effectively 99 per cent steam-free. Eight of the twenty-five have been spared the cutter's torch and yet – oddly, considering the enthusiasm for steam in the USA and the phenomenal wealth in that country – none is in running order. If it were, enthusiasts and camera crews would flock from around the world to see it.

Big Boy captured much of the spirit, and framed much of the substance, of American super-power steam. Visitors to North America were generally dumbfounded at first by the sheer size of steam locomotives in the United States and Canada. But, once they began fully to appreciate the scale of the dramatic landscape of the continent, locomotives like the Union Pacific Big Boys began to make sense. For all their might and splendour, the Big Boys were very much in a minority of US steam locomotives; where Big Boy was built for a specific route, the majority of American engines were generic, big, simple, strong machines which, except for differences in design details, liveries, and logos, could easily be mistaken for one another. In spite of there being so many private railroad companies, many of the best US steam locomotives were not just very similar in design, but they were built, for the most part, by a tiny handful of companies, the names of which – Alco, Baldwin, and Lima – are world-famous. Very few US railroads built their own locomotives, preferring to buy them from the major builders, although a number of companies did have strong and sometimes imaginative design teams who worked with engine builders to get what they felt they needed.

Otto Jabelmann was one of those railroad engineers, who worked closely with Alco to produce not just one but three of the great locomotives of the super-power steam era. These were the FEF ('four-eight-four') two-cylinder 4-8-4s of 1937–44, the later versions of the Challenger four-cylinder 4-6-6-4s of 1941–47, and the Big Boys of 1941–44. The FEFs were built in three batches, each an improvement on the first. It remains a wonder that FEF-3 844, the last of the series, and the last steam locomotive to be built for the Union Pacific, has never been retired from service. Today, this superb machine continues to run special passenger trains, and the occasional freight service, throughout and beyond the Union Pacific's extensive network. Designed for 100 mph running, and capable of at least 110 mph, this 5,500 ihp locomotive weighs 220 tons, its two 25 × 32 in cylinders packing a colossal 50 ton punch as they move trains away from rest.

On 14 March 1990, 844 worked a train of US veterans to Abilene in Kansas as part of the hundredth anniversary celebrations of the birth of Dwight D. Eisenhower, the Supreme Allied Commander in Europe at the time of D-Day, when the Union Pacific 4-8-4 was taking shape at Schenectady. There it stood close by the Gresley A4 Pacific 60008 *Dwight D. Eisenhower*; the British locomotive looked liked an 00-scale model in comparison. Everything about US locomotives and US railroading was built on a heroic scale, as if these companies and the machines that worked them were an outward sign of the American belief in 'manifest destiny' as the nation explored and conquered territory after territory from the Atlantic to the Pacific coast.

Jabelmann was a big character in every way. Born in Cheyenne, Wyoming, he joined the Union Pacific at the age of sixteen. His first job was to wake up crews to get them to the roundhouse on time. Working his way up the ranks, and with four years out to study mechanical engineering at Michigan and Stanford universities, Jabelmann rose from roundhouse superintendent at Cheyenne to become the Union Pacific's assistant general superintendent of motive power and machinery and, in 1936, head of a newly established department of research and mechanical standards; he became a vice president of the company in 1939.

'He was not endowed,' said a Union Pacific obituary, 'with the gift of eloquence and the results he accomplished were through tireless toil, indomitable courage, and an amazing intellect that won the respect and admiration of his legion of friends and associates.' In his swashbuckling and detailed history of the Union Pacific, Maury Klein describes Jabelmann as 'a tough, dour mechanical genius', a burly man with a prominent nose, 'who fired people almost as fast as Jeffers [Union Pacific's president] when they didn't meet his exacting standards'. The impression is of one of those people known, for better or worse, as 'forces of nature'. One Union Pacific shop-man described him as 'very, very bright' but 'probably the meanest man that was ever in the mechanical department'. Another recalled: 'He'd come in there and you better know what you was talkin' about. If you didn't, you was going to get your butt reamed.'

Working sixty-hour weeks, Jabelmann was on a mission, led by the railroad's dynamic William M. Jeffers. The son of first-generation Irish immigrants, Jeffers had started out, like Jabelmann, as a 'caller' at the tender age of fourteen; the two men were naturally close. The Union Pacific had been reconstituted in 1936, when the company took in a number of smaller railroads, and the following year Jeffers became president. Keen to create a highly effective modern railway, Jeffers took a keen interest not just in the way in which the Union Pacific performed, but in the way it looked. Its armour-yellow internal-combustion streamliners, black and anthracite steam locomotives, and the exemplary modern graphics it applied to both engines and trains, date from this period.

Jabelmann was not exclusively a steam man; what interested him was efficiency. He played a key role in the design of the Union Pacific's first streamliner, the M-10000 *City of Salina*, before he got a grip on the articulated freight locomotives and the 4-8-4s. A 100 mph lightweight aluminium Pullman, which toured sixty-eight US cities and was seen by over a million people before it went into service in 1934 between Kansas City and Salina, the *City of Salina* was a glimpse of a future that never quite took off. Powered by a 600 hp Winton distilled-fuel engine – diesel-electrics were on the way – this bright-yellow train made a big publicity splash and was followed by seven more Union Pacific streamliners, yet it was never really more than a sideshow. It was scrapped in 1942. Jabelmann's research department was staffed with experts in alloys, fuels, and lubricants. When the United States went to war in 1941, the Union Pacific was to play a major role working essential supply trains from the west to the east coast; the reliability as well as the sheer power of its new locomotives were the product of good initial design combined with expert maintenance, using the latest tools, techniques, and materials, some derived from experience with new forms of motive power and traction.

The Challengers emerged from a close collaboration between the Union Pacific's veteran general mechanical engineer, Arthur H. Fetters, Jabelmann, and Alco. The general layout of an articulated 4-6-6-4 which could work both high-speed freight and the heaviest passenger trains was laid down by late 1934. What the Union Pacific engineers had learned over the past few years was that it was one thing to build locomotives with a high nominal tractive effort to tackle heavy trains over steep hills, but it was quite another to build engines capable of producing and sustaining high rates of horsepower. It was horsepower that would give the Union Pacific the speed it wanted radically to transform the rate at which it moved heavy traffic through the Midwest and to raise productivity to unprecedented levels.

The first fifteen Challengers certainly boasted a high tractive effort – 97,400 lb – but were not as powerful as Jabelmann, in particular, wanted them to be. The later engines were modified with new exhaust ports, steam connections, hollow pistons, and lightweight valve gear, all designed to make the locomotives steam easily and freely. To watch one of these powerful engines – 3985 is preserved by the Union Pacific and runs special trains – from a car running parallel to the tracks at 70 mph is a thrilling yet almost perplexing sight; the Challenger's valve gear seems almost dainty, clicking away like sewing needles, while the locomotive rolls effortlessly and magisterially across the plains. Jabelmann had the wartime locomotive fitted with a new tapered boiler pressed to 280 psi, rather than the earlier 255 psi, a multiple blast-pipe – the 'pepperbox nozzle' designed by Leonard Botterton, one of his staff – roller bearings, Boxpok driving wheels, cast-steel frames, improved suspension and lubrication, and bigger, fourteen-wheeled tenders. Still further improvements were made to the last series of Challengers and some coal-burners were fitted with smoke deflectors which made them look even more modern and powerful than they were. On the Union Pacific's racing ground between Riverside and Los Angeles, these giants were recorded at up to 84 mph.

Challengers were also built by Alco for other US railroads, although naturally the Union Pacific was the biggest taker, with 105 out of the total of 252 engines built. The Union Pacific locomotives were withdrawn between January 1959 and July 1962. The Challengers had been a fine investment. The Big Boys followed, but the hurried effort to get these 4-8-8-4s out on the road undermined Jabelmann's health; in June 1941 he suffered a heart attack. In November 1942 he sailed to England as part of the newly formed US Transportation Corps to help with the pressing issue of locomotive maintenance. As no doctor in Omaha, the Union Pacific's home town, would let him go, Jabelmann took himself off to New York where a doctor gave him the necessary approval. He got to England, but on 6 January 1943 he dropped dead. He left a wife, Teresa Schauer, whom he had married in 1927, and he was missed by Jeffers and by fellow members of the Tangier Temple of the Ancient Arabic Order of the Nobles of the Mystic Shrine in Omaha, if not necessarily by some of those who had worked under this demanding and pugnacious man.

Perhaps the most extraordinary thing, though, about this giant of North American steam has to do with the suggestion made by William

W. Kratville in *The Challenger Locomotives* (1980) that Jabelmann was opposed to the idea of designing the very locomotives that made his name a legend in railway circles. 'It was Jabelmann,' Kratville writes, 'who, despite his affection for steam, had already opted for diesels by the time of the second big Challenger order, but the war prevented the change. It was well known that he would never have supported the new Challengers, Northerns [4-8-4s], or Big Boys because he could already see the diesel's advantage and he was often referred to as being "ten years ahead of his time".'

The diesel locomotive was certainly to push steam from US railroads in a remarkably short space of time. In June 1936, the Electro-Motive Division of General Motors began building diesel-electric locomotives at its new plant at La Grange, Illinois. By May 1952, diesel-electrics outnumbered steam locomotives, and by July 1961 there were no steam engines operating on class 1 US railroads. There were several key reasons for this, as we will discover, yet what is so extraordinary to the steam enthusiast is the way in which this revolution occurred at the very same time as the American steam locomotive itself had reached Olympian levels of power, speed, and endurance.

There had been a clearly recognizable and self-conscious era of super-power steam, beginning in 1925 when Lima's revelatory 2-8-4 prototype A-1 took to the rails, and ending with the Big Boys and other mountainous articulated freight engines and the long-distance express passenger engines of the New York Central and Pennsylvania Railroads in the immediate aftermath of the Second World War. Lima itself was to build its last steam locomotives – a batch of ten two-cylinder 2-8-4s for the Nickel Plate Road (the New York, Chicago & St. Louis Railroad) – in spring 1949, just a quarter of a century after the famous Ohio works had demonstrated that there was energetic new life to be had from the steam locomotive.

These twenty-five years were the glory days of North American steam. The size, power, speed, and sheer effect and glamour of the locomotives produced in this period were second to none. But these engineering wonders of the world were to prove short-lived. A comparison might be made between the last great commercial sailing ships – the clippers – or the last generation of piston-engine aircraft – the Britannias and Super-Constellations – and these glorious locomotives: they appeared at the very time that newer technologies were about to supersede them. Even then, perhaps there should have been contingency plans for new generations of US steam locomotives when the political cost and market price of oil disturbed the apparently smooth course of diesel railroading.

Super-power steam was the invention of William E. Woodard. The term 'super power' was the happy invention of Lima's advertising and public relations consultants. The genesis of A-1 came out of a drive to make the American steam locomotive very much more efficient than it had been to date. The design was intended to save coal in an era of economic uncertainty and the rising power of the United Mine Workers of America, the trade union whose successful efforts to boost its members' pay and better their working conditions had pushed up the price of coal by leaps and bounds. It was also prompted by a desire to increase the average speed of trains, which, for the most part, was very low across the United States at the very time that the automobile, along with the truck and long-distance bus, was seriously challenging the once indomitable position of the railroads. If the railroads were seen as complacent, it was Woodard's job to dispel that image.

Born in Utica, New York, Woodard was educated at Cornell University before joining the Baldwin locomotive works in Philadelphia. He moved on rapidly through Cramp's Shipyard, also in Philadelphia, and the Dickson Locomotive Works in Scranton, Pennsylvania, before being appointed chief draughtsman at the Schenectady Locomotive Company. This became Alco in 1916, when Woodard left to join Lima, the great Ohio locomotive factory, as vice president in charge of engineering.

A-1 was the result of progressive development over several years. 'My vision of the locomotive of the near future,' said Woodard in a talk to the New York Railway Club in January 1925, 'is one with a high boiler pressure, cylinders capable of developing from 3,000 to 3,500 hp, with a boiler and fire-box capable of producing an adequate amount of steam for the cylinders in an economic manner. Such locomotives will have larger fire-boxes than we have been accustomed to use. The coal will be burned at a low rate of combustion, to give a higher boiler efficiency. They will have a large gas area through flues and tubes to match the fire-box.' Evidently, Woodard had learned to see the steam locomotive as more of an organic whole than an assembly of components. This was something that, in France, Chapelon had understood. Here was the leap of the imagination that transformed the steam railway locomotive into a highly effective, very powerful and fast machine in the years leading up to the Second World War.

The visionary engine that appeared a month later was a 174 ton two-cylinder 2-8-4 – the first of this wheel arrangement, known as a 'Berkshire' – with cast-steel cylinders, a 100 sq ft grate, a high degree of superheating, streamlined internal steam passages, a feedwater heater to maintain a high temperature in the boiler as it was being refilled from the tender, a new type of ash-pan, a booster unit working on the trailing truck adding 13,500 lb to a tractive effort of 69,500 lb, and a host of other improvements. A-1 lived up to its name. It was first put on test on a very demanding 60 mile stretch of the New York Central Railroad between Selkirk and Washington, Massachusetts, in April 1925. On 14 April it was started eastbound from Selkirk at the head of a train of fifty-four freight cars, weighing 2,296 tons, 45 minutes behind one of Woodard's new H10b 2-8-2s, built by Alco, working a forty-six-car train of 1,691 tons. A-1 gained steadily on the lighter train.

By Chatham, New York, the two were running side by side. It must have been a thrilling sight. West of Canaan, and now 26 miles from Selkirk, A-1 pulled clear. By the time she stopped at North Adams junction, 20 miles down the line, she was 10 minutes ahead of the 2-8-2. Developing up to 3,675 ihp and 3,385 dbhp, A-1 was clearly a highly potent and markedly efficient machine, and used some 20 per cent less coal and water than the H10b during this test run. The 2-8-4 was subsequently demonstrated on a number of railroads and, from then until the end of steam, the Lima 2-8-4, along with variants built by other companies, became the closest thing to a US standard design.

The following year, Woodard built ten I1A 2-10-4s for the Texas and Pacific Railway. Making greater use of cast steel and with detailed improvements over A-1, the 4,200 ihp Texas 2-10-4s proved able, on a daily basis at work on the 450 mile Marshall to Big Springs line, to work trains 44 per cent heavier than the company's existing 2-10-2s, at 33 per cent higher speeds, while consuming 43 per cent less fuel. On the level, they pulled trains of up to seventy freight cars, weighing 2,750 tons, at 50 mph.

These were extraordinary figures by any standards. In its early days at least, Woodard's revolution was the American equivalent of Chapelon's in France in the late 1920s. The difference, though, between the two was in Chapelon's critical and scientific understanding of steam flow and the importance of a free-flowing exhaust. He calculated that a New York Central Niagara class 4-8-4 and a Pennsylvania Railroad 4-4-4-4 both needed 1,400 ihp simply to create the necessary draught from fire-box to smoke-box, because of the strong back-pressure engendered by their restricted exhaust from cylinder through blast-pipe to chimney. With the Chapelon treatment, including a Kylchap exhaust, the French engineer believed a Niagara could have produced 7,800 ihp at 100 mph – well above the 6,600 ihp recorded at 85 mph – with power peaking at 8,090 ihp at 120 mph. If he had been able to get his hands on the Big Boys, Chapelon claimed, he could have increased their power output to 12,000 dbhp with compound drive, a boiler-barrel preheater, and a boiler pressure of 330 psi. With a water-tube boiler pressed to 600 psi, triple-expansion drive, steam jackets, and re-superheating, power could be boosted to 16,000 dbhp. The mind boggles.

Woodard's insistence that horsepower was all-important for fast modern trains pushed on a very rapid development of high-speed steam locomotives and trains in the United States in the 1930s. The debut of his 2-8-4 A-1 coincided with the *Exposition international des arts décoratifs et industriels modernes* held in Paris in 1925. This event gave rise to art deco design and a fresh sense of elegant, luxurious modernity, the new spirit going hand in hand with jazz, streamlining, and the quest for speed. That this should all gel a few years later in the shadow of the Wall Street Crash might seem at first incomprehensible, but the new mood was also an escape into the future. It proved to be very short-lived; no sooner had it gathered momentum than the world was plunged into a savage war.

Cultural and economic imperatives aside, there were good technical reasons why steam sped up so very dramatically in the 1930s. One of these was the roller bearing. In 1929, after working hard without success to get an American railway to buy these for use on locomotives, the Timken Roller Bearing Company of Canton, Ohio, bought a 4-8-4 from Alco. Over the course of twenty-one months the *Four Aces* toured thirteen main lines, running a total of 119,600 miles without a single bearing overheating; until then, bearings had been an Achilles heel of the steam locomotive. In Chicago Union station, three young female office workers even pulled *Four Aces* a few feet along the track. This was no feat of magic: the rolling resistance of a locomotive fitted with roller bearings was 10 oz per ton.

The first really powerful and potentially very fast express passenger locomotives built in the US were the Hudson 4-6-4s designed by Paul W. Kiefer for the New York Central Railroad. Born in Delaware, Ohio, Kiefer studied at night school at the Cleveland YMCA before attending the Central Institute in Cleveland. Serving an apprenticeship as a machinist with the Lake Shore and Michigan Southern Railway from 1907, he moved on to the New York Central Railroad, where he was the company's representative at Baldwin and Alco. He was posted to the New York design office, rising to the position of chief motive power engineer in 1926. His first, and immediate, job was to work up the design of a new express passenger engine to take over crack trains on the company's famous Water Level Route to Chicago. This beautifully aligned and well-maintained line, much of it four-track, ran north from New York's Grand Central station up the Hudson river to Albany before heading west to Buffalo and along the shores of Lake Erie to Cleveland and through Toledo to Chicago's La Salle Street station, 960 miles from Manhattan. If the line was ideal for consistently fast running, its loading gauge was more restrictive than on most US railways, so its locomotives were always that bit more compact than their rivals.

The New York Central's route to Chicago was in direct competition with the Pennsylvania Railroad, for many decades the biggest of the US railroads and one of the world's largest business corporations. The 'Pennsy's' route headed south from Manhattan from the railroad's stunning terminus, a recreation of sorts by the architects McKim Meade and White of the ancient Roman Baths of Caracalla, attached to a magnificent train shed. (The building was foolishly demolished in 1961 and New York has never been able to forgive itself.) It ran on to Philadelphia, where the railway was based, and then west through Harrisburg and Altoona, where the Pennsy built its own engines, to Pittsburgh, Lima and Fort Wayne, and so into Chicago Union station, 903 miles from New York.

Traffic on these lines was extremely busy, a mix of heavy mineral and fast passenger trains, running through a vast coal belt. By the late 1920s, such was the weight of the new and luxurious trains coming into service that the New York Central's Pacifics were unable to cope with the demands being placed on them. Looking to Woodard's work at Lima, Kiefer schemed up a big, two-cylinder 4-6-4. Built by Alco, the first engine was assembled in nine days flat and delivered to the railroad on 14 February 1927. It was felt that this new type of locomotive merited a name. In an interview conducted in 1961 with Alvin F. Staufer, author of numerous books on American steam, Kiefer recalled: 'I asked Pat [Patrick E. Cowley, the New York Central's president] if we should name the engine or if he cared about that at all.

We were already calling the L class 4-8-2s Mohawks, after the Mohawk Valley and Indians. And then, I'll never forget that moment. He just looked at me; the sun was shining in from the west, it was late in the day. He swung around in his huge brown leather chair away from me. He stared out of the window for the longest time. He swung back and stared at me, his chin in his hand. Finally he spoke. "Let's call her the Hudson, after the Hudson river." I agreed immediately and that's how it was. The name stuck. It was a natural.'

Kiefer went on to oversee the design and construction of 275 Hudsons, in three closely related classes, for the New York Central Railroad. The last were the J3a series, elegantly streamlined by the industrial designer Henry Dreyfuss, who was as well known for his Big Ben alarm clocks for Westclox and vacuum cleaners for Hoover as for the look of ocean liners and trains. The Hudsons were initially fitted with boosters to enable them to start powerfully away from stops, as 4-6-4s had relatively little weight over their driving wheels for adhesion; they were always best as sprinters. Perhaps a little curiously, and despite the compelling streamlining of the J3a – which was assigned to work the famous long-distance express, the 20th Century Limited, at its zenith in the late 1930s – the New York Central's line limit was a carefully observed 85 mph. But to average a mile-a-minute, including five stops, from New York to Chicago was still impressive going, especially as a single locomotive ran the entire distance – or nearly the entire distance: the first 33 miles from Grand Central station had been electrified in 1907 when steam was banned from the city.

On test, the first J1, 5200, was able to sustain 75 mph and 4,300 ihp on the level with twenty-six coaches, weighing 1,700 tons. This made the class 27 per cent more powerful than the Pacifics they replaced, and they ran up to 18,000 miles per month, something few other railway locomotives, anywhere in the world, were asked to do. Kiefer was proving to be an expert in the design of large locomotives that could run hard, far, and fast. The J3a class of 1938, with a higher boiler pressure (275 psi in place of 225 psi) and many detailed improvements, could sustain 4,700 ihp. On test, a J3a was timed at 100 mph on level track with a train of 696 tons.

When the new-look 20th Century Limited entered service on 15 June 1938, the New York Central had shaped what surely must be the finest long-distance express train of the steam era. There were faster trains, but, from nose to tail, this superb expression of 1930s streamlining was very hard to beat. Its thirteen air-conditioned Pullman cars were painted two-tone grey, as were the Hudsons. They included double-bedded sleeping compartments, more exclusive 'roomettes' with private lavatories, a cocktail bar, dining car, barber's shop, and an observation car complete with a 'de-luxe suite' with its own living room, bedroom, and bathroom. Inside, Dreyfuss designed every last detail, from carpets and seat fabrics to napery, crockery, and menus. The last of these, printed in red with a graphic image of a stylised J3a on the cover, offers a Martini cocktail for 40 cents (make mine an Old Fashioned for 10 cents more), genuine Russian caviar on toast for $1.00 and – the most expensive item on a remarkably comprehensive list, complete with a variety of fresh salads and vegetarian options – Lobster Newburg 20th Century, with new wax beans fermière and julienne potatoes, at $2.25.

Drinks and dinner were served as the express cruised smoothly at the line limit, speedometers glowing from the carriage walls. As dusk fell, the locomotive's disc wheels were lit from inside the frames, casting a glow – beautiful in winter – around the train. After dinner, the dining car became a bar where swing and jazz were played from gramophones. Meanwhile, engaging advertising – always with the locomotives on show – stressed both comfort and glamour. The very first adverts posted in New York in 1938 boasted: 'It's Century time! A moment ago, outside the station, you were in the heart of a great city, with crowds, blaring taxis, newsboys shouting the evening headlines. Now you're in a different world as you follow that crimson carpet down the platform at Grand Central Terminal toward the softly

lighted, streamlined cars that will be your club on wheels for tonight.'
As for who else might be on the train, the advert was equally enticing:
'There is a fascination about your "dinner of the century". For nearby
may be a face you last saw in Technicolor, or one that would be news
on any financial page.'

With the 20th Century Limited, the New York Central had proved
that steam could indeed enjoy a new image. Diesels nudged their oily
way into service on the 20th Century Limited from 1945, although at
that time the train might just as commonly be hauled by a Hudson or
one of Kiefer's latest Niagara 4-8-4s as by a pair of new Electro-Motive
E7 diesel units. In 1945 the J3a locomotives lost the last of their
streamline casings, even though these had been carefully designed
to allow easy access to pistons and valve gear; they were easy to spot,
however, by their striking Scullin double-disc or Boxpok wheels.

For sheer speed, the rival Pennsylvania Railroad was always
faster than the New York Central. In fact, the high average speeds
maintained by even some of its veteran engines in the late 1930s
were positively eye-opening. In 1938, Donald Steffee recorded a run
on the Chicago Arrow, a fast, light train from Detroit. The five-car,
350 ton train was worked by 1649, one of eighty-three two-cylinder
E6 Atlantics designed by Alfred W. Gibbs, the Pennsylvania Railroad's
chief mechanical engineer, and built between 1910 and 1914. The
125 ton locomotive ran the 140.9 mile section between Fort Wayne
and Englewood, outside Chicago, in 113 minutes and 5 seconds – 2
minutes ahead of a very tight schedule – at an average speed of 74.3
mph, with a maximum of 93 mph.

As a vehicle, the steam locomotive is well suited to high-speed
running. From 29 May 1935, anyone travelling from Chicago to the
Twin Cities of Saint Paul and Minneapolis, Minnesota, by the brand-
new Hiawatha streamlined express of the Chicago, Milwaukee, St.
Paul and Pacific Railroad – known as the Milwaukee Road – discovered
just how fast steam trains could be. Here was the world's first steam
train designed to cruise at 100 mph, backed by a brilliant advertising

campaign – 'The Milwaukee Road presents the first of the Speedliners' – by Chicago's Roche, Williams & Cunnyngham.

The Milwaukee Road competed for passenger traffic between Chicago and the Twin Cities with two other first-class railways, the Chicago and North Western Transportation Company and the Chicago, Burlington & Quincy Railroad. Inevitably, there was an intense rivalry among the three, although a gentleman's agreement kept their schedules in tandem until the Milwaukee Road suddenly increased the running speed of its Hiawathas to 105 mph and introducing a sixty-minute schedule for the 85.6 miles between Chicago and Milwaukee.

On 2 January 1935, the Chicago and North Western introduced its 400 service, a train designed to run the 400 miles between Chicago and the Twin Cities in 400 minutes. At first the service was a little bit slower than over the Milwaukee Road's 408 miles, but in May a 6½ hour schedule was in force, maintained by four E2-a Pacifics, upgrades of a batch of ten engines built by Alco in 1923. Bereft of streamlining they may have been, yet these veterans could certainly move. In autumn 1935, one of the four is said to have run the 85 miles from Milwaukee to Chicago in 65 minutes, reaching 108 mph in the process. It may well have done.

On 21 April 1935, the Chicago, Burlington & Quincy's Twin Cities Zephyr pulled out of Chicago for the first time on its 427 mile route to the Twin Cities. This three-car, shot-welded, and streamlined stainless-steel diesel service was allowed six hours for the run, at an average speed of 71 mph. The pioneer Zephyr built the previous year by the Budd Company had already been timed at 112.5 mph. New six-car trains followed in 1936.

The Milwaukee Road had a lot to live up to. Its Hiawathas, though, were fleet of foot from the word go. On 15 May, on a trial run from Milwaukee to New Lisbon, with engineer Donahue at the controls of the new streamlined Atlantic No. 1, the train was run up to 112.5 mph. A special preview trip for 250 members of the Chicago Traffic Club saw the mercurial 4-4-2 holding a speed of 106 to 108 mph for twenty miles between Deerfield and Playfair, Illinois, on its way back to Chicago. The first grey, maroon, and orange service trains ran like clockwork and were extremely popular with the public; on 14 July, the *Chicago Tribune* ran a story about the crowds gathered at wayside crossings to watch the Hiawatha steam through in a blur of whirring rods. It was headlined 'Throngs Thrilled Nightly as Rail Flyer Races By'. Adverts for the new train taken out in newspapers roared: 'A silver and orange flash . . . America's first completely streamlined super-speed steam locomotive. Designed and built especially for the Hiawatha. Nothing faster on rails.' They also claimed that the oil-burning locomotive 'cruises easily at 100 miles per hour and is capable of a top speed of two miles a minute'. Was it?

The Hiawatha Atlantics, and indeed the trains themselves, were designed and built very quickly. The Milwaukee Road needed a simple and reliable locomotive that could run at very high speed without the expense of upgrading signalling and track. Its mechanical engineer, Charles H. Bilty, who had started out with the Milwaukee Road as an apprentice machinist in 1893 and stuck with it until he retired in 1943, had been very impressed by the fast running of the Pennsy's E6 Atlantics. He was happy with what seemed like an antiquated wheel arrangement – the 4-4-2 – because he wanted a light and fast engine for light and fast trains. The Hiawatha Atlantics would be expected to do nothing more than fly along with seven-car streamliners; they would haul no stopping passenger trains and certainly no freight trains.

Working with Alco, Bilty configured the new 125 ton, two-cylinder A class Atlantics – the first in the USA for twenty years – which featured high-pressure boilers (300 psi), roller bearings, Boxpok wheels, lightweight valve gear and coupling rods, and 7 ft 0 in driving wheels. Cylinders were 19 × 28 in and tractive effort was 30,700 lb. The streamline casing was partly the product of wind-tunnel tests carried out at New York University and partly a matter of style. Somewhere in the development of the Hiawatha, Otto Kuhler, the German-born industrial artist, worked his way into the Milwaukee Road's design team. Already working as an advertising consultant to Alco, Kuhler was to become an important part of the Hiawatha as the train grew in size and needed new locomotives and carriages within just sixteen months of its launch.

In practice, the A class Atlantics proved to be very fast. They needed to be. Aside from its five intermediate stops, some extended because of the need to take on water, the Hiawatha was faced with no fewer than fifty-eight service restrictions on its 410.1 mile run, twenty-three of them demanding that the train slow to below 60 mph. On a typical trip, recorded by Baron Vuillet on 15 June 1937, A1 No. 4, with 415 tons in tow, gained 24.5 minutes against the schedule, running at up to 106 mph, and running freely on the level at 100 mph with full regulator and 28 per cent cut-off. Vuillet described the trip as 'mainly a series of extremely energetic recoveries from slacks', with No. 4 demonstrating formidable acceleration at speeds above 60 mph. Throughout the journey, full pressure was maintained. 'The locomotive rode remarkably well,' Vuillet noted. 'At 96 mph I wrote my notes conveniently standing up and not leaning against anything. At 106 mph I took them quite comfortably, sitting down.'

The Milwaukee Road's track was excellent, with canted curves designed to be taken at a theoretical maximum of 116 mph. In a throwaway line in his *Railway Reminiscences of Three Continents*, Vuillet says: 'When tested on practically level track, a maximum speed of 125 mph was reached with six cars (310 tons).' It is hard to know for certain just how fast these well-balanced, two-cylinder locomotives were. They were rated at a maximum 3,450 ihp at 60 mph, tailing off to 2,700 ihp at 100 mph. Given that the braking distance of the Hiawathas was nearly two miles from 100 mph, perhaps no one was ever willing to go faster than the officially credited 112.5 mph. But, with a train as light as that of *Mallard* or the German 05 002, in proportion to the weight of the locomotive, it seems very likely that a Class A Atlantic could have topped 120 mph comfortably.

In August 1938, the Hiawatha Atlantics were replaced by much bigger two-cylinder F7 class Hudsons. The Hiawatha was now to be a heavier and even faster train, while the four A class engines were used to accelerate services elsewhere on the Milwaukee Road; they were withdrawn and scrapped in 1950–1. Six elegant class F7 4-6-4s were built by Alco, with design input from Bilty and his team, and styled by Kuhler; they even carried plates bearing the legend 'Speedlined by Kuhler'. The 153 ton locomotives boasted 23.5 × 30 in cylinders, 7 ft 0 in driving wheels, a 96.5 sq ft grate, and a boiler pressure of 300 psi. Tractive effort was 50,294 lb. Much use was made of steel casting, welding, roller bearings, and thermic siphons – two of them – to ensure a robust, easy-steaming, and free-running engine. The scale and power of these engines made the Hiawatha expresses a relatively easy proposition, compared with hauling heavy passenger trains. The coal-fired Hudsons, however, were designed to work all major Milwaukee Road expresses, no matter what the load; in this respect they were quite different machines from the Atlantics, which were custom-built for the lightweight streamliners.

In practice, the F7s could maintain the newly accelerated Hiawatha schedules with up to sixteen lightweight cars and run fast with twenty-car trains of standard heavy American passenger stock. During 1943, with a Hiawatha made up to the full sixteen cars, weighing 780 tons, an F7 ran the 85.6 miles from Milwaukee to Chicago in 63 minutes. The first 12 miles were covered in 12 minutes; the following 60 miles were reeled off in 37 minutes, at an average of 100.7 mph, with speed held between 99.5 and 102.5 mph. It was because such running was achieved so readily, and with low maintenance costs, that the Milwaukee Road proposed a sixty-minute schedule for the 85.6 miles between Chicago and Milwaukee – it could have been done, day in, day out. The Milwaukee Road's fastest schedule was the Morning Hiawatha taking 58 minutes for the 78.3 miles from Sparta to Portage, at 81 mph. It was the fastest steam timetable in the world, and it was never beaten.

One of these runs, the eastbound Morning Hiawatha, was timed by Eric Crickmay in 1940 with F7 No. 100 hauling a nine-coach train, weighing 465 tons (the equivalent in locomotive-to-train weight of an LNER A4 in charge of the King's Cross to Edinburgh Coronation streamliner). The Sparta to Portage section was run nicely on time, as was the entire journey with its seven intermediate stops and lightning acceleration away from each. The first 13 miles out of Sparta were allowed 12 minutes, despite a 9.75 mile climb away from the station at between 1-in-150 and 1-in-200, and two restrictions to 40 mph, but the F7 charged up this gradient at 80 to 82 mph. The pace and power were phenomenal. Crickway was further rewarded on his journey with three separate spells of sustained running at over 100 mph.

Rather frustratingly, Baron Vuillet had this to say of the maximum speed potential of the F7s: 'The load of the Hiawatha was at first increased to twelve cars (550 tons) but with such a load it was found that "the schedules were not fast enough to bring out the best performance of the engines". After accelerating to 105 mph . . . 25 per cent cut-off was sufficient for maintaining the required speed. With very little effort 120 mph was averaged for 4.5 miles on practically level track, the maximum speed being 125 mph.' Although we are never likely to know just how fast the Milwaukee Road Hudsons were, what we can be certain of is that these truly brilliant locomotives ran every day at between 100 and 110 mph; there is nothing in the annals of steam to compare with this marathon. Today, it is hard to imagine quite what it must have been like seventy years ago to stand by an ungated crossing somewhere out in the sticks watching one of these streamliners howl by. It seems sad that the steam Hiawathas were so short-lived; diesels made their appearance in 1951, the year that the last of the six Hudsons (or Baltics as Bilty insisted on calling them) was withdrawn. No Milwaukee Road streamliners were preserved.

As to just how fast an American steam locomotive ran, the jury is out and will probably remain so. Claims as wild as the West itself were very much a part of US railway lore, yet because few high-speed trains, even by the late 1930s, were accompanied by a dynamometer car, they could never be proved scientifically. It is just possible, though, that the Pennsylvania Railroad's unique four-cylinder S1 6-4-4-6, a duplex locomotive – two sets of cylinders and running gear mounted one behind the other underneath the boiler – built at the company's Altoona plant in 1939 for the New York World's Fair, may have outpaced an F7. Streamlined by Raymond Loewy, 6100 was the largest and, at 140 feet, certainly the longest passenger locomotive ever built. She was very powerful – about 7,000 ihp – and rode well, but because of her great size was restricted to the Pennsy mainline between Chicago and Crestline, Ohio. She was often seen at the head of such crack Chicago to New York trains as the General, the Trailblazer, and the Broadway Limited. In its December 1941 issue, *Popular Mechanics* claimed 133.4 mph for 6100 over this route. In March 1946, it was said to have topped 141 mph, and there were even claims of 156 mph. And what about 120 mph on the level with 1,600 tons? This would have demanded a far greater power output – something like 10,500 ihp – than the S1 was capable of. But, as the S1 was taken out of service in 1945 and scrapped four years later, all these claims remain the stuff of railway legend and superheated debate among steam enthusiasts.

More important than sheer speed in the late 1930s was the development of high speed and great power produced consistently over long runs. The work of Kiefer on the New York Central Railroad and of Jabelmann working with Alco resulted in some of the greatest of all US steam locomotives. Among these were the engines that met the new General Motors and General Electric diesels head-on in the aftermath of the Second World War. These were complemented by the controversial T-1 duplex locomotives built under the direction of William Kiesel at Altoona for the Pennsylvania Railroad, and the Norfolk and Western Railway's superb J class 4-8-4s.

The 4-8-4s, of which more than nine hundred were built by and for thirty-one US railroads, became the ultimate expression of super-power steam. This wheel arrangement offered a four-wheel leading truck for good riding at speed, eight driving wheels for traction, and a four-wheel trailing truck over which was slung a very large and deep fire-box, heating a very large boiler. The very first 4-8-4s were a batch of twelve for the Northern Pacific Railway – skirting the Canadian border from the Great Lakes to the Pacific – built by Alco in 1926–7. These locomotives gave their name to the type: Northerns. The Northern was developed steadily through the 1930s and during the Second World War.

The biggest American 4-8-4 was built by Baldwin at its Philadelphia works in three batches between 1938 and 1944 for the Atchison, Topeka and Santa Fe Railway, known as the Santa Fe. The engineer in chief at Baldwin was Ralph P. Johnson, author of *The Steam Locomotive: Its Theory, Operation and Economics* (1942). These 228 ton engines worked the heavy Santa Fe sleeping-car expresses from Chicago to San Francisco and Los Angeles west of La Junta, Colorado. This was difficult territory for trains of any sort, up and down through the see-saw mountain ranges of the continental divide and blazing deserts where there was precious little water. The gradients were so trying – up to 1-in-28.5 – that the Santa Fe's diesel streamliners sometimes had to be helped up them by the 4-8-4s; this must have been a wonderfully incongruous sight.

The Santa Fe 3765 class Northerns were oil-burners, equipped with 55 foot tenders which alone weighed 201.5 tons. They ran vast mileages. Arriving at Los Angeles after a through trip from La Junta – 1,234 miles – or even from Kansas City – 1,788 miles – they could be turned around in six hours and sent back east. Remarkably, given the long mountain gradients they had to climb, the Santa Fe Northerns were fitted with 6 ft 8 in driving wheels. But with 28 × 32 in cylinders, and boilers with a diameter of 8 ft 6 in pressed to 300 psi, they had a tractive effort of 66,000 lb and could sustain 5,500 ihp. They could also run at 100 mph wherever permitted by the track alignment or the railway's civil engineer. They certainly reached this speed on the 22 mile 1-in-91 downhill stretch west of Kingman on the 148.7 mile descent from Seligman, Arizona, to Needles, California, in the Mojave Desert.

The Northerns had to climb back the other way, of course, but they were outstanding hill-climbers. Cecil J. Allen cited a run with the westbound Chief express from Los Angeles with 3777 at the head of a fourteen-car train, weighing 780 tons. The 4-8-4 surmounted the 31 miles and 2,100 foot difference in altitude from Needles to Goffs 'with speed never once falling below 43½ mph, even up continuous 1-in-67 inclines'.

Goffs was once a busy desert peak town, created largely by the Santa Fe as a stop to water its engines. During the Second World War, when the 4-8-4s were at their busiest, some ten thousand US troops were stationed there at any one time. Today, Goffs is almost a ghost town, with the wind blowing the surrounding sands into ever-changing and hypnotic patterns. At times it can seem silent. When I stood there a few years ago – I had been driving the length of the legendary Route 66, which has bypassed the town for some years – I tried my best to imagine the sight and sound of one of these great 4-8-4s thundering up from the parched plains below, with its air-conditioned trainloads of Hollywood stars and business moguls heading west, iced cocktails in hand. Few Westerns of the time, with their galloping wagon trains, were as thrilling as these thunderous, long-distance expresses.

Over slightly easier terrain, Allen mentions a postal train weighing 1,590 tons sprinting the 134.5 miles from Dalies to Gallup, New Mexico, with a ruling gradient of 1-in-220, in 124 minutes. The slowest speed maintained uphill was 59 mph, with 90 mph and over wherever possible. Throughout the 80 mile uphill section, the 4-8-4 produced about 5,500 ihp. The Santa Fe was to make the most of its steam locomotives until the last of them was withdrawn in 1959.

The quest for athleticism and muscle had become something of an obsession for American railroads and their engineers in the late 1930s, as they aimed to meet ever more demanding requirements from their operating departments. In the event, their timing was spot-on, because when the war came in 1941, the country was to be well served by locomotives like the Santa Fe Northerns. In 1938, the Association of American Railroads conducted tests to see what horsepower was needed for a 1,000 US ton (892 imperial tons) passenger train to run on the level at 100 mph. And it wanted to know if any existing locomotive type was equal to this demanding target. The one locomotive that got close was the Jabelmann-Alco FEF 4-8-4 815, which reached 102.5 mph on a 1-in-500 to 1-in-2,000 falling gradient. In the reverse direction, 815 reached 89 mph.

A design developed during the war which could have managed this with ease was Kiefer's commanding Niagara class Northern for the New York Central Railroad. Designed jointly with and built by Alco, the Niagara was the biggest locomotive Kiefer could shoehorn into the New York Central's relatively restricted loading gauge; to keep within this, the steam dome, normally prominent on the crest of a locomotive's boiler, was replaced by a large internal steam-collector pipe. In his New York design office, Kiefer had drawn up plans for a prototype two-cylinder Niagara with interchangeable 6 ft 3 in and 6 ft 7 in driving wheels and a boiler pressure of either 275 or 290 psi, a four-cylinder 4-4-4-4 duplex, a 4-8-4 equipped with poppet rather than piston valves, and a standard production machine with 6 ft 7 in driving wheels, piston valves, and a 275 psi boiler. The duplex project was dropped early on, while tests were made on the other prototypes, which were soon joined by the first of the production engines.

There was not a great deal to choose between the variants. The production engines, class S1b, were thoroughly tested. They could produce a maximum 6,600 ihp at 85 mph and 5,050 dbhp at 62 mph, while their 8 ft 4 in diameter boilers generated steam at an impressive 110,000 lb per hour. Fitted with every possible labour-saving device, these 210 ton engines were as powerful and robust in everyday service as Kiefer and Alco had designed them to be. They ran heavy, fast, long-distance trains with easy competence and, with daily servicing reduced to two and a half hours, they were soon racking up 24,000 miles a month. The twenty-seven Niagaras were every bit as fast as, and exerted a much higher maximum power than, contemporary diesels, and even in terms of turnaround, maintenance, availability, and cost per mile, they ran the diesels that were to replace them within a decade a very close race indeed.

In June 1947, the Institution of Mechanical Engineers celebrated its centenary with events in London. These included a paper by Kiefer on the development, testing, and operation of rival forms of motive power on the New York Central Railroad. Back in New York, he had the paper published by the Steam Locomotive Research Institute as *A Practical Evaluation of Railroad Motive Power*. A copy of this small red book sits on my bookshelves between handsome illustrated tomes on American trains, locomotives, and railway history. It is a very prized volume indeed.

What Kiefer's book shows is just how close he came to making a case for modern super-power steam at the very moment that the diesel was about to take over – indeed, just a year before the New York Central itself declared an end to steam development, due, primarily, to the unreliability of coal supplies during the prolonged miners' strikes of 1946 and 1947. During 1946, six Niagaras were pitted against six 2,000 hp twin-unit E7 diesel-electric locomotives up and down the 928 mile Water Level route between Harmon, New York, and Chicago. The steam locomotives made 310 trips, the diesels 349, with fifteen coaches of air-conditioned stock weighing 1,005 US tons (897 imperial tons). Although the twin-unit diesels, which cost half as much again as a Niagara, could produce a maximum of 3,320 dbhp, compared to the 4-8-4s' 5,050 dbhp, the steam engines had been designed with a large degree of excess power capacity over that required in ordinary service; this was so that they could work the most demanding trains economically and be able to make up time easily if a service was held up for any reason.

The results really are nail-biting stuff. The acceleration tests remain fascinating. A Niagara could accelerate its train along level track from

0 to 60 mph in 3.5 minutes (the test reports were published using decimals), covering 2.1 miles as it did so. A twin-unit diesel-electric needed 4.73 minutes to reach the same speed, over 3.2 miles. Where the twin-unit diesel was up to 80 mph in 14.17 minutes over 14.8 miles, the Niagara was there in 6.36 minutes and 5.1 miles. A triple-unit diesel-electric could pip the 4-8-4 to 60 mph, in 3.06 minutes over 2 miles; but it was slower than the steam locomotive to 80 mph, taking 6.51 minutes and 6.1 miles; and way behind the Niagara as it stormed up to 100 mph, when the steam locomotive took 16.5 minutes and 21.3 miles, against the diesel-electric's 26.5 minutes and 37.8 miles. The Niagara was faster accelerating from delays, too, whether from 35 to 60 mph, 35 to 80 mph, or 60 to 80 mph – 2.86 minutes compared to the diesel's 3.45 minutes in the last instance.

Kiefer himself was careful to present a balanced picture. 'We have no sacred traditional standards, nor preconceived ideas or preferences with respect to the kinds of motive power used,' he wrote, 'but have striven to the limits of our collective abilities to provide units best suited to meet the changing necessities of transportation by rail in which numerous and varied problems are involved.' He was clearly proud of the Niagaras, although he made it clear that the long-term future lay with electric traction. He addressed the question of relative thermal efficiency, an issue often used by its critics to belittle the steam locomotive. Where a diesel-electric offered an overall efficiency of 22 per cent – that is, 22 per cent of the fuel it burned was converted into energy used to move a train – a steam locomotive could manage just 6 per cent. This figure does sound low – it was later doubled by Chapelon and Porta (see Chapter 7), and there is still a promise of greater things to come – but the diesel-electric appeared to be the better bet in terms of fuel usage. Even then, as Kiefer stressed: 'Although the overall thermal efficiency of the Diesel locomotive may be four to five times that of reciprocating steam, it should be recognized that without this advantage the cost of Diesel fuel oil would be prohibitive.'

With all the figures added up and computed, the total annual cost of the 4-8-4s was $1.22 per mile, and for the twin-unit diesels $1.11. Given that the price of diesel oil was to rise way above its 1946 level – and well above that of coal – the figures might have been in favour of the steam locomotive just a few years later. And if the New York Central Railroad had wanted to run even heavier or faster trains, then it would have been only fair to pit the Niagara against triple-unit diesel-electrics, producing 4,980 dhp, in which case the estimated cost per mile for the diesels would have risen to $1.48. Even then, three E7s were no match for a Niagara in full cry above 60 mph, when its drawbar horsepower was higher. However, it must be remembered that the low thermal efficiency of a Niagara meant that it burned three times the number of heat units for the same power output, so it would have needed a 50 per cent increase in the cost of oil above the 1946 price to equalize fuel costs.

Impressive though their showing was, the performance and economy of the Niagaras could have been improved. One abiding characteristic of so many US steam locomotives was the high exhaust pressure of their blast-pipes, which was necessary to produce sufficient draught for their high-output boilers. This resulted in power loss caused by back-pressure on the pistons and, partly as a result of this, the figure Kiefer cited for a Niagara of 16 lb steam to produce 1 ihp was higher than both the LNER A4 and LMS Coronation Pacifics, and considerably above the 11.2 lb of Chapelon's 5,500 ihp 242A1. If the 1,400 hp absorbed by draughting at maximum power in the Niagara could have been reduced to 500 hp by using a triple Kylchap exhaust – thereby reducing back-pressure – the locomotive could have produced a maximum of 7,500 ihp and used significantly less coal.

As it was, a series of annual coal strikes which began during the war led to large numbers of train cancellations in 1946 and again in 1947. The effect of these was so great that many railroads made the decision to drop their dependence on coal and to replace steam with diesel. The American railway press went so far as to describe the mining union's leader, John L. Lewis, as having done more to undermine steam than any living man. And the diesel lobby was anyway very much in the ascendant, armed with new business techniques which were to eliminate main-line steam within little more than a decade.

On a happier note, what was a Niagara like in regular service? I cherish a photocopy of an article, 'Riding a Niagara of the New York Central', written by Dr W. A. Tuplin, chief engineer of David Brown, a company specializing in the manufacture of gears and tractors, which went on to make the famous DB series of Aston Martin sports cars from 1947. '"Let's see it!" said the engineer from his seat ten feet above me after I had shouted that I had a permit to ride with him. After all, 7.30 on a Sunday morning is a strange time for a visitor, and the man in charge of the New York Central hauling the Mohawk from Buffalo to Albany was justifiably cautious about a proposed invasion of his eyrie. My letter from a Vice President immediately resolved his doubts.'

So up climbed the English engineer on to the spacious, almost room-like, footplate of Kiefer's finest. The 900 ton Mohawk was an express train from Chicago to New York, with forty points of call, booked to average 41 mph overall. Between these many stops, however, the big engine accelerated rapidly and was worked up to the line limit again and again, with mile-a-minute runs readily achieved between stations set as little as fifteen miles apart. All this was done with an easy competence that made the working of the Mohawk seem little more than a Sunday stroll.

So many things surprised Tuplin, a man who had ridden on the footplates of many British locomotives. At stations, the giant fire-bed – the mechanically stoked 8 × 12.5 ft grate – appeared to be lifeless, flaming into life only as the engineer, sitting comfortably in his leather-upholstered seat, controls ready at hand, cracked open the regulator and the exhaust draught set it ablaze. The exhaust seemed mild and tinny, while 'not even a turbine-driven engine could be expected to run any more smoothly than did the big two-cylinder engine, and no diesel locomotive is any easier to handle'. At 70 mph and above, the exhaust was all but inaudible, despite the fact that the Niagara was producing an average of 3,100 dbhp throughout the journey. Only once on his memorable ride did Tuplin hear the locomotive in any way extended, and that was as it climbed an 8 mile 1-in-132 gradient between the Mohawk river and the Hudson Valley. 'Although the engine appeared to be working in an effortless manner,' Tuplin enthused, 'the start-to-stop times on this journey were what would be regarded as phenomenal in Great Britain with an engine hauling five times her own weight.'

Plagued at one point by cracks in their silicon-steel boilers – designed to save 3 tons in weight – the Niagaras, refitted with normal carbon-steel boilers, were taken out of service between May 1955 and July 1956. On its last passenger run, with train No. 416 from Indianapolis to Cincinnati, 6015 left 34 minutes late, making up 28 minutes on the way. Clearly, it still retained a surplus of power. It had replaced a failed diesel. Sadly, no Niagara was preserved.

The Pennsylvania Railroad took a very different engineering path from the rival New York Central Railroad as average speeds and train loads increased in the late 1930s with the ending of the recession that had begun with the Wall Street Crash in 1929. Remarkably, the Pennsy relied almost entirely on its 425-strong fleet of two-cylinder K4 Pacifics, built between 1914 and 1928, to work its heaviest, fastest, and most prestigious express trains into the 1940s. These were excellent engines, but by this time they had to be worked in pairs to keep the fastest and heaviest trains to time. The Pennsy's main line from New York through Harrisburg, Pittsburgh, and Crestline to Chicago was sixty miles shorter than the New York Central's but, running further south, it had to cross the Allegheny Mountains. The magnificent 220 degree horseshoe curve that took the line west of Altoona, the Pennsylvania railway town where the company built and tested many of its own locomotives, presented a formidable challenge to engines and their crews. Going west, it climbed 12 miles at 1-in-52, curving all the way to Gallitzin, with 23 miles at 1-in-87 in the other direction.

On a 1945 visit to the USA, the British locomotive engineer Stewart Cox rode a heavy train hauled by a pair of K4s over the 114 miles from Altoona to Pittsburgh. The steaming of the locomotives was excellent. 'The other aspect,' Cox reported, 'was the deep carpet of smoke-box ash which flanked the line-side reaching up to a hundred feet into the pinewoods, and which was due to the terrific loss of unburned fuel arising from the very high combustion rates, accentuated by the pulverizing of fuel as it passed through the mechanical stokers. The load had to be got over the mountains, even if boiler efficiency was only 50 per cent, and the volcanic exhausts produced a symphony of sound the like of which we will never hear again.'

In 1937, F. W. Hankins, chief mechanical engineer of the Pennsy, formed a committee with S. B. Ennis, H. M. Glaezner of Baldwin, and W. E. Woodard of Lima to prepare designs for a locomotive to haul trains of 1,200 US tons (1,071 imperial tons) at 100 mph on level track and to develop 6,500 ihp at this speed. The result was 6100, the S1 class 6-4-4-6, built in 1938-9 in the Pennsy's Altoona shops. This was the railroad's first rigid-frame duplex locomotive with two sets of outside cylinders. A very large boiler with a 132 sq ft fire-grate made it necessary to use three-axle leading and trailing trucks. Despite its excellent performance, 6100's extreme length – 140 feet – restricted its route availability and the Pennsy asked the locomotive builders for a more compact duplex locomotive to haul 880 tons.

The result was the fifty-two T1 class 4-4-4-4s, a class of very fast, streamlined, four-cylinder duplex locomotives. Two prototypes were built by Baldwin in 1942 and the production batch in 1945-6 by Baldwin and the Altoona works. Sadly, the production engines lasted just two years in charge of crack Pennsy expresses, including the Broadway Limited from New York to Chicago, and were taken out of service altogether within five or six years of the last engine being delivered in August 1946.

The T1s were remarkable machines. The idea had been to shape an engine with smaller cylinders than the classic two-cylinder American

4-8-4 and so halve the piston thrusts, reduing piston speed and the 'hammer blow' that the heavy driving mechanism of large two-cylinder machines transmitted to the track. Clad in shark-nosed streamlining designed by Raymond Loewy, the first two locomotives – 6110 and 6111, the latter fitted with a Franklin booster on its trailing truck – were ready for testing in spring 1942. Visually, they were particularly striking machines, looking menacingly fast even when standing still. In practice, the streamlining encouraged exhaust steam and soot to drift over the boiler and into the cab; when the new engines were painted the Pennsy's almost malachite take on Brunswick green, they appeared to blacken after only a few days in service. Their specification was equally impressive. Hugely long, at 122 feet, which was 10 feet more than a Niagara, the engines sported 200 ton tenders mounted on two eight-wheeled trucks. Boilers were pressed to 300 psi, tractive effort was 64,650 lb, and, on test at Altoona, 6110 developed a peak of 6,666 ihp at 100 mph with 20 per cent cut-off, with a boiler evaporation rate of 105,500 lb per hour and a pressure drop of only 7 per cent between boiler and cylinders. The minimum specific steam consumption, at 5,000 ihp and 96 mph, was 13.6 lb per ihp per hour, the lowest recorded in forty years of testing at Altoona. On road tests, 5399 attained 94 mph on level track with a train of 1,178 US tons.

Performance, especially over the lightly inclined 280 mile section from Crestline to Chicago, could be sensational. On test, 6111 ran 69 miles at the head of a sixteen-car, 912 ton train at 102 mph, while with an almost identical load, 6110 is said to have run half of the 280 miles of the same route at a mean speed of 100 mph, with steam flowing freely through its large poppet valves. There were rumours throughout the brief lives of these charismatic machines of speeds of up to 125 mph. These should not be dismissed. The T1s were undoubtedly among the very fastest and most powerful of all passenger steam locomotives. Sadly, though, there are few details to back up such claims. But, although the T1s could fly, they – both the prototypes and the fifty production series that went into service between November

1945 and August 1946 – suffered from not one but several Achilles heels.

The first was slipping. Although careful driving could alleviate this problem to an extent, the two uncoupled sets of four driving wheels could easily slip differentially and at varying speeds. This could make hill-climbing tricky and acceleration irregular, while, from a maintenance aspect, the use of Franklin type A oscillating-cam poppet valves, with the driving gearboxes inaccessibly located, proved a problem. Johnson at Baldwin would have preferred rotary-cam poppet valves, with an easily accessible external Cardan shaft drive, similar to that used on the British Railways three-cylinder Pacific 71000 *Duke of Gloucester*.

The Pennsy's experience with Franklin oscillating-cam poppet valves had, though, proved to be remarkably successful when applied to one of the K4 Pacifics, 5399, in 1939 by Vernon Smith under the direction of William Kiesel, the railway's mechanical engineer, who had been closely involved in the design of the 4-6-2s more than a quarter of a century earlier. The result was a boost in power from around 3,500 ihp to a recorded 4,267 ihp, greater economy, and a higher top speed.

Before the last of the T1s had been placed in service in 1946, the Pennsy had decided to dieselize its non-electrified routes. By 1948, the Broadway Limited was diesel-hauled and within three years the T1s were redundant. The last was scrapped in 1953. In their brief heyday, these fleet-footed machines, sometimes likened to Bulleid's controversial Pacifics on England's Southern Railway, were trusted with fast, long-distance trains and must have been quite a sight streaking along between Crestline and Chicago.

The 73.1 mph bookings over the 123 miles from Fort Wayne to Gary, and 71.6 mph along the 140.9 miles from Fort Wayne to Englewood, outside Chicago, must have been an easy romp for these 6,500 hp, 100 mph-plus machines. But while the T1s were more than a match for a trio of E7 diesel-electrics in terms of high-speed performance, they were generally less reliable, especially during the very difficult time at the end of the war when servicing and maintenance standards were at a low level. The Pennsy borrowed a Norfolk and Western Railway J class 4-8-4 to see how this altogether simpler, and highly effective, locomotive could work the high-speed Pennsy expresses. The J class kept to time happily with 900 tons and attained 110 mph on easy falling gradients. This was impressive, but the Pennsy considered the 5 ft 10 in driving wheels of the J class to be too small for prolonged high-speed running.

Ralph Johnson, the Baldwin engineer, had certainly been very proud of the T1s when they first appeared. 'Many critics of the steam locomotive deplore the fact that it has changed so little in outward appearance,' he wrote in 1942. 'This criticism reflects ignorance of both engineering and economic facts, as no type of boiler commercially practicable has been developed which, subjected to the same space limitations, can generate more steam or generate it faster than the internally fired fire-tube boiler . . . however, the steam locomotive has always looked functional, rather than aesthetic, and while this is beautiful to a railroad man it was recognized that the traveling public might prefer the locomotive "dressed up". Therefore, Mr Raymond Loewy, one of the foremost industrial designers of this day, was retained to "streamline" these new four-cylinder locomotives.' Johnson added, as if an engineer's postscript: 'This styling was not carried out to an extreme as it left accessible all moving parts for inspection.'

As a last fling, along with the New York Central Railroad Niagaras, for express passenger steam in the United States, the T1s were something of a disappointment. They looked and performed the part, although in everyday service Loewy's streamlining was more of a hindrance than a help. The engineering of the locomotive's valves was too complex, especially for the Pennsy's rather run-down service and maintenance depots at the end of the war. If, however, the T1s had been fitted with boosters and more accessible Franklin type B rotary-cam poppet valves, they may well have been far more successful than they proved to be. Diesels triumphed very quickly on the Pennsy, and in 1945 even Johnson felt moved to write to E. C. Poultney, the author of *British Express Locomotive Development* (1952): 'On American roads, the Diesel locomotive sells – not so much on account of its superior thermal efficiency, but because of its superior availability.'

The diesel's availability and flexibility in service was recognized early on. This was a severe challenge for steam. As Kiefer wrote: 'Over the years it has been our increasing determination and practice to advance the design of this type of locomotive, not only to achieve progressively better results with it, but also to enforce ever higher standards for new and competing forms of motive power.'

These factors were, generally, as true for heavy freight as for express passenger steam. The Union Pacific's Big Boys were truly magnificent machines, and continued in regular service until 1959, but these were highly specialized machines designed to operate the heaviest of trains over one particular 176 mile stretch of track. It took three new 2,000 hp diesels to perform the work of a single Big Boy, but those same locomotives could run over virtually the entire Union Pacific system, and if they were ever found lacking in power, another 2,000 hp unit could be coupled on to help.

The mightiest of all US steam freight locomotives, though, were arguably not the Big Boys, but the sixty-eight four-cylinder Allegheny H8 class 2-6-6-6 Mallets designed and built by Lima for the Chesapeake and Ohio Railway and the Virginian Railway from 1941 to 1948. These muscular, yet lithe, machines, covered from smoke-box door to footplate in sand-boxes, brake-pumps, walkways, powerful lamps, and a plethora of ancillary equipment, looked like power stations on rails – although side on they displayed an elegant line –and perhaps this is exactly what these rail-bound leviathans were. Like the Union Pacific Big Boys, the Chesapeake and Ohio H8 Alleghenies, named after the mountain range they were designed to cross with enormous coal trains, were built primarily to work one particular line, although they were soon masters of others. The track for which they were built winds up to Allegheny, and precipitously down again through sharp curves and deep tunnels, between Clifton Forge and Hinton in West Virginia. The distance between the two towns is just 80 miles, but with 144-wagon coal trains, weighing 11,500 tons and with no roller bearings, the going was tough, as it is even for the strongest gangs of diesels today. The trains hauled by the class H8 Alleghenies crossed the summit at about 15 mph.

The idea had been that the H8s would be able to work this line single-handed with 5,750 tons westbound at speeds of up to 45 mph. In fact, like the Union Pacific Challengers and Big Boys, and the class A 2-6-6-4s of the Norfolk and Western, they proved to be fast engines and free running despite their great mass. They were the heaviest steam locomotives built in the USA, as well as the most powerful in terms of drawbar horsepower, yet they moved with a grace that belied their bulk. With their 5 ft 7 in driving wheels and ample steam-producing capacity, they would run happily up to 60 mph on freight trains, and were timed at 70 mph at the head of troop and hospital trains during the Second World War. Twenty-one H8s were fitted with steam-heating especially to work passenger trains.

Despite the Chesapeake and Ohio's original plans, the Allegheny proved to be an extremely powerful mixed-traffic locomotive, and the ultimate realization, perhaps, of Woodard's super-power steam concept. The railway used them, for the most part, to accelerate slow-moving coal trains on mountain sections, slogging at speeds often down to between 15 and 20 mph. For this kind of traffic the Chesapeake and Ohio was equipped with forty powerful T1 class 2-10-4s, capable of a maximum of 7,000 ihp, built by Lima in 1930. The Alleghenies shone on faster trains, as well as heavy mineral work. They were replaced by diesels from 1952, even though the last went into service in 1948, and the entire class was out of service by the end of 1956.

The design proposal had been drawn up the Advisory Mechanical Committee, formed in 1929, comprising motive power engineers from four railroads – the Chesapeake and Ohio Railway, the Erie Railroad, the Nickel Plate Road, and the Pere Marquette Railway, which was owned by the inseparable Van Sweringen brothers, Oris Paxton and Mantis James. The key members of the committee in terms of locomotive design were Daniel Ellis, its chairman, A. G. Turnbull, chief mechanical engineer, and M. J. 'Mitch' Donovan, who had emigrated to the United States from Scotland, where he had worked at the North British Locomotive Company in Glasgow. Detailed design work at Lima was by chief engineer Bert Townsend and project engineer James Cunningham.

The Chesapeake and Ohio had been designing and commissioning Mallet articulated locomotives since the H1 class compound 2-6-6-2 of 1910. With war looming and coal trains growing ever heavier, Lima was asked to build the H8 class in 1940. They had 22½ × 33 in cylinders, double blast-pipes and chimneys, and an excellent steam-flow circuit. When the first Allegheny – 1600 – was rolled out from Lima's works in December 1941, a veteran local journalist invited to the event is supposed to have said: 'When people have the will to build an engine like this, they're bound to win a war.'

The sheer power of the H8s remained unknown, because untested, until 6 August 1943 when 1608 was attached to a 14,075 ton freight train (imagine 400 British Railways Mark 1 carriages coupled together), with a dynamometer car attached, and worked at full power on the Chesapeake and Ohio's fairly level line between Russell and Columbus in south central Ohio. Working this train at 46 mph, 6108 developed a maximum of 7,498 dbhp, or at least 8,500 ihp. There are just enough recordings of these engines at work to imagine its deep bass exhaust rumbling like rolling thunder through Ohio. During the previous month, 6108, with another H8 banking, had sustained 6,879 dbhp with an 11,505 ton coal train over the Alleghenies on the line for which she was originally designed.

The power record was a case of friendly rivalry. When 1608 developed a peak of 7,498 dbhp, tears rolled down Daniel Ellis's cheeks; the Chesapeake and Ohio engine had beaten the neighbouring Norfolk and Western Railway's superb A class 2-6-6-4, and by some considerable margin (hauling a regular freight train in 1936, one of the new 2-6-6-4s had peaked at 6,300 dbhp, thought to be the US, and world, record at the time). In certain ways, the 347 ton H8s had reached the limit in terms of size for an American steam locomotive; axle loadings had risen to 37.5 tons. Photographs taken during their construction, from 1941 to 1948, show that their boilers only just fitted between the bays of Lima's erecting shop. Lima lost money on the first batch of $230,663 engines, but made about $75,000 profit on later orders from both the Chesapeake and Ohio Railway and the Virginian Railway, which bought eight. By 1948, the cost had risen to $248,438 (a New York Central Niagara cost $238,854 in 1946; an 8,000 hp diesel-electric, comprising four 2,000 hp units, would have cost approximately $700,000). Sadly for Lima, this profit was more than offset by the compensation it had to pay the Chesapeake and Ohio when their management discovered that the weight of the H8s was substantially above the 323 tons originally agreed – although the excess weight, which was primarily due to modifications insisted on by the advisory mechanical committee, had caused no damage to the track.

Spending much of their time working immensely long and heavy mineral trains at relatively low speeds, the fleet-footed Chesapeake and Ohio Alleghenies were scrapped between 1952 and 1956; their Virginian siblings, withdrawn in 1955, were cut up by 1960. Fortunately, two H8s survive – perhaps they will run again one day. A locomotive that could haul a 14,000 ton freight train – well over a mile long – over the Alleghenies could only ever have been a remarkable, almost dream-like, sight. What must it have been like to stand on the steel platform set in front of the smoke-box of one of these giants as it thundered up the steep, winding hills of rural Ohio?

Here was a railway apparently devoted to steam, and burning the coal that also provided the bulk of its traffic, that switched to diesel late in the day, with the arrival of an anti-steam president, Walter Tuohy, in 1956. The wholesale dieselization of US railways in the 1950s meant that manufacturers and suppliers of very many essential components either went out of business or switched production to meet the needs of the new form of traction. When it built the Alleghenies, for example, Lima had turned to at least fifty outside companies to supply anything from brake-shoes and cylinder cocks to mechanical stokers and smoke-box door hinges.

Even the Norfolk and Western Railway, one of the few American railways to design and build its own locomotives, and the last all-steam main-line railroad in the USA, was dependent on a host of specialist suppliers to turn drawings into fully operational steam locomotives. When these became unavailable, the railroad had to manufacture its own components, in small batches, at increased cost. Throughout the 1950s, however, the Norfolk and Western ran what was by almost any standards the most impressive and efficient steam locomotive operation in the world. Heavy mineral trains, representing very nearly three quarters of the railway's traffic, carried coal from the Pocahontas coalfield of West Virginia – one of the largest in the world – to the Midwest in one direction and to the Atlantic coast at Norfolk, Virginia, in the other. However, it also ran an excellent long-distance passenger service from Norfolk over the 677 miles, across the Alleghenies, to Cincinatti. Most remarkably, the great majority of these services – 84 per cent of passenger miles and more than 90 per cent of freight miles in 1955 – came to be worked by just three classes of steam locomotive, all of them powerful, modern, and highly capable. These were the A class four-cylinder 2-6-6-4, the Y-6b class four-cylinder compound 2-8-8-2, and the J class two-cylinder 4-8-4 – three of the finest classes of steam locomotives ever built. In 1955 the steam-powered Norfolk and Western was the most efficient American railway in terms of gross ton miles of freight operated per hour. For a while at least, steam reigned supreme.

At the railway's annual staff conference held in April 1951, H. C. Wyatt, the Norfolk and Western's assistant general superintendent of motive power, explained why the company was holding on to steam:

> Our situation differs from most other roads in two
> respects. First, we have available along our railroad
> in almost unlimited quantities, the cheapest known
> fuel – coal. It is coal of the finest quality for power
> generation. Second, when other railroads began to turn
> to other types of power, we already had in service a
> substantial number of modern coal-burning locomotives.
> The railroads on which the greatest number of steam
> locomotives were replaced by other types did not have
> fleets of steam power as reliable, efficient or as modern
> as our own Js, As, or Y-6s.

The quality and character of these highly distinctive locomotives, built at Roanoke, Virginia, between 1936 and 1952 is captured, subliminally, in the elegiac and technically brilliant railway photography of O. Winston Link. Link's beautiful book *Steam, Steel & Stars: America's Last Steam Railroad* (1987) bears comparison with the work of America's greatest photographers and painters. The black-and-white images, often shot at night with the help of a barrage of flashbulbs, caught a steam-driven world that seemed at once deeply old-fashioned and yet also a dynamic part of 1950s rock-'n-'roll America. One of Link's most famous photographs, taken in August 1956, shows A class 2-6-6-4 1242 speeding past the Laeger drive-in theatre at the head of a fast late-evening freight train. In the foreground, a young couple sit close together in the front seat of Link's bulbous 1952 Buick convertible, while on the screen a jet fighter (a Super Sabre?) shoots past. The shot is remarkable not just for its timing – the train passing at the exact moment the jet fighter darted across the silver screen, but because it shows steam powering confidently into the jet age. The two, as the

Norfolk and Western proved, did not have to be mutually exclusive.

Born in Brooklyn, Ogle Winston Link had been a steam enthusiast from earliest childhood. He went on to become a successful technical and commercial photographer, but when in 1955 he discovered that the Norfolk and Western had begun to buy diesels for the very first time, he made visit after visit to the railway to capture its last five years of steam operation. Today, the O. Winston Link Museum is housed in a former railway building in Roanoke, while the nearby Virginia Museum of Transportation is home both to the A class 2-6-6-4 1218 and to 611, one of the semi-streamlined J class 4-8-4s.

The four-cylinder A class 2-6-6-4, of which forty-three were built, was contemporary with the Union Pacific 4-6-6-4 Challengers. The first engines emerged from Roanoke in May 1936 and the last in April 1950. They were more powerful than their Union Pacific rivals, and, indeed, until the arrival of the Chesapeake and Ohio's Alleghenies and the Union Pacific Big Boys, they were among the most powerful locomotives in North America, and hence the world. Like the J class 4-8-4s, the 2-6-6-4s were designed in-house by the Norfolk and Western's mechanical engineers, Russell Henley and John Pilcher. They were intended primarily for fast freight services, and could work coal trains of up to 17,000 tons on the more lightly inclined Norfolk to Columbus main line, although their ability to run comfortably at 70 mph and more made them useful as passenger engines, especially during the Second World War, when trains could be very long and exceptionally heavy. The Norfolk and Western claimed that they were able to develop a peak output of 6,300 dbhp, or about 7,700 ihp; in a series of carefully monitored tests made against E7 diesel-electrics in 1952, 5,300 dbhp was sustained.

The compound Y6b 2-8-8-2 of 1948–52 was the ultimate development of a type of locomotive the Norfolk and Western had been using and improving, from an Association of American Railroads standard design, since 1919. These were engines designed to work coal trains over the mountain sections of the railway. They were massive-looking machines, especially with their huge outside low-pressure cylinders which, measuring no less than 39 × 32 in, looked like giant mechanical bear paws pulling these remarkable engines along. The 2-8-8-2s had a maximum starting tractive effort of 126,831 lb and could produce a sustained 5,500 dbhp at 25 mph, ideal for heavy mineral train operation over steep gradients. They could run at 50 mph when required.

In 1952, a Norfolk and Western test programme pitting the two classes of articulated freight engines against a General Motors four-unit F7 diesel-electric proved that Henley and Pilcher had created steam locomotives that the diesels were unable to beat conclusively. The results were declared a tie. On the almost-level line between Williamson and Portsmouth, west of Roanoke, the A class 2-6-6-4 ran a marginally heavier train than the four-unit 6,000 hp diesel slightly faster over the 111 miles. By international standards, the performance of the A class was without comparison: the big engine had averaged 31.6 mph with a train weighing 16,028 tons. The 2-8-8-2 was 15 per cent slower than the diesel climbing the 35 miles at 1-in-70 to 1-in-83 from Farm to Bluefield, but its train was 9 per cent heavier.

It was said that the Norfolk and Western had tuned up its test steam locomotives with a higher than usual boiler pressure (315 psi) and bored out cylinders to boost power; equally, it was claimed that General Motors had tweaked the four-unit diesel to give 7,000 hp. The 2-8-8-2 on test had certainly been 'supercharged' recently, using a booster valve to supply superheated steam at reduced pressure into the low-pressure cylinders during compound working – such was the ability of these engines' boilers to generate steam. In fact, Norfolk and Western steam did so well in these tests that its steam men liked to say that it had dieselized without diesels. In strictly commercial terms, the steam-driven Norfolk and Western Railway was also a success: it paid a dividend to shareholders of 6 per cent in the mid-1950s, compared to the 0.5 per cent paid by the fully electrified and dieselized Pennsylvania Railroad.

Not only were the new steam locomotives powerful and efficient, they were also backed up by modern servicing facilities, located in purpose-built depots at Shaffers Crossing (Roanoke), Bluefield, Williamson, and Portsmouth. Engines passing through brightly lit 'lubritoriums' were oiled and, if necessary, adjustments could be made very quickly. Even after the longest, hardest run, a large Mallet could be turned around in ninety minutes. The streamlined 4-8-4s could also be cleaned very easily, passing through automatic washes with spinning brushes and being hosed down by water-jets, just like a diesel or electric locomotive today. Photographs and films show that these depots employed modern, Bauhaus-style architecture and were exceptionally clean. The looks of the J class 4-8-4, new from Roanoke in October 1940, were a perfect match for these mechanized depots and the idea of fast, clean, and efficient steam trains that they promised.

The J class streamliners were a truly remarkable design for a railroad that had been, in terms of publicity and speed, somewhat out of the picture when compared with the Pennsy, the New York Central Railroad, the Southern Railway, the Milwaukee Road, or the Union Pacific. Here, though, was one of the most powerful of the American 4-8-4s, and possibly the fastest on record despite the locomotives' small 5 ft 10 in driving wheels. Designed and built at Roanoke under the direction of Russell G. Henley, the Js were beautifully streamlined, not by an industrial design consultant, but by Frank Noel, a foreman at Roanoke whose speciality was the construction of passenger cars. The first locomotive, attached to six new passenger cars, was packed off on a publicity tour of the railway on 24 October 1941. Finished in Indian red and gold over glossy black, 600 made a magnificent sight.

The J class engines weighed 220 tons. Their two cylinders measured 27 × 32 in. Boiler pressure was 275 psi and tractive effort 73,300 lb. Following performance tests made by the Norfolk and Western in 1945, these figures were raised to 300 psi and 80,000 lb. With 300 psi boiler pressure, 604 developed 5,100 dhbp at 40 mph. Their great power was a real boon to the Norfolk and Western during the war years, when the number of annual passenger journeys rose from 1,047,732 in 1939 to 5,168,580 in 1945. This figure was to fall rapidly in post-war years, as troop trains all but vanished and the new inter-state freeways and inter-city air routes began to take their toll on railway traffic.

The locomotives were built in three batches: five streamlined engines in 1941–2, five without streamlining in 1943, and a final four with streamline casing in 1950, although all ran in streamlined guise after the war. The 600 series were much faster than rivals had imagined; on loan to the Pennsy in 1944–5, 610 ran at 110 mph on the track between Crestline, Fort Wayne, and Chicago. Typical work for a J class engine on the Norfolk and Western included running the heavy Cavalier passenger train just over 200 hilly miles from Roanoke to Williamson, calling at nineteen stations on the way and averaging 30.5 mph in the process. Even the crack Powhattan Arrow, a fine-looking train composed of Tuscan red streamlined Pullman stock and launched in April 1946, averaged no more than 43 mph on its epic run from Norfolk to Cincinatti; however, the train made fifteen regular and two conditional stops, including five over the last 111.6 miles from Portsmouth to Cincinatti. What Norfolk and Western timetables hid – except to railwaymen and steam enthusiasts – was the vigorous acceleration required between stations over a challenging route; the power of the J class was never wasted.

More than speed, reliability was all-important, and the 600s were extremely reliable, racking up an average of 15,000 miles per month, despite moderate train speeds. They were comfortable engines to work on. With their neat, chrome-ringed instruments, well-placed controls, and general air of refinement, the J class was popular with the crews who worked them on trains like the Powhattan Arrow, up, down, and around the curves of a demanding main line which could be very challenging indeed in winter. Mechanical lubrication was provided to 220 points on the locomotive and tender, while a further seventy-two were lubricated using high-pressure hoses in the railroad's 'lubritoriums'.

In every respect – appearance, speed, power, comfort, utilization, and reliability – the J class 4-8-4s were among the very finest of all steam locomotives. Their end, and the finale for Norfolk and Western steam, came unexpectedly. On 1 April 1958, Stuart T. Saunders, a Virginia-born, Harvard-educated lawyer, took over from the veteran Robert 'Racehorse' Smith as president of the Norfolk and Western Railway. Whereas Smith, a man who had begun his working life on the railroad as a member of a permanent-way gang, and whose long, fast, striding walk earned him his nickname, believed very much in steam for the principal trunk routes, Saunders plumped for complete dieselization almost as soon as he assumed office. A man who did not mix with railroad staff, Saunders settled on 1 January 1960 as the first day of an all-diesel Norfolk and Western. The change from one form of highly successful traction to another was expedited at a faster rate than on any other class 1 US railroad, with a speed that left many working on the railway rubbing their eyes in disbelief.

Saunders hated what he thought of as 'dirty' steam locomotives. He swung into action with a zeal that would have impressed the puritan iconoclasts of seventeenth-century England. A Norfolk and Western passenger train timetable issued on 15 June 1958 featured a J class on its cover, set between profiles of two Native Americans; a new timetable published on 26 October depicted the Native Americans, but not the steam locomotive. The June timetable had clearly been at the printers, or already printed, before the announcement, made on 2 June, to the effect that the Norfolk and Western Railway was buying 268 diesel units to replace steam locomotive working entirely. So keen was Saunders to rid the railway of steam that he hired diesels from other companies and was content to see six- and seven-year-old main-line locomotives scrapped.

The subsequent cull was draconian. The last of the J class to run was 611, on 24 October 1959. Only a week before, on an excursion from Petersburg to Norfolk, 611 was said to have run up to 100 mph between Poe and Suffolk; sadly, there appears to be no record of the run. Given that a J could run at three-figure speeds on its home railway, logs of everyday runs demonstrating their power and acceleration over the Virginia hills would be riveting stuff. The A class 2-6-6-4 went the same year, while the last of the Y6bs soldiered on until 6 May 1960. Between June 1956 and May 1960, 233 modern Norfolk and Western steam locomotives, including all of the A, J, and Y6b classes, as well as seventy-five 0-8-0 switchers, some just five years old, were taken out of service.

While it was glorious to witness 611 back in steam on the Norfolk and Western – it ran special trains from 1982 to 1994, along with A class 2-6-6-4 1218 (from 1987) – and the 4-8-4 still looked sleekly modern and was clearly immensely powerful, her last run in regular service represented the final curtain for regular main-line steam in the United States. In fact, that curtain had fallen very quickly indeed on the Norfolk and Western, which, ironically, had by most measures been the finest of all North American steam railways. Given the astonishing power, speed, and overall operating efficiency of the last generation of American super-power steam, just why did this form of traction fall from commercial grace so very quickly? The reasons are not entirely obvious, yet together they must have added up to a convincing case as far as railway management was concerned.

*

The universality of the diesel-electric locomotive was quick to impress management, whether at an operational or commercial level. Whereas steam locomotives tended to be specialist machines – express passenger, heavy freight, shunting, and so on – diesel units could be coupled together in series, with only their final drive ratios varied to meet different requirements, so that any steam locomotive, no matter how powerful, could be challenged, equalled, and bettered. A single diesel unit might spend some time shunting or working local passenger and freight traffic; coupled together, a pair could haul an express train on most lines to exacting schedules. Because they were light on their wheels and caused no 'hammer blow' on the tracks, as steam locomotives did with their powerful piston thrusts and heavy running gear, diesels were popular with the railroads' civil engineers. They were easy to turn around at the end of long runs, clean compared to steam locomotives, and with their excellent acceleration from rest they could outpace most, if not all, contemporary steam locomotives on journeys with frequent stops.

The list could go on, and yet as the tests conducted by Kiefer on the New York Central Railroad in 1946 and Henley on the Norfolk and Western Railway in 1952 had proved, it was a close-run thing in terms of annual operating costs between the best of modern main-line steam and the latest diesels. And, given that a number of railroads sat on vast reserves of high-quality coal – especially those in the east of the country – it must have been sensible to burn coal rather than to use diesel oil. There were, of course, railroads operating in the parched and coal-less south-western states that had long had a problem with fuel and, especially, water supplies for steam locomotives. But the real reasons for the speed of dieselization lay elsewhere.

In late 1945, Joseph Ennis, a senior vice president of Alco, stated categorically that 'the future holds an expanding role for . . . the steam locomotive'. Yet Alco built its last steam locomotive in 1948. The company was out of business twenty-one years later, after building many diesel-electrics jointly with General Motors, by which time its old rivals Baldwin and Lima were history too. In an illuminating essay, 'Corporate Culture and Marketing in the American Railway Locomotive Industry', published in *Business History Review* in June 1995, Albert Churella, a senior lecturer at the Ohio State University, identified some of the key reasons why steam was banished with such astonishing pace in the United States.

Churella stresses the yawning gap in terms of corporate culture between steam locomotive makers like Alco and what were to be the two giants of the US, and global, diesel locomotive industry, General

Electric and General Motors. Taking their cue from the automotive industry, the newcomers used marketing as a tool and sold their wares direct to commercial railway management, rather than to operating and mechanical engineering management. Where the steam manufacturers were essentially craft-based and worked closely with railroad engineers and committed steam men, General Electric and General Motors were modern business corporations. They assembled cost-effective products, marketed them vigorously, and talked directly to the men whose main concern was profit and loss, not boiler pressures, cylinder diameters, and indicated horsepower.

'The inability of Alco executives to adapt their corporate culture to fit the emerging diesel locomotive market,' wrote Churella, 'had a dramatic effect. In 1917 Alco was the 52nd largest industrial corporation in the United States. By 1948, its ranking had fallen to 145th, and it continued to decline in the years that followed. With only two exceptions, Great Western Sugar and Willys-Overland, no industrial corporation in the history of American business fell so far so fast.'

Alco's senior management were steam men through and through. Although the company could have muscled in on the burgeoning diesel market early on, it chose not to. Significantly, Robert B. McColl, elected Alco president in December 1945, had begun his career in England with Robert Stephenson and Company. In many ways, these executives were far from competitive, with Alco, Baldwin, and Lima sharing working drawings and components with one another.

The diesel manufacturers, though, were creatures of the market and marketing, allied with first-rate design and production engineering. They offered easy-payment hire-purchase deals and extensive after-sales service. They ran courses to train US railroad workers in the ways of the new diesels. In May 1947, General Motors sent a diesel 'Train of the Future' off on a six-month tour of the USA to woo the travelling public. Booklets and advertising ensured that the American public was persuaded of the virtues of clean – or what appeared to be clean

– new diesels. An advertising campaign pursued between 1957 and 1959 saw General Motors place colour portraits of 'Men who build the future of American railroads' on the covers of *Railway Age*, the leading industry journal. These men of the future were, of course, General Motors' customers; the implication was that railway executives stuck in a black-and-white world of steam were a throwback to a grimy past.

There had been no conspiracy, no special lobby that had got one over steam in Washington, DC, or anywhere else. But the diesel industry was young, fuelled as much by new business management techniques as by oil, and a rapier in terms of sales and marketing to the steam industry's broadsword. The figures tell an astonishing success story. Although some railroads like the Norfolk and Western continued to build new steam locomotives for some years to come, order books at Alco, Baldwin, and Lima were empty by 1946. In 1945, diesels worked just 8 per cent of all passenger train miles; the figure was 34 per cent three years later. There were 3,882 diesels in service with US railroads at the end of 1945; there were 20,604 by the end of 1952, and nearly 28,000 by the time the Norfolk and Western's last Y6b ran in May 1960.

The end of main-line steam in the USA was caused as much by new business methods and new ways of seeing the world and how to get about it, as by new technology. It was not that the US steam locomotive at its best had been anything other than a magnificent machine, but its development in the 1940s was no match for the business proposition made to railway executives by General Motors. In 1945, orders had been coming in for some of the most impressive steam locomotives ever built; Alco was busy with Kiefer's Niagaras and Lima with the Allegheny 2-6-6-6 Mallets. It must have been difficult in those crucial years of the diesel-electric's takeover of the market for steam manufacturers to see the writing on the wall; they were making superb machines.

As late as February 1949, Lima prepared an advertisement to send out to US railroads for its latest design – by A. J. 'Bert' Townsend – for a fast freight 4-8-6 with all the modifications it thought necessary for this powerful engine to compete with diesels. The question of acceleration away from rest had been addressed with a new type of high-speed booster which would have provided increased tractive effort at speeds of up to 35 mph, the crucial speed at which the power characteristics of the steam locomotive begin to make themselves felt over and above diesels of the same nominal output. 'To get more power with less coal – investigate this new design.' But coal itself was being ousted by oil on the railways, and the project was dropped just two months later. Evidently heartbroken, Townsend resigned and died the following year. Significantly perhaps, the very last steam locomotives built by Lima were two-cylinder 2-8-4s for the Nickel Plate Road – the last descendants of Woodard's original and revolutionary super-power A-1 2-8-4 of a quarter of a century before.

With locomotives like the Chesapeake and Ohio Alleghenies and Union Pacific Big Boys, American steam had reached a limit in terms of sheer scale. Steam-cycle efficiency, however, was another thing, and while American steam engineers had shaped some of the most impressive, expressive, and memorable of all man-made machines, their development had reached an impasse. If the diesel lobby had not been so persuasive, might US steam have moved on again? It is hard to know, and yet Chapelon's firm belief that a Big Boy could be reworked to become much more efficient offered only a hint of how American steam might have developed from the 1950s onwards. Few in the 1930s truly understood just how troublesome the politics of oil would be in the years to come; the true cost of the diesel would be very high indeed.

CHAPTER 5

AROUND
THE WORLD

Red Stars, Southern Lights,
and Eastern Promise

The steam locomotive is not just the most expressive machine yet invented, but in many cases a work of art. Engineering art, yes, but art all the same. In France, André Chapelon worked with the artist Émile André Schefer on the styling of his later locomotives, while in Czechoslovakia, Vilém Kreibich collaborated with Vlastimil Mareš, a distinguished steam locomotive engineer who rose to become director of the machinery department at the ministry of railways in Prague. The working partnership between artist and engineer was to produce some of the finest and best-looking of all modern steam locomotives, while the story of late-flowering Czech steam was a remarkable one.

For a very brief period – between 1945 and 1948, when the Iron Curtain fell across Europe – Mareš worked closely with Chapelon, who had been appointed consultant locomotive engineer to the ČSD (Czech State Railways). Although just five 476.0 class three-cylinder compounds were built in 1949–50, Chapelon's influence could be seen in several other of Mareš's designs. These included the 475.1 class two-cylinder 4-8-2s (1947–55), the 498.1 class three-cylinder 4-8-2s (1949–55), the 556.0 class two-cylinder 2-10-0s (1952–8), and the 477.0 class two-cylinder 4-8-4Ts (1950–5) – a quartet of locomotive types that fused much of the very best of French, German, American, and, of course, Czech and Austrian design practice (Czechoslovakia, founded in 1918 and divided in 1992, had long been a part of the Austro-Hungarian Empire) to produce a fleet of eight hundred engines which could stand comparison with any built elsewhere in the world.

The main-line steam locomotive, despite regional variations and some specialist designs, belonged largely to four schools of engineering and design: those of France, Germany, Great Britain, and the United States. Most of the last generation of Stephensonian power represented alliances, partnerships, and what might be called marriages between these principal schools. Each had something to learn from the others, although Mareš did more than most to draw on the very best of international design. The sadness was not that he failed to design a number of quite brilliant classes of steam locomotive, but that he was able to collaborate with his colleagues beyond the Iron Curtain, especially André Chapelon, for no more than three years. After the communist coup of 1948, he was not allowed to communicate with them. And it was from then on that the Czech economy, once buoyed up by an exceptionally fine and inventive engineering tradition, sank into decline.

Even then, Mareš continued to develop Czech steam with engineers at the Škoda and ČSD works until an edict, effectively handed down from Moscow, insisted that steam development and manufacture must stop. This prevented the construction of his largest design, the 569.0 class three-cylinder simple-expansion 2-10-4 for heavy and fast freight; with 1.6 m (5 ft 3 in) driving wheels, 294 psi boiler pressure, and a 75 sq ft grate area, they would have run at up to 100 kph (62 mph). On a trip to communist Czechoslovakia in 1959, E. S. Cox, the British Railways design engineer, noted: 'One feels that satellite countries [of the USSR] are only allowed to deploy their native genius up to a certain point, and in this country the dead hand of Russian policy . . . evidently reached out and killed steam traction by a single blow.' Cox had been given a copy of the latest Škoda works brochure showing engines planned for Czech and overseas railways. On the inside of the back cover were printed the words: 'This catalogue of steam locomotives for railways had been elaborated before it had been decided that our locomotive works shall not continue building steam locomotives beginning with 1958 . . . in future our locomotive works will build diesel and electric locomotives only.' As Cox pointed out, there were at the time no Czech main-line diesels to replace steam. 'What is to be wondered at,' he wrote, given the above-average quality of modern Czech steam, 'is the world-wide contagion to be rid of steam at a rate beyond all common sense.' But, as Chapelon remarked when his SNCF locomotives went prematurely for scrap: *'C'est la mode.'*

Cox's first experience of a Czech locomotive was when he encountered 556-0370 at the border station at Cheb; this was one of Mareš's superb two-cylinder 2-10-0s. 'I have never heard a crisper, sharper exhaust,' Cox recalled, 'indicative of a perfect distribution and steam tightness at the front end.' Mareš's engines needed to be efficient. Lightly laid track, coal with a relatively low heat content, and heavily inclined routes demanded powerful locomotives with a light axle loading and a high tractive capacity to make the most of the modest fuel they burned. No wonder Mareš had turned to Chapelon for inspiration.

Certain aspects of the design of the class 476.0 compound 4-8-2s of 1949–50 were inspired by Chapelon's solitary 242A1 of 1946. The 108 ton engines featured double Kylchap exhausts and piston valves with double admission and exhaust. As with the Chapelon 4-8-4, on starting, steam was passed from the boiler (pressed to the same 294 psi as the 242A1) to the two outside low-pressure cylinders (at 206 psi), until the train was running at about 15 mph when it was directed to the single high-pressure cylinder between the frames and then on to the two low-pressure cylinders. The compounds proved capable of developing 2,900 ihp at 100 kph, despite burning low-grade coal. The reputation of the class, however, was marred when, on 27 November 1968, for some unfathomable reason, 476.002 overturned at 88 kph while heading the Chopin express from Prague to Košice through Nedakonice station: driver, fireman, and a passenger were killed.

Mareš developed two classes of simple-expansion 4-8-2s, both influenced by French practice. The first was the two-cylinder 475.1 class, an extremely fine-looking locomotive, of which 172 were built between 1947 and 1950. Twenty-five were shipped off to North Korea as a gesture of friendship between the two communist states at the time of the Korean War. With a similar all-welded boiler to the 476.0, but with thinner plates and a lower boiler pressure (235 psi), and larger (1.75 m or 5 ft 9 in) driving wheels, the 475s were slightly lighter machines and somewhat like the SNCF's 141R 2-8-2s. They performed exceptionally well as maids-of-all-work up until their withdrawal in 1980. Officially, the 475.1s were rated at 1,985 ihp and limited to 100 kph (62 mph), although in practice they could develop greater power. The Korean locomotives were still active in 1990, and possibly beyond. Since steam enthusiasts – considered, for some ineffable reason, by most communist states to be spies – have been just as unwelcome as any other visitors to the Democratic People's Republic of Korea, it is hard to say for certain what became of these Czech locomotives.

Borrowing from French and American practice, the 475.1s, like all Mareš's new locomotives, were equipped with double Kylchap exhausts and French-made mechanical stokers, as well as roller bearings, all-welded steel fire-boxes with Nicholson thermic siphons, and multiple-valve front-end throttles, rather than conventional regulators, to optimize the flow and use of steam. These features were added incrementally, so that later locomotives were more advanced in design than earlier examples, although the class was soon standardized in the drive for efficiency.

For heavy express passenger services, Mareš improved the 486.0 class three-cylinder 4-8-2s, essentially a 1934 design updated after the war. Forty-two of the class 498.0 engines were built by Škoda in 1946–9. Improved with double Kylchap exhausts and mechanical stokers, they were uprated from 1,830 to 2,200 ihp with a speed limit of 120 kph (74.5 mph). In September 2009, 486.007 and 498.022 were two of the locomotives used to haul a special train commemorating the trains organized in early 1939 by Nicholas Winton, the 'British Schindler', to convey Czech and Slovak Jewish children from Prague to safety in England, just before the German invasion of Czechoslovakia. The British leg of the journey, from Harwich to London, was powered by the brand-new three-cylinder A1 Pacific 60163 *Tornado*, and the Winton Train was met at Liverpool Street station by the 100-year-old Sir Nicholas Winton himself.

The 498.1s were similar to the 498.0s, but fitted with slightly larger fire-boxes and Witte smoke deflectors. Just fifteen were built before the Soviet crackdown on steam was announced in Moscow in 1956. That the 498.1s were free-running machines was never in doubt, even though there were few opportunities in Czechoslovakia for very fast running. On a test run made on 27 August 1964, however, 498.106 attained 162 kph (100.4 mph) over the Velim railway test circuit, near Poděbrady in central Bohemia. They were known as 'Albatrosses' – for their speed, endurance, and beauty, and with none of the negative connotations of the *Rime of the Ancient Mariner*. In 1962–3, the 498.1s were called on to run the Prague to Kolín expresses on the new electric schedule, something they did comfortably and successfully. It must have been a glorious sight to watch one of these fleet-footed modern engines rasping past with a crackling three-cylinder Kylchap beat.

The twenty-one three-cylinder 477.0 class 4-8-4Ts of 1951–5 were, with little doubt, the most impressive-looking tank locomotives ever built. With their massive appearance, all-enclosed cab, skyline casing, Witte-style smoke deflectors, powerful headlamps, and sheer scale, there was nothing to match them; they were truly extraordinary machines. They used the same boiler as the 475.1 4-8-2s and were the only tank engine to employ a mechanical stoker. Official power output and maximum permitted speed were the same as for the 4-8-2s.

Mareš's final design put into production, and the very last class of steam locomotives to be built in Czechoslovakia, was the two-cylinder 556.0 class 2-10-0s which had so impressed Stewart Cox at Cheb in 1959. The 93 ton engines were fitted with the same boiler as the 475.1 and 477.0 classes, with double Kylchap exhausts and mechanical stokers, and with the boiler pressure raised to 265 psi. The result, size for size, was one of the world's best-looking, best-performing, most reliable, and most efficient freight locomotives. On test on 11 September 1958, and with driver Zapletal at the controls, 556.0338 hauled a train weighing no less than 4,177 tons between Kojetín and Ostrava. The 510 members of the class, with 1.4 m (4 ft 7 in) driving wheels, were expected to run 1,200 ton trains on the level at a constant 80 kph (50 mph); they could exert a peak output of 2,500 ihp at that speed. They were also used as required on passenger trains. The last member of the class to enter service was 556.0510, on 31 May 1958. The very last scheduled steam train on the ČSD – one of the international passenger services connecting Czechoslovakia at České Velenice and Austria at Gmund – was powered by 556.0506, on 1 April 1981.

Fortunately, members of the 475.1, 477.0, 498.1, and 556.0 classes, as well as several other ČSD steam locomotives, have been preserved in running order and can be seen and heard in action on special trains. Czech steam offers one of the greatest treats the enthusiast can still experience. What is so impressive about the Mareš engines is that they were such a highly intelligent and effective welding together of the best modern steam design offered by France, Germany (and Austria), and the United States. Stewart Cox even spotted what appeared to be a very singular British contribution: his attention had been drawn to that 556.0 class 2-10-0 at Cheb by the sound of its Caledonian whistle. No other Czech class was fitted with this distinctive whistle; its provenance remains happily mysterious. Along with this catholic approach to design, Mareš brought standardization to something of a fine art – and yet his machines were also beautiful works of industrial art and, for all their underlying internationalism, they were also distinctly Czech locomotives.

What set Mareš locomotives apart from so many German-inspired and German-built Eastern European steam locomotives was their extraordinary good looks. For those who visited Czechoslovakia in the days of steam, the Mareš engines came as something of a shock, especially if they had been seen only in black-and-white photographs. Many, thanks to the happy collaboration between Mareš and Vilém Kreibich, were painted bright green with red wheels, or an extraordinarily lively bright blue with red wheels. In practice, this worked remarkably well – even, perhaps especially, on the largest locomotives.

Kreibich was the son of an engine driver on the Czech Western Railway. Trained at the Academy of Fine Arts in Prague, he began receiving commissions for paintings from the Škoda locomotive works in Plzeň during the First World War. In the late 1920s, he met the young Mareš and together they worked to shape a new look for Czech steam which culminated in the design of the high-stepping post-war 4-8-2s. The 498.1s were the first to be painted blue, with a white stripe running the length of the locomotive, white cab roofs, and red wheels. Eastern European steam locomotives tended to be uniformly black, so the Czech engines stood out from the Red Star crowd and, with the kind of paintwork more normally found on new diesel and electric locomotives around the world, they had a decidedly modern appearance. This was helped by Mareš's high-set boilers with a revealing space between boiler, bar frames, and driving wheels, and by French-style smoke deflectors, Kylchap exhausts, all-enclosed cabs, and massive, yet wholly resolved, front ends.

Good as it was, Czech steam could well have developed further in the 1950s and beyond. Improvements were made with the fitting of Giesl ejectors on a large scale between 1962 and 1967, but there was a limit to what could be done because from 1948 the country had been under the yoke of the Soviet Union. When it did try to go its own liberal way in the spring of 1968, Moscow retaliated in no uncertain terms. On 21 August, an army of 200,000 soldiers drawn from the USSR, Poland, Hungary, and Bulgaria, backed by two thousand tanks, invaded Czechoslovakia and brought the recalcitrant country to heel.

*

Steam had not, in fact, been an option for the Czechs or anyone else in the eastern bloc since 1957, when Lazar Kaganovich, the USSR's transportation and heavy industry commissar, was ousted by Nikita Khrushchev after attempting to stage a coup against the new Soviet leader. Unsurprisingly, Kaganovich's five-year plan to build six thousand new steam locomotives was denounced, and steam development came to an abrupt end in both the USSR and its satellite states. This was partly because of the Communist Party's wish to repudiate Kaganovich's policies, but was also partly because tests appeared to demonstrate the superiority of new diesel locomotives. Yet, as Soviet officials themselves would admit in private, the sudden decision to bring an end to steam was influenced as much by what was happening in the United States as by the decisive break with Kaganovich.

The Soviet Union launched the world's first satellite the year following Kaganovich's fall, and in later years anyone in search of steam was told, time and again, that there was no such thing as a steam locomotive in the Space Age USSR. Since taking photographs of railway engines was regarded as espionage, it was indeed hard to prove that steam locomotives were hard at work in the Soviet Union for many more years. Writing in *Trains* magazine in August 1958, J. N. Westwood recalled a conversation with a suspicious Soviet railway official – one that would be repeated in one form or another right up until Mikhail Gorbachev's policy of *perestroika* was introduced:

> 'Why were you photographing engines?' 'Because
> I am interested in railways.' 'What do you mean –
> interested?' 'In my country many people spend their

spare time watching and photographing locomotives. They sometimes travel hundreds of miles just to see a particular engine.' 'You are a fool to expect me to believe that! Why should anyone want to study the engines of his own country? Besides, the police in Western countries would never allow people to spy on the railways.'

I fondly remember the beat of a powerful steam locomotive at work, very late in the steam age, when I woke up early one winter morning on board the *Rossiya*, the Trans-Siberian Express, in eastern Siberia. When the train stopped, for water, I dropped down from my sleeping car, its underside laced with icicles, to make sure my ears were not deceiving me. At the front of the long and heavy green train stood one of the charismatic two-cylinder P36 class 4-8-4s. By the time breakfast was served, the steam locomotive had disappeared. Again, I was told that there was no steam in Russia. I must have been dreaming. And, in any case, what was I doing on the platform spying on the locomotive?

In this strange land, the steam locomotive developed along lines that, in certain ways, were very much its own. Although most steam locomotives were rugged two-cylinder machines exhibiting pronounced German and American traits, these were often camouflaged with flamboyant liveries, political slogans, and other decorations. Russian main-line railways had always been different from their counterparts in Western Europe – and indeed much of Eastern Europe – because of the choice of track gauge – 1,520 mm (4 ft 11⅚ in) compared with 1,435 mm (4 ft 8½ in – and because of the nature of both the physical and the political terrain. Much of Russia is all but flat, and even the Ural mountains are easily climbed, so there was never the same need for sheer power as there was in Britain, France, and the United States. Equally, centralized political control, whether exercised by imperial or Soviet tsars, placed a very high emphasis on the development of freight traffic. In practice, this meant that for very many years passenger trains were rarely much, if at all, faster than main-line freight trains. Again, this meant that very powerful and fast passenger locomotives were unnecessary.

Because the railways were centralized from so early on, steam locomotives were largely of standard types, built in vast numbers and sometimes over many decades. The very last steam engines in regular service were the prolific E class 0-10-0s originally designed by V. I. Lopushinsky, chief mechanical engineer of the Vladikavkazskaya railway, at the Lugansk works, and built there from 1912. Something like eleven thousand of these sturdy and reliable freight locomotives were built up until 1957. Modifications were, of course, made along the way. With a tractive effort of 58,640 lb, the later Er class locomotives were capable of pulling enormous freight trains, albeit at a maximum permitted speed of 65 kph (43 mph). Power rating was 1,479 ihp. My own memory of them, aside from many seen in sidings from windows of passing trains, is of an Er working hard in sensationally cold weather at the head of a passenger train through Karelia, on a thrilling journey from Pitkyaranta, and the frozen Lake Lagoda, to Olonets, in early 1985. This is a land of pine forests, which had been a part of Finland before the Russo-Finnish wars of 1939–40 and 1941–4. Lake Lagoda itself had been the scene of fierce battles between the armies of the two countries. For those few hours, though, there seemed no better place to be, in the depths of winter, than on board this dark-green Russian train storming, if at no great speed, through an enchanting landscape made all the more haunting by the great plumes of white steam hurled up from the 0-10-0.

Despite their great height – up to 17 ft, compared with the 13 ft of British locomotives – Russian steam engines were modest machines in terms of scale, power, and speed, until the 1930s. A drive under Stalin to catch up with the United States in everything from military equipment to architecture led to the first large Soviet locomotives. Five 2-10-4s from Alco and five Baldwin 2-10-2s were shipped to the Soviet Union for trials; with their 22 or 23 ton axle loadings, they were too heavy for most Russian routes. In a bid to meet ministerial demands for the biggest and most powerful freight locomotives – and, perhaps, to outdo the Americans – a huge two-cylinder 4-14-4 was built at Lugansk works in 1934. The 208 ton locomotive made a press trip to Moscow in January 1935, but for all her nominal power and the great impression she made, the AA-20-1 was soon purged, along with the man she was named after, Andrei Andreev, people's commissar of the NKPS, the Soviet state railway. The world's one and only 4-14-4 had great difficulty in negotiating curves in yards and depots, and its great length meant it was unable to fit on existing turntables.

The locomotive boasted the biggest boiler, with a diameter of 8 ft 5 in – ever built for a European steam engine, and there was talk of 5,000 ihp; in practice, AA-20-A1 exerted 3,700 ihp pulling a 2,800 ton train up a 1-in-100 gradient, but because it was said to be a diffident steamer, as well as too long, it proved unpopular and was sent into exile. Stored for a quarter of a century at the Shcherbinka test track on the outskirts of Moscow, perhaps with a view to preservation, this shadowy image of Soviet power was cut up in 1960.

The 4-14-4 had made its debut in the year that the Krivonosite movement exerted its grip on the Soviet railways and Kaganovich replaced Andreev. Giganticism was now very much on the railway agenda. In July of that year, driver P. F. Krivonos began driving his E class 0-10-0 much harder than normally permitted, raising the average speed of freight trains from 24 to 32 kph. This was a direct corollary of the work of Aleksei Grigorievich Stakhanov, a miner who, also in 1935, allegedly dug 102 tons of coal in 5 hours and 45 minutes – using a power tool, presumably – and thus fulfilled his norm fourteen times over. This gave rise to the wider Stakhanovite movement across the Soviet Union, whereby workers, factories, their managers, party officials, and politicians sought to increase production and productivity many times over. It soon came to the point where anyone who dared question the wisdom of this insane movement, which wrecked the lives of workers – and, in the case of the Krivonosites, caused excessive wear to locomotives – was labelled a 'wrecker', which could only mean the gulag, torture, or execution.

Although Soviet locomotive engineers of the time turned to the United States for inspiration, Britain played a tantalizing role, too. A 266 ton Beyer Garratt 4-8-2 + 2-8-4 with a tractive effort of 78,700 lb had been ordered from Beyer Peacock of Manchester in 1930. It was shipped from England to Leningrad in component form in December 1932. This was the biggest Garratt of all and the largest steam locomotive built in Europe. No. Ya-01 proved to be a success, working well in the Sverdlovsk region of central Russia with 2,500 ton trains in temperatures as low as –41 °C. But, according to Keith Chester in *Elements of Locomotive Development in Russia and the USSR* (2000), the Garratt 'ran into a wall of prejudice'. It appears that the 'Soviet Union simply could not afford to import sufficient quantities of Garratts from the UK, nor did it have the facilities to erect them under licence, let alone maintain them'. The lone Garratt soldiered on until April 1937, on the East Siberian railway, and is said to have been broken up that year.

One of the big questions facing Soviet steam engineers – and one that the Garratt answered positively – was that of axle loading. Traditionally, tracks were lightly laid across the huge Russian land mass and so locomotives, unless they were built with many axles to spread the load, had to be light. But with a slow upgrading of many lines in the early 1930s from an axle loading of 16 or 18 tons to one of 20 tons, it became possible to design and operate bigger and more conventional locomotives. The first of these – the Soviet Union's equivalent of US super-power steam – were the FD class 2-10-2s, of which 3,213, including a modified FD18 version, were built between November 1931 and the summer of 1942, under the design direction of L. S. Lebedyansky and K. N. Suschkin of the Central Locomotive Project Group. Based on first-hand experience of American design practice – with the Alco 2-10-4s and Baldwin 2-10-2s – the 135 ton FDs formed the basis of what became a line of standard two-cylinder locomotives which continued in various guises and wheel arrangements until the end of steam construction. The FDs had large combustion-chamber boilers pressed to 213 psi, a 75.8 sq ft grate area and 1.5 m (4 ft 11 in) driving wheels. They were initially limited to 65 kph (40 mph), but this figure was later raised to 85 kph (53 mph). Their tractive effort was 15–20 per cent higher than the E class 0-10-0s, and at speeds above 30 kph (18.5 mph), their maximum power was double that of the earlier type. They were named after Felix Dzerzhinsky, an aristocrat by birth who became the first head of the Cheka, the greatly feared Soviet secret police.

A passenger version – the IS (Josef Stalin) class 2-8-4 – followed in October 1932, it was designed by the same team, and 650 were built before Hitler's invasion of the USSR in June 1941. With a power output of up to about 3,200 ihp, or 2,500 ihp in normal operation, the 2-8-4s could pull 750 ton trains on the level at 100 kph (62 mph), their initial maximum permitted speed; this was later raised to 115 kph (71.5 mph). One – IS20-16 – was streamlined in 1937 and recorded at 155 kph (96 mph) on test. Both the FD and IS were successful, much-liked classes (despite the names they celebrated) and provided decades of reliable service.

Three streamlined, light-blue 4-6-4s were built in 1937–8 for the *Krasnaya Strela* (Red Arrow) express between Moscow and Leningrad. Designed under the direction of L. S. Lebedyansky and K. N. Suschkin at Kolomna works, these 4-6-4s, the first two with 2 m (6 ft 6 in) and the third with 2.2 m (7 ft 2½ in) driving wheels, were to have been heralds of a larger class of at least ten more locomotives which were to have accelerated the principal trains on the line most used by visiting foreigners as well as by Soviet officials. The aim of reducing the running time over the 404 miles between the two cities from ten to eight hours was not to be achieved before the Great Patriotic War of 1941–5. The engines themselves were certainly capable of high speeds; on test on 29 June 1938, one of the class reached 106 mph on level track, a record that still stands for Russian steam. The 4-6-4s were seen at work in the 1970s, but were rarely allowed to show their undoubted pace.

In the post-war era, Lebedyansky was the predominant steam locomotive designer, although all proposals were considered by a central research committee, as in previous decades. The L class 2-10-0 which emerged from Kolomna works on 5 October 1945 was so successful that in 1947 its name was changed from P (for *pobeda*, or victory) to L, for Lebedyansky, in honour of its designer, an accolade unique in Soviet railway history. Some 4,200 were built between 1945 and 1955. With their relatively light axle load and top speed of 80 kph (50 mph), these popular locomotives, with their maximum output of 2,200 ihp between 40 and 60 kph, could work virtually throughout the entire Soviet railway network.

Then in late 1949, the prototype of a true express passenger locomotive emerged from Kolomna, designed under the direction of Lebedyansky. This was the first of the two-cylinder P36 class 4-8-4s, a series of charismatic and extremely good-looking engines which promised mile-a-minute schedules over main lines where average speeds of 60 kph (37 mph) were the norm for even the most prestigious passenger trains. With its skyline casing housing the external main steam-pipe, massive smoke deflectors sweeping back seamlessly into the high running board, smoke-box decorated with a big red star, twelve-wheeled bogie tender, and its livery of light green offset with white lining and vermilion Boxpok wheels with white rims, the P36 was a strikingly handsome machine.

Production began in earnest in 1954 and there were to have been up to a thousand of these 3,000 ihp, 135 ton locomotives. The decision to abandon steam development and construction in 1956, however, meant that just 251 were built. Simple and robust, and heavily influenced by US design, the P36 was powered by a tapered boiler pressed to 213 psi and a mechanically or oil-fired 72.6 sq ft grate. Highly superheated steam passed to two 575 × 800 mm (22⅝ × 31½ in) cylinders. The driving wheels were 1.85 m (6 ft 0¾ in), tractive effort 39,686 lb, and speed limit 125 kph (77.5 mph). With a well-designed steam circuit, the optimum thermal efficiency of the P36 was up to 24 per cent higher than that of an IS class 2-8-4.

The P36s were a memorable sight at the head of expresses from Moscow to Leningrad or charging across the seemingly endless steppes with the *Rossiya*. Some were finished in a painterly light blue. They were often the first Russian steam engines encountered by the few foreign visitors who made it to the Soviet Union from the West; they proved excellent ambassadors for a country where travelling was often difficult and which was frequently incomprehensible to outsiders. Although popular with crews, running staff, and passengers, the P36s were effectively withdrawn by the end of 1976. Fortunately, many survived into preservation and today it is still possible to enjoy truly luxurious tourist trips across great tracts of the former Soviet Union with a blue or green P36 at the head of the train. The P36s were the last passenger steam locomotives built for Russian railways.

The last new class of mass-produced freight locomotives was the LV class 2-10-2s, of which 522 were built at the Voroshilovgrad (Lugansk) works between 1954 and 1956. These led on from a prototype of 1952. The LVs were essentially a lengthened L class 2-10-0, with a larger fire-box and grate area; they featured a number of technical improvements over the L class, including a higher degree of superheating, a feedwater heater, bar frames, roller bearings, and a mechanical stoker. They were also equipped with an ingenious mechanism that could adjust weight distribution between coupled wheels; this allowed a variation in axle load of between 18 and 19 tons, and a boost to starting power as the locomotive accelerated from rest with heavy freight trains. Maximum power was 2,420 ihp between 50 and 60 kph (31–37 mph). With its partial skyline casing, but for the red star on the smoke-box door, an LV could easily have been mistaken for an American freight engine. At the height of the Cold War, Soviet and American steam locomotives were closer than cousins.

Before Kagonovich's fall and exile, there was one last shout for new Soviet steam with a project for a much higher-powered freight locomotive with a 20 ton axle load. This was Lebedyansky's hugely impressive four-cylinder P38, a 2-8-8-4 Mallet, of which just two appear to have been built in 1954–5. The first – P38-0001 – boasted a dramatic, almost art deco, shroud around its smoke-box which gave the massive engine a slightly otherworldly appearance. This was not fitted to the remaining member (or members) of the class; as a result, they looked much like American Mallets. With four 575 × 800 mm (22.6 × 31½ in) cylinders, a grate area of 115 sq ft, 213 psi boiler pressure, and 1.5 m (4 ft 11 in) driving wheels, the Soviet Mallets promised much in the way of tractive effort and power at speeds of up to a permitted 85 kph (53 mph). On test on the Krasnoyarsk railway in 1955, one of these machines hauled a 3,500 ton train up a 1-in-110 gradient at a steady 23 kph (14.3 mph), developing 3,600 dbhp, or about 4,600 ihp, in the process. But the die had been cast and, although as powerful as the latest diesels and electrics except at very low speeds, the P38s had little or no chance to prove themselves; they were taken out of service in July 1959. Packed off to the Belgorodsky district, they were dismantled and their boilers used in sugar-beet factories.

'I am for the steam locomotive and against those who imagine that we will not have any steam locomotives in the future; this machine is sturdy, stubborn, and won't give up.' So Lazar Kaganovich had said in his speech of 1954 when he had proposed thousands of new steam locomotives. Three years later, this former henchman of Josef Stalin was dispatched into exile to run a small potassium factory in the Urals. Expelled from the Communist Party for good in 1961, Kaganovich returned to Moscow and lived on until the end of the Soviet Union in 1991. 'In years to come,' wrote H. M. Le Fleming and J. H. Price in *Russian Steam Locomotives* (1960), 'his name will probably be honoured by steam traction enthusiasts, for his obduracy gave the world some most interesting steam locomotives.' Actually, not even the most fervent steam enthusiast should ever honour the memory of Lazar

Kaganovich. This ardent Stalinist was one of those directly responsible for the politically motivated death by starvation of millions of Ukrainians during the *Holodomor* ('killing by hunger') of 1932–3. He was also in charge of putting down strikes by workers, gratuitously demolishing historic buildings, and signing the death warrants of hundreds of those who fell foul of Stalin's regime.

A country, though, abounding in new supplies of hydroelectricity and with its own easy access – at the time – to oil reserves, was perhaps inevitably thinking of a switch from steam to diesel and electric technology. Even so, there is no question that the sudden decision to drop steam was a political act. When Khrushchev took power in 1956, denouncing Stalin, the boss he had served so loyally until the dictator's death in 1953, he wanted to push the Soviet Union into the forefront of modern technology and ahead of the United States. Whether in terms of the space race, military hardware, or railway traction, the USSR was on the march anew from the mid-1950s, in double-quick time. Steam locomotives were, however, to run in daily service until the early 1990s and, pleasingly, they were kept in spick-and-span condition. Who couldn't help 'spying' on them?

As for Lev Sergeyevich Lebedyansky, the Soviet Union's finest locomotive engineer of the 'Super Steam' era, he too met a sorry end. And, it was politics – of a very petty nature – that appears to have brought a premature end to his stellar career. This was especially sad, as not only was Lebedyansky a particularly fine engineer, but the Soviet state had long recognized his achievements. He was awarded the Order of Lenin and held two Orders of the Red Banner for Labour, and when the L-class 2-10-0s were named in his honour, he was made a laureate of the Stalin Prize, which was high praise indeed.

A graduate of the Petrograd Polytechnic Institute, Lebedyansky was employed from 1922 until 1963 at the Kolomna locomotive works – 114 kms south-east of Moscow by rail – where he rose to become principal designer and chief of construction. He survived Kaganovich's fall. On 29 June 1956, Lebedyansky held a celebratory event at the

Kolomna works to commemorate the simultaneous production of its last steam locomotive, P36-0251, and of its first diesel loco, TE3-1001. The twin-unit 1,972 hp Co-Co diesel was, in fact, very much a Lebedyansky-led design with the prototype emerging from Khar'kov works as early as 1953. Production of this highly successful class of freight locomotives continued until 1973 by which time no fewer than 6,809 were in service.

Lebedyansky went on to lead the design of the 2,959 hp, 160 kph TEP60 Co-Co diesel-electric, the Soviet Union's first purpose-built express passenger diesel; 1,241 were built between 1960 and 1985. At the same time, Lebedyansky developed a new generation of gas-turbine electric locomotives, the first of which, G1-01 – a singularly handsome machine – was built at Kolomna in 1959. It was this promising machine that brought about Lebedyansky's tragic fall.

G1-01 was demonstrated at an exhibition of the latest Soviet locomotives in April 1963. Khruschev was present. The Soviet leader, it seems, was informed that the G1-01 was not as efficient as the latest diesel-electrics. Lebedyansky had the temerity – or the naivety of the apolitical engineer – to suggest otherwise. Soon afterwards, he was summoned to a meeting with the director of the Kolomna works and told that all work on the gas-turbine electric would cease forthwith. Again, Lebedyansky remonstrated; in the ensuing row with his chief, the engineer suffered a heart attack. An ambulance took him to hospital. His resignation followed, and then he was hit by a stroke that paralysed the right side of his body.

Lebedyanksy lived for a further five years, a victim of the capriciousness and sheer nastiness of Soviet politics. Since then, however, a memorial plaque has been affixed to the house – 330 October Revolution Street, Kolomna – where he lived for the last twenty-eight years of his life, while an L-class 2-10-0 – No 0012 – stands on a plinth close by in a street named after him. The centenary of the engineer's birth was marked with a plaque fixed on the management block of Kolomna works. Happily, Lebedyansky's handsome steam locomotives speed on at the head of special trains today.

*

Remarkably, Russian and Russian-derived steam did live on in a country that even today is a communist state, despite running the world's most successful capitalist economy. This geographical and political enigma is the People's Republic of China. Here, production of the 3,000 ihp, two-cylinder QJ (*Qian Jin* or 'march forward') class 2-10-2, derived from the Russian LV class, continued until 1988. In 1987, I witnessed the production of these engines at Datong works in Inner Mongolia; even at the time it was hard to believe that steam locomotives of this scale were still being built for a state railway. And, given that this was a communist country, and despite a gaping language barrier, it was a particular delight to be treated courteously and without the slightest sign of suspicion. Perhaps this was because I was in Mongolia and among Mongols, rather than in China proper. The odd thing for me was that I had not known that steam was still under construction at Datong. I had come all this way to see the remarkable sixth-century Hanging Monastery perched miraculously on the side of Heng Shan mountain, some forty miles south-east of Datong. An architect-engineer working on some essential repairs told me about the railway works. How we got into a conversation about steam, I cannot now remember, but a love of steam is a shared passion and its language a global one.

What I did not know at the time was that the finest moment of these 2-10-2s was to be some years in the future, with the opening of the Jitong railway in 1995. Running 587 miles through Inner Mongolia between Jining and Tongliao, through Datong, this was the world's last brand-new steam main line. Like many steam enthusiasts at the time, I thought that there must have been some mistake, in translation perhaps. But no, the railway was quite real. More pragmatic than the Soviet Russians, the communist Chinese believed that the best use should be made of appropriate fuel resources and technology. As the new railway ran through coal belts, and Datong was along the line, steam made economic sense. There was, though, no desire on the part of the vast majority of Chinese officials to prolong the life of steam. Far from it. Most were committed modernizers who would, soon enough, abandon steam on the Jitong railway. What mattered in 1995, and for the following ten years, was that steam was cheap in terms of both capital cost and the cost of fuel.

The Jitong railway was worked by steam until 8 December 2005. This ten-year period of grace gave many enthusiasts the opportunity to see powerful steam locomotives working hard at the head of heavy freight trains, along a line that passed through several areas of natural grandeur. The Jinpeng pass became a mecca for steam enthusiasts in that astonishing decade. Here, too, was the chance to ride long-distance, steam-hauled, sleeping-car trains, to ride on the footplate, to see locomotives being serviced, and to stay with the families of Datong's tolerant steam men. I came this way in 1996 and was enchanted. This, truly, was the last great blast of regular main-line steam.

For whatever reason, the Chinese authorities appeared to allow 'foreign devils', or 'ghost people', as they call us, something of a free hand in and around Datong. What few local hostels existed in this bleakly beautiful part of the world were rather grim places, so it was a delight to be able to stay with the families of locomotive crews. A little disappointingly for me, most of the men were looking forward to the day when diesels would arrive. In a bitterly cold climate, they wanted enclosed cabs and engines that could be easily switched off and parked for the night – no fire to rake out, no ashes to dispose of, little in the way of soot and oily grime. The men, however, threw themselves into their work with gusto.

Between 1956 and 1988, no fewer than 4,714 QJs were built, accounting for about half of all steam locomotives produced from the Chinese revolution of 1949 until 1988, a decade after the country's 'second revolution', the economic reforms led by Deng Xiaoping.

Mass production of the class began in 1964. Significantly, the first QJ emerged from the Dalian works soon after the last Russian LV 2-10-2 was built. Over the years, various improvements were made, including an unofficial Chinese version of the Giesl ejector exhaust, and experiments with gas-producer fire-boxes, but the class remained essentially creatures of the late 1940s, modified for Chinese conditions.

Hard-riding and unrefined in many ways, the QJs were nonetheless the workhorses of the Chinese railways in the 1970s and 1980s. They could be worked very hard and yet were generally liked by their crews. They steamed well, were simple to maintain, and many featured a WC in the tender, a luxury unknown to 99 per cent of the world's steam locomotive crews. Restricted to a maximum speed of 80 kph (50 mph) – they were fitted with 1.5 m (4 ft 11 in) driving wheels – the QJs were rated at a maximum of 2,980 ihp, although on test 3,580 ihp was recorded at 41 mph. It was certainly thrilling to ride the footplate of a QJ, klaxon sounding and whistle blowing, as it led a second member of the class at full regulator and 45 per cent cut-off up and around the curving concrete viaduct through the Jinpeng pass at the head of an enormous coal train, with twin plumes of steam trailing back through the snow-sheathed mountains.

The SY (*Shang You*, or 'reach upward') class 2-8-2, of which some were still at work on colliery railways in 2012, was built between 1960 and 1999. More than 1,800 of these light mixed-traffic engines were put into service. The design of the SY, the world's last mass-produced main-line steam locomotive, dates back almost a century. The locomotives owe their ancestry to the Japanese *Mi Ka Ro* 2-8-2, brought to China in 1934 at the time of the Japanese occupation of Manchuria. In turn, the *Mi Ka Ro* was based on Alco 2-8-2s supplied to Japanese-occupied Korea in the 1920s. Despite attempts elsewhere to radically improve and even to completely rethink the conventional Stephensonian locomotive, it is significant that this final ambassador for main-line steam was a simple, modestly powered, yet rugged, two-cylinder machine, which would have fitted in quite readily to the railways of 1920s America before Woodard and super-power steam.

An important British contribution to Chinese motive power was the Kf class 4-8-4, of which twenty-four were built by the Vulcan Foundry in 1934–5 to the design specifications of Kenneth Cantlie, technical adviser to the Chinese National Railways from 1930 to 1937. Cantlie was much in favour in China, as his father had saved Sun Yat-sen, first president of the Chinese Republic, from return to China and certain execution when, as a medical student in London, he was kidnapped by agents of the imperial government. Built for the heavily inclined Canton–Hangkow line, Cantlie's 4-8-4s were powerful and impressive machines. When the locomotives were withdrawn in 1980, Hua Kuofeng, the Chinese railways minister, who had been a railway operating trainee when the British 4-8-4s were built, told Cantlie that they were among the finest locomotives in China and that he would like one to be taken back to England as a tribute to the engineer's work. This was duly done, which is why a Kf 4-8-4 resides today at the National Railway Museum in York.

*

Steam survived late in the day in a number of countries, including India as well as China, but here again steam locomotive development never really advanced much after the 1940s. The pinnacle of 1940s steam design on railways outside of Britain, France, Germany, and the United States was, perhaps, the South African Railways class 25 and 25NC 4-8-4s, of which 140 were built by Henschel in Kassel and the North British Locomotive Company in Glasgow, between 1953 and 1955. These impressive and muscular machines, which ran in regular mainline service into the 1990s, have often been likened to scaled-down New York Central Railroad Niagara 4-8-4s, and, in many ways, that is what these heavily American-influenced locomotives were. What made them remarkable was the fact that they were designed and built for South Africa's 3 ft 6 in gauge national railway and yet, despite this limitation, they were big and imposing as well as powerful machines.

In terms of design, they were in advance of the Standard classes of locomotives built by British Railways in the 1950s. In fact, many of Britain's most impressive steam locomotives were built for use in Africa and other parts of the former British Empire. There were several reasons for this, including the scale and nature of the landscapes the African railways ran through, a pressing need to conserve fuel and water, and the need for robust construction, reliability, and easy maintenance. There was, though, something else: the freedom of thought that some locomotive engineers working far away from Britain seem to have enjoyed. Meanwhile, the chief mechanical engineers of the South African Railways themselves worked closely, like their American peers, with commercial manufacturers.

The 25s and 25NCs were, in fact, part of a pattern of locomotive development that dated back to before the Second World War and had paved the way for standardized engines of great power and efficiency. That these locomotives were also good-looking was not so much a bonus as a consequence of a mindset that believed that the railways deserved the very best. In the 1930s, the South African management tried to increase the speed of its trains up to rates previously unknown south of Algeria, where streamlined French Garratts ran at up to 75 mph on expresses between Oran and Algiers.

An attempt to raise the speed limit on key main lines to 70 mph was blocked by the chief civil engineer, although not before Allan Griffiths Watson, chief mechanical engineer from 1929 to 1936 and mastermind of the standardization programme, had designed six magnificent 16E class Pacifics, built by Henschel, which could run very happily at more than 70 mph. Sadly, the railway's blanket speed limit was raised to 110 kph (68.3 mph) – and then only on certain sections of the famous Blue Train route – only after the 16Es had been withdrawn from service in 1973. These two-cylinder Pacifics were extremely impressive. With massive boilers, huge, 63 sq ft grates, a high degree of superheating, 24 × 28 in cylinders, and Lentz rotary-cam poppet valves, they steamed well and ran freely. Their 6 ft 0 in driving wheels were the largest ever fitted to 3 ft 6 in gauge locomotives. Weighing 98 tons and as long and as high as British Pacifics, with a tractive effort of 39,985 lb, they were imposing and powerful machines and South Africa's speediest locomotives – one was tested at 90 mph. They were also built more than fifteen years before British Railways' two-cylinder Britannia Pacifics, their British equivalents.

Watson, born in Hopetown, Cape Province, had spent five years in Glasgow between 1895 and 1900 working at the North British Locomotive Company and studying at the city's technical college. A draughtsman with a fine eye, he had considerable experience of the day-to-day running of locomotives before he was appointed chief mechanical engineer of South African Railways and Harbours, at the age of fifty-three. He brought the country's locomotive works up to date and, while maintaining excellent relations with the North British Locomotive Company in Glasgow and Henschel in Kassel, laid the foundations for one of the world's finest fleets of modern steam locomotives, marrying the best traditions and innovations from Britain, Germany, the United States, and, increasingly, South Africa itself. Like many of his generation, he is an unsung hero in South Africa today.

In 1935, Watson designed the 15F class, a very large, mixed-traffic 4-8-2, with 5 ft 0 in driving wheels, a grate area of 63 sq ft, and a tractive effort of 46,771 lb. Watson was also responsible for the excellent 19C class light 4-8-2s for branch and secondary lines, with rotary-cam poppet valve gear; and the 19D class 4-8-2s, with piston valves, built from 1937 to 1948. I rode behind several of these locomotives at the time of the elections that brought Nelson Mandela to power, especially on the sublime George–Knysna line, running along the south coast of South Africa. The way in which these engines accelerated away from stations set on sharp curves, and up gradients slippery after rain, was deeply impressive and remains one of my fondest steam memories to date. Here was a steam locomotive as well adapted to its environment as a mountain goat.

The 16E Pacifics, however, were not sufficiently powerful to tackle the heaviest post-war passenger trains. Work on what became the 25 and 25NC class 4-8-4s began in the late 1940s, when experiments with enlarged boilers and condensing equipment were carried out under the direction of H. J. L. du Toit, working under Dr M. M. Loubser, who was chief mechanical engineer from 1939 to 1949, in collaboration with Henschel. The orders for the 4-8-4s were finally placed by L. C. Grubb, chief mechanical engineer from 1949 to 1954.

A massive 6 ft 4 in diameter boiler, pressed to 225 psi, was fired by a welded-steel 70 sq ft grate. The combustion chamber was adopted from German practice established by Richard Wagner. Steam was passed to two 24 × 28 in cylinders. Driving wheels were 5 ft 0 in; tractive effort was 51,400 lb. Roller bearings were used throughout the engines. Free running and packing a tremendous punch on starting, the 4-8-4s proved to be ideal locomotives for several routes on a railway characterized by heavy passenger and freight trains worked up steep gradients from frequent stops. In autumn 1968, O. S. Nock made a trip to South Africa and in the June 1969 issue of *Railway* magazine wrote up a very typical run made by these greatly respected machines. He rode the eighteen-coach 08.55 stopping train from Kimberley to De Aar, a 146 mile trip. The load was 730 tons. No. 3449 took this heavy train in its stride. The train made fifteen intermediate stops in its journey across the rolling plains, with an average running speed of 57.6 kph (35.8 mph).

Given that stations were often as little as five and a maximum of fifteen miles apart, and that the line limit was 90 kph (56 mph), this was very good going. 'The evidence of extremely hard work from every start was manifested in a continuous roar from the exhaust,' Nock observed. 'There was also some long and uphill slogging, on gradients of around 1-in-100, with magnificently sustained speeds of 38 to 40 mph . . . the making of relatively short runs of around ten miles, start to stop, at average running speeds of 40 mph was extraordinarily good work.' It was rather like the work Kiefer's Niagaras were put to at the end of their working lives on the New York Central Railroad, with trains between New York and Chicago making stops every twenty to thirty miles.

'Here was a country,' wrote the British engineer Stewart Cox in *Locomotive Panorama* (vol. 2, 1966), thinking of these mighty, Cape-gauge 4-8-4s, 'where steam had run its course of development to the very limits of size and weight . . . As in the case of the USA, it is hard to see what further development would have been possible, was electrification not being deployed to take its place.' This is interesting, because Cox reveals just how unaware steam locomotive engineers were of the potential for further development at the very time that the steam locomotive itself was most under threat. It was, in fact, in South Africa, some fifteen years after Cox's *Locomotive Panorama* was published, that David Wardale rebuilt a class 25 into a substantially more powerful and efficient steam locomotive, *The Red Devil* (see Chapter 7).

Designed under the direction of their chief engineer, Dr Richard Roosen, ninety of the new 4-8-4s were equipped with Henschel condensing equipment including vast condensing tenders. The aim was to reduce water consumption dramatically when operating steam in arid regions like the Great Karoo, between Touws River and De Aar, and across South-West Africa. Exhaust steam from the cylinders passed through a receiver to a turbine-driven draughting fan in the smoke-box, which replaced the conventional blast-pipe, and then through large-diameter pipes to a low-pressure turbine at the front of the tender, before finally passing to condensing pipes at the sides of the tender. The low-pressure turbine was geared to drive five condenser air-cooling fans mounted along the top of the tender. Condensation was collected in a well at the bottom of the tender and then returned to the boiler using two turbine-driven rotary pumps. Although complex, this arrangement allowed the 25s to run up to five hundred miles between water stops. The 25s consumed 90 per cent less water than the conventional 25NCs (non-condensing), using the same water up to eight times over, while the use of hot recycled feedwater also led to a 10 per cent decrease in coal consumption. With their huge tender, lute-shaped smoke-box, and whining exhaust, the 25s cut a very particular dash across the scorching veldt.

Inevitably, maintenance costs were higher than for the non-condensing 25s, and as they were replaced on the Karoo main line by diesels and electrics between 1973 and 1980, they were converted into 25NCs. Cheap coal and global fuel crises kept South Africa in steam until relatively late in the day, although ardent modernizers were at work here as elsewhere. Even during the oil scares of the late 1970s, at a time when South African industry was being asked to go easy on the use of oil, diesel locomotives were ordered to replace steam. This was unnecessary and barely justified: tests proved that the 25s compared well with the new diesels in terms of running costs. Exceptionally hard-working locomotives, the 25s could be turned at the end of a five-hundred-mile run with the heaviest of trains and sent back in the opposite direction, with minimal maintenance. Steam, though, had to go, whatever the cost; common sense was not always part of the management agenda.

The 25s worked a substantial amount of passenger and freight traffic in their long heyday; powerful, much liked by crews, and generally popular, they were a fine example of a late-flowering, heavy-duty, mixed-traffic locomotive which could have been developed further as a class in terms of both power output and efficiency. The class was essentially intact as late as 1988. Unfortunately, decisions made at government level to transfer freight to the roads made an increasing number of locomotives redundant. Today, it is heartbreaking to see the wilful destruction of historic locomotives and to witness how the conservation of steam, which is hugely popular with visitors to the country, is met with official obstruction, being regarded in some narrow-minded quarters as a legacy of colonialism. South Africa appears to be turning its back on this particular aspect of its history.

*

Sadly, the once highly efficient East African Railways have gone much the same way. It seems beyond belief that such a fine international railway network, connecting Kenya, Uganda, and Tanzania, was allowed to fall into precipitous decline. The damage to the economies of these three countries has been enormous, as battered and often dangerous and unreliable lorries have taken the place of trains hauled by a fleet of magnificent, well-maintained and spotless locomotives. The greatest of these was without doubt the class 59 4-8-2 + 2-8-4 Garratt built in Gorton, Manchester, in 1955–6 by Beyer Peacock. These thirty-four machines were the largest, heaviest, and most powerful steam locomotives – capable of producing 3,500 ihp when fitted with Gisel ejectors – built for a metre-gauge line anywhere in the world. From 1960, by which time the American Mallets and 4-8-4s had gone, they were among the most powerful steam locomotives running anywhere in the world.

Resplendent in highly polished maroon paintwork, with gleaming cabs, usually manned by devoted Sikh crews, the class 59s, which were all named after African mountains, were built to work both heavy long-distance freight and passenger mail trains up from the Kenyan coast at Mombasa to Nairobi. This long, single-track line – all 329 miles of it – boasted a ruling uphill gradient of 1-in-66. It climbed from sea level at Mombasa to 5,600 feet at Nairobi; further on towards Kampala, the line peaked first at 7,690 feet at Uplands on the eastern scarp of the Great Rift Valley, and then, once across this daunting geographical divide, climbed yet again to 9,136 feet east of Timboroa. With a weight of 252 tons and a tractive effort of 83,350 lb, the 59s were masters of this demanding and exceptionally beautiful line, working 1,200 ton trains with relative ease – loads 70 per cent greater than before their arrival. The sight and sound of these glorious engines pounding up steep escarpments and steaming past prides of lions and other wildlife, or winding their way down the roller-coaster track back to Mombasa, must have been thrilling.

The story of the East African Railways was certainly a dramatic one.

After much heated debate, Westminster agreed to the construction of a 584 mile railway from Mombasa on the Indian Ocean up to Nairobi and on through the Kenyan Highlands to Port Florence (Kisumu) on the eastern bank of Lake Victoria. The £5 million line was built in a breathtakingly fast five years, between 1896 and 1901, opening to traffic in 1903. 'The British art of "muddling through" was here seen in one of its finest expositions,' wrote Winston Churchill, an early visitor to the new railway. 'Through everything – through the forests, through the ravines, through troops of marauding lions, through famine, through war, through five years of excoriating Parliamentary debate – muddled and marched the railway.'

The future British prime minister and war leader was not exaggerating. Maasai tribesmen massacred five hundred railway workers after the rape of two girls. During the construction of a bridge across the Tsavo river in 1898, a pair of male lions killed at least twenty-eight African and Indian labourers. The 'Man-Eaters of Tsavo' were eventually shot by Lieutenant Colonel John Henry, the engineer in charge of building the bridge, who made their skins into rugs which he sold for $5,000 a piece in Chicago. At Mackinnon Road, a small lowland town between Mombasa and Voi, trains still pass a lineside mosque where travellers stop to visit the tomb of Seyyid Baghali, a Punjabi foreman who had been working on the construction of the railway before being eaten by a lion. (At the time that the 59 class Garratts were arriving in Mombasa from Manchester, Mackinnon Road was best known for its detention camp, where Mau Mau soldiers and suspects, fighting against the British and fellow Kenyans, were held during the uprising of 1952–60.)

The railway was amalgamated with Tanganyika Railways in 1948 to form the East African Railways and Harbours Administration. A big-engine policy was adopted almost immediately, spearheaded by William Ellerington Bulman, a former GWR engineer, who had also worked with the Canadian Pacific, and rose to become chief mechanical engineer of the East African Railways. 'He was one of the old generation CMEs who could walk around his drawing office and comment with experience on almost any detail under way,' recalled A. E. 'Dusty' Durrant, a young engineer who left Swindon for Nairobi in 1955. 'When in a good mood he would regale us with his experience in the Canadian Rockies, where double-headed and banked 2-10-2s and 2-10-4s clawed over the Great Divide with never an anxious moment on steaming capacity.'

Bulman collaborated closely with Beyer Peacock on the design of his masterpiece, the 59 class, travelling to the company's Gorton works to obtain exactly what he wanted. He was assistant chief mechanical engineer at the time and the design of the 59s was carried out under the overall direction of G. Gibson, the East African Railways' chief mechanical engineer. Bulman insisted, for example, on a 7 ft 6 in rather than a 7 ft 0 in boiler; he wanted maximum steam production for maximum power output. And brilliant performers though these locomotives were, Bulman wanted even more power. He and his engineers worked on design proposals for a far bigger engine, the 61 class 4-8-2 + 2-8-4 Garratt with a tractive effort of 115,000 lb but a much heavier axle load than the 59s. The boilers of the 61s, pressed to 250 psi, would have had a diameter of no less than 8 ft 6 in. Durrant, meanwhile, went even further and outlined a 4-12-2 + 2-12-4 with the same axle loading as a class 59 and a tractive effort of 125,000 lb.

These machines would have been the most powerful steam locomotives outside the United States. The 59s, however, proved able, especially when fitted from 1959 with Giesl ejector exhausts, to handle everything then required by the East African Railways, and so they were eventually succeeded not by bigger Garratts, but by diesel-electrics. On test, a Giesl-fitted 59 hauled a 1,200 ton train up the 1-in-66 gradient from Nairobi to Uplands 33 per cent faster than a 59 with a single blast-pipe, which burned 15 per cent more oil.

Up until the end, in 1980, the 59s were cherished by all who had a hand in their working. The best-kept member of the class was 5918 *Mount Gelai* (since preserved), whose regular crew worked the red

Garratt for sixteen unbroken years. According to Colin Garratt, a particularly well-travelled railway photographer: 'Her cab interior is more akin to a Sikh temple than a locomotive footplate for its boiler face abounds in polished brasswork, embellished with mirrors, clocks, silver buckets, and a linoleum floor.' Indeed, one of her regular drivers, Kirpal Singh Sandhu, who died in 2010, had a bar fitted in his home in Mombasa made from components from the cab of a retired 59. It was a happy sight and proof of just how well loved these remarkable locomotives were.

*

Virtually everywhere they ran, in fact, Garratts were to prove extremely popular. These articulated engines were invented by Herbert William Garratt, who began his career as a steam locomotive engineer at the Bow works of the North London Railway, before moving to marine engineering in Sunderland and then back to locomotives. He worked in Argentina, Cuba, and Peru before resettling in London in 1906. It was while observing horse-drawn carriages in motion that Garratt had the idea for an articulated locomotive which would align itself freely to swing through sharp curves like no other. A boiler and fire-box were to be carried on a girder frame pivoted above fore and aft engine units. This layout allowed for large boilers with wide and deep fire-boxes, unrestricted by the presence of axles. It was a brilliant idea, effectively two locomotives in one, and ideal for lines with restricted axle loading. Beyer Peacock took up Garratt's 1907 patent with little enthusiasm but were eventually to build a total of 1,023 Garratts for fifty-six railways in thirty-six countries.

The first Garratt was one of a pair of 2 ft gauge 0-4-0 + 0-4-0s built in 1909 for the Tasmanian government's North East Dundas Tramway; the Garratts worked the line successfully until it closed in 1929. The last Garratts, built by Hunslet-Taylor in Germiston, South Africa, after the closure of Beyer Peacock, was an NG16 class 2-6-2 + 2-6-2 built in 1968 for the 2 ft gauge lines of South African Railways. Happily, both these historic locomotives are at work today on the Welsh Highland

Railway, a glorious 25 mile line, completed in 2011, which steams through Snowdonia between Caernarfon and Porthmadog.

Between these poles, Garratts were built for service in many parts of the world, but perhaps most notably in Africa. The most remarkable, and unexpected, were the twenty-nine 231-132BT 4-6-2 + 2-6-4 express passenger Garratts built at Raismes, in northern France, between 1936 and 1941 by the Société Franco-Belge de Matériel de Chemins de Fer, in association with Beyer Peacock, for the Algerian railways, operated first by the PLM and then by the state-owned Chemins de Fer Algériens. These semi-streamlined machines, weighing 212.6 tons, were to feature double PLM-type exhausts, electrically controlled Cossart drop-piston valve gear, mechanical stokers, and a boiler pressure of 284 psi. Their starting tractive effort was 66,000 lb. Their 1.8 m (5 ft 10¾ in) driving wheels were the largest of any Garratt.

These striking machines were complex and yet peerless in terms of performance when carefully serviced and maintained. On test in France between Paris and Calais, an Algerian driver had the massive locomotive spinning along at 132 kph (82 mph) between La Falaise and Ailly-sur-Noye, and generating 3,000 dbhp on the climb to the summit at Survilliers. This was the highest speed ever recorded by a Garratt – or, indeed, by any other articulated steam locomotive, including the Union Pacific Challengers and Big Boys. The Algerian Garratt was capable of developing 3,600 ihp for extended periods.

In Algiers, and taking over from ex-PLM 4-6-0s, these locomotives accelerated the principal Algiers–Oran passenger trains by two hours from 1937; the run of 422 kilometres (262 miles), with a train of 450 tons, making nineteen intermediate stops, was now made in seven hours. This demanded rapid acceleration and spells of running at 120 kph (74.5 mph). The relative complexity of their design, along with the effects of poor local water, proved to be the Achilles heel of these otherwise exceptional machines; denied the care they needed in wartime and the years following, they were retired in 1951 after what, for a Garratt, was a very short life. Sadly, none survives.

The British experience of Garratts was far less satisfactory. This had nothing to do with the inherent qualities of the Beyer Peacock locomotives, but was a consequence of interference by the LMS motive power superintendent, J. E. Anderson. The LMS took delivery of thirty-three four-cylinder 2-6-0 + 0-6-2 Garratts between 1927 and 1930. They worked heavy coal trains for the most part, over the Midland main line from Toton (Nottingham) to Brent (London). Unfortunately, Anderson had insisted on changes to the design, with the result that the engines were beset by wholly unnecessary problems, including inadequately sized and poorly lubricated axle boxes, and short-lap, short-travel piston valves. The Garratts nonetheless did much hard work, replacing pairs of 4F class 0-6-0s on heavy coal trains. They survived until 1958, but were little loved. The only other main-line British Garratt was one built at Gorton with Nigel Gresley in 1925; the solitary six-cylinder U1 2-8-0 + 0-8-2 was used for banking heavy coal trains up 1-in-40 inclines in south Yorkshire; it was retired in 1955.

The one design for a Garratt that could have truly helped the LMS was a six-cylinder express passenger compound 4-6-2 + 2-6-4 Garratt, with 6 ft 9 in driving wheels, worked up as a very convincing proposal by Beyer Peacock in 1930. In all probability it would have been a great success, but when William Stanier came to the LMS from Swindon with a powerful four-cylinder Pacific in mind, the express Garratt was dropped. Beyer Peacock did try once more, with a proposal made to British Railways in 1949 for a four-cylinder 4-6-2 + 2-6-4, with 5 ft 9 in driving wheels, for use in Scotland. It never got beyond the drawing board, partly because at the time there was only one train daily – the Perth–Inverness sleeper – that weighed more than a single Stanier class 5 4-6-0 could manage.

No, the Garratt's great stamping ground was Africa. Even today – certainly in 2011 – a handful of Garratts, returned to service in 2004–5, can be seen at work now and again around Bulawayo in Zimbabwe, though whether Garratt-hauled trains to Victoria Falls will ever return remains to be seen.

*

There were, of course, interesting locomotive developments in various outposts – advanced, developing, and remote – of the steam world. Other countries – Canada, Australia, New Zealand, India, and Japan among them – created impressive and much-admired machines which often operated in demanding or downright inhospitable terrain, but the majority of steam locomotives built for or by them were, as ever, heavily influenced by British, American, German, and sometimes, especially in terms of thermodynamics, French experience. None, however, demanded the high steam-cycle efficiency achieved by the likes of Chapelon in France, or the sustained high speeds that characterized the steam railways of Britain and the United States. Indeed, many steam locomotives served railways that for any number of reasons – political, economic, geographic, the nature and quality of local fuel supplies – were unable to work trains at great speeds. It was often impossible to commission or build extremely powerful locomotives because of track conditions and axle-loading limits. These were considerations that applied to even the most ambitious countries. I was certainly thrilled to see a Japanese National Railways C62 class two-cylinder 4-6-4 in action at the head of a special train in the early 1990s. My immediate impressions were of a miniature version of a US Hudson and of the dense and voluminous clouds of thick black smoke trailing behind what was otherwise a delightful machine.

In fact, the C62 class was, marginally, the most powerful and fastest steam locomotive to serve Japan's railways and, despite some distinctive local design details, it really was an American Hudson at heart. With its disc wheels, powerful headlamps, and haunting chime whistles, the C62 could be nothing else. The thick black smoke was caused by poor-quality local coal. The low calorific value of Japanese coal was one reason why Japanese steam was limited in terms of power output; the other was a 15 ton maximum axle loading. The C62s, of which forty-nine were built between 1947 and 1949 by Hitachi, Kawasaki, and Kisha Seizo Kaisha, were metre-gauge locomotives and weighed no more than 88.8 tons. With their 520 × 660 mm (20½ × 26 in) cylinders, 228 psi boiler pressure, and 1.75 m (5 ft 9 in) driving wheels, they developed a starting tractive effort of 30,690 lb. They were rated at 1,620 ihp and were limited to a top speed of 100 kph (62 mph), although on 15 December 1964, C62 17 2 was worked up to 129 kph (80 mph) on the Tōkaidō main line, a record for Japanese steam.

It was that same year that the revolutionary standard-gauge *Shinkansen* 'Bullet Train' expresses came into service between Tokyo and Osaka. Intelligently, the Japanese made the transition straight from 100 kph steam expresses, which, given their limited dimensions and poor fuel, did their job as well as could be expected, to ultra-fast electrics running on dedicated new lines and capable of 130 mph. This quantum leap in railway engineering and operating made Japan's railways equal best in the world, along with those of France. Ironically, the *Shinkansen* project had begun in 1955, the year of British Railways' misjudged Modernization Plan. The Japanese had not run down steam as the British had done, but replaced well-maintained steam only when the new high-speed electric railways were ready. Even then, some of the Hudsons were transferred to Hokkaido, Japan's north island, where, often double-headed, they worked boat trains over the heavily inclined Otaru to Oshamanbe line until 1973, providing a most captivating sight and sound in winter snow.

Significantly, one of the key designers of the C62s, working at the end of the Second World War, with Colonel Howard G. Hill, an American military locomotive engineer, was Hideo Shima. Born in Osaka and trained in engineering at Tokyo Imperial University, Shima worked his way up in the railways; in 1955 he was appointed to lead the design development of the *Shinkansen* trains. He went on to become head of Japan's National Space Development Agency and an expert in hydrogen-powered rockets. But Shima never lost his love of steam. He simply progressed from 100 kph steam to 210 kph electrics to 40,000 kph space rockets. Each had its place in engineering and economic development. Steam was neither to be looked down on nor despised.

*

It was elsewhere, though, in Malaysia, that steam was to be developed along the kind of sophisticated lines rarely found outside Europe. The locomotives in question were the fascinating O class, three-cylinder Pacifics designed by Hugh Murton Le Fleming, a Cambridge-educated and Swindon-trained engineer who was chief draughtsman and then assistant chief mechanical engineer on the Federated Malay States Railways.

Laid lightly through the jungles, the first section of what was then Malaya's 860 mile metre-gauge railway had opened in 1885; it reached Singapore in 1923 and was completed by 1931. Its locomotives needed to be light, yet powerful, in order to manage steep gradients and sharp curves. Its first Pacifics, built by Kitson and Company in Hunslet, Leeds, were delivered in 1907, a year before Churchward unveiled *The Great Bear* at Swindon. The O class was developed to haul passenger and mail trains along the length of the railway's west coast route and to run on the east coast line. Working with the North British Locomotive Company, Le Fleming produced the first of twenty-six three-cylinder O class Pacifics – later designated classes 56.1, 56.2, and 56.3 – in 1938–9, followed by forty more class 56.4s in 1945–6. For the period, these were notably advanced engines, with bar frames, nickel-steel boilers, welded-steel fire-boxes, reliable Lentz rotary-cam poppet valves, thermic siphons, and roller bearings. Everything was done to keep weight to a minimum, given the railway's governing axle loading of just 12.75 tons. The locomotives were fitted with boilers pressed to 250 psi, 12½ × 24 in (later enlarged to 13 × 24 in) cylinders and 4 ft 6 in driving wheels. Tractive effort was 23,940 lb. Normally, these three-cylinder Pacifics were limited to 50 mph, although they could run freely at between 60 and 70 mph, and perhaps a little more when given their head. Excellent steamers and reliable locomotives, they survived the brutal Japanese occupation of Malaya in the early

1940s and attacks on the railways by communist insurgents during the 1950s. Forty were still in service at the end of steam in Malaysia in 1974.

One of these remarkable engines – 564.36 *Temerloh* – was restored at Sentul works, Kuala Lumpur, in 1996, on the initiative of the enthusiastic ex-chief mechanical engineer, Dalip Singh, and for a memorable, if all too brief, period she powered a regular Peninsular Line mail train between Gemas and Tampin. Painted royal blue, the Pacific made a splendid sight. To many who came from abroad to ride behind her in handsomely renovated and luxurious carriages, this highly sophisticated, lightweight, three-cylinder Pacific was a revelation. Machines like this were a rarity in tropical countries, and yet a part of what makes steam railways so fascinating is just this kind of experience of the unexpected. In this instance, the experience was captured by the artistry of Hugh Le Fleming, who was a talented painter as well as locomotive engineer, and the posters he designed for the Federated Malay States Railways in the 1930s were both colourful and enticing – almost inevitably, they feature a passing steam locomotive as well as lush tropical countryside. A notable book with ninety-two of his paintings of locomotives from around the world, with descriptions by A. E. 'Dusty' Durrant, was published by the Institution of Mechanical Engineers in 1972 – although sadly, the original paintings, donated to the IME by his widow, were stolen and have never been traced.

*

The particular mechanical artistry of the steam locomotives that once clawed their way through jungles and over mountains in the southern hemisphere, or powered massive coal trains across the plains and valleys of central Europe, has not been entirely lost; it lives on in the imagination of subsequent generations of enthusiasts and engineers. And yet many of the world's modern steam locomotives owed a debt not just to the Stephensons, Chapelon, and 'Hot Steam Willy' Schmidt, or to the common sense and engineering might of manufacturers in the United States, but to the engineers of one small European country which, although all too often overlooked, made a major contribution to steam railway locomotive development. This was Belgium, one of the first countries on the European continent to build railways; the first, in 1835, ran the twenty kilometres (12.5 miles) from Brussels to Mechelen (Malines).

One of the country's most distinguished locomotive engineers was Egide Walschaerts, who started work as a mechanic on the state railway, which then owned only a part of the network, at Mechelen, and became workshop foreman at Brussels in 1844. That year, a patent in Walschaerts's name was taken out for new system of steam distribution for locomotives. This was first applied to a series of 2-2-2s built by Malines Arsenal and Cockerill in 1854–5. Applied sparingly in Belgium, it was taken up with increasing enthusiasm in the USA, especially after 1900, at the very end of Walschaerts's life – not least for its simplicity compared to other systems, and its reliability. It later became the most commonly used of all valve gears.

Alfred Belpaire also had a widespread influence on international steam locomotive design practice. Born in Ostend, he was trained in Paris at the École Centrale des Arts et Manufactures, and went on to become chief mechanical engineer of the Belgian railways, a position he held from 1864 to 1884. His distinctive square-topped fire-boxes, first introduced in 1864, were fitted to nearly all Belgian railway locomotives over the next thirty years. Their principal advantage over round-topped fire-boxes was the larger water and steam space above the crown of the inner fire-box, the zone in which steam generation is most intense. Curiously, a change of regime after Belpaire saw the Belgian railways reverse the square-topped fire-box policy and order round-topped locomotives from Neilson, Reid of Glasgow, which were virtually identical to the two-cylinder express passenger Dunalastair III class 4-4-0s designed by John Farquharson McIntosh, chief mechanical engineer of the Caledonian Railway. In fact, between 1898 and 1913 hundreds of Scottish locomotives were put to work on the Belgian railways.

Continental order was restored by Jean-Baptiste Flamme, chief mechanical engineer from 1904 to 1914, who designed two extremely powerful four-cylinder, superheated, simple-expansion classes, the type 10 Pacific and the type 36 2-10-0. These brought Belgium early on into the realm of what the Americans would call super-power steam. Both types had round-topped fire-boxes, and large grates of 53.8 sq ft. With tractive efforts of 44,000 lb and 60,000 lb, the Pacifics and the 2-10-0s were well equipped to work heavy trains on the steep Brussels to Luxembourg main line, with its ruling gradient of 1-in-62 – so much so that the type 10s remained the principal passenger locomotive on this route until its electrification in 1956.

The type 10 Pacific, of which fifty-eight were built, had an unusual outline, with the smoke-box set well back behind decking plates designed to be lifted in order to provide easy access to the inside cylinders and motion below. In 1934, a Flamme Pacific was exchanged with the French Nord railway for one of the latter's Chapelon compound Pacifics. The French locomotive showed fuel economies of about 35 per cent. It was not surprising, then, that in 1938 the type 10s were 'Chapelonized' with improved steam circuit and double Kylchap exhaust; these modifications increased their maximum power by 20 per cent, with an appreciable reduction in fuel consumption.

The type 36 2-10-0, of which 136 were built, had meanwhile greatly impressed a Lancashire and Yorkshire Railway delegation visiting Belgium in 1911. An attempt was made to get a similar locomotive – the type 36 was the most powerful European freight locomotive – into production as late as 1922; its size and weight, however, were unacceptable to the railway's civil engineer.

In 1932, Raoul Notesse, the newly appointed locomotive design engineer, working for chief mechanical engineer Fernand Legein, prepared designs for a four-cylinder Pacific intended to be faster and more powerful than the Flamme type 10s. Notesse visited Britain the following year to study Stanier's new Princess Royal four-cylinder Pacific. The result was the type 1 – the heaviest of European Pacifics, at 126 tons – a class of thirty-five engines with 2 m (6 ft 6 in) driving wheels, boiler pressure of 256 psi, and large double-admission piston valves. The type 1s developed a maximum of 3,400 ihp at 100 kph (62 mph), making them, along with Stanier's Coronation class, the most powerful simple-expansion European Pacifics.

Then, in 1939 the Belgian railways introduced what was at the time the fastest steam-hauled train in the world, covering the 92.9 kilometres (57.7 miles) from Brussels to Bruges, en route to Ostend, in 46 minutes each way, start to stop, at an average speed of 121.3 kph (75.3 mph). To work these trains, Notesse designed the type 12 streamlined Atlantics, elegant dark-green machines, weighing 89 tons. To minimize disturbing forces at high speed, the two cylinders were located inside the frames, but with external drive to the valve gear; four of the Atlantics had Walschaerts valve gear, one had Dabeg rotary-cam valves, and one Caprotti valve gear. With very large steam-chests to optimize steam flow, double blast-pipe and chimney, 256 psi boiler pressure, 2.1 m (6 ft 10¾ in) driving wheels, and a grate of 39.8 sq ft, these were fast, free-steaming, and powerful locomotives. On test, they developed 2,500 ihp and one reached 165 kph (102.5 mph). The high-speed train was usually loaded with just three or four coaches, weighing up to 220 tons, and limited to 150 kph (93 mph).

Sadly, the German invasion of Belgium in 1940 put an end to the high-speed trains, although the type 12s continued to run on heavier express trains and semi-fasts until the last of them was withdrawn in 1962. (No. 12.004 was preserved and has been in steam since, notably for the 150th anniversary of the Belgian railways, in 1985.) At the time of the invasion, Notesse was working on two very large and powerful three-cylinder types, a 4-8-4 passenger and 2-10-2 freight locomotive, the former designed for 5,000 ihp. With massive 2.1 m (6 ft 11 in) diameter boilers, triple blast-pipes and chimneys, and mechanical stokers, they promised a great deal. But the Second World War put a stop to these notable designs and Notesse, who came to Britain with the Belgian government-in-exile, was killed by a V-2 ballistic missile at Harrow-on-the-Hill in July 1944. For all its efficacy and apparent innocence, the steam locomotive and its designers, whether in Czechoslovakia, the Soviet Union, China, South Africa, or Belgium, have never been free from the depredations of politics and war.

The *Hiawatha* departs Chicago Union station in 1935 in the first year of her fast-as-an-arrow flight over the four hundred miles to Minneapolis. The streamlined A-class Atlantics ran smoothly, day-in, day-out at over 100 mph.

Dramatic 1938 publicity shot of one of Paul Kiefer's beautiful and highly effective new J3-a Hudsons, streamlined by the industrial artist Henry Dreyfuss for service on the New York Central's *20th Century Limited*. Running at a mile-a-minute from New York to Chicago, this was one of the world's greatest, and certainly its most stylish, trains.

Best known for the legendary Union Pacific Big Boy 4-8-8-4s, Otto Jabelmann (right) pursued maximum horsepower wherever possible. Here he is, in December 1938, inspecting General Electric's 5,000 hp steam-turbine electric locomotive with UP President, W. M. Jeffers (left), and GE vice-president H. L. Andrews (centre); Big Boys proved to be more powerful and far more successful than this intriguing machine.

Designed and styled in-house by the Norfolk and Western Railway, the J-class 4-8-4s of 1941 were, indisputably, all-time greats. On loan to the Pennsylvania Railroad, No. 610 spun a 15-car, 1,050-train up to 110 mph.

Livio Dante Porta, one of the great steam locomotive engineers of recent decades, seen here in 1971 sporting a pair of goggles given to him by Andre Chapelon on the footplate of No 1802, a General Belgrano Railway C-16 4-8-2. Porta modified this metre-gauge Argentinian engine, built by Baldwin in 1948, between 1969 and 1974, making it highly efficient.

'Better to carry out than to promise', is the slogan emblazoned along Porta's streamlined 4-8-0, *Argentina*. What Porta carried out in 1948 was the transformation of a metre-gauge Cordoba Central Railway Pacific, into a locomotive with a power-to-weight ratio equal to Chapelon's mighty SNCF 240P.

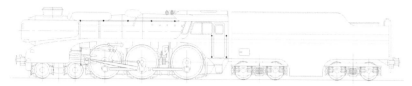

Outline drawing of the 5AT [Advanced Technology] Project, a high-speed locomotive designed by David Wardale between 1998 and 2012. The aim had been to create a 200 kph locomotive that could run across the British railway network. The project was put on hold due to lack of funding.

Bill Hoole was a celebrated East Coast driver who retired from Kings Cross in 1959. Photographed on the footplate of A4 Pacific 60034 *Lord Farringdon*, Hoole set a post-war record that year for British steam: 112 mph, with A4 60007 *Sir Nigel Gresley*.

CHAPTER 6

EXPERIMENTATION
Reinventing the *Rocket*

The photograph is telling. Standing on the buffer beam of No. 10000, an experimental high-pressure, four-cylinder 4-6-4, at the buffer stops of King's Cross station are the two crews in soot-stained overalls who have just brought the non-stop Flying Scotsman express up from Edinburgh. The date is 31 July 1930. The platform clock shows the time as 18.25. The train had arrived ten minutes earlier, exactly on time. The men look exhausted. Standing on the platform to their right beside the whale-like, battleship-grey locomotive is its designer, Nigel Gresley. He looks intensely serious. It is hard not to think that the chief mechanical engineer and crews were simply relieved that No. 10000 had run the 393 miles from Scotland without incident and to schedule. Not that the 1930 timing was especially demanding; with eight and a quarter hours allowed from Edinburgh Waverly, the Flying Scotsman trotted and occasionally cantered, but never had to gallop, much less fly. To steam non-stop over such a distance, however, was no mean achievement.

Doubtless, the men cheered up after a wash-up and a few beers. As for Gresley, what might he have been thinking? Did this unusual locomotive at King's Cross point the way to the future, or was it nothing more than an engineering sidetrack? From its inception at the beginning of the nineteenth century, engineers had experimented with the steam locomotive. Although the Stephensons had established the fundamentals of a design that was to endure until the end of regular main-line steam on the world's railways, there was always a belief that somehow the low thermal efficiency of the steam railway locomotive could be radically improved. The Union Pacific's Big Boys and the Chesapeake and Ohio's Alleghenies were to be hugely powerful, while Chapelon's 240Ps and 141Ps were to set new standards of thermal efficiency – but were locomotive engineers missing a trick?

Gresley was certainly willing to experiment, and No. 10000, the one and only member of the LNER W1 class, was his most radical design. Completed in November 1929, No. 10000 was taken out of service in October 1936. It had spent more than half of its time in the workshops. The following year, it reappeared as a conventional, three-cylinder simple-expansion locomotive, a 4-6-4 version, with a larger P2 boiler, of Gresley's magnificent streamlined A4 Pacifics which had first entered service in 1935. What is clear from the rebuilding is that, ultimately, Gresley had decided that any marginal fuel savings were more than offset by the increased servicing and maintenance costs, which ruled out any multiplication of the W1 type.

The engine itself took five years to design and build, and had emerged from Doncaster in late 1929 from behind a veil of the greatest secrecy; this was why No. 10000 was known as the 'Hush-Hush' locomotive, although some said the nickname was inspired by the engine's exceptionally soft exhaust. The heart of this big express engine was its high-pressure water-tube boiler. Designed originally for marine work, the water-tube boiler differs fundamentally from a fire-tube boiler. In the latter, heat produced by combustion in the fire-box is transferred as convected heat through the fire-tubes in the water barrel. In the water-tube boiler, water is heated and converted into steam in vertical banks of tubes linking lower and upper water drums. By the time Gresley designed No. 10000, water-tube boilers had been at work in factories, ships, and power stations for several decades.

Indeed, Francis Webb, the inventive chief mechanical engineer of the LNWR, had employed water-tube boilers in a pair of tiny 0-4-0 tank engines operating at Crewe works as early as 1875.

The advantage of the water-tube over the fire-tube boiler lies in its ability to work at a much higher pressure. With their high working pressures and multiple-stage expansion of steam, marine steam engines tended to be far more efficient than steam railway locomotives. The difficulty Gresley faced was fitting an efficient water-tube boiler to a locomotive within the tight limitations of the British loading gauge.

Some of the only large-scale locomotives at work in the 1920s with water-tube boilers, or hybrid water-tube and fire-tube boilers, were four experimental engines built by the Delaware and Hudson Railway in the United States, where the loading gauge was far more generous. Gresley followed the design of these with great interest. The first, in 1924, was a monstrous two-cylinder compound 2-8-0 built by Alco, which looked as if a factory boiler had been lowered on to on a locomotive chassis. Numbered 1400 and named *Horatio Allen*, this 174 ton engine – the world's largest 2-8-0 – was equipped with a 350 psi water-tube boiler (at a time when 200 psi was the norm for conventional boilers), designed by the Delaware and Hudson's consultant engineer, John E. Muhlfeld. Water-tube side walls with top and bottom drums formed the fire-box, while the boiler barrel itself was of a conventional superheated fire-tube design. With Young valve gear, which allowed a maximum cut-off of an exceptionally high 90 per cent, a booster engine on the two axles at the rear of the tender, high adhesive weight, and a tractive effort, with the booster, of 102,560 lb (simple) or 88,620 lb (compound operation), *Horatio Allen* was prodigiously strong. She was recorded hauling 3,217 US tons at 26.5 mph up a 1-in-200 gradient with a drawbar thermal efficiency of 8.72 per cent, twice that of a conventional contemporary US steam locomotive. This prototype, however, did require frequent and specialist servicing and maintenance.

Two more two-cylinder compound 2-8-0s with similar hybrid boilers – 1401 *John B. Jervis*, with a boiler pressure of 400 psi, and 1402 *James Archibald*, with a 500 psi boiler pressure – followed in 1927 and 1930. The Delaware and Hudson went further in 1933 with 1403 *L. F. Loree*, named after the railway's long-serving president. This 190 ton triple-expansion 4-8-0 was an impressive machine, although it looked rather top-heavy. It was also complex. Steam pressed to 500 psi was passed to a 20 × 32 in high-pressure cylinder located under the right side of the cab, and then to a medium-pressure 27½ × 32 in cylinder under the left side; it was then exhausted to two 33 × 32 in low-pressure cylinders positioned between the bogie wheels at the front of the locomotive. Connecting rods from the fore and aft cylinders drove the second pair of driving wheels, with steam distribution through rotary-cam poppet valves. A six-wheeled booster working at 500 psi replaced the rear truck of the tender. *L. F. Loree* duly proved able to haul a 6,103 ton freight train up a 1-in-200 gradient, although at no more than walking pace. This, though, was quite some achievement, especially as her maximum drawbar thermal efficiency was 12.5 per cent – although one Delaware and Hudson employee was overheard to say, with some exaggeration: 'Every time we sent her out, a machine shop had to go with her.'

There were two further American experiments with high-pressure steam. The first was a 350 psi, three-cylinder compound 4-10-2 with a water-tube boiler, built by Baldwin in 1926. It produced an impressive 4,515 ihp on test at the Pennsylvania Railroad's Altoona test plant – the limit of the test plant and not that of the locomotive – and gave generally excellent results, running one hundred thousand miles over the territories of six US railroads. Mechanical engineers, however, disliked the fact that the locomotive needed special water-tube descaling treatment; they prized simplicity, and no matter how effective she was, the 4-10-2 needed special treatment. The second was the New York Central Railroad's HS-1a, No. 800, a handsome 850 psi, three-cylinder compound 4-8-4, built by Alco in 1931. This had much the same complex Schmidt-Henschel water-tube boiler as the LMS's high-pressure 4-6-0 *Fury*. The locomotive did little main-line work and was soon relegated to shunting at the New York Central's Selkirk yard, a duty for which she was unsuited. She was scrapped in 1939.

If anything, Gresley's plans were even more ambitious. His 450 psi, water-tube compound 4-6-4 was intended for high-speed and long-distance express passenger work. It was intended to be a more efficient version of the LNER's fleet-footed A1 Pacifics. Development took place over five years. Working closely with the shipbuilder and philanthropist Harold Yarrow of Yarrow Shipbuilders, based at Scotstoun on the river Clyde, the Canadian locomotive engineer Lawford H. Fry developed a water-tube boiler suitable for one of Gresley's Pacifics. Initial drawings, however, showed an A1 with a boiler so long that there was precious little room for a cab. As a result, the Pacific's frame was stretched to a 4-6-4 arrangement, although because the rear axles were independent of one another, No. 10000 was really a 4-6-2-2.

The locomotive's streamlined external cladding was devised by O. V. S. Bulleid and William Ernest Dalby, professor of civil and mechanical engineering at Imperial College, London. An early expert in applied aerodynamics, Dalby started work aged fourteen as an apprentice machinist at the Stratford works of the Great Eastern Railway. At Crewe with the LNWR from 1884, he studied part-time for a BSc degree in engineering at London University, before helping to set up the new engineering department at Cambridge University in 1891.

The 'Hush-Hush' locomotive was not a failure; equally, it was not a complete success, particularly as servicing and maintenance costs were appreciably higher than for a standard Pacific. A major problem with poor steaming, however, was overcome with Chapelon's help; in June 1935, No. 10000 was fitted with a double Kylchap exhaust and a separate low-pressure superheater, eliminating the condensation formed in the low-pressure cylinders which had hampered performance. Thus modified, it produced 1,701 dbhp at 57 mph and could meet mile-a-minute schedules with 450 ton trains between York and Darlington. However, with the introduction of the A4 Pacifics that year, giving 10 to 15 per cent more power than the extremely able A3s, Gresley felt unable to justify further work on No. 10000, especially with the arrival at the LNER in 1936 of a new general manager with the mind of an accountant.

There had been plans to name No. 10000 *British Enterprise* and, perhaps, for the engine to be the prototype of an extended class of water-tube compounds. Instead, in 1937 the locomotive was transformed into a three-cylinder 4-6-4 along the lines of a Gresley A4 and ran in this guise until 1 June 1959, when she was withdrawn and scrapped. The sole member of the W1 class, and now numbered 60700, the former 'Hush-Hush' locomotive was very nearly named *Pegasus*, but because non-standard British Railways locomotives were culled at the end of the 1950s, the name plates cast for her were never fitted. The water-tube boiler, meanwhile, steamed on until 1965 under a cover of industrial bricks at Darlington, where No. 10000 had been assembled, used for pressure-testing and space-heating. The locomotive's eight-wheeled corridor tender runs on today behind the preserved A4 60009 *Union of South Africa*.

Meanwhile, the truly furious *Fury* emerged from the North British Locomotive Company in Glasgow a few weeks after No. 10000 made its debut at Darlington. This semi-compound variation on the three-cylinder Royal Scot 4-6-0s of 1927 was rooted in German rather than American research. Dr Robert Hartmann, engineering director of the Schmidt Superheated Steam Company, had devised a special type of hybrid water-tube boiler in a bid to increase heat and efficiency. The idea was to raise steam in banks of vertical water-tubes, forming the fire-box walls, to top drums in a closed primary circuit of distilled water at very high pressure, between 1,400 and 1,800 psi. This steam was transferred via tubes to raise pressure at 900 psi in a further drum above the fire-box. Finally, now mixed with steam generated at 250 psi in the fire-tube boiler barrel, it was fed to one 11½ × 26 in high-pressure cylinder and, after being re-superheated, on to a pair of 18 × 26 in low-pressure cylinders. The aim was to reduce fuel and water consumption. The LMS was intrigued. On 15 December 1928, it ordered its first high-pressure locomotive. The boiler was built by the Schmidt Superheated Steam Company, with advice from Henschel in Kassel, while the fire-tube boiler barrel was from the North British Locomotive Company. No. 6399 was ready for testing on 30 January 1930.

Faith in this daring and rather terrifying-looking machine was severely tested less than a fortnight later. Passing through Carstairs station on its first main-line run, *Fury* exploded – or at least a high-pressure fire-box tube did. The ensuing rush of steam through the fire-hole door at a pressure of 1,000 psi and more mortally wounded Louis Schofield, the Superheated Steam Company's representative, who died the following day in hospital in Edinburgh. *Fury*'s boiler was repaired and further tests were made under Stanier in 1932 and 1933; the results were poor. There was, though, a happy ending of sorts. In 1935, she was transformed by Tom Coleman, under the direction of William Stanier, into 6170 *British Legion*, prototype of the rebuilt Royal Scots, a class of freshly invigorated express passenger locomotives completed in 1955. These tapered-boiler, three-cylinder machines proved to be among the most efficient of all British steam locomotives.

*

The latest ships and power stations at the time No. 10000 and *Fury* first steamed were worked with high-pressure boilers feeding steam turbines. Invented by Charles Algernon Parsons in 1884 from an idea that had originated with Hero of Alexandria, the multi-stage steam turbine was, when combined with vacuum condensing, one of the most efficient of all power units, and remains so. Could its smooth-spinning sorcery be made to work effectively in railway service? A small experimental 0-2-2-0 tank engine designed by Professor Giuseppe Belluzzo had been built as early as 1907, by Officine Meccaniche

SA of Milan. Four turbines drove the 26 ton engine's four wheels independently through a series of reduction gears. A conversion of a locomotive dating from 1876, the Belluzzo prototype was not a success; it was dismantled in 1921. Belluzzo himself went on to design two more turbine locomotives for the Italian railways. One was a 2-8-2 with high- and low-pressure turbines, built by Breda in 1931; the other, in 1933, was a rebuild of a class 685 2-6-2, with a single forward turbine, which made a number of runs between Florence and Pistoia. Both locomotives led shadowy lives and quickly disappeared. As for their inventor, Belluzzo – a committed fascist – he became a minister in Mussolini's government. From 1942, he worked closely with the German SS on the development of a turbine-driven flying bomb which, had it flown, might have been mistaken for a flying saucer.

Various other more or less complicated attempts at a practical steam-turbine locomotive had been made by the time William Stanier, by now chief mechanical engineer of the LMS, became interested in the idea. The most successful had, in fact, been the Beyer Peacock Ljungström 2,000 hp twin-unit condensing turbine of 1926, which had been tested by the LMS on 600 ton fast freight trains from London to Leeds in 1928.

Stanier sailed to Sweden with representatives of the turbine division of the Metropolitan Vickers Company to see the three 1,270 hp 2-8-0 non-condensing steam-turbine locomotives designed by Birger and Fredrik Ljungström to work heavy iron-ore trains on the Grängesberg–Oxelösund railway. Built between 1930 and 1936, these were successful machines, kept busy at work until the line to the port at Oxelösund was electrified in 1953; all three have survived into preservation. Impressed by them, Stanier commissioned a turbine version of his new four-cylinder Princess Royal Pacific, based on the Ljungström locomotives. An elegant and well-resolved machine, 6202 did not look like an experiment and it achieved considerable success. In later years, when he was chairman of Power Jets, the British government's gas-turbine organization, Stanier told Joseph Cliffe, a

Doncaster-trained mechanical engineer on his team, that he would have liked to have had fifty turbine-driven Pacifics.

The Turbomotive, as 6202 was known, proved to be slightly more efficient in terms of thermodynamics and power distribution than the Princess Royals. On test, she beat the four-cylinder Pacifics, if marginally, in terms of water and coal consumption, and she climbed Shap and Beattock more rapidly and with less chance of slipping at the head of heavy express trains. The Turbomotive was also smooth, powerful, and easy to drive. Nominally, the forward turbine with its eighteen rows of blades developed 2,600 hp with the engine travelling at 62 mph. The driver could select between one and six nozzles each blasting steam to the turbine and so raising or lowering the power output. Rotary turbine drive offered smooth torque characteristics, ensuring smoother and more slip-free starts and hill-climbing. A small, four-bladed reverse turbine was engaged by a clutch. Design complexity was kept to a minimum.

Rather than the fan of the Beyer Peacock Ljungström locomotive, a conventional blast-pipe was fitted to exhaust steam and generate draught for the fire, while the vacuum condensing equipment that had been specified by Beyer Peacock was dispensed with, providing a major simplification at the expense of lower thermal efficiency. Soft exhaust from the double chimney clouded the crews' view ahead and so smoke deflectors – the first on an LMS Pacific – were soon fitted to lift exhaust clear of the cab. The boiler, pressed to 250 psi, was similar to those fitted to the reciprocating Pacifics, but with a larger superheater. A maximum tractive effort of 40,000 lb was maintained at a slightly higher level than with the Princess Royals at comparable speeds, with the result that the Turbomotive was slightly more powerful on hills and at higher speeds than the reciprocating Pacifics.

The Turbomotive made quite a name for itself on its regular runs with the fast and heavy 08.30 Euston to Liverpool Lime Street and the return working, the 17.25 Liverpool to London express, of the mid- to late 1930s. Often loaded to 480 tons, the London-bound train was booked to run the 152.6 miles from Crewe to Willesden at an average speed of 64.5 mph. A clear run tended to be the exception, so locomotives assigned to this important train had to be able to accelerate briskly from signals and sprint when necessary. O. S. Nock recorded an occasion when 6202 made up five minutes by running the 61.6 miles from Weedon to Wembley in 47.5 minutes, at an average speed of 77.8 mph.

Unsurprisingly for a prototype, there were teething problems. The main forward turbine spindle broke one day when 6202 was bowling along the west coast main line near Leighton Buzzard at 60 mph; luckily, the turbine casing remained intact. Occasionally, a failure in the transmission system would cause the driving wheels to seize up and main-line services would be severely delayed until the front end could be jacked up and the locomotive towed away. There were also oil leaks from the enclosed triple-reduction gearing and transmission shafts, a detail Bulleid might have been aware of – this was to be one of the bugbears of his radical Merchant Navy and light Pacifics.

Inevitably, standards of maintenance fell as the Second World War ground on. The Turbomotive was out of service, awaiting parts, and her annual wartime mileage was just 28,500 miles, compared with the 53,000 miles run by the Princess Royals and 73,000 miles by the more powerful Coronation Pacifics. She had, however, run 66,200 miles in 1938, a very creditable achievement for a prototype. When one stormy wartime evening, Cecil J. Allen needed to catch a heavy combined Liverpool and Manchester express from Crewe, he feared the worst when he saw the Turbomotive rolling into Crewe with the Liverpool portion of the train. 'I'm afraid we're going to lose time,' he told his engineer companion. To Allen's surprise, 6202 gained 11.5 minutes between Crewe and Watford at the head of its seventeen-coach, 610 ton train.

In 1946 Roland Bond, then deputy chief mechanical engineer of the LMS, read a paper to the Institution of Locomotive Engineers on the railway's experience with 6202. Despite teething problems, the Turbomotive had been much admired. 'On present indications,' said

Bond, 'the next five years should show up the turbine locomotive in an increasingly favourable light. It has, in the author's opinion, already proved itself well worth persevering with, and it is not beyond the bounds of possibility that a limited number of non-condensing turbine locomotives, in a more highly developed form based on the experience with No. 6202, will be regularly employed on the heaviest and fastest express trains, with profit to their owners.'

It was not to be. Having run 440,000 miles, 6202 was taken out of service in 1949, re-emerging from Crewe on 15 August 1952 as a conventional reciprocating four-cylinder Pacific. Numbered 46202 and named *Princess Anne*, this elegant engine – a happy cross between a Princess Royal and a Coronation – was destined for a tragically brief life. On 8 October 1952, she was one of four locomotives involved in a horrific multiple crash at Harrow and Wealdstone, 11.4 miles north of Euston. The late-running 20.15 Perth to Euston sleeper, hauled by Coronation Pacific 46242 *City of Glasgow*, passed signals set to danger at 60 mph and smashed into the rear of the 07.31 Tring to Euston stopping train, standing in the station behind a Fowler 4MT 2-6-4T; a few moments later, the double-headed, fifteen-car 08.00 Liverpool and Manchester express, climbing up from Euston at between 50 and 60 mph, rode into the wreckage. Its locomotives were the Jubilee class three-cylinder 4-6-0 45637 *Windward Islands* and 46202 *Princess Anne*. Both locomotives were written off and scrapped. The former Turbomotive had run just 11,442 miles in its new and regal guise. The accident was the worst of its kind in English railway history: 112 people died and 340 were injured.

The steam-turbine railway locomotive did appear to promise great things: smooth power; a solution to the problem of the 'hammer blow' on the tracks made by large reciprocating locomotives; lower fuel and water bills. In practice, however, most seemed to be beset by problems, some mechanical, others political. French and German locomotives built from the late 1920s to the early 1940s were caught out by the Second World War before they could be fully evaluated. Some, like the ungainly 2,000 hp Krupp-Zoelly condensing turbine locomotive T18 1001, a Pacific built in 1924, and the 2,700 hp Maffei condensing turbine engine T18 1002 of 1926, were damaged by allied bombing. Others, like the SNCF's 232Q1 built by Schneider and Creusot in 1940, and resembling a rather dumpy Gresley A4, seemed promising. On test between Le Creusot and Montchanin, the 4-6-4 produced 2,600 hp and ran freely at up to 140 kph (87 mph). It was sabotaged beyond repair by retreating German troops on 3 September 1944. What also told against it was its fuel and water consumption, which was some 10 to 15 per cent higher than Chapelon 4-8-0s and 141Ps.

One turbine engine, influenced by Stanier's Turbomotive, that did look very promising was the Pennsylvania Railroad's S2 6-8-6, built by Baldwin in 1944, with turbines by Westinghouse Electric. This massive and purposeful-looking machine, with a conventional fire-tube boiler pressed to 300 psi, 5 ft 8 in driving wheels, and a tractive effort of 70,500 lb, generated no less than 6,900 hp and powered thousand-ton trains happily at 100 mph and more on the lightly inclined 280 mile Crestline to Chicago main line. On a visit to the United States in 1947, E. S. Cox rode the footplate of 6200 on this section and a top speed of 100 mph was maintained for twelve minutes before the train had to be slowed.

Although 6200 showed up well at high speed on the main line, it suffered from a problem shared by all these experimental turbine engines. Relatively efficient at full speed, their turbines were inefficient at low speed, while their rotary inertia was such that sudden changes in speed were both difficult to obtain without heavy use of the engine's brakes and potentially damaging to the driving mechanism. Turbines are best run – as they normally are in power stations and ships – within a narrow speed range. Despite its undeniable power and speed, 6200 was withdrawn in 1949 and scrapped.

*

Other attempts to use steam turbines using electrical transmissions and traction motors proved to be fascinating, if complex. The first attempt had been Britain's very first turbine locomotive, the Reid-Ramsey Turbine Electric, built by the North British Locomotive Company in 1910. With a conventional boiler at one end, capped with a bulbous chimney enclosing an exhaust fan, and condensing equipment at the other, this curious 4-4-0 + 0-4-4 machine had a push-me-pull-you appearance which lacked, to say the least, the gentle grace and refined elegance of contemporary express passenger locomotives. The boiler fed an impulse turbine coupled to a dynamo which energized four 275 hp traction motors. The locomotive was not a success and in 1924 it was rebuilt into the Reid-Macleod Turbine, equipped with high- and low-pressure turbines, but without the complication of electric motors, and promising 1,000 hp at 60 mph. This machine was shown at the British Empire Exhibition at Wembley in 1924 and perhaps, with its submarine-like profile, it may have had the look of a locomotive of the future. Trials made between March 1926 and April 1927, however, were decidedly disappointing. Its one big chance was a run from Glasgow to Edinburgh and back. On the way out it suffered axle-box problems; on the way back, a turbine failed. It never ran again.

The idea of the steam-turbine electric locomotive continued to inspire railway engineers. The most ambitious experiments, all of them failures, were made in the United States between 1938 and 1954, by the Union Pacific Railroad, the Chesapeake and Ohio Railway, and the Norfolk and Western Railway. The feeling was that the new diesel-electrics might just be rivalled by a new generation of steam-turbine electrics which not only looked like diesels but had similar speed and tractive effort characteristics. In April 1939, at the instigation of Otto Jabelmann, General Electric delivered a pair of striking 277 ton, vacuum-condensing, oil-fired, steam-turbine electric 4-6-6-4s (or 2-C + C-2s) to the Union Pacific; the railroad returned this twin 5,000 hp machine to the manufacturers for modifications just two months later. Encased in a long-nosed, diesel-style casing, each oil-fired 2,500 hp unit featured a semi-flash 1,500 psi water-tube boiler for rapid steam raising, high- and low-pressure turbines, two electric generators, six air-cooled traction motors, and dynamic electric braking. After further trials on the New York Central Railroad and the Great Northern Railway, the twins were retired in late 1943; wartime conditions were not conducive to prototype locomotive development.

In 1946, the Chesapeake and Ohio Railway proposed to introduce a high-speed 'Chessie' passenger service between Washington, DC, and Cincinatti. High power would be required for climbs through and over the Alleghenies. Mainly for this service, the railway ordered three 6,000 hp, non-condensing, steam turbo-electrics. Built by Baldwin with Westinghouse Electric in 1947–8, these 154 ft, multi-axle machines, weighing 367 tons, promised 6,000 hp and 100 mph, and a glimpse into the future. Their large 310 psi fire-tube boilers, similar to those of the Pennsy's S2 class 6-8-6, supplied steam to a Westinghouse impulse turbine working in its economic range between 3,600 and 6,000 rpm and driving a pair of twin-armature generators. While all this sounded impressive, there was a fundamental flaw with the design. The turbine designers had not been told by Baldwin that the turbine would be exhausting against a 25 psi back-pressure to draught the boiler. They had assumed that the exhaust would be at atmospheric pressure. The result of this misunderstanding was a reduction in maximum turbine power output of 20 per cent. Dr Adolph Giesl-Gieslingen, the Austrian engineer and inventor of the Giesl exhaust ejector, who had already fitted one of these devices to a Chesapeake and Ohio 0-8-0 switcher (shunter), designed a special twin ejector for the turbo-electrics to reduce back-pressure enough to raise maximum power to 5,600hp. It was, however, too late. The new Chesapeake and Ohio president, Walter J. Touhy, cancelled the 'Chessie' high-speed train project and the Giesl ejectors were never fitted to the other turbo-electrics. The locomotives were put to work on heavy freight trains instead, and withdrawn in 1951.

One final attempt was made by the Norfolk and Western Railway in 1954 with 2300 *Jawn Henry*. Named after the legendary construction worker, John Henry, who took up a challenge to outperform a steam-hammer and won, only to collapse and die, this formidable-looking, glossy black, 4,500 hp, non-condensing machine, with its Babcock & Wilcox 600 psi water-tube boiler, twelve electric traction motors, and 6-6-6-6 (or C-C-C-C) wheel arrangement, was itself the stuff of legend. *Jawn Henry* could move a heavy coal train away from rest with greater aplomb than one of the railway's magnificent Y6b Mallets. '*Jawn* rides smoothly and makes the dynamometer car needles move with gusto,' reported David Morgan, editor of *Trains* magazine, in May 1953. 'Once while starting, the tractive effort measurement read 224,000 pounds. Impressive!' Impressive indeed: a Y6b had a maximum tractive effort of 152,000 lb. In tests over mountain sections in 1954, 2300 hauled loads on average 18.27 per cent heavier than the Y6bs, and although at speeds 4 to 13 per cent lower, these runs were achieved with fuel savings over the Mallets of between 20 and 30 per cent.

Following these tests, the Norfolk and Western decided to purchase up to twenty further turbo-electrics, with power raised to 5,250 hp. Unfortunately, this decision coincided with the crisis leading to the withdrawal of Baldwin from locomotive building and the arrival of the new Norfolk and Western president, Stuart Saunders, who was determined to abandon steam in any form in favour of diesel-electrics. This was especially sad as the Norfolk and Western test report on *Jawn Henry*, published on 26 April 1955, had stated: 'There is a definite place and need for a coal-burning locomotive on some American railroads. The advantages of the turbine-driven over the reciprocating engine are being recognized. Further development of the oil-burning turbine-electric locomotive is assured. Other railroads are interested. The 2300 points the way.'

Jawn Henry was a descendant of the intriguing Heilmann steam-electric locomotives invented by Alsace-born Jean-Jacques Heilmann, proprietor of the Le Havre-based Société Industrielle de Moteurs Électriques et à Vapeur, in 1890. These were the first self-propelled locomotives in which the prime mover (steam, diesel, or gas turbine) operated in its efficient speed range with electrical transmission providing a variable speed drive to the road wheels. Heilmann's first steam-electric locomotive was *La Fusée Électrique* (The Electric Rocket), built in Paris in 1892–3 in collaboration with the Winterthur locomotive works and Bown, Boveri & Cie. A cab-in-front design, the 118 ton machine had a special Lentz boiler with a stay-less corrugated circular fire-box. Steam passed to a twin opposed-cylinder, 790 hp, compound engine, driving a 400 kW DC generator which, in turn, powered eight 80 hp traction motors, one mounted on each of the locomotive's eight axles, carried in two bogies.

On a trial run with the Ouest railway on the Paris to Nantes main line, *La Fusée Électrique* covered 58.33 kilometres (36.25 miles) of undulating line with a load of 183 tons at an average speed of 70.4 kph (43.75 mph), topping 100 kph (62 mph). Two more powerful, 124 ton, 1,350 hp locomotives, with conventional fire-tube boilers and Willans six-cylinder triple-expansion engines, were built in 1897–8. On test, the first of these, No. 8001, ran happily at 120 kph (74.5 mph) with loads of 250 tons. With 100 per cent adhesion – the engine's entire weight rested on its driving wheels – good acceleration, and quiet running, the Heilmann locomotives were a real success. They accelerated strongly and worked on the Paris–Versailles suburban service until the line was electrified. The Ouest railway, however, required that they carry a crew of three – driver, fireman, and electrician – a fact that did nothing to help their cause, while their power-to-weight ratio was low compared with that of the best new French compound Atlantics.

Intriguingly, the idea of a heavy-duty American reciprocating steam-electric locomotive was revived in the 1990s in a project by two British engineers, Robin Comyns-Carr and George Carpenter. Designed for heavy freight work, this 4,500 hp, vacuum-condensing Co-Co locomotive was to have used a coil-tube, semi-flash boiler working at 1,700 psi, feeding a twelve-cylinder triple-expansion engine, driving electrical transmission.

Attempts to combine the reciprocating steam engine with electric power were also tried at various times, with varying degrees of failure and success. One unusual development was the conversion during the Second World War of several veteran Swiss federal railways 0-6-0 tank engines into steam-electric locomotives. Fitted with pantographs, the E3/3 class locomotives drew power from 15 kV overhead lines. This fed electric heating elements in the boiler through transformers rated at 480 kW. At a time when Switzerland was desperately short of coal – it has no indigenous supply – yet rich in hydroelectricity, it seemed only sensible to power steam locomotives in this way. The E3/3s could be coal-powered when necessary. The idea was a wartime expedient, though; in Swiss conditions, ultimately it made more sense simply to build electric locomotives.

*

Steam-diesel hybrids, meanwhile, were investigated by railways in Britain, Russia, and Italy. As both forms of traction were seen to have their advantages, perhaps a combination of the two might be a winner, with steam providing power at starting and thus making it unnecessary to equip diesel engines with variable-speed transmission. The idea was patented in 1917 by William Joseph Still, a London engineer, who presented its virtues at a meeting of the Royal Society of Arts chaired by Charles Algernon Parsons. Still's invention was a reciprocating engine with double-acting cylinders. The top half of the cylinder was diesel, the bottom half steam. At starting, steam was supplied from an oil-fired boiler. Once running, it was generated by hot diesel exhaust gas and steam propulsion could be used as a booster to the diesel cylinders when necessary.

The first Still engines were used to power ships. In 1924, *Dolius*, an 11,533 ton Blue Funnel Line freighter, built by Scott's of Greenock, set off on her maiden voyage from Cardiff to Algiers. She averaged 11.45 knots and burned a total of 8.4 tons of fuel per day. This was widely noted in the shipping industry: it was a fine and economical performance. But the ship required engineers trained for both steam and internal-combustion working.

The first such engine on rails was the Kitson-Still locomotive, a 2-6-2T built by Kitson & Company of Leeds, for trials on the LNER in 1926. The cylinders sat below the small, high-pitched, oil-exhaust-gas-fired boiler. The engine unit had two horizontally opposed banks of four cylinders on either side of the crankshaft, in parallel with the driving axles. The 85 ton oil-fired engine had 5 ft 0 in driving wheels, a 200 psi boiler pressure, and a tractive effort of 28,000 lb. Starting under steam, diesel power cut in at 5 mph and the locomotive could run up to 43 mph at a maximum engine speed of 450 rpm.

The Kitson-Still machine proved to be a strong starter and could manage 400 ton goods trains, restarting these on gradients as steep as 1-in-50. Maximum diesel power was 800 hp, with up to about 200 hp more when boosted by steam, although 80 to 90 per cent of running was diesel only. Fuel consumption compared well with much later British Railways main-line diesel locomotives. But it was no match for Gresley's conventional steam locomotives, and because great strides had been made with electric transmission for diesel engines in the course of the 1930s, the justification for the Kitson-Still engine was diminished. A fascinating and not unsuccessful experiment, the locomotive was broken up by Kitson and Company in late 1935.

Russia was one of the very few countries (another was Italy) to pursue the idea of a steam-diesel locomotive. The *Teplopaorvozi* (diesel-steam) locomotive was built at Voroshilovgrad in 1939. A hunched and massive-looking 2-8-2, No. 8000 was equipped with four opposed pistons mounted centrally outside its frames, each pair driving the coupled wheels through connecting rods and jackshafts. Up to 20 kph (12.5 mph), steam acted on the outside of the pistons and internal combustion on the inner. Above this speed, internal combustion took the dominant role, although steam continued to drive the outer piston faces on their inward movements. Its smoke-box door emblazoned with the legend '*Stalinets*' ('Follower of Stalin'), 8000 was meant to have produced 3,000 ihp and run at up to 130 kph (81 mph). Trials began in October 1939, when 2,950 ihp was developed at 78 kph (48.5

mph), and continued until 1943. Although testing resumed in 1946 after the Great Patriotic War of 1941–5, the locomotive was stored two years later and preserved. Apparently it suffered from cracked cylinders and a poor ride, and with its 25 ton axle loading it was in any case too heavy for almost all Russian track.

A second, quite remarkable, Soviet steam/internal-combustion locomotive made its unlikely debut from Kolomna works on 26 December 1939. This was the TP-1 2-10-2, a cab-in-front design with opposed pistons, powered by pulverized and gasified anthracite for the internal-combustion cycle, and by steam raised from the pulverized coal left over from the gas-producing cycle. This was a complex process, made more intricate and demanding still by the fact that this was a condensing locomotive complete with a turbine exhaust fan. The driver sat in the diesel-style enclosed cab at the front of the dark-blue and red engine, while the fireman regulated steam and gas production from a conventional steam locomotive footplate – although, this being Russia, one fully protected from the elements.

The valve gear was immensely complex and, in action, must have looked rather like a spider cycling. Mounted more or less in the centre of the frames, TP-1's eight pistons drove the engine's wheels through four crossheads on each side, via jackshafts and rocking levers. This bizarre machine was intended to match the performance of a highly competent FD class 2-10-2. The gas cycle was to have produced 2,000 ihp and the steam cycle a further 1,000 to 1,500 ihp. In the event, TP-1 made seventy-six runs around the Shcherbinka test track, covering a total of 1,790 kilometres (1,112.25 miles). It seems that it did work as planned, but only up to about 30 kph (18.5 mph). Above this speed, the gas cycle gave up the ghost. Kolomna engineers worked hard to improve TP-1's performance, but again the war intervened and there was no time, let alone will, to continue such experiments. Later, in 1948, a third opposed-piston steam/internal-combustion locomotive was built, to a pre-war design, at Voroshilovgrad, but although this eight-cylinder 2-10-2, numbered

8001 and weighing 153 tons, was less complex than TP-1, it was considered to be a complete failure.

The idea of using pulverized fuel, however, had also interested German engineers in the lead-up to the Second World War, especially as the country had large deposits of lignite. The Deutsche Reichsbahn's 05 003 4-6-4 was the third of this small class of high-speed streamliners. Here, the conventional layout of boiler barrel and fire-box was reversed, with the fire-box at the front immediately behind the driver's cab. The entire machine was encased so that when steam was shut off it could easily have been mistaken for a new diesel or electric locomotive. With the fire-box remote from the tender, the grate was fed by pulverized coal blown through delivery pipes by a centrifugal compressor. Unlike its super-fast siblings, though, and despite its promising looks, 05 003 was a relative failure; it was converted into a conventionally arranged and fired 4-6-4 by Adolf Wolff, Krauss Maffei's post-war technical director, in 1950.

Attempts to improve the way in which power was delivered – ways, that is, of reducing torque fluctuation when transmitting cylinder thrust to driving wheels – led to a number of fascinating experiments in the 1930s with multi-cylinder engine units designed to power two or more axles and thus adopt one of the great advantages of diesel engines: smoothly transmitted power, especially from starting. In France in 1939, the SNCF's Vitry test plant produced the solitary 221TQ, a 1,200 hp 4-4-2 tank engine. This boasted a high-speed steam V12 engine, mounted longitudinally, driving two axles through a transmission shaft and helical gears. The prototype had been ordered by Dabeg, manufacturers of locomotive poppet valves and feedwater heaters, and was intended for secondary-line service. The war put a stop to its development and, when in 1946, the SNCF announced an end to all unconventional types, 221TQ was scrapped.

In July 1941, however, V19 001, the eight-cylinder 2-8-2 masterminded by Friedrich Witte, head of testing for Deutsche Reichsbahn, with Richard Roosen of Henschel, began trials. Streamlined in the same style as the record-breaking 05 Baltics, V19 001 was intended for speeds of up to 175 kph (109 mph). Each axle was powered by a V2 engine. The war put an abrupt end to this promising experiment. The Witte-Roosen 'V8' certainly looked the part but, disappointingly, steam consumption rates were higher than those for the 05s. The locomotive, however, drew considerable attention from US Army Transportation Corps engineers – perhaps the idea of a 'V8' engine appealed – and V19 001 was shipped to the United States. After enduring years of neglect, she was scrapped in 1957.

*

Certain features developed through some of these experimental designs did meet with wider acceptance, although these were often the simplest elements. From 1910, cab-in-front design, for example, revolutionized steam operation on the Southern Pacific Railroad's demanding route through the Sierra Nevada. Here, trains ran through miles of tunnels and snow sheds on a steeply inclined line. Working through these with a conventionally arranged steam locomotive, with fumes and excessively high cab temperatures (which could rise to 60–70 °C), was not just unpleasant but downright dangerous. The Southern Pacific's two hundred or more oil-fired, cab-in-front 4-8-8-2s, built up until 1944, solved the problem. The crew worked from a cab at the front of these powerful and greatly respected locomotives, with the fire-box behind them; this gave them a clear view of the twisting, climbing, snow-covered track ahead, and ensured they were not troubled by fumes because the chimney, a long way behind, faced the tender and exhaust was carried back over the train.

Equally successful were the many Shay-geared locomotives built by Lima over the decades from 1880. These delightful and highly effective engines were designed for use on lightly laid, often narrow-gauge, railways, where very steep and slippery gradients and tight curves were the norm. Employed widely in the logging industry, some even ran on wooden rails. To ensure optimum adhesion and the smooth delivery of power, albeit at low speeds, the Shay locomotives were fitted with three vertical cylinders mounted on one side, driving a longitudinal shaft (as in a lorry or car), geared to the road axles of the bogies they rode on.

What became, however, one of the holy grails of some steam locomotive designers in the mid-twentieth century was the idea of a modern main-line steam locomotive with mechanical drive and the total adhesion enjoyed by double-bogie diesels and electrics. Such a machine would have a cab at both ends. It would be fast, powerful, and economical to run, with excellent acceleration. Sheathed in sheet-steel casing, it would be easy to clean. It would make turntables redundant. It would not just prolong, but might even revolutionize, the story of the steam railway locomotive.

As it was, the first locomotives of this type were the metre-gauge Co-Cos built by Sentinel in 1933 for Colombia's railways, with Woolnough semi-flash boilers working at 550 psi and two-cylinder compound engine units driving each axle. One engineer who was attracted to the concept, and who clung to it with some tenacity, was Oliver Bulleid, when he was chief mechanical engineer of the Southern Railway and, later, of the CIE in Ireland. The locomotive he developed, in the face of mounting opposition within his own mechanical engineering department on the Southern Railway and, from 1948, the management of the new British Railways, was the legendary Leader 0-6-6-0T of 1949. Here was a steam locomotive that really could be mistaken for a diesel.

Curiously, the Leader project began, in 1944, with a request by the Southern Railway's general manager for proposals for twenty-five general-purpose tank engines. This gradually developed into an all-purpose locomotive that would modernize locomotive operation on the non-electrified sections of the Southern Railway. Indeed, in a paper published in *Modern Transport* on 26 October 1947, entitled 'New Conception of Steam Locomotive Design – Lessons for the Immediate Future', Bulleid asked: 'What sort of locomotive may we expect to see if it is to meet the majority of our future requirements?' Answering his own question, he wrote: 'The locomotive should be built (1) to run over the majority of company lines; (2) to be capable of working all classes of train up to 90 mph; (3) to have its whole weight available for braking and the highest percentage thereof for adhesion; (4) to be equally suited to running in both directions without turning with unobstructed look-out; (5) to be ready for service at short notice; (6) to be almost continually available; (7) to be suited for complete "common use"; (8) to run not less than 10,000 miles between general overhauls with little or no attention at the running sheds; (9) to cause minimum wear and tear to the track; and (10) to use substantially less fuel and water per drawbar horsepower developed [than conventional steam locomotives].' (As it turned out, of these desiderata only numbers 3 and 4 were fully achieved.)

With these points in mind, Bulleid declared that 'a new type of Southern engine has been designed, the construction of five has been authorized. The engine will incorporate the following features . . . The locomotive is carried on two six-wheeled bogies, the general design of which follows that of the bogies I designed for use under the company's electric locomotives [they were, in fact, designed by the Southern Railway's Percy Bolland] . . . the engine develops a torque, the uniformity of which is comparable with that of a nose-suspended electric traction motor but has a higher speed range and the unsprung weight is less. The capacity of the boiler has been made greater, relative to the cylinder horsepower, than in the case of any previous Southern locomotive. The cabs at both ends will give an improved lookout . . . The engines are intended for working fast passenger trains of 480 tons weight over the difficult Southern main line, and goods and mineral trains of up to 1,200 tons; that is to say, something above the heaviest trains that would be required on the system.'

Material for the first five Leaders had been ordered in December 1946. The locomotive, 36001, that emerged from the Brighton works, painted a uniform grey, was certainly like no steam locomotive that had ever been seen before. It promised a great deal, but in the event proved to be a troublesome prototype which was attempting to apply several undeveloped design features. The British Railways locomotive design team, led by E. S. Cox under 'Robin' Riddles, steeped in the ideas of Stanier, standardization, austerity, and simplicity, were never going to be sympathetic to such a radical and complex machine unless its new features were quickly proven to be reliable – particularly since the Stanier class 5 4-6-0, and later the British Railways Standard class 5 4-6-0, could do pretty much anything the Leader could do, with exemplary reliability and economy.

'As a man, I liked Bulleid and we got on well,' said Riddles after the latter's death. 'But he was an individualist who wanted to do it his own way and some of what he did was questionable. I couldn't fathom some of his thinking . . . Was there a job for Bullied after Nationalization? No; how could there be? Having been king of his own dung heap, how could he suddenly come and serve in mine? The surprise to me was that having failed on the Southern, he went to Ireland and failed there too.'

This uncharacteristically tart comment by the generally broad-minded Riddles shows just how strongly more conventionally inclined engineers than Bulleid felt about the Leader and its successor, the Irish Railways' turf-burning locomotive, CC1, built at Inchicore in 1957. And sadly, the age of austerity, when the British public still shopped with wartime ration books and national finances were very tight indeed, meant that there was little room for prolonged experiments like the Leader, which had no guarantee of success and was paid for by the public purse.

Although 36001 had been retired in March 1951 and construction of the remaining four Leaders halted, the *Sunday Dispatch* nonetheless led its 18 January 1953 edition with the headline 'Railways' Biggest Fiasco'. The popular Sunday newspaper had sent its reporters to investigate the scandal of '£500,000 being wasted on three useless engines'. 'The engines, 67-foot-long monsters of the Leader class with driving cabins at each end, were built in 1948 and 1949 to "revolutionize" train travel. They were part of a £750,000 experiment undertaken by Mr O. V. Bulleid, Chief Mechanical Engineer of British Railways, Southern Region. I can reveal,' thundered the anonymous *Dispatch* reporter, 'that the region's officials regard the experiment as one of their biggest failures.'

Other stories on the front page of that edition of the *Dispatch* told of a twenty-year-old from Glasgow winning the first heat of the National Bathing Beauty Championship and of Manny Shinwell, 'a former Socialist Minister for Defence and Secretary of State for War, attacking plans for Queen Elizabeth's Coronation because standard bearers at this great state occasion were to be drawn from the aristocracy and particularly from the military'. And, at the bottom of the page, a small headline reading 'Fares Rise Now May Be Queried at Westminster' gave the game away. Fares rises were unpopular then, as now, and so British Railways could be taken to task for demanding higher revenues while throwing money away on 'white elephants'.

The problem with the Leader was that too many experiments were carried out on one locomotive at one time and with inadequately proven components. The three-cylinder bogies had chain drives coupling the centre driving axle with the outer axles. The valve gear was housed in an oil bath which was liable to leak, and sleeve valves, more often associated with car engines than steam railway locomotives, were subject to steam leakage and seating-ring breakage. The stubby 280 psi welded boiler was offset to one side of the locomotive's frames to allow for a passageway giving access to the fireman's compartment. Furthermore, since the chosen fuel for the Leader was coal rather than oil, the fireman was tucked into a tiny and blisteringly hot cubbyhole, nicknamed 'The Chinese Laundry', inside the engine's casing. And because of the nature of the fire-box, in which the sides were provided by firebrick walls which needed thickening in service, the grate area was just 26 sq ft, rather than the 43 sq ft originally planned. Meanwhile, just 2,500 gallons of water were carried, which meant that the locomotive needed to make frequent stops to replenish her tanks. The weight grew during the design and construction stage from

110 to 130.5 tons – much of this due to the ballast needed to balance the offset boiler – and, given its axle loading of 21.75 tons, the chief civil engineer would only allow 36001 to run on lines cleared for the Merchant Navy Pacifics and, initially, at a maximum of 50 mph.

On the plus side, the bogies and brakes were excellent. The former, derived from a design by Percy Bolland for Bulleid's Southern Railway Co-Co electric locomotives, were later used on British Railways class 40, 45, and 46 diesel-electrics, as well as Southern Region express electric multiple units of the 1950s and 1960s. But if 36001 was a fine-riding vehicle, running very comfortably at 70 mph on test, it was beset by all too many problems. Worst of all, it was dogged by its inability to steam consistently and needed frequent stops to regain boiler pressure after long, arduous climbs. On 19 November 1949, British Railways issued a directive putting a halt to work on sister locomotives 36002, which was just two days away from completion, and 36003.

What was particularly frustrating is that, on a good day, and with Bulleid allegedly paying crews £1 bonus to 'go for it', 36001 could put up some reasonable performances. When full pressure was maintained, she would climb up banks with relative ease – working, for example, a test train of five coaches up the 4.75 miles from Buxted to Crowborough, Sussex, in just 4.5 minutes, or half the time demanded by contemporary timetables. As it was, final tests were made in late 1950. On 17 October, and after modifications made at the Brighton works, the locomotive was scheduled to pull a thirteen-coach train weighing 480 tons from Eastleigh to Basingstoke, Woking, and Guildford, and back again. Among those on the footplate was Roland Bond, a Stanier man and, later, chief mechanical engineer of British Railways. Apart from an embarrassing moment at Basingstoke when the Leader refused to move forwards or backwards while attempting to take on water, the locomotive behaved well – so much so that a further test with a fifteen-coach, 480 ton train was planned for 2 November.

Pulling away up the gradient northwards from Eastleigh, 36001 was half a minute early through Worting Junction, covering the 25.8 miles to Basingstoke in 46 minutes, or about 42 minutes net allowing for a 1.5 minute signal stop along the way. In sustaining 40 mph up the long 1-in-252 gradient with 480 tons, 36001 was developing about 1,000 dbhp, or about 1,250–1,300 ihp. Unfortunately, however, cinders and chunks of coal falling inside the locomotive from the chimney on the long climb threatened to set its wooden floor alight and the test had to be abandoned at Basingstoke. Uncoupled from her train, 36001 ran back to Eastleigh light engine, reaching – or so the optimists claimed – her intended 90 mph. It was the last journey she made. The Leader never made it into revenue-earning service. Management was pleased to see her go – aside from a fundamental difference in design philosophies between Riddles and Bulleid, British Railways did not have the money to invest, or indulge, in further modifications to 36001 to make it a reliable and traffic-worthy machine.

Bulleid's reaction to the termination of the Leader experiment is hard to determine. An article he wrote in the US journal *Mechanical Engineering* in 1950 suggests that he was confident that Leader would succeed, while looking forwards to a future generation of steam locomotives that might well be quite different from 36001:

> While in this Leader class of engine the development of
> the steam locomotive has been carried a stage further,
> there is still much work to be done. The use of the
> blast to create draught should give way to fans so that
> we can control the production of steam accurately.
> The exhaust steam should not be allowed to escape to
> the atmosphere but should be returned to the boiler.
> Experimental work already done encourages the thought
> that these two problems can be solved and I commend
> them to young engineers as worthy of investigation.
> I shall feel more than recompensed if I have shown
> that while the Stephenson locomotive may in some
> circumstances be dead or dying, this cannot be said of

steam traction itself. If new designs be developed in the light of our present greater knowledge and the servicing of the locomotive be brought up to date – in short, if we can demolish the conservatism which is destroying the steam locomotive rather than give up any of its customary ways – then we can look forward to a revival of steam traction.

In his history of the project, *Leader: Steam's Last Chance* (1988), Kevin Robertson came to the conclusion that this daring locomotive never really stood a chance: 'Certainly Bulleid tried to point the way forward. The problem really comes down to a matter of timing and, in this respect, the onset of nationalization meant that No. 36001 was really condemned before she ever turned a wheel. It would have required a faultless performance from the outset to alter this. In the form No. 36001 took, the timing of her birth would never have been right, she was a hybrid and in essence stillborn.'

Sadly, if perhaps inevitably, 36001 was cut up, rather than being preserved as a curiosity – if nothing else. If the locomotive had survived into the preservation era, she would very probably be running today in the care of enthusiastic owners and engineers determined to make her run as well as Bulleid had planned. What a sight 36001 would make at the head of a special passenger train on the main line, painted perhaps in British Rail blue with yellow warning panels and the double-arrow InterCity logo. And she would, in all probability, be named too: *O. V. S. Bulleid*.

Bulleid himself made one more attempt at a double-bogie locomotive which might just have given steam a new lease of life, and this time he used a very different and non-polluting source of fuel. This was CC1, his experimental turf-burning locomotive for the CIE. Bulleid had left British Railways in September 1949, moving on to a new lease of professional life as chief mechanical engineer in Ireland. During the Second World War, the Irish railways had started using turf as fuel for steam locomotives because supplies of imported coal were severely limited. There were very few coal mines in Ireland and what coal they produced was low-quality stuff compared with the high-calorific produce of Yorkshire and Wales. The supply of oil, even had it been affordable, was also severely limited throughout the war years. The one fuel that Ireland did have in abundance was turf, or peat. This was being burned with some degree of success in Irish power stations, but with its small grate a steam railway locomotive was not the ideal turf-burning vehicle.

Bulleid was quick to pick up on the idea and had soon converted a venerable ex-Great Southern & Western Railway K3 class two-cylinder 2-6-0 into a complex and, despite a few heroic test runs, unsuccessful turf-burner. Looking like a plumber's nightmare, the poor machine, painted in a dazzling coat of aluminium paint, had the words 'Experimental Turf-Burning Locomotive' emblazoned across its tender. Crews were quick to cover over the first six letters of 'Experimental' – to impress upon their workmates, and any CIE passenger who might have seen it at work, what they thought about it.

Undeterred, Bulleid began again from scratch in 1952 when, with Roland Bond's permission, two of his former Eastleigh colleagues, Ron Pocklington and John Click, then at British Railways' Rugby locomotive testing plant, were seconded to work on the design of a brand new turf-burning locomotive. Click had worked on the Leader and had played a major role in the design of CC1, so much so that among CIE staff CC1 was often referred to as 'Click's Clever Invention'.

The locomotive that first steamed on 6 August 1957 was very nearly a success. It was smaller than the Leader, measuring 60 ft long and weighing 120 tons. It had four 12 × 14 in cylinders, rather than six, and conventional piston rather than sleeve valves. The boiler, comprising two barrels, one on either side of the fire-box, was pressed to 250 psi, the diameter of the driving wheels was 3 ft 7 in, compared with the Leader's 5 ft 1 in, and the tractive effort was 19,926 lb. Turf was supplied to the 22.75 sq ft grate by a pair of steam-powered

Archimedes' screws, while the crew worked comfortably in a pair of cabs positioned at the centre of the locomotive, which, however, offered far more restricted views than the driver of 36001 enjoyed. Draught and exhaust were both generated by steam-driven fans. As with 36001, final drive was by chains, although soft-grease lubrication was used instead of the Leader's leaky oil baths.

The locomotive was built at Inchicore, alongside the assembly of the CIE's new diesel-electric locomotives, ordered by Bulleid. In fact, it was Bulleid who supervised – successfully – the dieselization of the CIE, although the decision to abandon steam was taken above his head. The turf-burner was viewed by CIE management, and probably by Bulleid too, as an experiment, but one that, should it prove successful, might well be built as a standby for the new diesels in case of problems with imported fuel supplies or mechanical failures.

On 7 August 1957, Bulleid's friend, Louis Armand, general manager of the SNCF, rode with the chief mechanical engineer on the footplate of CC1 up and down the yard at Inchicore, at speeds of up to 30 mph. Photographs show both men clearly enjoying themselves. Now in his seventies, Bulleid was certainly a lucky man, able to indulge in experimental work on steam when his contemporaries were long retired. Runs on the main line to Kildare followed. The locomotive proved to be smooth-riding, fast – it could easily run at 70 mph – and almost dangerously quiet. With little more than the smooth hum of its fans, CC1 sounded nothing like a reciprocating steam locomotive, and drivers quickly got used to sounding its whistle long and loud as it approached crossings, tunnels, and wayside stations. With the light trains it hauled, acceleration and braking were excellent.

There were the usual problems with oil leaks, broken valve rings, and rapid wear to the drive chains. Ejecting partly burned turf, the exhaust set fire to carriage roofs on test trains several times. Steaming was patchy. After it had run some two thousand miles, Click wrote a measured report on CC1. He considered it to be fairly successful for a prototype, but, as with the Leader, he believed it to be too complex, recommending a simpler machine with a cab at one end for series production. If this had gone ahead, the CIE's future turf-burners would have looked very much like the thousands of single-cab diesel-electrics that perform the mainstay of work on US railroads today. Someone needed to fight for turf-burners on the rapidly dieselizing CIE. But Click had been back in England for some time when, at the end of May 1958, at the age of seventy-five, Bulleid finally retired. CC1, although freshly turned out in a coat of handsome green paint, retired with him. She was never to steam again and, sadly, was broken up in 1963, when she should have been preserved.

*

By this time, new steam locomotive development was coming to a halt worldwide. There were to be no more revolutionary schemes to reinvent the steam railway locomotive in modified form after the late 1950s, although several attempts were made, with varying degrees of success, to improve the economy and thermal efficiency of existing locomotives. In Italy, Ing. Attilio Franco and Dr Piero Crosti had in 1913 devised a new form of locomotive boiler and water pre-heater that promised substantial reductions in fuel consumption. This was the Franco-Crosti boiler, which was first applied to a very large and complex triple-unit, 0-6-2 + 2-4-2-4-2 + 2-6-0 machine, 31 m (102 ft) long and rated at 3,000 ihp, built by Tubize in Belgium in 1932. The centre unit carried the main boiler, with twin barrels on either side of a central fire-box, and two four-coupled engine units at either end. This unit was in turn flanked by two outboard units, linked by knuckle-joints. Each of these housed a large tubular drum through which boiler flue gases passed, via flexible pipe connections, from the adjacent smoke-box on the centre unit, to preheat the boiler feedwater to about 160 °C, thus considerably reducing the heat transfer required to convert water into steam in the boiler.

The Tubize locomotive was tested over the heavily inclined Brussels–Luxembourg line, hauling a 1,214 ton train at 24 kph (15 mph) up the 1-in-62 ruling gradient. There was no buyer for this impressive, if complex, machine because of the severe economic recession of the time. Finally, in 1943, the constituent parts of the Tubize locomotive were rebuilt to form two 2-6-2 + 2-6-0 four-cylinder, twin-unit machines with conventional boilers. These were then sent to work in the German naval dockyards at Kiel. In 1945 they passed to the Polish railways, the last being withdrawn in 1955. This enormous machine had, however, proved that the Franco-Crosti boiler and pre-heater concept worked. The underlying idea had been to maximize the use of heat in exhaust gases which would otherwise have been discharged up the chimney. Recycling these hot gases through tubes in a second drum enabled further heat to be extracted from them in pre-heating the boiler. This maximized heat retention within the steam cycle of the locomotive and lowered fuel consumption.

In 1936, just before the death of Attilio Franco, the Italian railways rebuilt a 670 class saturated (i.e. non-superheated), four-cylinder, cab-in-front 4-6-0 with a Franco exhaust pre-heater in the tender. Tested the following year, it showed substantial fuel economies over the standard 670s. In 1937, Piero Crosti, Franco's collaborator, tested a more efficient pre-heater with two drums, one on each side of the boiler, through which exhaust gas was piped from the main smoke-box. This gas was exhausted through oblong chimneys at the rear end of each drum, drawn by exhaust steam from the cylinders passing through triple-jet blast-pipes.

Steam enthusiasts who visited Italy in post-war years will associate Franco-Crosti boilers with the inside-cylinder Gr 623 class 2-6-0s, a class of thirty-five engines rebuilt from Gr 625s dating from 1910–23, the ninety-three 743 class 2-8-0s with twin-drum pre-heaters, and the eighty-one members of the Gr 741 class of 2-8-0s, rebuilt from 1954 with single-drum pre-heaters located under the boiler and a single oblong chimney. With their side-mounted pre-heater boiler drums and oblong chimneys along the flanks of their boilers, just ahead of the fire-box, these machines were decidedly odd-looking, yet they were undeniably efficient. The 60 ton Gr 623 class 2-6-0s developed

920 ihp, compared with the 800 ihp of the Gr 625s, while burning 15 per cent less fuel. The single feedwater boiler of the Gr 741s was mounted below the main boiler, giving a cleaner, if slightly top-heavy, appearance. The effectiveness of the single-drum Franco-Crosti pre-heater system attracted engineers and operating management in both Germany and Britain. But what had seemed to be such a successful invention in Italy met with little success in other countries.

In Germany, the Deutsche Bundesbahn equipped two class 42 2-10-0s with single-drum Franco-Crosti pre-heaters in 1951. These gave a fuel economy of 15 per cent over standard 42s. These were followed in 1958–9 by thirty-one class 50 2-10-0s. These featured stainless-steel pre-heater drum smoke-boxes, obviating the corrosion problem that had been experienced with mild-steel drums, where the low-temperature gas at dew point produced sulphuric acid. So equipped, the modified 2-10-0s also showed a 15 per cent fuel saving. The Franco-Crosti machines were significantly more economical at higher power outputs than conventional locomotives because the exit-gas temperature from the primary boiler barrel was higher, thus increasing the heat transfer to feedwater in the pre-heater drum.

In Britain, British Railways decided to equip ten new 9F class 2-10-0s built at Crewe in 1955 with single-drum Franco-Crosti pre-heater boilers. An arrangement was made by which British Railways would pay Dr Crosti a full royalty if the Franco-Crosti engines made an 18 per cent saving on coal burnt compared with a regular 9F. A part-royalty would be paid if the saving was between 12 and 18 per cent, and none if it was below 12 per cent. Dr Crosti was truly aghast when tests made on the Glasgow and south-western main line between 92023, with a Franco-Crosti boiler, and the unmodified 92050, revealed a saving of just 4 per cent. At the suggestion of Dennis Carling, superintending engineer at the Rugby locomotive testing plant, André Chapelon, who was visiting Britain in 1959, was asked to verify or refute the reports, which he did. The upshot was a polite payment made by British Railways to Crosti and, soon afterwards, an end to the experiment.

British crews were generally happy when the pre-heaters were disconnected and the ten modified 9Fs returned to normal working. The side exhaust in front of the fire-box had restricted the crew's view from the right-hand side of the locomotives, while in a crosswind exhaust smoke made the cabs dirtier than usual. And Dr Crosti himself may have found it hard to grasp how efficient the 9F 2-10-0s actually were. These were conventional Stephensonian locomotives, but well designed and as capable of heading heavy express passenger trains at 90 mph on mile-a-minute schedules as of running heavy goods trains at 60 mph. No Italian steam locomotive, ancient or modern, was ever asked to work as hard as a 9F. As it was, Crosti had many successes with Italian locomotives rebuilt from older machines, and good results were also obtained in Germany in the 1950s with the 2-10-0s; further installations were planned before steam construction was halted at the end of the decade.

Meanwhile, the Austrian engineer Dr Adolph Giesl-Gieslingen achieved much in raising the power and efficiency, and lowering the fuel consumption, of steam locomotives around the world in the 1950s and 1960s. A graduate of Vienna Technical University, Giesl was employed from 1928 as a design engineer with the Vienna locomotive works. In 1931 he went to the United States, working in technical universities there before returning to Vienna on the weekend of the Austrian *Anschluss*, in March 1938. Giesl was appointed sales manager of the Vienna locomotive works; he believed he had been returning to Austria to take on the role of managing director, but this was given to two pro-Nazis who shared the job. Giesl, however, was still able to develop the ejector that bears his name and which was initially applied to ten industrial 0-6-0T shunters.

In the aftermath of the war, in 1948, Giesl returned to the United States, where he hoped to fit many inefficiently draughted locomotives with his highly efficient ejector. In the event, he equipped just one large Chesapeake and Ohio Railway 0-8-0 switcher (shunter), while his design for a special twin ejector for three 6,000 hp Chesapeake and Ohio turbo-electrics was abandoned when all work was stopped on steam development in 1951. That same year, Giesl returned to Austria, where he made an agreement with the Schoeller Bleckmann steelworks licensing them to manufacture the Giesl ejector, of which over 2,500 were eventually made.

The Giesl ejector was a blast-pipe comprising a longitudinal row of nozzles which discharged steam through a deep oblong chimney. The ejector's great step forward was in minimizing the 'shock loss' in conventional draughting. This reduced back-pressure on the pistons, while simultaneously allowing for a stronger draught through the boiler tubes from the fire-grate, and a higher degree of superheating. This meant that lower grades of coal could be burned at higher rates of combustion. In East Germany, for example, a lignite-burning class 50 2-10-0 fitted with a Giesl ejector developed 1,600 ihp at 50 kph (31 mph), compared with 1,100 ihp for the standard machine. It is hardly surprising that 390 Deutsche Reichsbahn class 50 and class 52 2-10-0s were so equipped.

Initial approaches to British Railways, in 1957, were rejected, but after the matter had been raised in parliament, British Railways agreed grudgingly for a trial installation on a double-chimneyed class 9F 2-10-0, on the proposition that the locomotive would be able to produce the same power using lower-grade, and thus cheaper, coal. The Giesl ejector fitted to 92250 showed no more than a 4.5 per cent reduction in coal consumption, and little in the way of increased power, in tests made at Rugby in 1959, burning normal Blidworth coal at moderate firing rates. Burning lower-grade coal, however, was the point of the exercise, and in this respect the experiment was never properly seen through, creating the erroneous impression that the Giesl ejector was not nearly as efficient as its designer claimed.

Then, in 1962, 34064 *Fighter Command*, an unrebuilt Bulleid Battle of Britain light Pacific, was fitted with a Giesl ejector. The objective was to minimize spark emission, which was a serious problem with the unrebuilt Bulleids, causing many line-side fires in southern

England, for which compensation had to be paid to farmers. Thus equipped, *Fighter Command* proved so successful that it was decided to fit all forty-nine unrebuilt Bulleid light Pacifics with Giesl ejectors. The British Railways board, however, vetoed the agreement that had been drawn up with Schoeller Bleckmann, on the grounds that the locomotives had only a three- to four-year working life ahead of them.

If *Fighter Command* was so improved by a Giesl ejector, then what might have been the result if the device had been fitted to hundreds, or thousands, of other British Railways locomotives? We shall never know. There was, anyway, no rational answer to be had. From 1963, British Railways was determined to rid itself of steam as quickly as possible and management had little appetite to improve a form of traction it considered old-fashioned. This does seem a shame, as the Giesl ejector performed wonders elsewhere in the world, on locomotives both old and new. Indeed, in a letter to the *Railway Magazine* in November 1966, the steam locomotive engineer Kenneth Cantlie took issue with those who dismissed the Giesl ejector based on British Railways' one-off experience with 92250: 'In Kenya . . . a class 59 Garratt hauls 1,170 to 1,200 tons on the long 1-in-66 grades of the main line. When fitted with Giesl ejectors, they have hauled 1,500 tons at slightly higher speeds. Other classes have shown similar increases. In Nigeria, where increased hauling power is also the requirement, ejector-fitted River class locomotives have taken 780 tons at the same speeds as the normal 660 ton trains.'

Cantlie went on to explain the particular way in which the Giesl ejector helped to improve locomotive performance: 'The increase in power of locomotives fitted with Giesl ejectors comes not from additional steam production, though this is possible, but from better utilization of the steam produced. By reducing exhaust pressure by 50 to 75 per cent considerably greater cylinder mean effective pressure is obtained; on the locomotives I tested in Africa the extra power averaged about 20 per cent. For hauling the same trains, therefore, less steam and thus less coal and water is required. On the other hand the extra power can be utilized in hauling heavier trains or running at higher speed.' And Cantlie concluded: 'Roughly, the cost of 100 Giesl ejectors, when fitted, is the same as one diesel locomotive and the annual average return on capital varies from 100 to 300 per cent . . . as a result I was convinced that the Giesl ejector was the finest draughting system in the world.'

No matter how effective some of these latest developments were, railway management the world over had become convinced that steam had to make way for diesel and, where possible or expedient, electric traction. The main-line steam locomotives that were built in the three decades following Cantlie's paean to the Giesl ejector were rugged, simple machines designed to provide, as Riddles and his team had done for British Railways, the maximum tractive effort, and perhaps power, for the minimum cost. Doubtless a great deal of money could have been saved on many railways in the short term if existing steam locomotives had been modified along the lines of *Fighter Command*, the East African class 59 Garratts, and the Gresley A3 and A4 Pacifics and V2 2-6-2s fitted with double Kylchap exhausts. Indeed, the enhanced performance of the last was such that British Railways Eastern Region motive power engineers called for more Kylchap-fitted V2s and fewer new, less powerful, and far less reliable, diesels.

Such calls were to go unheeded; what mattered most to management was modernization, that blinkered and invariably illusory rush towards a brighter, cleaner, and super-efficient new world. Even so, and very much against the odds, a number of spirited and highly intelligent engineers continued to believe that there was a future for steam on the world's railways. And what they called for was not a revolutionary form of steam locomotive, but a Stephensonian machine that would use the steam it generated far more effectively.

CHAPTER 7

THE FUTURE
Keeping the Faith

If the steam railway locomotive has a future, the origins of its renaissance will date back to the years immediately following the Second World War. This was not primarily in Europe, where André Chapelon continued to put forward proposals for advanced compound and triple-expansion locomotive types until the 1970s, and much less so in the United States, where the diesel-electric was about to trounce its characterful predecessor. No. Perhaps unexpectedly, today's putative steam renaissance was nurtured largely in Argentina, and the year of its inception can be pinpointed accurately. It was 1948, the year that the Argentine steam engineer Livio Dante Porta, a disciple of Chapelon, began converting the metre-gauge Córdoba Central Railway B22 class Pacific No. 2011 into a streamlined, four-cylinder compound 4-8-0. It was named *Argentina* and it was one of the most efficient steam railway locomotives yet built, with the equal highest power-to-weight ratio ever, sharing this particular honour with Chapelon's mighty SNCF 240P.

What was all the more remarkable is that this was the 27-year-old engineer's very first locomotive. Born in Paraná and educated at the Salesian missionary school in Rosario, Porta trained as a civil engineer at the National University of the Littoral, going on to become a brilliant and provocative theoretician as well as an exceptionally fine hands-on locomotive engineer. Typically, he trained as a fireman and engine driver before designing *Argentina*. He became fluent in French, Italian, English, and German, and somehow managed to raise a close and loving family of five children with his cherished wife, Ana Maria Bosco; they married in 1950.

The energetic young engineer, who had by now set up his own workshop, the Livio Dante Porta Locomotive Factory, in La Plata, went to see Argentina's charismatic populist President Juan Perón personally in order to gain funding for the project. Keen on technological development, Perón ensured that funds were released from the Argentine National Bank to Porta's engineering company. The result was a 68 ton locomotive capable of developing 2,100 dbhp, an astonishing feat made possible by Porta's thorough reappraisal, in the light of Chapelon's work in France (the two corresponded regularly until the Frenchman's death), of how steam flowed through a locomotive and how this flow could be optimized. No contemporary – or even much later – diesel locomotive could match this pugnacious performance on a power-to-weight basis. It was like a bantamweight boxer packing the punch of Mike Tyson.

Argentina was equipped with steam passages that were bigger in cross-section than even Chapelon's, had a high boiler pressure (285 psi), and featured compounding and a substantial degree of superheating and re-superheating. Exhaust was through a Kylchap nozzle, although Porta was soon to develop his own system which he claimed was even more efficient than Chapelon's. The real secret to *Argentina*'s astonishing power, however, was Porta's first attempt at what was to be his gas-producer combustion system (GPCS). This transformed the fire-box into a sophisticated gas producer, with air drawn across the fire not just through the ash-pan and holes in the fire-door, but also through apertures at various levels in the fire-box sides above the grate. The result was a fire-box where coal burned very effectively at a more even temperature, with combustion gases passing through the boiler's fire-tubes, carrying very little in the way of unburnt particles. A GPCS-fitted locomotive was not only considerably more powerful than one fitted with a conventional fire-box, it was also unlikely to cause line-side fires or to hurl smuts through the dining-car windows on to the luncheon plates, or into the eyes of passengers looking out of the carriage windows.

As Porta continued his researches into improving the GPCS system, he found that virtually any solid fuel could be burned cleanly and effectively, including wood, charcoal mixed with oil, waste from sawmills, and even bagasse, the waste from crushed sugar cane. What Porta was beginning to prove with *Argentina* is that a new-generation steam locomotive would not only be very much more efficient than its predecessors, it would also be a very much cleaner machine. Indeed, with its white and blue livery – the colours of the Argentine flag – *Argentina* would have shown dirt more easily than the vast majority of steam locomotives. As one of the main arguments against the steam is that it is dirty and polluting, Porta was learning to pull the carpet from under the anti-steam lobby's feet.

Mounted on 1.27 m (4 ft 2 in) driving wheels, smaller than most standard-gauge freight locomotives, *Argentina* was nevertheless designed to run at a maximum speed of 120 kph (74.5 mph). In the event, the state of Argentine metre-gauge tracks meant that she never ran at more than about 105 kph (65 mph), although at this speed she rode as steadily as a Pullman car. With her bullet-shaped flanks emblazoned with two favourite sayings of President Perón – *'Mejor que decir es hacer'* ('Better to do than to say') and *'Mejor que prometer es realizar'* ('Better to carry out than to promise') – in 1949 *Argentina* made extensive trials, at which Chapelon himself was present. The locomotive pulled a 1,200 ton unfitted freight train at 105 kph (65 mph) with almost casual ease, and had no problem restarting a 2,000 ton train up a steep gradient and cruising at 80 kph (50 mph) on the level. An axle loading of just 13.5 tons meant that *Argentina* could run over most local lines. Meanwhile, coal and water consumption was half that of much larger, standard-gauge locomotives of the same power. Thermal efficiency was measured at 11.9 per cent – about twice that of contemporary US steam locomotives – and 13 per cent appeared to be possible. *Argentina* was, quite simply, a phenomenon, although Porta saw her as simply a starting point for a new breed of steam locomotives.

The all-conquering 4-8-0, renamed *Presidente Perón* for the occasion, was put on display in central Buenos Aires; either delightfully or tellingly, she was towed into place by horses. *Argentina* returned to the rails and worked the Mira Pampa to Olavarría line, south-west of Buenos Aires, until 1961, when she was withdrawn and laid aside at La Plata depot. She was meant to have been a prototype for a production series of locomotives, but this never happened. Despite being a brilliant success, clearly nothing could persuade railway management in Argentina, as elsewhere, that steam could possibly be better than diesel power. Porta attempted to return the locomotive to steam in 2000, hoping to use it as a test bed for all that he had learned over the intervening forty years. Sadly, this never happened, and the great locomotive was to be found some years later abandoned, stripped of most of its components, rusting, and vandalized, at the wrecked Mate de Luna depot in a suburb of San Miguel de Tucumán in the north-west of the country.

After *Argentina*, Porta modernized a fleet of broad-gauge 8C class two-cylinder 2-6-2T and 8E class three-cylinder 2-6-4T tank engines which ran suburban passenger services in and around Buenos Aires. He fitted these with his latest invention, the Lempor (Lemaître-Porta) ejector, a highly modified version of the Lemaître exhaust in which hot gases from the boiler tubes were mixed with used steam from the cylinders and expelled with considerably less friction than in earlier exhausts. Like Chapelon, Porta was not simply a gifted thermodynamicist, he also saw the internal workings of the steam locomotive as an organic whole, rather than a collection of components: the organism might be fashioned from steel, but it needed to breathe well to work at new levels of efficiency.

The power of the Argentine Railways 8Es was increased from a maximum of 900 ihp to 1,200 dbhp, while the fully modernized 8C 2-6-2T No. 3477 produced a maximum of 1,400 dbhp, enough to tackle trains normally hauled by locomotives twice its size, such as the three-cylinder PS11 class Pacifics, while burning up to 40 per cent less coal. Management remained indifferent, and even if these powerful tank engines had produced three or four times the power they did when first built and used 100 per cent less fuel, and even if they had proved themselves 200 per cent superior to any new diesel locomotive on the market, they would still have been sent for scrap. Porta's logic was not shared by a management drooling over the latest glossy catalogues from General Motors.

In 1957, Porta was appointed general manager of the Río Turbio railway and Río Gallegos coal port and here, in Patagonia, he demonstrated beyond doubt how the operation of an entire railway could be revolutionized by major advances in the design of the steam locomotive. The 750 mm gauge Ramal Ferro Industrial de Río Turbio (RFIRT) itself was new. Completed in 1951, the railway stretched 255 kilometres between the south Atlantic port of Río Gallegos to the coal mines at Río Turbio, close to the Chilean border. Savagely cold winds blowing for days at 100 kph (62 mph), with gusts of over 200 kph, sweep across this bleak, undulating, and often all but featureless country. In winter, temperatures fall to –20 °C as snow falls and the rails are coated in frost. It is no wonder that few people had settled here before the opening up of the coal mines in the 1950s. An abundance of coal, however, spelt a steam railway.

When Porta arrived in this almost lunar landscape, trains were worked by ten Mitsubishi-built, two-cylinder 2-10-2s, weighing 48 tons and generating up to 925 dbhp on test, although continuous output in service was rated at 700 dbhp. Fitted with GPCS and Kylpor (Kylala-Porta) exhausts, the engines were soon developing a sustained 1,200 dbhp. As this would be like increasing the continuous power output of a Stanier Coronation Pacific from 2,500 to more than 4,000 dbhp, or the maximum output of a Union Pacific Big Boy from 7,500 ihp to 12,000 ihp, at a stroke, it is easy to see why Porta's work was sometimes likened to sorcery.

A second batch of ten 2-10-2s ordered by Porta from Mitsubishi in 1963, incorporating further advances in design, saw sustained power increased to 1,340 dbhp. The twenty-strong class worked 1,700 ton coal trains, day in, day out, at the line's maximum of 50 kph (30 mph) from the Patagonian mines to the Atlantic coast. I was lucky enough to see this operation for myself in the early 1990s, as part of an extended trip to Buenos Aires. Like other visitors to the railway – a very rare species – I was treated with great civility and travelled the length of the line in a caboose fitted out with a stove and benches. It did seem hard to believe that trains a kilometre long could be worked so effectively and quietly by such small locomotives. Riding the footplate of one of the 1963 batch of 2-10-2s back towards the coast was my introduction to the work of Livio Dante Porta. Once on the move, the train could be worked under easy steam and, despite the ferocious weather, the crew were full of praise for their locomotive. It was impossible not to be enthralled by the efficacy of this relatively small machine and in awe of the brilliance of its designer.

In 1961, Porta headed back north to the sophistication and warmth of Buenos Aires, to work, at first, for the recently created Centre for Industrial Power and Fuel Efficiency and then to head up the department of thermodynamics at the National Institute of Industrial Technology, a role he held until his retirement in 1982. He kept in regular touch with the RFIRT and in the mid-1960s one of the 2-10-2s was rebuilt with his latest cyclonic GPCS fire-box. In this new design, air ducts and steam jets produced a swirling flow of fire-box gases, and coal particles caught up in this 'cyclone' were burnt completely. The result was greater heat and power from a given amount of fuel than ever before, and a clean exhaust. On test No. 118 worked a train of 3,190 tons on level track at 30–35 kph (around 20 mph) at full regulator and 35 per cent cut-off – on a 2 ft 6 in gauge track with a maximum axle load of 7.6 tons. Perhaps Porta really was a wizard.

In the early 1970s, Porta proposed a replacement for the hard-working and extremely reliable 2-10-2s. This was due not to any fault in these superb machines, but to the fact that the Río Turbio mines were expected to increase production by over 300 per cent. To work heavier trains, the track was to be upgraded throughout, permitting an axle load of 14 tons. Rather remarkably, a ministry of transport committee found that steam working would be twice as economical as replacement diesel traction and three times cheaper than installing and running electric trains in this remote, wind-blasted, and coal-rich region.

If the plan had gone ahead, the new Porta engines would have been a class of 178 ton 2-12-12-0 Mallets, developing a tractive effort of 110,000 lb, producing a continuous 4,000 dbhp, and running non-stop from the mines to the ocean at up to 75 kph (46.5 mph). The Argentine government asked the United Nations Industrial Development Organization for assistance in financing the upgraded RFIRT. Intriguingly, one of the members of the committee of experts the UN brought in to consider the case was John Click, who had done so much to try to make Bulleid's experimental Leader and CC1 turf-burner work in everyday service. Click was hugely impressed by what Porta had already achieved with the modified RFIRT 2-10-2s. In his report to the UN of December 1977 he noted, after a footplate ride over the line with a heavy train in tow, the evident thermal efficiency of these deeply impressive machines:

> Of greater interest in the dark was the amount of sparking from the chimney top. The locomotive was clean to ride on, but just how little was leaving the chimney top partly burnt was surprising after dark. Even on the last assault up to the Río Turbio station . . . when the locomotive was working very hard in 50–55 per cent cut-off with the regulator wide open at about

18 mph (where the author would have expected a trail
of fire from the chimney) there were only a few (almost
countable!) pea-sized sparks with an occasional one the
size of an olive that lay, after bouncing, a few seconds
on the frozen ground before becoming invisible. It did
not go unnoticed either that the locomotive, after many
hours of steaming, blew off at the safety valves the
instant the regulator was shut in Río Turbio yard.

As late as 1978, it looked as if the Mallets might be built. Unfortunately, these magnificent machines remained firmly on the drawing board in Buenos Aires at a time of increasing financial difficulty in Argentina. With the rise of a vicious military dictatorship in 1976 and the onset of the seven-year-long Dirty War, during which Porta's own fifteen-year-old daughter was one of the tens of thousands of *desaparecidos* ('the disappeared') taken away at gunpoint in the middle of the night and murdered by the security forces, Argentina imploded.

The pathetic and cruel military regime was finally toppled with the country's crushing defeat by the British in the Falklands War of 1982. A civilian government was returned to power the following year. Argentina was now caught up in the mad rush to privatize its state-owned enterprises, encouraged by General Pinochet in Chile and his close friend and ally, Margaret Thatcher, in Britain. One of the state companies privatized in the 1990s was the RFIRT. As private management cut costs, the number of trains fell dramatically and the steam locomotives were replaced, in November 1996, not by 4,000 dbhp Mallets, but by a handful of second-hand Romanian diesel-hydraulics. Not surprisingly, the RFIRT ground to a halt within five years. Plans to resurrect it as a steam-hauled tourist railway by extending it twenty-eight miles east over the Andes into Chile were announced by the steam engineer Shaun McMahon in 2005. Well thought through, and perfectly practicable, these remain little more than a glorious pipe dream.

In the late 1970s, meanwhile, and at the instigation of the industry ministry, Porta drew up designs for a general-purpose, three-cylinder compound 2-10-0 for use on Argentina's metre-gauge railways. This modern machine would have been rated at 5,000 ihp, with a maximum service speed of 130 kph (81 mph). Such a locomotive would have been a great asset to railways in Africa and South East Asia as well as South America. Porta believed, along with many level-headed railway engineers, that steam had a future, at least for the medium term, in countries where its simplicity, ruggedness, and ability to burn a variety of local fuels, including rice husks, orange peel, bark, and peat, made it a more commonsensical choice than costly and complex imported diesels running on even costlier imported fuel.

In 1969 Porta had presented to the Institution of Locomotive Engineers a highly successful and much discussed paper, written jointly with George Carpenter, entitled 'Steam Locomotive Development in Argentina: Its Contribution to the Future of Railway Technology in the Under-Developed Countries'. Yet many politicians, administrators, and railway managements in those very countries shied away from the notion that they were 'under-developed'. Why should they have steam railways when others had shiny new diesels and electrics? Why should they have pick-up trucks and Land Rovers when their peers in the developed world drove around in air-conditioned Mercedes? Porta proved – very clearly – that a new generation of steam locomotives could compete with the latest diesels. Yet none of this mattered to those who wanted to expend, and even squander, resources on forms of motive power that were perceived as luxurious, smart, and, above all, modern.

One country that did listen, for a while at any rate, was Cuba. Forced into ever-increasing self-sufficiency by a petulant US trade embargo – still in place today – this nominally communist Caribbean state ran many veteran wood-burning US steam locomotives throughout the 1990s on the island's numerous and extensive sugar plantations. While these were a joy to watch, ride, fire, and drive, and although they were cheaper to run than modern diesels, they were hardly a byword for efficiency. In 1999, after six years of discussions with the Cuban ministry of transport, during times of great economic difficulty, Porta converted a two-cylinder 2-8-0, orginally built by Alco in 1919, into Cuba's most efficient steam railway locomotive. The aim was to run the Ministry of Sugar's No. 1816 on bagasse, the sugar-cane husks left over from sugar production, or other biomass fuels, including timber grown specially for the purpose on dedicated plantations. Work on No. 1816 led to proposals for an entirely new class of biomass-fuelled, three-cylinder compound 0-6-2 tank engines. Production was scheduled for 2002, but with the death that year of the dynamic and cheerful Manuel Alepuz, director of the Cuban Transport Research Institute and Porta's champion, as well as a dramatic downturn in sugar production in 2003, the project ground to a halt. Porta himself, who, after Chapelon, made the greatest lifetime contribution to the development of the steam locomotive, died the same year.

Porta believed that a blinkered approach to steam locomotive engineering had held its development back during much of the twentieth century, as rival forms of traction became ever more appealing to railway management and politicians. He was unimpressed by the kind of experimental locomotives examined in the previous chapter. 'André Chapelon,' he wrote, 'was the engineer clever enough to realize that the answer was not to be sought in exotic designs, but in eliminating from the Stephensonian scheme a number of absurd imperfections, perhaps the most significant [of which] were poor internal streamlining and flagrant violations of thermodynamic fundamentals. He discovered this when, after sweating to keep up the 16 atm boiler pressure when firing PLM locomotives, his drivers destroyed his painful efforts by throttling ("strangling", one should say) the pressure down to 10 atms at the cylinders. His drivers? No. The mechanical running engineers were responsible!'

Porta knew he was fighting an all but impossible battle on behalf of the steam locomotive, and yet he never let go – and indeed he did prove that a steam locomotive could be cleaner than and as efficient as its diesel rivals. For the future, he proposed triple-expansion, high-pressure (870 psi) locomotives which would achieve a thermal efficiency of 21 per cent. Cleaner, cheaper, faster, and more powerful on a power-to-weight basis, steam would compete effectively with diesel technology.

In 1980, Porta was invited for the first time to, of all countries, the United States, where oil shortages and fears about the reliability of future supplies from the Middle East encouraged a short-lived enthusiasm for a new generation of coal-burning locomotives. As vice president of research and development of American Coal Enterprises (ACE), a company formed in 1980 by the US financier and steam enthusiast Ross Rowland Jr, Porta helped work up the design of the ACE 3000, a twin-unit locomotive with each unit having a front-end cab. This 4,000 ihp, 70 mph 4-8-2 looked very like an elongated diesel-electric locomotive and was intended to compete head-on with General Motors' contemporary EMD GP-40. The power unit had a four-cylinder compound drive. The 300 psi tapered boiler was mated to a computer-controlled cyclonic GPCS firebox. A second-support-unit, borne on two three-axle bogies, carried fuel and a vacuum condenser. By the time trials were to have been carried out on the Chesapeake and Ohio Railway in the mid-1980s, many different versions of the ACE locomotive had been drawn up. The final proposal – none was ever built – was for the 6000G, effectively a 6,000 dbhp 2-8-0 + 0-8-2 Garratt.

As it was, a fall in oil prices of 30 per cent between 1981 and 1985 led to the project being dropped. Porta himself was highly dubious about the complexity of the ACE 3000 and later ACE designs, especially since his American colleagues were so keen on the extensive use of microprocessors to integrate steam production and usage to precise degrees in the engine units. The reciprocating steam locomotive is not an ideal environment for such potentially delicate electronic control mechanisms. The idea, though, was that wholly automated power controls would allow the ACE 3000 to be worked by crews who had grown up exclusively with diesels. Here was steam at the press of a button and the turn of a handle, while the overall diesel-like outline of the ACE machines was intended to attract railway managers who still thought of steam as old-fashioned.

Meanwhile, Porta stressed the importance of improving what he referred to as 'museum' or preserved locomotives, issuing a warning that one day these might well be banned on grounds of environmentally unacceptable smoke emissions and their capacity to cause line-side fires. Initially, he had been not just uninterested in museum locomotives but positively against them, believing that they did nothing to advance steam development. But the sheer growth of the preservation movement and the rise in the number of steam trains operating around the world by the 1980s encouraged him to change his mind. And if equipped with his latest GPCS fire-boxes, he argued, such locomotives would keep emissions to a theoretical minimum and produce less of the dangerous and obnoxious exhaust fumes associated with diesels.

Indeed, when Porta learned in 1992 of a bravura plan by the British A1 Steam Locomotive Trust to build a brand-new, three-cylinder express passenger LNER Peppercorn A1 class Pacific, for work on the main line with special trains for steam enthusiasts and day trippers with a fondness for steam, his response was to write a 200-page paper, 'A Proposal for the Tornado Project', on ways in which the Pacific could be built to look like a 1948 locomotive while packing the punch and meeting the higher levels of power and efficiency expected of a twenty-first-century steam locomotive. The fact that 60163 *Tornado* was built at all is a minor modern miracle. It took the best part of twenty years to raise the necessary funding and complete the project, and no one can doubt that the new A1 has been a hugely popular success. Porta, though, believed that *Tornado* should be a flag-bearer for modern steam. With certain modifications to the 1940s design, the new three-cylinder Pacific would be capable of running at 112 mph and producing around 5,000 ihp at 105 mph. (In their original condition, A1s could touch 100 mph and sustain a maximum of 2,800 ihp, or possibly 3,000–3,300 ihp for short bursts, as has been confirmed by *Tornado* on several occasions.)

Porta couched his address to the A1 Steam Locomotive Trust in soothing, yet challenging, terms: 'The unsurpassed elegance [of the Peppercorn A1], like that of Michelangelo's David, cannot be improved nor altered. But, under forms and liveries scrupulously respected, it is possible to introduce substantial design alterations leading to the above figures [4,000 dbhp and 180 kph], this justifying an effort whose greatness does not detract from but enhances Gresley's name.'

David Elliott, the former British Railways engineer who diligently built *Tornado*, read Porta's paper with great interest and wrote a considered public reply, explaining why the A1 Trust had rejected the concept, in the letters column of *Steam Railway* in October 1993. 'There are,' Elliott remarked, 'a large number of rather radical proposals in Porta's ideas which would make the A1 markedly different from its predecessors, but they were nevertheless given the detailed consideration they deserved . . . However, setting aside the theoretical benefits of the various proposed modifications made by Porta, there was also the question of technical risk to consider. Many of these innovative ideas have not been tried anywhere in the UK before, and nowhere in the world have they all been applied on a single locomotive. As a consequence, Porta himself prudently suggests that no fewer than 20,000 miles of test running might be required to "iron out the bugs" and optimize the performance. Considering how difficult the 71000 Trust found organizing a 200 mile test run with *Duke of Gloucester*, such a programme would hardly be realistic, so we have had to approach such a swathe of innovation with some caution.'

Even so, Elliott promised to investigate a number of useful and readily applicable improvements to the original A1 design, but as the whole point of the project was to build an A1 – a type of locomotive that had slipped the preservationists' net – and not an A1 mark 2,

Tornado emerged from Darlington's Hopetown works in 2003 very much as her siblings had done, from Darlington and Doncaster, more than half a century earlier.

The dream, though, of a super-fast and super-efficient new steam locomotive racing along British rails did not go away. In an article in *Steam Railway* in April 1998, David Wardale, an inspired former British Railways steam locomotive engineer and Porta's chief apostle, published an article titled 'Whither Steam Now?' in which he referred to a 'locomotive of class 5 4-6-0 format that would outperform any British Pacific'. Wardale's design for such a locomotive, the 5AT (Advanced Technology), was revealed in 2001. A small team of businessmen and women, engineers, and scientists gathered around Wardale to form the 5AT Project with the aim of building the engine, ideally by 2010. The aim was to shape a modern two-cylinder 4-6-0 drawing on the researches of Chapelon, Porta, and Wardale himself, which would look, sound, and in most ways feel like a classic British steam locomotive, while packing a 3,500 ihp punch which no previous engine of its weight – 80 tons – could possibly have equalled. The idea was for a medium-sized locomotive with wide route availability and low running costs which could run enthusiasts and other special trains at electric and diesel line speeds. This meant a cruising speed of 113 mph and a top speed, where necessary, of 125 mph. Burning light oil and coupled to an eight-wheeled, double-bogie tender, 5AT would run 228 miles between water stops and 343 miles between fuel stops when fully extended.

With its Witte-style German smoke deflectors, double Lempor exhaust, semi-streamlining, all-enclosed cab, and massive tender, 5AT would look rather different from a Stanier or British Railways Standard class 5 4-6-0. The real differences, though, were beneath the skin. The 305 psi boiler fed valves and pistons fitted with diesel-quality rings to avoid steam leakages. Insulation would ensure minimal heat loss. Lightweight rods, pistons, valves, and roller bearings would not just reduce friction but would keep 'hammer blow' on the tracks to a minimum. Clasp brakes would be highly efficient, while an air-sanding system would ensure that 5AT would get away with minimum slipping. Throughout, an insistence on CAD/CAM modelling, exacting tolerances, and new materials would result in a thoroughly well-designed and precision-built locomotive with smooth riding and minimal need for maintenance.

Wardale completed his fundamental design calculations in 2004, while Network Rail told the *Guardian* newspaper that it would be happy to consider high-speed running with 5AT. At this time, steam locomotives with driving wheels of 6 ft 2 in and over were restricted to a maximum speed of 75 mph. They still are, and this includes 60163 *Tornado*, even though it is a new locomotive and would have no difficulty in running at 90–100 mph. When announced, the cost of building 5AT was estimated to be £1.7 million; this, though, had risen to £10 million by 2010 and there was little sign, especially as the global economy plunged into recession, that adequate funding would come the project's way. Sadly, the project has been mothballed; it seems that those willing to fund steam locomotive construction prefer to invest in replicas of previous types rather than new development.

Even if 5AT is never built, Wardale's work will not have been entirely in vain, as his highly detailed research and calculations will provide the basis for new steam projects in years to come. And there will be a need for a new generation of steam locomotives if the blossoming of steam enthusiasm and tourism continues, and railways insist, quite rightly, that locomotives operating over their lines meet stringent modern safety requirements.

What no one can doubt is the validity of Wardale's calculations. Here is one of the world's great steam locomotive engineers, who has proved that steam can be competitive with rival forms of traction; he is also a man who refuses to wear professional blinkers or the enthusiasts' rose-tinted glasses. His extraordinary book, *The Red Devil and Other Tales from the Age of Steam* (1996), a 520-page tome printed in tiny type which should – eye strain permitting – be read by anyone interested in the future as well as the recent history of the steam locomotive, is often quite damning in its criticisms of particular schools of steam locomotive engineering. Nor does Wardale – quite clearly a perfectionist – ever spare himself. *The Red Devil*, taking its title from the nickname of his superb class 26 4-8-4 for South African Railways, must be one of the most painfully honest as well as informative and riveting books written by an engineer on any subject.

'Who is going to like this book?' asks Wardale in the opening sentence of his preface. 'Steam enthusiasts will not like it because it reveals how steam's performance did not match up to the levels enshrined in their cherished beliefs, this because there can be no balanced view if steam's weaknesses are glossed over and the strengths of its rivals ignored. Steam's detractors will not like it because it finally glorifies something they probably do not understand, and what is not understood is all too often thought of as "wrong". The railway administrations which are portrayed will certainly not like it, because it discloses too much of their way of doing things. And even I do not like it, because it repeats the word "I", a fault which can only be accepted by the realization that the "I" concerned is simply a convention.'

One of the main thrusts of his compelling book is Wardale's belief, shared by Porta, that both railway management and engineers were, and still are, too conservative in their approach to the development of the steam locomotive. For if the steam locomotive had been improved substantially late in the twentieth century, huge amounts of fuel would have been saved and there would have been much less need to manufacture, and market, other forms of traction in parts of the world that could barely afford to buy them, or the oil they required for fuel, let alone maintain them to proper standards. But as Wardale discovered, as he took his skills around the world, once railway management had decided that steam was out, there was, it seemed, no going back, no matter how well – even brilliantly – he could make existing locomotives work.

Wardale began his engineering career with British Railways in 1967. Studying part-time, he graduated from Portsmouth Polytechnic in 1971 and worked for British Railways until 1973, when he left for South Africa. At the time, South African Railways was still something of a steam paradise and Wardale wanted to work with steam. Working in the chief mechanical engineer's department from 1974 to 1983, he radically improved the performance of a 19D class light 4-8-2 and one of South African Railways' powerful main-line 4-8-4s. He came to international attention in 1981 when his class 26 4-8-4, named *L D Porta* but popularly known as *The Red Devil*, put up one memorable performance after another on trials that year. The bright-red locomotive was a major reconstruction of an existing class 25NC 4-8-4. The project had been triggered by a dramatic rise in oil prices in 1978, which encouraged at least some South African Railways engineers to think very seriously about a long-term future for steam.

A gradual move away from steam had begun in 1955, even though a comprehensive South African Railways report that year revealed that there was no real difference in operating costs between heavy modern main-line steam and the latest diesel-electrics, while the railway's Garratts were actually significantly cheaper to run than diesels. Despite these findings, the report, as Wardale records, came down in favour of diesel traction as a matter of fashion. The giveaway line in the report stated there was a need to go with diesels 'to obviate the purchase of further main-line steam locomotives which might prove a further embarrassment to the Administration in a few years'.

Nevertheless, when Wardale joined South African Railways in 1974, the company still owned far more steam locomotives – 1,953 of them – than electrics (1,436) or diesels (737). The steam fleet was of a high calibre and, in general, engines were worked hard and well maintained. But even the best, although they had been built into the mid-1950s, were very much products of 1940s thinking and design. Forty years down the line, they could – and, in Wardale's opinion, should – have been working to far greater levels of efficiency. In 1979, Wardale was authorized to rebuild No. 3450, a class 25NC delivered to South Africa from Henschel in 1952, in response to a sudden rise in the cost of oil. With a budget of just 20,000 rands, Wardale equipped 3450 with a GPCS fire-box, enlarged superheater, improved piston valves, a double Lempor exhaust, a feedwater heater, and many other detailed improvements. In deference to the age of the boiler, its pressure remained at 225 psi.

The result was revelatory. Completed at Salt River works in Cape Town in February 1981 – and with great help, by correspondence, from Porta in Argentina – No. 3450 soon proved capable of sustaining 4,492 ihp at 75 kph (46.5 mph), with the promise of an absolute maximum of 5,029 ihp at 100 kph (62 mph). She could pull a 640 ton passenger train up a 1-in-100 gradient at a steady 100 kph and ran smoothly at up to 120 kph (74.5 mph) on 3 ft 6 in gauge track normally limited to 90 kph (56 mph). Comparative tests were made, in identical conditions, between 3450 and 3428, a standard 25NC in excellent condition, on the Pretoria to Witbank line in November 1981. *The Red Devil* proved to be 43 per cent more powerful than the standard 25NC, while burning 28 per cent less coal and consuming 30 per cent less water. Overall, No. 3450 achieved 21 per cent higher dbhp output than the standard 25NC, and 39 per cent lower specific fuel consumption per dbhp per hour.

Senior officials were at least curious and a team of them made their way to see No. 3450 at Pretoria. Despite what had been achieved, H. J. L. du Toit, deputy general manager of South African Railways and one of the engineers who had drawn up the specification for the original 4-8-4s years earlier, turned to Wardale and said: 'This engine is no better than a standard 25 class.' This amounted, says Wardale, to being told he had done nothing – 'a rather interesting inversion of the oft-quoted words said to Chapelon by his CME after a test of his rebuilt Paris–Orléans Railway 4-6-2 3566 ("*Chapelon, vous avez fait quelque chose*")'. As it was, No. 3450 remained in service from 1981 to 1991 and was often in charge of passenger trains between Kimberley and De Aar. With loads of 650 to 820 tons, she could, and would, easily run ahead of time, running at, or sometimes above, the 90 kph (56 mph) line limit for the entire journey and with great consistency. Most journeys were made at an average speed of 85 kph (53 mph).

Despite what he had achieved – and this was a rebuild of a thirty-year-old engine and not a brand new locomotive – Wardale knew that du Toit's attitude was not only typical of South African Railways management but entrenched within it. Even if he had got *The Red Devil* to beat *Mallard*'s speed record while developing more power than a Chesapeake and Ohio Allegheny and using less fuel than the smallest branch-line tank engine, Wardale's work would have been to no avail. He wrote a final, 115-page report for South African Railways on 3450 in late 1983. One of its conclusions reads:

> The object of all research and development work on
> steam traction is to reduce costs through improved
> performance. In view of the prediction by world
> authorities that oil supplies are limited and will be
> exhausted when coal is still abundantly available, as
> well as the prohibitive cost of electrification . . . it would
> appear to be worthwhile to invest some effort into coal-
> burning steam locomotives, so that their advantages
> can be developed and exploited and their present
> disadvantages minimized or eliminated. However, if the
> engineering and management support which the current
> steam locomotive development work in this organization
> has received continues at its present level, such work will
> remain a largely futile exercise.

Wardale left South Africa at the end of the year. For him, *The Red Devil* had been merely a stepping stone along the iron road to a new generation of steam locomotives. Typically, he insists that 3450 had many faults, although it was a very impressive machine indeed. The locomotive last ran on 29 September 2003 and, given the current South African regime's apparent neglect of – indeed, active hostility towards – not just steam but railways as a whole, its future is by no means assured.

Moving on to work with Porta on the short-lived ACE project in the United States, Wardale took his talents to China in 1985. From speaking at a conference held at Datong works in June that year, Wardale was invited to join the engineering team there, led by Xu Hong Pei. Although Wardale was keen to build a new Garratt class, Pei insisted that work must be concentrated on the QJ class 2-10-2, still in production at Datong. At this time, 70 per cent of all Chinese locomotives were steam, working 60 per cent of all traffic. Datong works itself had a staff of eight thousand, including at least six hundred engineers and technicians, of whom, Wardale says, sixty were engaged in design.

Wardale set to work, drawing up plans for a new design QJ that, with as little modification as possible, would reduce coal consumption by 25 per cent while increasing maximum power to 4,500 ihp. It was difficult, though, to move forwards with any degree of haste at the very time that it was important to do so if steam's reputation was to be enhanced, rather than degraded, in China. Meetings – the bane of creative and active people worldwide – dominated working life at Datong, while locomotive crews were impatient for the better working conditions that diesels promised.

'Even the most dedicated steam enthusiast would have had a hard time maintaining his enthusiasm for long in the real world of locomotive operation as it is experienced throughout North China in wintertime,' wrote Wardale, 'when temperatures can be below –40 °C, and it must be remembered that the vast majority of China's footplate staff were not enthusiasts . . . painful though this might be to steam enthusiasts, the men in China did not share their romantic vision of life on the footplate. They, along with the maintenance staff, were forcefully agitating for change, and such men were not likely to put much effort into making a success of any new design of steam locomotive.'

The end came in 1988, when it was announced that steam production would end at Datong and, together with it, the improved QJ. As he returned to Britain, Wardale could only conclude that the steam locomotive had no future beyond the world of conservation and 'tourism'. He pinpointed the key reasons why the steam locomotive has not been developed as well as it should have been, and why it has very nearly vanished except for working special trains and specialist railways like the narrow-gauge mountain railways of Wales, the sugar-plantation railways of Cuba, and the vast collieries of China: steam's image, and the crudely banal concerns of management. He quotes Warren Fox, director of sales and service for General Motors' Electro-Motive Division, speaking to the *Wall Street Journal* in January 1985 about the company's research into a modern coal-fired locomotive: 'You have to get the image out of your mind of a thing chugging down the track and throwing off black smoke. All it will do is haul freight and make money.'

'So that is *all* it will do?' retaliated Wardale. 'But that is not all it did, its real worth did not lie there. A pox on your view, Mr Fox; its real worth lay in the smoke that thundered which you seem to have hated. The forces of the universe have nothing to do with efficiency and cleanliness, and least of all with making money. They are overwhelmingly powerful, like the power of a thunderstorm compared to the monotonous drizzle of our ever more synthetic world. And the steam locomotive was of the same nature as those elemental forces: you saw it in the billowing exhaust of steam and smoke, you heard it in the stack talk, you felt it when adhesion was lost and driving wheels, rods, and motion span out of control in a dizzying blur. You became one with it in your consciousness, which brought you ever closer to an awareness of your own dynamic essence, nothing else and nothing less than that fundamental universal power.'

Wardale, the engineer, is also something of a poet and philosopher too, ably and beautifully expressing just why the steam locomotive keeps us in its thrall. It is a machine of elemental force, power, and beauty. No matter how efficient, it will always be the antithesis of the clinical, money-driven, and ultimately soulless modern management-driven world. Even the tiniest model steam locomotive can never be accused of being dull. The continuing, indeed blossoming, fascination with steam in an era of clever digital technology proves that humans are still moved by poetry and beauty.

*

Since steam came to an official end in Britain in 1968, around the world there have been at least forty serious proposals to build new main-line steam locomotives for everyday working. Brand-new locomotives have been built since Datong works saw an end to steam in 1988, although these have nearly all been for narrow-gauge railways and mostly for those serving tourism. *Tornado*, the new Peppercorn A1 class Pacific, highlighted a second trend, that of building replicas, or slightly modified versions, of historic locomotives for work on main-line specials. As yet, no engineer has been able to convince a railway, or other backers, to invest in a thoroughly new and truly high-performance locomotive like Wardale's 5AT or a Porta 2-10-0, which might yet have a very useful role to play in developing countries. Steam, it seems, is merely to be tolerated by railway management and enjoyed by enthusiasts as a some sort of pet or mascot.

Even so, Porta's disciples have done much to raise the standing of steam among operators who understand why its appeal is unlikely to go away so long as human beings retain a soul, an ear for rhythm, and a feeling for mechanical sorcery and bewitchment. When, for example, the Brienz Rothorn Bahn, a Swiss mountain rack railway, needed new locomotives to handle heavier trains in the early 1990s, it might have bought the latest diesels. The railway's management understood, though, that few passengers wanted to be bullied up the mountainside by a diesel when steam was an option. Roger Waller of the Swiss Locomotive and Machine Works in Winterthur designed the all-new H2/3 class of two-cylinder 0-4-2T rack locomotives which first entered service in 1992.

Heavily influenced by Porta, these locomotives retained the visual charm of their predecessors, which were built by the Swiss Locomotive and Machine Works between 1891 and 1933. Designed for driver-only operations and with steel fire-boxes, modern draughting, light-oil firing, extensive thermal insulation, all-welded boilers, and roller bearings, the H2/3s are highly efficient and modern locomotives. They can retain a head of steam overnight and can be moved instantly, requiring just ten to fifteen minutes in the morning to reach full pressure. After boiler wash-outs, steam is raised without thermal stresses in the boiler, with water flowing by gravity to a circulation pump which forces it back to the boiler through an external electrical heater. The H2/3 class weigh 25 per cent less than their veteran shed mates, while offering 36 per cent more power and a 56 per cent higher maximum speed. Fuel consumption is 41 per cent less, while power-to-weight ratio is up by 82 per cent.

Waller, an engineer born and trained in Switzerland, worked as an assistant to David Wardale on the design and construction of *The Red Devil* in South Africa. Unsurprisingly, when his turn came to rebuild a standard-gauge main-line locomotive, to work the Orient Express, the results were equally impressive. The donor locomotive was a class 52 German *Kriegslok*, 8055, built in 1942–3 at Grafenstaden, then in German-occupied France. Work was completed in 1999 and power was raised from 1,600 to 2,000 dbhp and top speed from 70 to 100 kph (43.5 to 62mph).

The result is a quiet, powerful, reliable, and impressive-looking locomotive with light-oil firing which, very importantly for the steam lobby, emits approximately 80 per cent less toxic gases than a new diesel-electric. It is thus an extremely clean locomotive to work on. With exceptional powers of acceleration, 52 8055 works comfortably between electric trains on tight schedules in territory, normally between Zurich and Schaffhausen, where demanding gradients and tight curves prevail. Since 2000, Waller has gone on to head a new company, Dampflokomotiv- und Maschinenfabrik AG, which, as of

2003, owns the 2-10-0. In 2010 the company demonstrated a pair of fireless 0-6-0T shunting locomotives complete with cab-roof-mounted solar panels.

Other Porta disciples include the British engineers Phil Girdlestone and Nigel Day, and the Irish engineer Shaun McMahon, who, between them, have successfully modified narrow-gauge and standard-gauge main-line locomotives on railways in parts of the world as disparate as North Wales, Australia, Sudan, South Africa, the United States, and Tierra del Fuego. The case for steam locomotives continuing to work preserved and tourist railways as well as main-line special trains is well proven and, although railway managers with a dislike of steam – and of life lived fully and joyously – will pop up from time to time with yet another jargon-fuelled reason for it to go, no one today seriously anticipates steam-free railways in the future.

As to whether or not steam will ever return to regular use on scheduled trains on main-line railways, much turns on what sort of fuels will be available for use by railways in the future. How long will the world want to fight wars for oil? Might the steam locomotive's more or less proven ability to burn a great variety of fuels redeem it? And will dedicated steam locomotive engineers be available to bring the steam locomotive truly up to date in terms of automated boiler controls, traction control, dynamic braking, multiple-unit working, and crew comfort?

If they had the opportunity and the funding, I think a new generation of engineers could, while learning the lessons of the past, nurture a highly efficient form of steam railway locomotive for the future which could serve railways in remote corners of the world, in poor countries, as well as those that accept that there are many people who simply like the idea of riding behind steam and are willing to pay for it, even if only on high days and holidays. In the world of civil aviation, for example, jets have not entirely replaced turboprops. Saab and Fokker, Bombardier and Embraer, among others, have proved the case for turboprop air travel over a certain sort of route. These aircraft are aerodynamically sophisticated and their engines – and propellers – are at the leading edge of design and engineering. They are economical, and reasonably sound from an environmental point of view too. Could modern steam be to diesel-electric as turboprops are to jetliners? Modern fuels mean that there is no reason why steam railway locomotives of the future would have to be regarded as dirty, especially as their thermal efficiency – the use they make of fuel – could be so very much higher than it has been to date. Different technologies can, after all, exist comfortably together – the letterpress book with the Kindle, bicycles with cars, pens and paper with laptop computers, sailing boats with nuclear submarines. So the steam railway locomotive could still play its part – and its unmistakable rhythmic beat and characterful presence still encourage fond glances and broad smiles.

I have been in awe of steam railway locomotives, and loved them, since as a little boy born in London at the end of the regular steam era, I watched and listened to them under the great glazed train sheds of stations where diesels were already brooding noisily at every turn of the head. Since then, I have learned to fire and drive them, and I have worked and ridden behind them in Great Britain and France, Germany and Poland, Russia and Inner Mongolia, Cuba and Vietnam, India and Pakistan, South Africa and Argentina, Jordan and elsewhere. When the last steam expresses ran from Waterloo, to Southampton and beyond, I wanted to be a doctor, a missionary, a fighter pilot, and an engine driver, yet I cannot remember thinking I wanted to be a steam locomotive engineer. Perhaps intuitively, I knew that the time for such a career had run its course; and yet as I have learned about the ways in which these dedicated men worked more for the love of Stephensonian steam than for money or position, and how they tried to develop the steam locomotive, all too often against the odds, in the era of General Motors, the oil lobby, modernization, and the culture of management, I still wish I could have been part of their world. Instead, I became a writer, and this book is my modest contribution to celebrating both the very idea and the genius of steam and the steam locomotive. And I have gone about it with the regulator wide open and accompanied by an inner soundtrack of pulsating exhaust, singing injectors, an insistence of pistons, a chattering of motion, safety valves on the point of lifting, chiming whistles, and the clatter and thrum of fast-retreating rails.

GLOSSARY OF TECHNICAL TERMS

adhesive weight

Weight carried by the driving wheels.

articulated locomotive

Locomotive with two engines (the unit comprising cylinders, valve gear, and wheels) pivoted under a single frame: for example, Mallets and Beyer Garratts.

ash-pan

Steel receptacle below the fire-grate designed to collect ash and regulate the flow of air, normally through damper doors controlled by the fireman, into the grate.

Atlantic

Popular name for 4-4-2 locomotives, derived from their early use on the Atlantic Coast Line Railroad and the Philadelphia and Reading Railway, which ran the type to Atlantic City, New Jersey.

Baltic

Popular name for 4-6-4 locomotives in Europe, derived from the Nord railway 4-6-4s of 1911 designed to work Paris to St Petersburg expresses – from the Seine, that is, to the Baltic. The type was known as the Hudson in the USA. The first American 4-6-4s were built for the New York Central Railroad in 1927, its principal main line running north from New York up the Hudson Valley.

bar frame

Locomotive frames constructed from steel bars, square in section; first used in England, by Edward Bury in 1830, it was a common feature of the majority of US locomotives from 1840.

Belpaire boiler

Type of boiler developed by Belgian locomotive engineer Alfred Belpaire between 1860 and 1864, characterized by a flat-topped fire-box.

big end

The crank-pin end of the connecting rod, where stresses are higher (or 'bigger') than at the cross-head end – the Achilles heel of many steam locomotives.

blast-pipe

Pipe carrying exhaust steam from the cylinders into the centre of the smoke-box; the gap between the blast-pipe and the chimney above it creates a vacuum which draughts the boiler, drawing heat from the fire-box through the boiler tubes and thus raising steam.

blower

Device providing a draught for a locomotive's fire, through jets of live steam, when steam to the cylinders is shut off. A safety device, too, it ensures that fire is not blown back through the fire-box door by draughts from the chimney back through the boiler tubes.

Boxpok wheels

Disc driving wheels, as opposed to the usual spoked wheels, patented by General Steel Castings of Granite City, Illinois, and popular in the USA in late steam locomotive design. They were easier to cast and easier to balance than spoked wheels. Variations included the lighter Bulleid Firth Brown wheels fitted to Bulleid's steam locomotives for the Southern Railway.

brick arch

Constructed from firebricks or concrete inside the fire-box, this is designed to direct air from the fire-hole to the hot gases, ensuring complete combustion before they reach the boiler fire-tubes. It also helps prevent particles of fuel from being drawn into the fire-tubes and helps maintain even heat within the fire-box.

Caprotti valve gear

Camshaft-operated valve gear using poppet valves invented by Italian engineer and architect Dr Arturo Caprotti in 1921. More costly to make and to fit than conventional piston valves, this was a more efficient option.

chimney

Known as a 'stack' in the USA, the chimney exhausts steam from the blast-pipe, ejects hot gases, as well as smoke and poorly combusted fuel particles, from the smoke-box, and is a key element in the draughting and steam process. Its shape was raised to something of a fine art in Great Britain.

compound

System using steam twice in high- and then low-pressure cylinders, increasing the work done by expanded steam. Compound locomotives were often highly efficient.

connecting rod

Steel rod connecting the piston rod with the crank on the driving axle or driving wheel, and converting the to-and-fro motion of the piston into the rotary action necessary to turn the driving wheels.

cut-off

Point at which steam is cut off from entering cylinders. Controlled by the driver through a reverser screw gear or a ratchet lever in the

cab, the cut-off can be set anywhere, but is normally between 10 and
75 per cent of the piston stroke. When starting, the driver will work
the locomotive at a high percentage cut-off to maximize the flow and
force of steam in the cylinders, reducing this as the locomotive gets
into its stride.

dome

Fitting, usually in the shape of a dome or a bowler hat on top
of the boiler, designed to collect steam and housing the regulator
valve – the valve, operated by the regulator (or 'throttle'), that
admits steam to the cylinders – and, sometimes, safety valves.
It was originally designed to raise the entry to the main steam-
pipe above the boiler to stop boiling water from flowing into the
cylinders. Domeless boilers were a feature of late-generation
steam locomotives.

drawbar horsepower (dbhp)

The net power a locomotive has to pull its train. In practice, this
was measured by dynamometer cars equipped with the necessary
measuring and recording instruments. Calculated as: dbhp = tractive
effort × speed ÷ 375.

grate

Grill of fire-bars at the bottom of the fire-box on which the fire rests.
Gaps between the bars create currents of air to assist combustion.

'hammer blow'

Force exerted by the thrust of the connecting rod on the crank and
transmitted through the driving wheels to the rails.

horsepower (hp)

Measurement of power, equivalent to 550 ft-lb per second, or the
equivalent of 745.7 W. The true maximum output of a horse is about

15 hp. A healthy human can manage up to about 1.2 hp and an Olympic athlete can double that.

indicated horsepower (ihp)
Power developed in the cylinders of a locomotive, calculated from a measurement of the pressure in the cylinders using an 'engine indicator'. This equipment was housed in a timber shelter erected around the front end of a locomotive – an interesting place for engineers to spend up to several hours as the engine was worked up to maximum power.

injectors
Operated by the fireman, these feed water into the boiler from a tank or tender using live steam from the boiler or exhaust steam from the cylinders. Anyone who has made a cappuccino with a traditional espresso machine will be familiar with the concept.

Mallet
Type of locomotive with two sets of engines mounted on bogie frames and set below a single boiler, designed by the Swiss engineer Anatole Mallet in 1884. Mallets grew to prodigious size in the United States. With the front engine unit articulated, American Mallets were able to negotiate tight bends despite their immense length.

Mikado
Locomotive with 2-8-2 wheel arrangement. The name was given to the Bt4/6 class 2-8-2s built by Baldwin of Philadelphia for the Japanese Nippon Railway in 1893. After the Japanese attack on Pearl Harbor on 7 December 1941, some US railroads, including the Chesapeake and Ohio and Union Pacific, adopted the name MacArthur for the type, after General Douglas MacArthur, chief of staff of the US Army in the 1930s who was recalled to active duty in 1941.

Mogul

Name for locomotives with 2-6-0 wheel arrangement, from the first British 2-6-0 type, the Great Eastern Railway's No. 527 *Mogul*, designed by William Adams and built by Neilson and Company in Glasgow, in 1878.

motion

The sequence of piston rods, connecting rods, and valve gear that power and turn the driving wheels of a locomotive.

Mountain

Name for locomotives with 4-8-2 wheel arrangement. Named after the first locomotives of this type, the Alco-built 4-8-2s of 1911, designed to work heavy passenger trains single-handed over steeply inclined mountain sections of the Chesapeake and Ohio Railway in the Alleghenies.

Pacific

Name for locomotives with 4-6-2 wheel arrangement. The first true Pacifics were the thirteen Q class 4-6-2s built by Baldwin to designs by Alfred Luther Beattie, chief mechanical engineer of the New Zealand railways in 1901. The locomotives were shipped across the Pacific. The last was withdrawn in 1957. None was preserved.

pannier tank

A tank locomotive with water tanks carried on either side of the boiler and raised clear of the running board. An apt name for locomotives that were very often the mules of the steam railway world.

poppet valves

Steam-chest valves opened and closed by rotary or oscillating cams. Theoretically, but not always, more efficient than conventional

piston valves. The best known poppet valve set-ups were designed
and manufactured by Caprotti, Franklin, Lentz, and Redlinger.

regulator
The throttle on a steam locomotive, opening a valve at the top of the
boiler to admit steam to the cylinders, operated by the driver through
a number of different types of levers mounted in the cab.

reverser
Forward and reverse control also used to 'cut off' steam entering
valves and cylinders. The equivalent of gears in a car and used in
tandem with the regulator.

saturated steam
Steam that has not been superheated.

superheater
The first superheaters, designed by Wilhelm 'Hot Steam Willy'
Schmidt, were fitted to locomotives of the Prussian State Railways
in 1898. The equipment, formed of coils of pipes inside large boiler
flues, re-heats and 'dries' saturated steam produced in the boiler. The
thermal efficiency of superheated locomotives was up to 50 per cent
greater than that of saturated steam locomotives.

thermic siphon
Heat-exchanging device comprising flattened funnels directing water
from the tender or tank to the hottest areas in and around the fire-
box so as to speed up and increase steam production. Patented by US
engineer, John L. Nicholson, in 1928.

tractive effort
The force exerted by a locomotive at the point of contact between
wheel rim and rail, and a measure of the locomotive's ability to pull

or push a train away from rest. Not the same thing as horsepower, which is a determinant of speed. A high tractive effort is essential for heavy freight locomotives, but not for high-speed locomotives designed to haul light passenger trains. Tractive effort falls with speed, while power rises. Calculated as: TE = piston diameter squared × piston stroke × 85 per cent of boiler pressure ÷ diameter of driving wheels. A three-cylinder engine has 50 per cent greater tractive effort than a two-cylinder engine; a four-cylinder engine has 100 per cent greater tractive effort than a two-cylinder engine.

Walschaerts valve gear

Form of valve gear patented by Belgian engineer Egide Walschaerts in 1844. Gradually it became the most popular, reliable, and easy to maintain steam railway locomotive valve gear and was adopted worldwide.

SELECT BIBLIOGRAPHY

Allen, Cecil J.
Locomotive Practice and Performance in the Twentieth Century (W. Heffer & Sons, 1949)
British Pacific Locomotives (Ian Allan, 1962)
Two Million Miles of Train Travel (Ian Allan, 1965)

Atkins, Philip
Dropping the Fire: The Decline and Fall of the Steam Locomotive (Irwell Press, 1999)

Ball, Don, Jr, and Whitaker, Rogers E. M.
Decade of the Trains: The 1940s (New York Graphic Society, 1977)

Barnes, Robin
Some 20th Century British Locomotives That Never Were (Jane's Publishing, 1985)

Bellwood, John, and Jenkins, David
Gresley and Stanier: A Centenary Tribute (NRM York, 1976)

Blakemore, Michael, and Rutherford, Michael
Duchess of Hamilton: Ultimate in Pacific Power (NRM York, 1990)

Bond, Roland
A Lifetime with Locomotives (Goose & Son, 1975)

Broncard, Yves, and Fenino, Felix
French Steam (Ian Allan, 1970)

Brown, William
Hush-Hush: The story of LNER 10000 (Kestrel Railway Books, 2010)

Bruce, Alfred W.

The Steam Locomotive in America – Its Development in the Twentieth Century (W. W. Norton, 1952)

Bulleid, H. A. V.

Master Builders of Steam (Ian Allan, 1963)
Bulleid of the Southern (Ian Allan, 1977)

Carter, Ernest F.

Unusual Locomotives (Frederick Muller Ltd, 1960)

Catchpole, Paul

The Steam Locomotives of Czechoslovakia (published by the author, 1995)

Chacksfield, J. E.

Sir Henry Fowler: A Versatile Life (The Oakwood Press, 2000)
Sir William Stanier: A New Biography (The Oakwood Press, 2001)

Chapelon, André

La Locomotive à Vapeur, 2nd edn 1952, trans. by George W. Carpenter (Camden Miniature Steam Services, 2000)

Chester, Keith R. (ed.)

Russian and Soviet Steam Locomotives, 2 vols (Trackside Publications, 2000)

Clay, John F.

The Stanier Black Fives (Ian Allan, 1972)

Clay, John F. (ed.)

Essays in Steam (Ian Allan, 1970)

Clay, John F., and Cliffe, J.

The West Coast Pacifics (Ian Allan, 1976)

Cox, E. S.

Locomotive Panorama, 2 vols (Ian Allan, 1965–6)
Chronicles of Steam (Ian Allan, 1967)
World Steam in the Twentieth Century (Ian Allan, 1969)

Day-Lewis, Sean
Bulleid: Last Giant of Steam (George Allen & Unwin, 1964)

Drury, George H.
Guide to North American Steam Locomotives: History and Development of Steam Power since 1900 (Kalmach Books, 1993)

Durrant, A. E.
The Steam Locomotives of Eastern Europe, 2nd edn (David & Charles, 1972)

Durrant, A. E., Lewis, C. P., and Jorgensen, A. A.
Steam in Africa (Hamlyn, 1981)

Fryer, Charles
Experiments with Steam (Patrick Stephens, 1990)

Giesl-Gieslingen, A.
Anatomie der Dampflokomotive (Verlag Josef Otto Stezak, 1986)

Glancey, Jonathan
The Train: An Illustrated History (Carlton Books, 2004)
Tornado: 21st Century Steam (Books on Track, 2010)

Gottwaldt, Alfred B.
Baureihe 05: Schnellste Dampflok der Welt (Franckh'sche Verlagshandlung, 1981)

Gruber, John, and Solomon, Brian
The Milwaukee Road Hiawathas (Voyageur Press, 2006)

Heywood, A. J., and Button, I. D. C.
Soviet Locomotive Types (Frank Stenvalls Forlag, 1995)

Hirsimaki, Eric
Lima: The History, 2nd edn (Hundsman Publishing, 2004)

Hollingsworth, Brian
An Illustrated Guide to Modern Trains (Salamander Books, 1985)

Huddleston, Eugene L., and Dixon, Thomas W.
The Allegheny: Lima's Finest (Huddleston Dixon, 1984)

Kiefer, P. W.
>A Practical Evaluation of Railroad Motive Power (Steam Locomotive Research Inc., 1947)

Klein, Maury
>Union Pacific, vol. 2: The Rebirth 1894–1969 (Doubleday, 1990)

Kratville, William W.
>The Challenger Locomotives (Kratville Publications, 1980)

Lamb, J. Parker
>Perfecting the American Steam Locomotive (Indiana University Press, 2003)

Le Fleming, H. M., and Price, J. H.
>Russian Steam Locomotives (David & Charles, 1960)

Maillet, M.
>L'Oeuvre d'André Chapelon à la SNCF et son Influence Mondiale (Les Editions du Cabri, 1983)

Mierzejewski, Alfred C.
>Hitler's Trains: The German National Railway and The Third Reich (Tempus, 2005)

Miller, Kenneth L.
>Norfolk and Western Class J: The Finest Steam Passenger Locomotive (Roanoke Chapter National Railway Historical Society, 2000)

Mullay, A. J.
>Streamlined Steam: Britain's 1930s Luxury Expresses (David & Charles, 1994)

Nock, O. S.
>William Stanier: A Biography (Ian Allan, 1964)
>British Locomotives at Work (George Allen & Unwin, 1967)
>Railways of the USA (A. & C. Black, 1979)
>British Locomotives of the 20th Century, vol. 2: 1930–60 (Book Club Associates, 1984)
>Locomotive Practice & Performance, vol. 1: The Age of Steam, 1959–68 (Ian Allan, 1989)

Péroche, Marcel
Pacific Senator, trans. by Roland Wilson (Argyll Publishing, 1984)

Powell, A. J.
Living with London Midland Locomotives (Ian Allan, 1967)

Ransome-Wallis, P.
On Railways at Home and Abroad (Batchworth, 1951)
Engines in Britain and France (Ian Allan, 1957)

Ransome-Wallis, P. (ed.)
The Concise Encyclopaedia of World Railway Locomotives (Hutchinson, 1959)

Reed, Brian (ed.)
Locomotives in Profile, 4 vols (Profile Publications, 1971–4)

Riemsdijk, Van J. T.
Compound Locomotives: An International Survey (Pendragon Books, 1994)

Robertson, Kevin
Leader: Steam's Last Chance (Alan Sutton, 1988)

Rogers, Col. H. C. B.
Chapelon: Genius of French Steam (Ian Allan, 1972)
G. J. Churchward (George Allen & Unwin, 1975)
Transition from Steam (Ian Allan, 1980)
Express Steam: Locomotive Development in Great Britain and France (Ian Allan, 1990)

Rutherford, Michael
Castles and Kings at Work (Ian Allan, 1984)

Shepherd, Ernie
Bulleid and the Turf Burner (K R B Publications, 2004)

Talbot, Edward
The Coronation Scot: The Streamline Era on the LMS (published by the author, 2002)

Vuillet, Gerard
Railway Reminiscences of Three Continents (Thomas Nelson & Sons, 1968)

Wardale, David
The Red Devil and Other Tales from the Age of Steam (published by the author, 1998)

Westwood, J. N.
Soviet Railways Today (Ian Allan, 1963)
Locomotive Design in the Age of Steam (Sidgwick & Jackson, 1977)

Whitehouse, P. B.
Steam in Europe (Ian Allan, 1966)

Ziel, Ron, and Huxtable, Nils
Steam beneath the Red Star (Amereon Ltd, 1995)

Zimmerman, Karl R.
20th Century Limited (MBI Publishing, 2002)

MAGAZINES

Modern Railways; *Railway Magazine*; *Railway World*; *Steam Railway*; *Trains Illustrated*

WEBSITES

Martin Bayne's Steam and Travel Pages: www.martynbane.co.uk
Steam Index: www.steamindex.com
Ultimate Steam Page: www.trainweb.org/tusp

LIST OF ILLUSTRATIONS

LIST OF PEOPLE

Louis Armand (1905–71), France
Chief Mechanical Engineer, Western Region SNCF; chief of
Resistance–Fer; General Manager SNCF

Max Baumberg (1906–78), Germany
Chief of Locomotive Design, Deutsche Reichsbahn (East Germany)

Roland Bond (1903–80), Great Britain
Chief Mechanical Engineer, British Railways

Jean Gaston du Bousquet (1839–1910), France
Chief Mechanical Engineer, Chemin de Fer du Nord

Alfred W. Bruce (1879–1955), USA
Director of Steam Engineering, Alco (American Locomotive
Company)

Oliver Bulleid (1882–1970), Great Britain
Chief Mechanical Engineer, Southern Railway and BR Southern
Region; CME (Coras Impair Eireann)

Kenneth Cantlie (1899–1986), Great Britain
Consulting Engineer, Chinese Ministry of Railways; technical advisor
to Locomotive Manufacturers Association

George Carpenter (b. 1923), Great Britain
Locomotive engineer, historian

Marc de Caso (1893–1985), France
Principal locomotive design engineer, Chemin de Fer du Nord, SNCF

André Chapelon (1892–1978), France
Principal locomotive design engineer, P.O-Midi Railway; Chief
Engineer, SNCF

George Jackson Churchward (1857–1933), Great Britain
Chief Mechanical Engineer, Great Western Railway

Daniel Kinnear Clark (1822–96), Great Britain
Locomotive superintendent, Great North of Scotland Railway

Tom Francis Coleman (1885–1958), Great Britain
Chief locomotive draughtsman, London Midland & Scottish Railway;
chief locomotive and rolling stock draughtsman, BR London Midland
Region

Ernest Stewart Cox (1900–92), Great Britain
Executive officer design, British Railways

Thomas Russell Crampton (1816–88), Great Britain
Civil and locomotive engineer; inventor of the Crampton locomotive

Ctesibius (*fl.* 285–222 BCE)
Pioneer of pneumatics

Nicolas Joseph Cugnot (1725–1804), France
Inventor of steam vehicle

Rudolf Diesel (1858–1913), Germany
Mechanical engineer; inventor of the diesel engine

Joseph B. Ennis (1879–1955), USA
Senior Vice President, Engineering, Alco

Lawford H. Fry (1874–1949), USA
Director of research, steam locomotive research division, Steam Locomotive Institute

Herbert William Garratt (1864–1913), Great Britain
Mechanical engineer; inventor of the Garratt locomotive

Adolph Giesl-Gieslingen (1903–92), Austria
Locomotive design engineer; inventor of Giesl ejector

Alfred George de Glehn (1848–1936), France
Chief Mechanical Engineer, Société Alsacienne de Constructions Mécaniques

Herbert Nigel Gresley (1876–1941), Great Britain
Chief Mechanical Engineer, Great Northern Railway, London and North Eastern Railway

Hero of Alexandria (c.10–70 CE)
Inventor of first steam powered device

Otto Jabelmann (1891–1943), USA
Vice president, Research, Union Pacific Railroad

Ralph P. Johnson, (1890–1980) USA
Chief Engineer, Baldwin Locomotive Works

361

Russell G. Henley, (1884–1953) USA
Design engineer, Norfolk and Western Railway

Paul Kiefer (1888–1968), USA
Chief motive power engineer, New York Central Railroad

Kyösti Kylälä (1873–1938), Finland
Inventor of Kylala steam/gas exhaust

Lev Sergeyevich Lebedyansky, (1898–1968) Russia
Head of Construction, Kolomensky Machine Building Design Bureau

A. I. Lipetz (1881–1950), USA
Chief consulting engineer, Alco

Anatole Mallet (1837–1919), Switzerland
Inventor of Mallet articulated locomotive

Vlastimil Mareš (1896–1979), Czechoslovakia
Chief Mechanical Engineer, railways, Czechoslovak Ministry of
Transport

Raoul Notesse (1898–1944), Belgium
Locomotive design engineer, SNCB

John Pilcher (1868–1949), USA
Design engineer, Norfolk and Western Railway

Livio Dante Porta (1922–2003), Argentina
Steam locomotive engineer; inventor of gas-producer firebox

R. A. 'Robin' Riddles (1892–1983), Great Britain
Railway executive member for mechanical and electrical engineering,
British Transport Commission

Wilhelm 'Hot Steam Willy' Schmidt (1858–1924), Germany
Inventor of practical superheater

Hideo Shima (1901–98), Japan
Head of rolling stock, Japanese Government Railways, Vice president
for engineering, Japanese National Railways; President, National
Space Development Agency

William Stanier (1876–1965), Great Britain
Chief Mechanical Engineer, London Midland and Scottish Railway

**George Stephenson (1781–1848) Robert Stephenson (1803–59),
Great Britain**
Mechanical and civil engineers; creators with Marc Seguin (1786–
1875) of mainline steam railway locomotive

A. J. 'Bert' Townsend (1892–1953), USA
Chief engineer, Lima locomotive works

Richard Trevithick (1771–1833), Great Britain
Inventor and builder of first steam railway locomotive

Richard Wagner (1882–1953), Germany
Reichsbahnöberrat: Chief of design, Deutsche Reichsbahn

Egide Walschaerts (1820–1901), Belgium
Mechanical engineer; inventor of Walschaerts valve gear

David Wardale (b. 1946), Great Britain

Locomotive engineer; famous for *Red Devil* and 5AT Project

James Watt (1736–1819), Great Britain

Inventor and mechanical engineer; revolutionized the early steam engine

Friedrich Witte (1900–77), Germany

Chief of Locomotive Design, Deutsche Bundesbahn(West Germany)

Adolf Wolff (1894–1964), Germany

Chief design engineer, Borsig Lokomotivwerke

William E. Woodard (1873–1942), USA

Chief Engineering Director, Lima locomotive works; originator of 'super-power' steam

ACKNOWLEDGEMENTS

This book has worked itself up to full pressure over many years. A lifetime, I suppose. I have loved steam railway locomotives, I'm told, since before I can remember doing so. Trying to thank all the people around the world and across half a century who have nurtured my interest in the steam locomotive and steam technology in general has to be an impossible task. Yet to all the many railwaymen, engine drivers and engineers, managers and historians, who have told me so much, and along the way allowed me to clean, oil, ride, fire, and drive steam locomotives, from the miniature and narrow-gauge to some of the fastest and most powerful, I can only say you would make up one of the most appreciated trainloads of people imaginable. Only the most powerful, most efficient, and best-looking triple-expansion, high-pressure compound could even begin to move so many of you away from rest in an appropriately deserving style.

Special thanks to George Carpenter, whose keen intelligence, vast knowledge, extraordinary memory, captivating story-telling, generosity, and friendship have kerbed my rash judgements, corrected my many errors, and deepened and tempered my understanding of steam locomotive design and engineering. George has read, added to, and dismembered my manuscript where necessary to ensure a proper degree of accuracy, although any errors – of fact and judgement – are mine alone. Thanks too, of course, to Angus MacKinnon, my wise and knowledgeable commissioning editor, Sarah Norman, formerly at Atlantic Books, and David Atkinson who copy-edited the manuscript. Sarah Chalfant, my agent, knows that I move forward through green signals with her advice and help.

INDEX